Romola

ROMOLA

BY
GEORGE ELIOT

VOL. I

TORONTO
THE MUSSON BOOK COMPANY
LIMITED
EDINBURGH AND LONDON: WILLIAM BLACKWOOD & SONS

CONTENTS.

GEORGE ELIOT

CHAPTER		PAGE
I.	INTRODUCTORY	vii
II.	CHILDHOOD AND EARLY HOME	xiii
III.	YOUTHFUL STUDIES AND FRIENDSHIPS	xxiii
IV.	TRANSLATION OF STRAUSS AND FEUERBACH — TOUR ON THE CONTINENT	xxxix
V.	THE 'WESTMINSTER REVIEW'	xlix
VI.	GEORGE HENRY LEWES	lxiii
VII.	SCENES OF CLERICAL LIFE	lxxii
VIII.	ADAM BEDE	lxxxiii
IX.	THE MILL ON THE FLOSS	xcvi
X.	SILAS MARNER	cvi
XI.	ROMOLA	cxiv
XII.	HER POEMS	cxxiii
XIII.	FELIX HOLT AND MIDDLEMARCH	cxxxiii
XIV.	DANIEL DERONDA	cxlv
XV.	LAST YEARS	cliv

ROMOLA

	PROEM	7

BOOK I

I.	THE SHIPWRECKED STRANGER	15
II.	BREAKFAST FOR LOVE	29
III.	THE BARBER'S SHOP	34
IV.	FIRST IMPRESSIONS	46
V.	THE BLIND SCHOLAR AND HIS DAUGHTER	50
VI.	DAWNING HOPES	65
VII.	A LEARNED SQUABBLE	82

CONTENTS.

CHAPTER		PAGE
VIII.	A Face in the Crowd	88
IX.	A Man's Ransom	101
X.	Under the Plane-Tree	109
XI	Tito's Dilemma	121
XII.	The Prize is Nearly Grasped	125
XIII.	The Shadow of Nemesis	138
XIV.	The Peasants' Fair	146
XV.	The Dying Message	162
XVI	A Florentine Joke	171
XVII.	Under the Loggia	185
XVIII.	The Portrait	192
XIX.	The Old Man's Hope	199
XX.	The Day of the Betrothal	203

GEORGE ELIOT.

CHAPTER I.

INTRODUCTORY.

Speaking of the contributions made to literature by her own sex, George Eliot, in a charming essay written in 1854, awards the palm of intellectual pre-eminence to the women of France. "They alone," says the great English author, "have had a vital influence on the development of literature. For in France alone the mind of woman has passed, like an electric current, through the language, making crisp and definite what is elsewhere heavy and blurred; in France alone, if the writings of women were swept away, a serious gap would be made in the national history."

The reason assigned by George Eliot for this literary superiority of Frenchwomen consists in their having had the courage of their sex. They thought and felt as women, and when they wrote, their books became the fullest expression of their womanhood. And by being true to themselves, by only seeking inspiration from their own life-experience, instead of servilely copying that of men, their letters and memoirs, their novels and pictures, have a distinct, nay, unique, value for the student of art and literature. Englishwomen, on the other hand, have not followed the spontaneous impulses of nature. They have not allowed free play to the peculiarly feminine element, preferring to mould their intellectual products on the masculine pattern. For that reason, says George Eliot, their writings are "usually an absurd exaggeration of the masculine style, like the swaggering gait of a bad actress in male attire."

This novel theory, concerning a specifically feminine manifestation of the intellect, is doubly curious when one compares it with Madame de Stael's famous saying, "*Le génie n'a pas de sexe.*" But an aphorism, however brilliant, usually contains only one half the truth, and there is every reason to think that women have already, and will much more largely, by-and-by, infuse into their works certain intellectual and emotional qualities which are essentially their own. Shall we, however, admit George Eliot's conclusion that Frenchwomen alone have hitherto shown any of this original bias? Several causes are mentioned by her in explanation of this exceptional merit. Among these causes there is one which would probably occur to every one who began to reflect on this subject. The influence of the "Salon" in developing and stimulating the finest feminine talents has long been recognized. In this school for women the gift of expression was carried to the utmost pitch of perfection. By their active co-operation in the discussion of the most vital subjects, thought became clear, luminous, and forcible; sentiment gained indescribable graces of refinement; and wit, with its brightest scintillations, lit up the sombre background of life.

But among other causes enumerated as accounting for that more spontaneous productivity of Frenchwomen, attributed to them by George Eliot, there is one which would probably have occurred to no other mind than hers, and which is too characteristic of her early scientific tendencies to be omitted. For according to her, the present superiority of Frenchwomen is mainly due to certain physiological peculiarities of the Gallic race Namely, to the "small brain and vivacious temperament which permit the fragile system of woman to sustain the superlative activity requisite for intellectual creativeness," whereas "the larger brain and slower temperament of the English and Germans are in the womanly organization generally dreamy and passive. So that the *physique* of a woman may suffice as the substratum for a superior Gallic mind, but is too thin a soil for a superior Teutonic one."

So knotty and subtle a problem must be left to the scientist of the future to decide. Perhaps some promising young physiologist, profiting by the "George Henry Lewes Studentship" founded by George Eliot, may some day satisfactorily elucidate this question. In the meanwhile it is at least gratifying to reflect that she does not deny the future possibilities of even English and German women. She admits that conditions might arise which in their case also would be favorable to the highest creative effort; conditions which would modify the existing state of things according to which, to speak in her own scientific phraseology: "The woman of large capacity can seldom rise beyond the absorption of ideas; her physical conditions refuse to support the energy required for spontaneous activity; the voltaic pile is not strong enough to produce crystallizations."

But was the author of 'Adam Bede' not herself destined to be a triumphant refutation of her theory? Or had those more favorable circumstances mentioned as vague possibilities already arisen in her case? Not that we believe, for that matter, in the superior claims of illustrious Frenchwomen. It is true George Eliot enumerates a formidable list of names. But on the whole we may boast of feminine celebrities that need not shrink from the comparison.

There is, of course, much truth in the great Englishwoman's generous praise of her French compeers. "Mme. de Sévigné remains," she says, "the single instance of a woman who is supreme in a class of literature which has engaged the ambition of men; Mme. Dacier still reigns the queen of bluestockings, though women have long studied Greek without shame; Mme. de Stael's name still rises to the lips when we are asked to mention a woman of great intellectual power; Mme. Roland is still the unrivalled type of the sagacious and sternly heroic yet lovable woman; George Sand is the unapproached artist who, to Jean Jacques' eloquence and deep sense of external nature, unites the clear delineation of character and the tragic depth of passion."

Shall we be forced to admit that the representative women of England cannot justly be placed on as high a level? Is it so certain that they, too, did not speak out of the fulness of their womanly natures? That they, too, did not feel the genuine need to express modes of thought and feeling peculiar to themselves, which men, if at all, had but inadequately expressed hitherto?

Was not Queen Elizabeth the best type of a female ruler, one whose keen penetration enabled her to choose her ministers with infallible judgment? Did not Fanny Burney distil the delicate aroma of girlhood in one of the most delightful of novels? Or what of Jane Austen, whose microscopic fidelity of observation has a well-nigh scientific accuracy, never equalled unless in the pages of the author we are writing of? Sir Walter Scott apparently recognized the eminently feminine inspiration of her writings, as he says: "That young lady had a talent for describing the involvements, and feelings, and characters of ordinary life, which is for me the most wonderful I ever met with. The Bow-wow strain I can do myself like any now agoing; but the exquisite touch, which renders ordinary commonplace things and characters interesting from the truth of the descriptions and the sentiment, is denied to me." Then turning to the Brontës, does not one feel the very heartbeats of womanhood in those powerful utterances that seem to spring from some central emotional energy? Again, does not Mrs Browning occupy a unique place among poets? Is there not a distinctively womanly strain of emotion in the throbbing tides of her high-wrought melodious song? And, to come to George Eliot herself, will any one deny that, in the combination of sheer intellectual power with an unparalleled vision for the homely details of life, she takes precedence of all writers of this or any other country? To some extent this wonderful woman conforms to her own standard. She undoubtedly adds to the common fund of crystallized human experience, as literature might be called, something which is specifically feminine. But, on the other hand, her intellect excels precisely in those qualities habitually believed to be masculine, one of its chief characteristics consisting in the grasp of abstract philosophical ideas. This faculty, however, by no means impairs those instinctive processes of the imagination by which true artistic work is produced; George Eliot combining in an unusual degree the subtlest power of analysis with that happy gift of genius which enabled her to create such characters as Amos Barton, Hetty, Mrs Poyser, Maggie, and Tom Tulliver, Godfrey Cass, and Caleb Garth, which seem to come fresh from the mould of

Nature itself. Indeed, she has hardly a rival among women in this power of objective imagination by which she throws her whole soul into natures of the most varied and opposite types, whereas George Sand only succeeds greatly when she is thoroughly in sympathy with her creations.

After George Eliot's eulogium of Frenchwomen, one feels tempted to institute a comparison between these two great contemporaries, who occupied the same leading position in their respective countries. But it will probably always remain a question of idiosyncrasy which of the two one is disposed to rank higher, George Eliot being the greatest realist, George Sand the greatest idealist, of her sex. The works of the French writer are, in fact, prose poems rather than novels. They are not studies of life, but life interpreted by the poet's vision. George Sand cannot give us a description of any scene in nature, of her own feelings, of a human character, without imparting to it some magical effect as of objects seen under the transfiguring influence of moonlight or storm clouds; whereas George Eliot loves to bathe her productions in the broad pitiless midday light, which leaves no room for illusion, but reveals all nature with uncompromising directness. The one has more of that primitive imagination which seizes on the elemental side of life — on the spectacle of the starry heavens or of Alpine solitudes, on the insurrection and tumult of human passion, on the shocks of revolution convulsing the social order — while the other possesses, in a higher degree, the acute intellectual perception for the orderly sequence of life, for that unchangeable round of toil which is the lot of the mass of men, and for the earth in its homelier aspects as it tells on our daily existence. In George Sand's finest work there is a sweet spontaneity, almost as if she were an oracle of Nature uttering automatically the divine message. But, on the other hand, when the inspiration forsakes her, she drifts along on a windy current of words, the fatal facility of her pen often beguiling the writer into vague diffuseness and unsubstantial declamation.

In this respect, also, our English novelist is the opposite of George Sand, for George Eliot invariably remains the master of her genius: indeed, she thoroughly fulfils Goethe's demand that if you set up for an artist you must command art. This intellectual self-restraint never forsakes George Eliot, who always selects her means with a thorough knowledge of the ends to be attained. The radical difference in the genius of these two writers, to both of whom applies Mrs. Browning's apt appellation of "large-brained woman and large-hearted man," extends naturally to their whole tone of thought. George Sand is impassioned, turbulent, revolutionary, the spiritual daughter of Rousseau, with an enthusiastic faith in man's future destiny. George Eliot, contemplative, observant, instinctively conservative, her imagination dearly loving to do "a little Toryism on the sly," is as yet the sole outcome of the modern positive spirit in imaginative literature — the sole novelist who has incorporated in an artistic form some of the leading ideas of Comte, of Mazzini, and of Darwin. In fact, underlying all her art there is the same rigorous teaching of the inexorable laws which govern the life of man. The teaching that not liberty but duty is the condition of existence; the teaching of the incalculable effects of hereditary transmission, with the solemn responsibilities it involves; the teaching of the inherent sadness and imperfection in human nature, which render resignation the first virtue of man.

In fact, as a moral influence, George Eliot cannot so much be compared with George Sand, or with any other novelist of her generation, as with Carlyle. She had, indeed, a far more explicit ethical code to offer than the author of 'Sartor Resartus.' For though the immense force of the latter's personality, glowing through his writings, had a tonic effect in promoting a healthy moral tone, there was little of positive moral truth to be gathered from them. But the lessons which George Eliot would fain teach to men were most unmistakable in their bearing — the lessons of pitying love towards fellow-men; of sympathy with all human suffering; of unwavering faithfulness toward the social bond, consisting in the claims of race, of country, of family; of unflagging aspiration after that life which is most beneficent to the community, that life, in short, towards which she herself aspired in the now famous prayer to reach

> "That purest heaven, be to other souls
> The cup of strength in some great agony,
> Enkindle generous ardor, feed pure love,
> Beget the smiles that have no cruelty —
> Be the sweet presence of a good diffused,
> And in diffusion ever more intense."

CHAPTER II.

CHILDHOOD AND EARLY HOME.

MARY ANN EVANS, better known as "George Eliot," was born on November 22nd, 1819, at South Farm, a mile from Griff, in the parish of Colton, in Warwickshire. Both the date and place of her birth have been incorrectly stated, hitherto, in the notices of her life. The family moved to Griff House in March of the following year, when she was only six months old. Her father, Robert Evans, of Welsh origin, was a Staffordshire man from Ellaston, near Ashbourne, and began life as a carpenter. In the kitchen at Griff House may still be seen a beautifully fashioned oaken press, a sample of his workmanship. A portrait of him, also preserved there, is known among the family as "Adam Bede." It is not as good a likeness as that of a certain carefully painted miniature, the features of which bear an unmistakable resemblance to those of the daughter destined to immortalize his name. A strongly marked, yet handsome face, massive in structure, and with brown eyes, whose shrewd, penetrating glance is particularly noticeable, betoken the man of strong practical intelligence, of rare energy and endurance. His career and character are partially depicted in Adam Bede, Caleb Garth, and Mr. Hackit — portraitures in which the different stages of his life are recorded with a mingling of fact and fiction. A shadowing forth of the same nature is discernible in the devotion of Stradivarius to his noble craft; and even in the tender paternity of Mr. Tulliver there are indications of another phase of the same individuality.

Like Adam Bede, Mr. Evans from carpenter rose to be forester, and from forester to be land-agent. It was in the latter capacity alone that he was ever known in Warwickshire. At one time he was surveyor to five estates in the midland counties — those of Lord Aylesford, Lord Lifford, Mr. Bromley Davenport, Mrs. Gregory, and Sir Roger Newdigate. The last was his principal employer. Having early discerned the exceptional capacity of the man, Sir Roger induced him to settle in Warwickshire, and take charge of his estates. Sir Roger's seat, Arbury Hall, is the original of the charming description of Cheverel Manor in 'Mr. Gilfil's Love Story.' It is said that Mr. Evans's trustworthiness had become proverbial in the county. But while faithfully serving his employers he also enjoyed great popularity among their tenants. He was gentle, but of indomitable firmness; and while stern to the idle and unthrifty, he did not press heavily on those who might be behindhand with their rent, owing to ill-luck or misfortune, on quarter days.

Mr. Evans was twice married. He had lost his first wife, by whom he had a son and a daughter, before settling in Warwickshire. Of his second wife, whose maiden name was Pearson, very little is known. She must, therefore, according to Schiller, have been a pattern of womanhood; for he says that the best women, like the best ruled states, have no history. We have it on very good authority, however, that Mrs. Hackit, in 'Amos Barton,' is a faithful likeness of George Eliot's mother. This may seem startling at first, but, on reflection, she is the woman one might have expected, being a strongly marked figure, with a heart as tender as her tongue is sharp. She is described as a thin woman, with a chronic liver-complaint, of indefatigable industry and epigrammatic speech; who, "in the utmost enjoyment of spoiling a friend's self-satisfaction, was never known to spoil a stocking." A notable housewife, whose clock-work regularity in all domestic affairs was such that all her farm-work was done by nine o'clock in the morning, when she would sit down to her loom. "In the same spirit, she brought out her furs on the first of November, whatever might be the temperature. She was not a woman weakly to accommodate herself to shilly-shally proceedings. If the season didn't know what it ought to do, Mrs. Hackit did. In her best days it was always sharp weather at 'Gunpowder Plot,' and she didn't like new fashions." Keenly observant and quick of temper, she was yet full of good nature, her sympathy showing itself in the active helpfulness with which she came to the assistance of poor Milly Barton, and the love she showed to her children, who, however, declined kissing her.

Is there not a strong family resemblance between this character and Mrs. Poyser, that masterpiece of George Eliot's art? Mary Ann's gift of pointed speech was therefore mother-wit, in the true sense, and her rich humor and marvellous powers of observation were derived from the same side, while her conscientiousness, her capacity, and that faculty of taking pains, which is so large a factor in the development of genius, came more directly from the father.

Mr. Evans had three children by his second wife, Christiana, Isaac, and Mary Ann. "It is interesting, I think," writes George Eliot, in reply to some questions of an American lady, "to know whether a writer was born in a central or border district — a condition which always has a strongly determining influence. I was born in Warwickshire, but certain family traditions connected with more northerly districts made these districts a region of poetry to me in my early childhood." In the autobiographical sonnets, entitled 'Brother and Sister,' we catch a glimpse of the mother preparing her children for their accustomed ramble, by stroking down the tippet and setting the frill in order; then standing on the door-step to follow their lessening figures "with the benediction of her gaze." Mrs. Evans was aware, to a certain extent, of her daughter's unusual capacity, being anxious not only that she should have the best education attainable in the neighborhood, but also that good moral influences should be brought to bear upon her: still, the girl's constant habit of reading, even in bed, caused the practical mother not a little annoyance.

The house, where the family lived at that time, and in which the first twenty years of Mary Ann Evans's life were spent, is situated in a rich verdant landscape, where the "grassy fields, each with a sort of personality given to it by the capricious hedge-rows," blend harmoniously with the red-roofed cottages scattered in a happy haphazard fashion amid orchards and elder-bushes. Sixty years ago the country was much more thickly wooded than now, and from the windows of Griff House might be seen the oaks and elms that had still survived from Shakespeare's forest of Arden. The house of the Evans family, half manor-house, half farm, was an old-fashioned building, two stories high, with red brick walls thickly covered with ivy. Like the Garths, they were probably "very fond of their old house." A lawn, interspersed with trees, stretched in front towards the gate, flanked by two stately Norway firs, while a sombre old yew almost touched some of the upper windows with its wide-spreading branches. A farm-yard was at the back, with low rambling sheds and stables; and beyond that, bounded by quiet meadows, one may still see the identical "leafy, flowery, bushy" garden, which George Eliot so often delighted in describing, at a time when her early life, with all its tenderly hoarded associations, had become to her but a haunting memory of bygone things. A garden where roses and cabbages jostle each other, where vegetables have to make room for gnarled old apple-trees, and where, amid the raspberry-bushes and row of currant-trees, you expect to come upon Hetty herself, "stooping to gather the low-hanging fruit."

Such was the place where the childhood of George Eliot was spent. Here she drew in those impressions of English rural and provincial life, of which one day she was to become the greatest interpreter. Impossible to be in a better position for seeing life. Not only was her father's position always improving, so that she was early brought in contact with different grades of society, but his calling made him more or less acquainted with all ranks of his neighbors, and, says George Eliot, "I have always thought that the most fortunate Britons are those whose experience has given them a practical share in many aspects of the national lot, who have lived long among the mixed commonalty, roughing it with them under difficulties, knowing how their food tastes to them, and getting acquainted with their notions and motives, not by inference from traditional types in literature, or from philosophical theories, but from daily fellowship and observation."

And what kind of a child was it who loitered about the farm-yard and garden and fields, noticing everything with grave, watchful eyes, and storing it in a memory of extraordinary tenacity? One of her schoolfellows, who knew her at the age of thirteen, confessed to me that it was impossible to imagine George Eliot as a baby; that it seemed as if she must have come into the world fully developed, like a second Minerva. Her features were fully formed at a very early age, and she had a seriousness of expression almost startling for her years. The records of her child-life may be deciphered, amid some romantic alterations, in the early history of Tom and Maggie Tulliver. Isaac and Mary Ann Evans were playmates, like these, the latter having all the tastes of a boy; whereas her sister Chrissy, said to be the original of Lucy Deane, had peculiarly dainty feminine ways, and shrank from out-door rambles for fear of soiling her shoes or pinafore. But Mary Ann and her brother went fishing together, or spinning tops, or digging for earth-nuts; and the twice-told incident of the little girl being left to mind the rod and losing herself in dreamy contemplation, oblivious of her task, is evidently taken from life, and may be quoted as a reminiscence of her own childhood: —

"One day my brother left me in high charge
   To mind the rod, while he went seeking bait,
And bade me, when I saw a nearing barge,
   Snatch out the line, lest he should come too late.

"Proud of the task I watched with all my might
   For one whole minute, till my eyes grew wide,
Till sky and earth took on a new, strange light,
   And seemed a dream-world floating on some tide.

"A fair pavilioned boat for me alone,
   Bearing me onward through the vast unknown.

"But sudden came the barge's pitch-black prow,
   Nearer and angrier came my brother's cry,
And all my soul was quivering fear, when lo!
   Upon the imperilled line, suspended high,

> "A silver perch! My guilt that won the prey
>   Now turned to merit, had a guerdon rich
> Of hugs and praises, and made merry play
>   Until my triumph reached its highest pitch
>
> "When all at home were told the wondrous feat,
>   And how the little sister had fished well.
> In secret, though my fortune tasted sweet,
>   I wondered why this happiness befell.
>
> "'The little lass had luck,' the gardener said;
>   And so I learned, luck was to glory wed"

Unlike Maggie, however, little Mary Ann was as good a hand at fishing as her brother, only differing from him in not liking to put the worms on the hooks.

Another incident taken from real life, if somewhat magnified, is the adventure with the gypsies. For the prototype of Maggie also fell among these marauding vagrants, and was detained a little time among them. Whether she also proposed to instruct the gypsies and to gain great influence over them by teaching them something about "geography" and "Columbus," does not transpire. But, indeed, most of Maggie's early experiences are autobiographic, down to such facts as her father telling her to rub her "turnip" cheeks against Sally's to get a little bloom, and to cutting off one side of her hair in a passion. At a very early age Mary Ann and her brother were sent to the village free school at Colton, in the parish of Griff, a not unusual custom in those days, when the means of tuition for little children were much more difficult to procure than now. There are still old men living who used to sit on the same form with little Mary Ann Evans learning her A, B, C, and a certain William Jacques (the original of the delightfully comic Bob Jakins of fiction) remembers carrying her pick-a-back on the lawn in front of her father's house.

As the brother and sister grew older they saw less of each other, Mary Ann being sent to a school at Nuneaton, kept by Miss Lewis, for whom she retained an affectionate regard long years afterwards. About the same time she taught at a Sunday-school, in a little cottage adjoining her father's house.

When she was twelve years old, being then, in the words of a neighbor, who occasionally called at Griff House, "a queer, three-cornered, awkward girl," who sat in corners and shyly watched her elders, she was placed as boarder with the Misses Franklin at Coventry. This school, then in high repute throughout the neighborhood, was kept by two sisters, of whom the younger, Miss Rebecca Franklin, was a woman of unusual attainments and ladylike culture, although not without a certain taint of Johnsonian affectation. She seems to have thoroughly grounded Miss Evans in a sound English education, laying great stress in particular on the propriety of a precise and careful manner of speaking and reading. She herself always made a point of expressing herself in studied sentences, and on one occasion, when a friend had called to ask after a dying relative, she actually kept the servant waiting till she had framed an appropriately worded message. Miss Evans, in whose family a broad provincial dialect was spoken, soon acquired Miss Rebecca's carefully elaborated speech, and, not content with that, she might be said to have created a new voice for herself. In later life every one who knew her was struck by the sweetness of her voice, and the finished construction of every sentence, as it fell from her lips; for by that time the acquired habit had become second nature, and blended harmoniously with her entire personality. But in those early days the artificial effort at perfect propriety of expression was still perceptible, and produced an impression of affectation, perhaps reflecting that of her revered instructress. It is also believed that some of the beauty of her intonation in reading English poetry was owing to the same early influence.

Mary Ann, or Marian as she came afterwards to be called, remained about three years with the Misses Franklin. She stood aloof from the other pupils, and one of her school-fellows, Miss Bradley Jenkins, says that she was quite as remarkable in those early days as after she had acquired fame. She seems to have strangely impressed the imagination of the latter, who, figuratively speaking, looked up at her "as at a mountain." There was never anything of the schoolgirl about Miss Evans, for, even at that early age, she had the manners and appearance of a grave, staid woman; so much so, that a stranger, happening to call one day, mistook this girl of thirteen for one of the Misses Franklin, who were then middle-aged women. In this, also, there is a certain resemblance to Maggie Tulliver, who, at the age of thirteen, is described as looking already like a woman. English composition, French and German, were some of the studies to which much time and attention were devoted. Being greatly in advance of the other pupils in the knowledge of French, Miss Evans and Miss Jenkins were taken out of the general class and set to study it together; but, though the two girls were thus associated in a closer fellowship, no real intimacy apparently followed from it. The latter watched the future "George Eliot" with intense interest, but always felt as if in the presence of a superior, though socially their positions were much on a par. This haunting sense of superiority precluded the growth of any closer friendship between the two fellow-pupils. All the more startling was it to the admiring schoolgirl, when one day, on using Marian Evans's German dictionary, she saw scribbled on its blank page some verses, evidently original, expressing rather sentimentally a yearning for love and sympathy. Under this granite-like exterior, then, there was beating a heart that passionately craved for human tenderness and companionship!

Inner solitude was no doubt the portion of George Eliot in those days. She must already have had a dim consciousness of unusual power, to a great extent isolating her from the girls of her own age, absorbed as they were in quite other feelings and ideas. Strong religious convictions pervaded her life at this period, and in the fervid faith and spiritual exaltation which characterize Maggie's girlhood, we have a very faithful picture of the future novelist's own state of mind. Passing through many stages of religious thought, she was first simple Church of England, then Low Church, then "Anti-Supernatural." In this latter character she wore an "Anti-Supernatural" cap, in which, so says an early friend, "her plain features looked all the plainer." But her nature was a mixed one, as indeed is Maggie's too, and conflicting tendencies and inclinations pulled her, no doubt, in different directions. The self-renouncing impulses of one moment were checkmated at another by an eager desire for approbation and distinguishing pre-eminence; and a piety verging on asceticism did not exclude, on the other hand, a very clear perception of the advantages and desirability of good birth, wealth, and high social position. Like her own charming Esther in 'Felix Holt,' she had a fine sense, amid somewhat anomalous surroundings, of the highest refinements and delicacies which are supposed to be the natural attributes of people of rank and fashion. She even shared with the above-mentioned heroine certain girlish vanities and weaknesses, such as liking to have all things about her person as elegant as possible.

About the age of fifteen Marian Evans left the Misses Franklin, and soon afterwards she had the misfortune of losing her mother, who died in her forty-ninth year. Writing to a friend in after life she says, "I began at sixteen to be acquainted with the unspeakable grief of a last parting, in the death of my mother." Less sorrowful partings ensued, though in the end they proved almost as irrevocable. Her elder sister, and the brother in whose steps she had once followed "puppy-like," married and settled in homes of their own. Their different lots in life, and the far more pronounced differences of their aims and ideas, afterwards divided the "brother and sister" completely. This kind of separation between people who have been friends in youth is often more terrible to endure than the actual loss by death itself, and doth truly "work like madness in the brain." Is there not some reference to this in that pathetic passage in 'Adam Bede': "Family likeness has often a deep sadness in it. Nature, that great tragic dramatist, knits us together by bone and muscle, and divides us by the subtler web of our brains, blends yearning and repulsion, and ties us by our heartstrings to the beings that jar us at every movement . . . we see eyes — ah! so like our mother's, averted from us in cold alienation."

For some years after this Miss Evans and her father remained alone together at Griff House. He offered to get a housekeeper, as not the house only, but farm matters, had to be looked after, and he was always tenderly considerate of "the little wench," as he called her. But his daughter preferred taking the whole management of the place into her own hands, and she was as conscientious and diligent in the discharge of her domestic duties as in the prosecution of the studies she carried on at the same time. One of her chief beauties was in her large, finely shaped, feminine hands — hands which she has, indeed, described as characteristic of several of her heroines; but she once pointed out to a friend at Foleshill that one of them was broader across than the other, saying, with some pride, that it was due to the quantity of butter and cheese she had made during her housekeeping days at Griff. It will be remembered that this is a characteristic attributed to the exemplary Nancy Lammeter, whose person gave one the idea of "perfect, unvarying neatness, as the body of a little bird," only her hands bearing "the traces of butter-making, cheese-crushing, and even still coarser work." Certainly the description of the dairy in 'Adam Bede,' and all the processes of butter-making, is one which only complete knowledge could have rendered so perfect. Perhaps no scene in all her novels stands out with more lifelike vividness than that dairy which one could have sickened for in hot, dusty streets: "Such coolness, such purity, such fresh fragrance of new pressed cheese, of firm butter, of wooden vessels perpetually bathed in pure water; such soft coloring of red earthenware and creamy surfaces, brown wood and polished tin, gray limestone and rich orange-red rust on the iron weights and hooks and hinges."

This life of mixed practical activity and intellectual pursuits came to an end in 1841, when Mr. Evans relinquished Griff House, and the management of Sir Roger Newdigate's estates, to his married son, and removed with his daughter to Foleshill, near Coventry.

CHAPTER III.

YOUTHFUL STUDIES AND FRIENDSHIPS.

THE period from about twenty to thirty is usually the most momentous in the lives of illustrious men and women. It is true that the most abiding impressions, those which the future author will reproduce most vividly, have been absorbed by the growing brain previous to this age; but the fusion of these varied impressions of the outward world with the inner life, and the endless combinations in which imagination delights, rarely begin before. Then, as a rule, the ideas are engendered to be carried out in the maturity of life. Alfred de Vigny says truly enough:

> "Qu'est-ce qu'une grande vie ?
> Une pensée de la jeunesse, exécutée par l'âge mur."

Moreover, it is a revolutionary age. Inherited opinions that had been accepted, as the rotation of the seasons, with unhesitating acquiescence, become an object of speculation and passionate questioning. Nothing is taken upon trust. The intellect, stimulated by the sense of expanding and hitherto unchecked capacity, delights in exercising its strength by critically passing in review the opinions, laws, institutions commonly accepted as unalterable. And if the intellect is thus active, the heart is still more so. This is emphatically the time of enthusiastic friendship and glowing love, if often also of cruel disenchantment and disillusion. In most biographies, therefore, this phase of life is no less fascinating than instructive. For it shows the individual while still in a stage of growth already reacting on his environment, and becoming a motive power according to the measure of his intellectual and moral endowments.

It is on this state of George Eliot's life that we are now entering. At Foleshill she acquired that vast range of knowledge and universality of culture which so eminently distinguished her.

The house she now inhabited, though not nearly as picturesque or substantial as the former home of the Evanses, was yet sufficiently spacious, with a pleasant garden in front and behind it; the latter, Marian Evans was fond of making as much like the delicious garden of her childhood as was possible under the circumstances. In other respects she greatly altered her ways of life, cultivating an ultra-fastidiousness in her manners and household arrangements. Though so young, she was not only entire mistress of her father's establishment, but, as his business required him to be abroad the greater part of each week, she was mostly alone.

Her life now became more and more that of a student, one of her chief reasons for rejoicing at the change of residence being the freer access to books. She had, however, already amassed quite a library of her own by this time. In addition to her private studies, she was now also able to have masters to instruct her in a variety of subjects. The Rev. T. Sheepshanks, head master of the Coventry Grammar-school, gave her lessons in Greek and Latin, as she particularly wished to learn the former language in order to read Æschylus. She continued her study of French, German, and Italian under the tuition of Signor Brezzi, even acquiring some knowledge of Hebrew by her own unassisted efforts. Mr. Simms, the veteran organist of St. Michael's Coventry, instructed her in the pianoforte; and probably Rosamond Vincy's teacher in 'Middlemarch' is a faithful portraiture of him. "Her master at Mrs. Lemon's school (close to a country town with a memorable history that had its relics in church and castle) was one of those excellent musicians here and there to be found in the provinces, worthy to compare with many a noted Kapellmeister in a country which offers more plentiful conditions of musical celebrity." George Eliot's sympathetic rendering of her favorite composers, particularly Beethoven and Schubert, was always delightful to her friends, although connoisseurs considered her possessed of little or no strictly technical knowledge. Be that as it may, many an exquisite passage, scattered up and down her works, bears witness to her heartfelt appreciation of music, which seems to have had a more intimate attraction for her than the fine arts. She shows little feeling for archæological beauties, in which Warwickshire is so rich: in her 'Scenes of Clerical Life' dismissing a fine monument of Lady Jane Grey, a genuine specimen of old Gothic art at Astley Church, with a sneer about "marble warriors, and their wives without noses."

In spite of excessive study, this period of Marian's life is not without faint echoes of an early love-story of her own. In the house of one of her married half-sisters she met a young man who promised, at that time, to take a distinguished position in his profession. A kind of engagement, or semi-engagement, took place, which Mr. Evans refused to countenance, and finally his daughter broke it off in a letter, showing both her strong sense and profoundly affectionate nature. At this time she must have often had a painful consciousness of being cut off from that living fellowship with the like-minded so stimulating to the intellectual life. Men are not so subject to this form of soul hunger as women; for at their public schools and colleges they are brought into contact with their contemporaries, and cannot fail to find comrades amongst them of like thoughts and aspirations with themselves. A fresh life, however, at once vivifying to her intellect and stimulating to her heart, now began for Marian Evans in the friendship she formed with Mr. and Mrs. Charles Bray of Rosehill, Coventry. Rahel — the subtly gifted German woman, whose letters and memoirs are a treasury of delicate observation and sentiment — observes that people of marked spiritual affinities are bound to meet some time or other in their lives. If not entirely true, there is a good deal to be said for this comforting theory; as human beings of similar nature seem constantly converging as by some magnetic attraction.

The circle to which Miss Evans now happened to be introduced was in every sense congenial and inspiring. Mr. Bray, his wife, and his sister-in-law were a trio more like some delightful characters in a first-rate novel than the sober inhabitants of a Warwickshire country town. Living in a house beautifully situated on the outskirts of Coventry, they used to spend their lives in philosophical speculations, philanthropy, and pleasant social hospitality, joining to the ease and *laisser aller* of continental manners a thoroughly English geniality and trustworthiness.

Mr. Bray was a wealthy ribbon manufacturer, but had become engrossed from an early age in religious and metaphysical speculation as well as in political and social questions. Beginning to inquire into the dogmas which formed the basis of his belief, he found, on careful investigation, that they did not stand, in his opinion, the test of reason. His arguments set his brother-in-law, Mr Charles C. Hennell, a Unitarian, to examine afresh and go carefully over the whole ground of popular theology, the consequence of this close study being the 'Inquiry concerning the Origin of Christianity,' a work which attracted a good deal of attention when it appeared, and was translated into German at the instance of David Strauss. It was published in 1838, a few years after the appearance of the 'Life of Jesus.' In its critical examination of the miracles, and in the sifting of mythological from historical elements in the Gospels, it bears considerable analogy to Strauss's great work, although strictly based on independent studies, being originally nothing more than an attempt to solve the doubts of a small set of friends. Their doubts were solved, but not in the manner originally anticipated.

Mrs. Bray, of an essentially religious nature, shared the opinions of her husband and brother, and without conforming to the external rites and ceremonies of a creed, led a life of saintly purity and self-devotion. The exquisite beauty of her moral nature not only attracted Marian to this truly amiable woman, but filled her with reverence, and the friendship then commenced was only ended by death.

In Miss Sara Hennell, Marian Evans found another congenial companion who became as a sister to her. This singular being, in most respects such a contrast to her sister, high-strung, nervous, excitable, importing all the ardor of feeling into a life of austere thought, seemed in a manner mentally to totter under the weight of her own immense metaphysical speculations. A casual acquaintance of these two young ladies might perhaps have predicted that Miss Hennell was the one destined to achieve fame in the future, and she certainly must have been an extraordinary mental stimulus to her young friend Marian. These gifted sisters, two of a family, all the members of which were remarkable, by some are identified as the originals of the delightful Meyrick household in 'Daniel Deronda.' Each member of this genial group was already, or ultimately became, an author of more or less repute. A reviewer in the *Westminster*, writing of Mr. Bray's philosophical publications, some years ago, said: "If he would reduce his many works to one containing nothing unessential, he would doubtless obtain that high place among the philosophers of our country to which his powers of thought entitle him." His most popular book, called 'The Education of the Feelings,' intended for use in secular schools, deals with the laws of morality practically applied. Mrs. Bray's writings, on the same order of subjects, are still further simplified for the understanding of children. She is the authoress of 'Physiology for Schools,' 'The British Empire,' 'Elements of Morality,' etc. Her 'Duty to Animals' has become a class book in the schools of the midland counties, and she was one of the first among those noble-hearted men and women who have endeavored to introduce a greater degree of humanity into our treatment of animals.

George Eliot, writing to Mrs. Bray in March 1873 on this very subject, says:

"A very good, as well as very rich, woman, Mrs. S——, has founded a model school at Naples, and has the sympathy of the best Italians in her educational efforts. Of course a chief point in trying to improve the Italians is to teach them kindness to animals, and a friend of Mrs. S—— has confided to her a small sum of money — fifty pounds, I think — to be applied to the translation and publication of some good books for young people, which would be likely to rouse in them a sympathy with dumb creatures.

"Will you kindly help me in the effort to further Mrs. S——'s good work by sending me a copy of your book on animals, and also by telling me the periodical in which the parts of the book first appeared, as well as the titles of any other works which you think would be worth mentioning for the purpose in question?

"Mrs. S—— (as indeed you may probably know) is the widow of a German merchant of Manchester, as rich as many such merchants are, and as benevolent as only the choicest few. She knows all sorts of good work for the world, and is known by most of the workers. It struck me, while she was speaking of this need of a book to translate, that you had done the very thing."

A few days later the following highly interesting letter came from the same source:

"Many thanks for the helpful things you have sent me. 'The Wounded Bird' is charming. But now something very much larger of the same kind must be written, and you are the person to write it — something that will bring the emotions, sufferings, and possible consolations of the dear brutes vividly home to the imaginations of children: fitted for children of all countries, as Reineke Fuchs is comprehensible to all nations. A rough notion came to me the other day of supposing a house of refuge, not only for dogs, but for all distressed animals. The keeper of this refuge understands the language of the brutes, which includes differences of dialect not hindering communication even between birds and dogs, by the help of some Ulysses among them who is versed in the various tongues, and puts in the needed explanations. Said keeper overhears his refugees solacing their evenings by telling the story of their experiences, and finally acts as editor of their autobiographies. I imagine my long-loved fellow-creature, the ugly dog, telling the sorrows and the tender emotions of gratitude which have wrought him into a sensitive soul. The donkey is another cosmopolitan sufferer, and a greater martyr than Saint Lawrence. If we only knew what fine motives he has for his meek endurance, and how he loves a friend who will scratch his nose!

"All this is not worth anything except to make you feel how much better a plan you can think of.

"Only you must positively write this book which everybody wants — this book which will do justice to the share our 'worthy fellow-laborers' have had in the groaning and travailing of the world towards the birth of the right and fair.

"But you must not do it without the 'sustenance of labor,' — I don't say 'pay,' since there is no pay for good work. Let Mr. . . . be blest with the blessing of the unscrupulous. I want to contribute something towards helping the brutes, and helping the children, especially the southern children, to be good to the creatures who are continually at their mercy. I can't write the needed book myself, but I feel sure that you can, and that you will not refuse the duty."

Mrs. Bray's answer to this humorous suggestion may be gathered from George Eliot's amiable reply.

"I see at once that you must be right about the necessity for being simple and literal. In fact I have ridiculous impulses in teaching children, and always make the horizon too wide.

"'The Wounded Bird' is perfect of its kind, and that kind is the best for a larger work. You yourself see clearly that it is an exceptional case for any one to be able to write books for children without putting in them false morality disguised as devout religion. And you are one of the exceptional cases. I am quite sure, from what you have done, that you can do the thing which is still wanted to be done. As to imagination, 'The Wounded Bird' is full of imagination."

These extracts pleasantly illustrate both the writer and recipient of such humane letters; and, though written at a much later period, not only give an idea of the nature of Mrs Bray's literary pursuits, but of the friendly relations subsisting to the end between her and George Eliot.

Of Miss Hennell's work it is more difficult to speak without entering more deeply into her subject-matter than is compatible with the scope of the present work. In one of her best-known books, entitled 'Thoughts in Aid of Faith,' she makes the daring attempt to trace the evolution of religion, her mode of thought partaking at once of the scientific and the mystical. For the present she seems to be one of the very few women who have ventured into the arena of philosophy; and, curiously enough, her doctrine is that there should be a feminine method in metaphysics as well as a masculine, the sexes, according to this singular theory, finding their counterpart in religion and science. It may be remembered that George Eliot, in one of her essays, is of opinion that women should endeavor to make some distinctively feminine contributions to the intellectual pursuits they engage in, saying, "Let the whole field of reality be laid open to woman as well as to man, and then that which is peculiar in her mental modification, instead of being, as it is now, a source of discord and repulsion between the sexes, will be found to be a necessary complement to the truth and beauty of life. Then we shall have that marriage of minds which alone can blend all the hues of thought and feeling in one lovely rainbow of promise for the harvest of happiness." Something of the same idea lies at the root of much in Miss Hennell's mystical disquisitions.

This circumstantial account of the circle to which Miss Evans was now introduced has been given, because it consisted of friends who, more than any others, helped in the growth and formation of her mind. No human being, indeed, can be fully understood without some knowledge of the companions that at one time or other, but especially during the period of development, have been intimately associated with his or her life. However vastly a mountain may appear to loom above us from the plain, on ascending to its summit one always finds innumerable lesser eminences which all help in making up the one imposing central effect. And similarly in the world of mind, many superior natures, in varying degrees, all contribute their share towards the maturing of that exceptional intellectual product whose topmost summit is genius.

The lady who first introduced Marian Evans to the Brays was not without an object of her own, for her young friend — whose religious fervor, tinged with evangelical sentiment, was as conspicuous as her unusual learning and thoughtfulness — seemed to her peculiarly fitted to exercise a beneficial influence on the Rosehill household, where generally unorthodox opinions were much in vogue.

Up to the age of seventeen or eighteen Marian had been considered the most truly pious member of her family, being earnestly bent, as she says, "to shape this anomalous English Christian life of ours into some consistency with the spirit and simple verbal tenor of the New Testament." "I was brought up," she informs another correspondent, "in the Church of England, and have never joined any other religious society; but I have had close acquaintance with many dissenters of various sects, from Calvinistic Anabaptists to

Unitarians." Her inner life at this time is faithfully mirrored in the spiritual experiences of Maggie Tulliver. Marian Evans was not one who could rest satisfied with outward observances and lip-worship: she needed a faith which should give unity and sanctity to the conception of life; which should awaken "that recognition of something to be lived for beyond the mere satisfaction of self, which is to the moral life what the addition of a great central ganglion is to animal life." At one time Evangelicalism supplied her with the most essential conditions of a religious life: with all the vehemence of an ardent nature she flung her whole soul into a passionate acceptance of the teaching of Christianity, carrying her zeal to the pitch of asceticism.

This was the state of her mind, at the age of seventeen, when her aunt from Wirksworth came to stay with her. Mrs. Elizabeth Evans (who came afterwards to be largely identified with Dinah Morris) was a zealous Wesleyan, having at one time been a noted preacher; but her niece, then a rigid Calvinist, hardly thought her doctrine strict enough. When this same aunt paid her a visit, some years afterwards, at Foleshill, Marian's views had already undergone a complete transformation, and their intercourse was constrained and painful; for the young evangelical enthusiast, who had been a favorite in clerical circles, was now in what she afterwards described as a "crude state of freethinking." It was a period of transition through which she gradually passed into a new religious synthesis.

Her intimacy with the Brays began about the time when these new doubts were beginning to ferment in her. Her expanding mind, nourished on the best literature, ancient and modern, began to feel cramped by dogmas that had now lost their vitality; yet a break with an inherited form of belief to which a thousand tender associations bound her was a catastrophe she shrank from with dread. Hence a period of mental uncertainty and trouble. In consequence of these inward questionings, it happened that the young lady who had been unwittingly brought to convert her new acquaintances was converted by them. In intercourse with them she was able freely to open her mind, their enlightened views helping her in this crisis of her spiritual life; and she found it an intense relief to feel no longer bound to reconcile her moral and intellectual perceptions with a particular form of worship.

The antagonism she met with in certain quarters, the social persecution from which she had much to suffer, are perhaps responsible for some of the sharp, caustic irony with which she afterwards assailed certain theological habits of thought. It is not unlikely that in some of her essays for the *Westminster Review* she mainly expressed the thoughts which were stirred in her by the opposition she encountered at this period of her life — as, for example, in the brilliant paper entitled 'Worldliness and Other-Worldliness,' which contains such a scathing passage as the following:

"For certain other elements of virtue, which are of more obvious importance to untheological minds, — a delicate sense of our neighbor's rights, an active participation in the joys and sorrows of our fellow-men, a magnanimous acceptance of privation or suffering for ourselves when it is the condition of good to others, in a word, the extension and intensification of our sympathetic nature, we think it of some importance to contend, that they have no more direct relation to the belief in a future state than the interchange of gases in the lungs has to the plurality of worlds. Nay, to us it is conceivable that to some minds the deep pathos lying in the thought of human morality — that we are here for a little while and then vanish away, that this earthly life is all that is given to our loved ones, and to our many suffering fellow-men, lies nearer the fountains of moral emotion than the conception of extended existence. . . . To us it is matter of unmixed rejoicing that this latter necessity of healthful life is independent of theological ink, and that its evolution is insured in the interaction of human souls as certainly as the evolution of science or of art, with which, indeed, it is but a twin ray, melting into them with undefinable limits."

It was, of course, inevitable that her changed tone of mind should attract the attention of the family and friends of Marian, and that the backsliding of so exemplary a member should afford matter for scandal in many a clerical circle and evangelical tea-meeting. Close to the Evanses there lived at that time a dissenting minister, whose daughter Mary was a particular favorite of Marian Evans. There had been much neighborly intimacy between the two young ladies, and though there was only five years' difference between them, Marian always inspired her friend with a feeling of awe at her intellectual superiority. Yet her sympathy — that sympathy with all human life which was the strongest element of her character — was even then so irresistible that every little trouble of Mary's life was intrusted to her keeping. But the sudden discovery of their daughter's friend being an "infidel" came with the shock of a thunder-clap on the parents. Much hot argument passed between the minister and this youthful controversialist, but the former clinched the whole question by a triumphant reference to the dispersion of the Jews throughout the world as an irrefutable proof of the divine inspiration of the Bible. In spite of this vital difference on religious questions, Miss Evans was suffered to go on giving the minister's daughter lessons in German, which were continued for two or three years, she having generously undertaken this labor of love twice a week, because she judged from the shape of her young friend's head — phrenology being rife in those days — that she must have an excellent understanding. But, better than languages, she taught her the value of time, always cutting short mere random talk by simply ignoring it. Altogether the wonderful strength of her personality manifested itself even at this early period in the indelible impression it left on her pupil's memory, many of her sayings remaining graven on it as on stone. As, for instance, when one day twitting Mary's too great self-esteem she remarked, "We are very apt to measure ourselves by our aspiration instead of our performance." Or when on a friend's asking, "What is the meaning of Faust?" she replied, "The same as the meaning of the universe." While reading '*Wallenstein's Lager*' with her young pupil, the latter happened to say how life-like the characters seemed: "Don't say *seemed*," exclaimed Marian; "we know that they *are* true to the life." And she immediately began repeating the talk of laborers, farriers, butchers, and others of that class, with such close imitation as to startle her friend. Is not this a foreshadowing of the inimitable scene at the 'Rainbow'?

By far the most trying consequence of her change of views was that now, for the first time, Marian was brought into collision with her father, whose pet she had always been. He could not understand her inward perplexities, nor the need of her soul for complete inward unity of thought, a condition impossible to her under the limiting conditions of a dogmatic evangelicalism, "where folly often mistakes itself for wisdom, ignorance gives itself airs of knowledge, and selfishness, turning its eyes upwards, calls itself religion." She, on the other hand, after a painful struggle, wanted to break away from the old forms of worship, and refused to go to church. Deeply attached though she was to her father, the need to make her acts conform with her convictions became irresistible. Under such conflicting tendencies a rupture between father and daughter became imminent, and for a short time a breaking up of the home was contemplated, Marian intending to go and live by herself in Coventry. One of the leading traits in her nature was its adhesiveness, however, and the threat of separation proved so painful to her that her friends, Mr. and Mrs. Bray, persuaded her to conform to her father's wishes as far as outward observances were implied, and for the rest he did not trouble himself to inquire into her thoughts or occupations.

From a letter written at this period it appears that the 'Inquiry Concerning the Origin of Christianity' had made a most powerful impression on her mind. Indeed, she dated from it a new birth. But so earnest and conscientious was she in her studies, that before beginning its longed-for perusal, she and a friend determined to read the Bible through again from beginning to end.

The intimacy between the inmates of Rosehill and the girl student at Foleshill meanwhile was constantly growing closer. They met daily, and in their midst the humorous side of her nature expanded no less than her intellect. Although striking ordinary acquaintances by an abnormal gravity, when completely at her ease she at times bubbled over with fun and gayety, irradiated by the unexpected flashes of a wit whose full scope was probably as yet unsuspected by its possessor. Not but that Miss Evans and her friends must have been conscious, even at that early age, of extraordinary powers in her, destined some day to give her a conspicuous position in the world. For her conversation was already so full of charm, depth, and comprehensiveness, that all talk after hers seemed stale and common-place. Many were the discussions in those days between Mr. Bray and Marian Evans, and though frequently broken off in fierce dispute one evening, they always began again quite amicably the next. Mr. Bray probably exercised considerable influence on his young friend's mind at this impressible period of life; perhaps her attention to philosophy was first roused by acquaintance with him, and his varied acquirements in this department may have helped in giving a positive direction to her own thoughts.

Mr. Bray was just then working out his 'Philosophy of Necessity,' the problems discussed being the same as those which have occupied the leading thinkers of the day: Auguste Comte in his 'Positive Philosophy;' Buckle in his 'History of Civilization;' and Mr. Herbert Spencer in his 'Sociology.' The theory that, as an individual and collectively, man is as much subject to law as any of the other entities in nature, was one of those magnificent ideas which revolutionize the world of thought. Many minds, in different countries, of different calibre, were all trying to systematize what knowledge there was on this subject in order to convert hypothesis into demonstration. To what extent Mr. Bray may have based his 'Philosophy of Necessity' on independent research, or how much was merely assimilated from contemporary sources, we cannot here inquire. Enough that the ideas embodied in it represented some of the most vital thought of the age, and contributed therefore not a little to the formation of George Eliot's mind, and to the grip which she presently displayed in the handling of philosophical topics.

In 1842 the sensation created by Dr. Strauss's *Leben Jesu* had even extended to so remote a district as Warwickshire. Some persons of advanced opinions, deeply impressed by its penetrating historical criticism, which was in fact Niebuhr's method applied to the elucidation of the Gospels, were very desirous of obtaining an English translation of this work; meeting at the house of a common friend, the late Mr. Joseph Parkes of Birmingham, they agreed, in the first blush of their enthusiasm, to raise amongst them whatever sum might be required for the purpose. Mr. Hennell, the leading spirit in this enterprise, proposed that the translation should be undertaken by Miss Brabant, the accomplished daughter of Dr. Brabant, a scholar deeply versed in theological matters, who was in friendly correspondence with Strauss and Paulus in Germany and with Coleridge and Grote in England. The lady in question, though still in her teens, was peculiarly fitted for the task, as she had already translated some of Baur's erudite writings on theological subjects into English. But when she had done about one half of the first volume, her learned labors came to an unexpected conclusion, as she became engaged to Mr. Hennell, who to great mental attainments joined much winning buoyancy of manner. And on her marriage with this gentleman she had to relinquish her task as too laborious.

Miss Brabant's acquaintance with Marian began in 1843, and in the summer of that year the whole friendly group started on an excursion to Tenby. During their stay at this watering-place the lady who had begun, and the lady destined eventually to accomplish, the enormous labor of translating the 'Life of Jesus,' gave tokens of feminine frivolity by insisting on going to a public ball, where, however, they were disappointed, as partners were very scarce. It should be remembered that Marian Evans was only twenty-three years old at this time, but, though she had not yet done anything, her friends already thought her a wonderful woman. She never seems to have had any real youthfulness, and her personal appearance greatly improved with time. It is only to the finest natures, it should be remembered, that age gives an added beauty and distinction; for the most persistent self has then worked its way to the surface, having modified the expression, and to some extent the features, to its own likeness.

There exists a colored sketch done by Mrs. Bray about this period, which gives one a glimpse of George Eliot in her girlhood. In those Foleshill days she had a quantity of soft pale-brown hair worn in ringlets. Her head was massive, her features powerful and rugged, her mouth large but shapely, the jaw singularly square for a woman, yet having a certain delicacy of outline. A neutral tone of coloring did not help to relieve this general heaviness of structure, the complexion being pale but not fair. Nevertheless the play of expression and the wonderful mobility of the mouth, which increased with age, gave a womanly softness to the countenance in curious contrast with its framework. Her eyes, of a gray-blue, constantly varying in color, striking some as intensely blue, others as of a pale, washed-out gray, were small and not beautiful in themselves, but when she grew animated in conversation, those eyes lit up the whole face, seeming in a manner to transfigure it. So much was this the case, that a young lady, who had once enjoyed an hour's conversation with her, came away under its spell with the impression that she was beautiful, but afterwards, on seeing George Eliot again when she was not talking, she could hardly believe her to be the same person. The charm of her nature disclosed itself in her manner and in her voice, the latter recalling that of Dorothea, in being "like the voice of a soul that has once lived in an Æolian harp." It was low and deep, vibrating with sympathy.

Mr. Bray, an enthusiastic believer in phrenology, was so much struck with the grand proportions of her head that he took Marian Evans to London to have a cast taken. He thinks that, after that of Napoleon, her head showed the largest development from brow to ear of any person's recorded. The similarity of type between George Eliot's face and Savonarola's has been frequently pointed out. Some affinity in their natures may have led her, if unconsciously, to select that epoch of Florentine life in which he played so prominent a part.

Though not above the middle height Marian gave people the impression of being much taller than she really was, her figure, although thin and slight, being well-poised and not without a certain sturdiness of make. She was never robust in health, being delicately strung, and of a highly nervous temperament. In youth the keen excitability of her nature often made her wayward and hysterical. In fact her extraordinary intellectual vigor did not exclude the susceptibilities and weaknesses of a peculiarly feminine organization. With all her mental activity she yet led an intensely emotional life, a life which must have held hidden trials for her, as in those days she was known by her friends "to weep bucketfuls of tears."

A woman of strong passions, like her own Maggie, deeply affectionate by nature, of a clinging tenderness of disposition, Marian Evans went through much inward struggle, through many painful experiences, before she reached the moral self-government of her later years. Had she not, it is hardly likely that she could have entered with so deep a comprehension into the most intricate windings of the human heart. That, of course, was to a great extent due to her sympathy, sympathy being the strongest quality of her moral nature. She flung herself, as it were, into other lives, making their affairs, their hopes, their sorrows, her own. And this power of identifying herself with the people she came near had the effect of a magnet in attracting her fellow-creatures. If friends went to her in their trouble they would find not only that she entered with deep feeling into their most minute concerns, but that, by gradual degrees, she lifted them beyond their personal distress, and that they would leave her presence in an ennobled and elevated frame of mind. This sympathy was closely connected with her faculty of detecting and responding to anything that showed the smallest sign of intellectual vitality. She essentially resembled Socrates in her manner of eliciting whatsoever capacity for thought might be latent in the people she came in contact with: were it only a shoemaker or day-laborer, she would never rest till she had found out in what points that particular man differed from other men of his class. She always rather educed what was in others than impressed herself on them; showing much kindliness of heart in drawing out people who were shy. Sympathy was the keynote of her nature, the source of her iridescent humor, of her subtle knowledge of character, and of her dramatic genius.

CHAPTER IV.

TRANSLATION OF STRAUSS AND FEUERBACH. — TOUR ON THE CONTINENT.

Miss Brabant's marriage to Mr. Charles Hennell occurred some months after this excursion to Tenby. In the meanwhile it was settled that Miss Evans should continue her translation of Dr. Strauss's *Leben Jesu*. Thus her first introduction to literature was in a sense accidental. The result proved her admirably fitted for the task; for her version of this searching and voluminous work remains a masterpiece of clear nervous English, at the same time faithfully rendering the spirit of the original. But it was a vast and laborious undertaking, requiring a large share of patience, will, and energy, quite apart from the necessary mental qualifications. On this occasion, to fit herself more fully for her weighty task, Marian taught herself a considerable amount of Hebrew. But she groaned, at times, under the pressure of the toil which had necessarily to be endured, feeling tempted to relinquish what must often have seemed almost intolerable drudgery. The active interest and encouragement of her friends, however, tided her over these moments of discouragement, and after three years of assiduous application, the translation was finally completed, and brought out by Dr. (then Mr.) John Chapman in 1846. It is probably safe to assume that the composition of none of her novels cost George Eliot half the effort and toil which this translation had done. Yet so badly is this kind of literary work remunerated, that twenty pounds was the sum paid for what had cost three years of hard labor!

Indeed, by this time, most of the twelve friends who had originally guaranteed the sum necessary for the translation and publication of the 'Life of Jesus' had conveniently forgotten the matter; and had it not been for the generosity of Mr. Joseph Parkes, who volunteered to advance the necessary funds, who knows how long the MS. translation might have lain dormant in a drawer at Foleshill? It no sooner saw the light, however, than every one recognized the exceptional merits of the work. And for several years afterwards Miss Evans continued to be chiefly known as the translator of Strauss's *Leben Jesu*.

Soon after relieving Miss Brabant from the task of translation, Miss Evans went to stay for a time with her friend's father, Dr. Brabant, who sadly felt the loss of his daughter's intelligent and enlivening companionship. No doubt the society of this accomplished scholar, described by Mr. Grote as "a vigorous self-thinking intellect," was no less congenial than instructive to his young companion; while her singular mental acuteness and affectionate womanly ways were most grateful to the lonely old man. There is something very attractive in this episode of George Eliot's life. It recalls a frequently recurring situation in her novels, particularly that touching one of the self-renouncing devotion with which the ardent Romola throws herself into her afflicted father's learned and recondite pursuits.

There exists a letter written to an intimate friend in 1846, soon after the translation of Strauss was finished, which, I should say, already shows the future novelist in embryo. In this delightfully humorous mystification of her friends, Miss Evans pretends that, to her gratification, she has actually had a visit from a real live German professor, whose musty person was encased in a still mustier coat. This learned personage has come over to England with the single purpose of getting his voluminous writings translated into English. There are at least twenty volumes, all unpublished, owing to the envious machinations of rival authors, none of them treating of anything more modern than Cheops, or the invention of the hieroglyphics. The respectable professor's object in coming to England is to secure a wife and translator in one. But though, on inquiry, he finds that the ladies engaged in translation are legion, they mostly turn out to be utterly incompetent, besides not answering to his requirements in other respects. The qualifications he looks for in a wife, besides a thorough acquaintance with English and German, being personal ugliness and a snug little capital, sufficient to supply him with a moderate allowance of tobacco and *Schwarzbier*, after defraying the expense of printing his books. To find this phœnix among women he is sent to Coventry on all hands.

In Miss Evans, so she runs on, the aspiring professor finds his utmost wishes realized, and so proposes to her on the spot; thinking that it may be her last chance, she accepts him with equal celerity, and her father, although strongly objecting to a foreigner, is induced to give his consent for the same reason. The lady's only stipulation is that her future husband shall take her out of England, with its dreary climate and drearier inhabitants. This being settled, she invites her friends to come to her wedding, which is to take place next week.

This lively little *jeu d'esprit* is written in the wittiest manner, and one cannot help fancying that this German Dryasdust contained the germ of one of her very subtlest masterpieces in characterization, that of the much-to-be-pitied Casaubon, the very Sisyphus of authors. In the lady, too, willing to marry her parchment-bound suitor for the sake of co-operating in his abstruse mental labors, we have a faint adumbration of the simple-minded Dorothea.

But these sudden stirrings at original invention did not prevent Miss Evans from undertaking another task, similar to her last, if not so laborious. She now set about translating Ludwig Feuerbach's *Wesen des Christenthums*. This daring philosopher, who kept aloof from professional honors, and dwelt apart in a wood, that he might be free to handle questions of theology and metaphysics with absolute fearlessness, had created a great sensation by his philosophical criticism in Germany. Unlike his countrymen, whose writings on these subjects are usually enveloped in such an impenetrable mist that their most perilous ideas pass harmlessly over the heads of the multitude, Feuerbach, by his keen incisiveness of language and luminousness of exposition, was calculated to bring his meaning home to the average reader. Mr. Garnett's account of the 'Essence of Christianity' in the 'Encyclopædia Britannica,' admirably concise as it is, may be quoted here, as conveying in the fewest words the gist of this "famous treatise, where Feuerbach shows that every article of Christian belief corresponds to some instinct or necessity of man's nature, from which he infers that it is the creation and embodiment of some human wish, hope, or apprehension.... Following up the hint of one of the oldest Greek philosophers, he demonstrates that religious ideas have their counterparts in human nature, and assumes that they must be its product."

The translation of the 'Essence of Christianity' was also published by Mr. Chapman in 1854. It appeared in his 'Quarterly Series,' destined "to consist of works by learned and profound thinkers, embracing the subjects of theology, philosophy, biblical criticism, and the history of opinion." Probably because her former translation had been so eminently successful, Miss Evans received fifty pounds for her present work. But there was no demand for it in England, and Mr. Chapman lost heavily by its publication.

About the same period Miss Evans also translated Spinoza's *De Deo* for the benefit of an inquiring friend. But her English version of the 'Ethics' was not undertaken till the year 1854, after she had left her home at Foleshill. In applying herself to the severe labor of rendering one philosophical work after another into English, Miss Evans, no doubt, was bent on elucidating for herself some of the most vital problems which engage the mind when once it has shaken itself free from purely traditional beliefs, rather than on securing for herself any pecuniary advantages. But her admirable translations attracted the attention of the like-minded, and she became gradually known to some of the most distinguished men of the time.

Unfortunately her father's health now began to fail, causing her no little pain and anxiety. At some period during his illness she stayed with him in the Isle of Wight, for in a letter to Mrs. Bray, written many years afterwards, she says, "The 'Sir Charles Grandison' you are reading must be the series of little fat volumes you lent me to carry to the Isle of Wight, where I read it at every interval when my father did not want me, and was sorry that the long novel was not longer. It is a solace to hear of any one's reading and enjoying Richardson. We have fallen on an evil generation who would not read

'Clarissa' even in an abridged form. The French have been its most enthusiastic admirers, but I don't know whether their present admiration is more than traditional, like their set phrases about their own classics."

During the last year of her father's life his daughter was also in the habit of reading Scott's novels aloud to him for several hours of each day; she must thus have become deeply versed in his manner of telling the stories in which she continued to delight all her life; and in speaking of the widening of our sympathies which a picture of human life by a great artist is calculated to produce, even in the most trivial and selfish, she gives as an instance Scott's description of Luckie Mucklebackit's cottage, and his story of the 'Two Drovers.'

But a heavy loss now befell Marian Evans in the death of her father, which occurred in 1849. Long afterwards nothing seemed to afford consolation to her grief. For eight years these two had kept house together, and the deepest mutual affection had always subsisted between them. Marian ever treasured her father's memory. As George Eliot she loved to recall in her works everything associated with him in her childhood; those happy times when, standing between her father's knees, she used to be driven by him to "outlying hamlets, whose groups of inhabitants were as distinctive to my imagination as if they belonged to different regions of the globe." Miss Evans, however, was not suffered to mourn uncomforted. The tender friends who cared for her as a sister, now planned a tour to the Continent in hopes that the change of scene and associations would soften her grief.

So they started on their travels, going to Switzerland and Italy by the approved route, which in those days was not so hackneyed as it now is. To so penetrating an observer as Miss Evans there must have been an infinite interest in this first sight of the Continent. But the journey did not seem to dispel her grief, and she continued in such very low spirits that Mrs. Bray almost regretted having taken her abroad so soon after her bereavement. Her terror, too, at the giddy passes which they had to cross, with precipices yawning on either hand — so that it seemed as if a false step must send them rolling into the abyss — was so overpowering that the sublime spectacle of the snow-clad Alps seemed comparatively to produce but little impression on her. Her moral triumph over this constitutional timidity, when any special occasion arose, was all the more remarkable. One day when crossing the Col de Balme from Martigny to Chamounix, one of the side-saddles was found to be badly fitted, and would keep turning round, to the risk of the rider, if not very careful, slipping off at any moment. Marian, however, insisted on having this defective saddle in spite of the protest of Mrs. Bray, who felt quite guilty whenever they came to any perilous places.

How different is this timidity from George Sand's hardy spirit of enterprise! No one who has read that captivating book, her *Lettres d'un Voyageur*, can forget the great Frenchwoman's description of a Swiss expedition, during which, while encumbered with two young children, she seems to have borne all the perils, fatigues, and privations of a toilsome ascent with the hardihood of a mountaineer. But it should not be forgotten that Miss Evans was just then in a peculiarly nervous and excitable condition, and her frequent fits of weeping were a source of pain to her anxious fellow-travellers. She had, in fact, been so assiduous in attendance on her sick father, that she was physically broken down for a time. Under these circumstances an immediate return to England seemed unadvisable, and, when her friends started on their homeward journey, it was decided that Marian should remain behind at Geneva.

Here, amid scenes so intimately associated with genius — where the "self-torturing sophist, wild Rousseau," placed the home of his '*Nouvelle Héloïse*,' and the octogenarian Voltaire spent the serene Indian summer of his stirring career; where Gibbon wrote his 'History of the Decline and Fall of the Roman Empire;' where Byron and Shelley sought refuge from the hatred of their countrymen, and which Madame de Stael complainingly exchanged for her beloved Rue du Bac — here the future author of 'Romola' and 'Middlemarch' gradually recovered under the sublime influences of Nature's healing beauties.

For about eight months Miss Evans lived at a boarding-house, "Le Plongeau," near Geneva. But she was glad to find a quieter retreat in the family of an artist, M. D'Albert, becoming much attached to him and his wife. Established in one of the lofty upper stories of this pleasant house, with the blue shimmering waters of the lake glancing far below, and the awful heights of Mont Blanc solemnly dominating the entire landscape, she not only loved to prosecute her studies, but, in isolation from mankind, to plan glorious schemes for their welfare. During this stay she drank deep of Rousseau, whose works, especially *Les Confessions*, made an indelible impression on her. And when inciting a friend to study French, she remarked that it was worth learning that language, if only to read him. At the same period Marian probably became familiarized with the magnificent social utopias of St. Simon, Proudhon, and other French writers. Having undergone a kind of mental revolution herself not so long ago, she must have felt some sympathy with the thrilling hopes of liberty which had agitated the states of Western Europe in 1849. But, as I have already pointed out, her nature had conservative leanings. She believed in progress only as the result of evolution, not revolution. And in one of her most incisive essays, entitled 'The National History of German Life,' she finely points out the "notable failure of revolutionary attempts conducted from the point of view of abstract democratic and socialistic theories." In the same article she draws a striking parallel between the growth of language and that of political institutions, contending that it would be as unsatisfactory to "construct a universal language on a rational basis" — one that had "no uncertainty, no whims of idiom, no cumbrous forms, no fitful shimmer of many-hued significance, no hoary archaisms 'familiar with forgotten years,'" — as abruptly to alter forms of government which are nothing, in fact, but the result of historical growth, systematically embodied by society.

Besides the fascinations of study, and the outward glory of nature, the charm of social intercourse was not wanting to this life at Geneva. In M. D'Albert, a very superior man, gentle, refined, and of unusual mental attainments, she found a highly desirable daily companion. He was an artist by profession, and it is whispered that he suggested some of the traits in the character of the delicate-minded Philip Wakem in the 'Mill on the Floss.' The only portrait in oils which exists of George Eliot is one painted by M. D'Albert at this interesting time of her life. She inspired him, like most people who came into personal contact with her, with the utmost admiration and regard, and, wishing to be of some service, he escorted Miss Evans to England on her return thither. Curiously enough, M. D'Albert subsequently translated one of her works, probably 'Adam Bede,' without in the least suspecting who its real author was.

It is always a shock when vital changes have occurred in one's individual lot to return to a well-known place, after an absence of some duration, to find it wearing the same unchangeable aspect. One expects somehow that fields and streets and houses would show some alteration corresponding to that within ourselves. But already from a distance the twin spires of Coventry, familiar as household words to the Warwickshire girl, greeted the eyes of the returning traveller. In spite of all love for her native spot of earth, this was a heavy time to Marian Evans. Her father was dead, the home where she had dwelt as mistress for so many years broken up, the present appearing blank and comfortless, the future uncertain and vaguely terrifying. The question now was where she should live, what she should do, to what purposes turn the genius whose untried and partially unsuspected powers were darkly agitating her whole being.

As has been already said, Marian Evans had a highly complex nature, compounded of many contradictory impulses, which, though gradually brought into harmony as life matured, were always pulling her, in those days, in different directions. Thus, though she possessed strong family affections, she could not help feeling that to go and take up her abode in the house of some relative, where life resolved itself into a monotonous recurrence of petty considerations, something after the Glegg pattern, would be little short of crucifixion to her, and, however deep her attachment for her native soil may have been, she yet sighed passionately to break away from its associations, and to become "a wanderer and a pilgrim on the face of the earth."

For some little time after her return from abroad Marian took up her residence with her brother and his family. But the children who had toddled hand-in-hand in the fields together had now diverged so widely that no memories of a mutual past could bridge over the chasm that divided them. Under these circumstances the family at Rosehill pressed her to make their home permanently hers, and for about a year, from 1850 to 1851, she became the member of a household in fullest sympathy with her. Here Mr. Bray's many-sided mental activity and genial brightness of disposition, and his wife's exquisite goodness of heart, must have helped to soothe and cheer one whose delicately strung nature was just then nearly bending under the excessive strain of thought and feeling she had gone through. One person, indeed, was so struck by the grave sadness generally affecting her, that it seemed to him as if her coming took all the sunshine out of the day. But whether grave or gay, whether meditative or playful, her conversation exercised a spell over all who came within its reach.

In the pleasant house at Rosehill distinguished guests were constantly coming and going, so that there was no lack of the needed intellectual friction supplied by clever and original talk. Here in a pleasant garden, planted with rustling acacia-trees, and opening on a wide prospect of richly wooded, undulating country, with the fitful brightness of English skies overhead, and a smooth-shaven lawn to walk or recline upon, many were the topics discussed by men who had made, or were about to make, their mark. Froude was known there. George Combe discussed with his host the principles of phrenology, at that time claiming "its thousands of disciples." Ralph Waldo Emerson, on a lecturing tour in this country, while on a brief visit, made Marian's acquaintance, and was observed by Mrs. Bray engaged in eager talk with her. Suddenly she saw him start. Something said by this quiet, gentle-mannered girl had evidently given him a shock of surprise. Afterwards, in conversation with her friends, he spoke of her "great calm soul." This is no doubt an instance of the intense sympathetic adaptiveness of Miss Evans. If great, she was not by any means calm at this period, but inwardly deeply perturbed, yet her nature, with subtlest response, reflected the transcendental calm of the philosopher when brought within his atmosphere.

George Dawson, the popular lecturer, and Mr. Flower, were more intimately associated with the Rosehill household The latter, then living at Stratford-on-Avon, where he was wont to entertain a vast number of people, especially Americans, who made pilgrimages to Shakespeare's birthplace, is known to the world as the benevolent denouncer of "bits and bearing-reins." One day this whole party went to hear George Dawson, who had made a great sensation at Birmingham, preach one of his thrilling sermons from the text "And the common people heard him gladly." George Eliot, alluding to these days as late as 1876, says, in a letter to Mrs. Bray:

"George Dawson was strongly associated for me with Rosehill, not to speak of the General Baptist Chapel, where we all heard him preach for the first time (to us). . . . I have a vivid recollection of an evening when Mr. and Mrs. F —— dined at your house with George Dawson, when he was going to lecture at the Mechanics' Institute, and you felt compassionately towards him, because you thought the rather riotous talk was a bad preface to his lecture. We have a Birmingham friend, whose acquaintance we made many years ago in Weimar, and from him I have occasionally had some news of Mr. Dawson. I feared, what you mention, that his life has been a little too strenuous in these latter years."

On the evening alluded to in this letter Mr. Dawson was dining at Mrs. Bray's house before giving his lecture on 'John Wesley,' at the Mechanics' Institute. His rich sarcasm and love of fun had exhilarated the whole company, and not content with merely "riotous talk," George Dawson and Mr. Flower turned themselves into lions and wild cats for the amusement of the children, suddenly pouncing out from under the table-cloth, with hideous roarings and screechings, till the hubbub became appalling, joined to the delighted half-frightened exclamations of the little ones. Mr. Dawson did the lions, and Mr. Flower, who had made personal acquaintance with the wild cats in the backwoods of America, was inimitable in their peculiar pounce and screech.

Thus amid studies and pleasant friendly intercourse did the days pass at Rosehill. Still Marian Evans was restless, tormented, frequently in tears, perhaps unconsciously craving a wider sphere, and more definitely recognized position. However strenuously she, at a maturer time of life, inculcated the necessity of resignation, she had not then learned to resign herself. And now a change was impending — a change which, fraught with the most important consequences, was destined to give a new direction to the current of her life. Dr. John Chapman invited her to assist him in the editorship of the *Westminster Review*, which passed at that time into his hands from John Mill. They had already met, when Marian was passing through London on her way to the Continent, on some matter of business or other connected with one of her translations. Dr. Chapman's proposition was accepted; and although Marian suffered keenly from the wrench of parting with her friends, the prompting to work out her powers to the full overcame the clinging of affection, and in the spring of 1851 she left Rosehill behind her and came to London.

CHAPTER V.

THE 'WESTMINSTER REVIEW'

Dr. and Mrs Chapman were at this time in the habit of admitting a few select boarders, chiefly engaged in literary pursuits, to their large house in the Strand, and Miss Evans, at their invitation, made her home with them. Thus she found herself at once in the centre of a circle consisting of some of the most advanced thinkers and brilliant *littérateurs* of the day; a circle which, partly consisting of contributors to the *Westminster Review*, was strongly imbued with scientific tendencies, being particularly partial to the doctrines of Positive Philosophy.

Those were in truth the palmy days of the *Westminster Review*. Herbert Spencer, G. H. Lewes, John Oxenford,

James and Harriet Martineau, Charles Bray, George Combe, and Professor Edward Forbes were among the writers that made it the leading expositor of the philosophic and scientific thought of the age. It occupied a position something midway between that of the *Nineteenth Century* and the *Fortnightly*. Scorning, like the latter, to pander to the frivolous tastes of the majority, it appealed to the most thoughtful and enlightened section of the reading public, giving especial prominence to the philosophy of the Comtist School; and while not so fashionable as the *Nineteenth Century*, it could boast among its contributors names quite as famous, destined as they were to become the foremost of their time and country. With this group of illustrious writers Miss Evans was now associated, and the articles she contributed from the year 1852 to 1858 are among the most brilliant examples of periodical literature. The first notice by her pen is a brief review of Carlyle's 'Life of Sterling' for January 1852, and judging from internal evidence, as regards style and method of treatment, the one on Margaret Fuller, in the next number, must be by the same hand.

To the biographer there is a curious interest in what she says in her first notice about this kind of literature, and it would be well for the world if writers were to lay it more generally to heart. "We have often wished that genius would incline itself more frequently to the task of the biographer, that when some great or good personage dies, instead of the dreary three- or five-volumed compilations of letter, and diary, and detail, little to the purpose, which two-thirds of the public have not the chance, nor the other third the inclination, to read, we could have a real 'life,' setting forth briefly and vividly the man's inward and outward struggles, aims, and achievements, so as to make clear the meaning which his experience has for his fellows. A few such lives (chiefly autobiographies) the world possesses, and they have, perhaps, been more influential on the formation of character than any other kind of reading." Then again, speaking of the 'Memoirs of Margaret Fuller,' she remarks, in reference to the same topic, "The old-world biographies present their subjects generally as broken fragments of humanity, noticeable because of their individual peculiarities, the new-world biographies present their subjects rather as organic portions of society."

George Eliot's estimate of Margaret Fuller (for there can be little doubt that it is hers) possesses too rare an interest for readers not to be given here in her own apposite and pungent words: "We are at a loss whether to regard her as the parent or child of New England Transcendentalism. Perhaps neither the one nor the other. It was essentially an intellectual, moral, spiritual regeneration — a renewing of the whole man — a kindling of his aspirations after full development of faculty and perfect symmetry of being. Of this sect Margaret Fuller was the priestess. In conversation she was as copious and oracular as Coleridge, brilliant as Sterling, pungent and paradoxical as Carlyle; gifted with the inspired powers of a Pythoness, she saw into the hearts and over the heads of all who came near her, and, but for a sympathy as boundless as her self-esteem, she would have despised the whole human race! Her frailty in this respect was no secret either to herself or her friends. . . . We must say that from the time she became a mother till the final tragedy when she perished with her husband and child within sight of her native shore, she was an altered woman, and evinced a greatness of soul and heroism of character so grand and subduing, that we feel disposed to extend to her whole career the admiration and sympathy inspired by the closing scenes.

"While her reputation was at its height in the literary circles of Boston and New York, she was so self-conscious that her life seemed to be a studied act, rather than a spontaneous growth; but this was the mere flutter on the surface; the well was deep, and the spring genuine; and it is creditable to her friends, as well as to herself, that such at all times was their belief."

In this striking summing-up of a character, the penetrating observer of human nature — taking in at a glance and depicting by a few masterly touches all that helps to make up a picture of the real living being — begins to reveal herself.

These essays in the *Westminster Review* are not only capital reading in themselves, but are, of course, doubly attractive to us because they let out opinions, views, judgments of things and authors, which we should never otherwise have known. Marian Evans had not yet hidden herself behind the mask of George Eliot, and in many of these wise and witty utterances of hers we are admitted behind the scenes of her mind, so to speak, and see her in her own undisguised person — before she had assumed the *rôle* of the novelist, showing herself to the world mainly through her dramatic impersonations.

In these articles, written in the fresh maturity of her powers, we learn what George Eliot thought about many subjects. We learn who were her favorite authors in fiction; what opinions she held on art and poetry; what was her attitude towards the political and social questions of the day; what was her conception of human life in general. There is much here, no doubt, that one might have been prepared to find, but a good deal, too, that comes upon one with the freshness of surprise.

A special interest attaches naturally to what she has to say about her own branch of art — the novel. Though she had probably no idea that she was herself destined to become one of the great masters of fiction, she had evidently a special predilection for works of that kind, noticeable because hitherto her bent might have appeared almost exclusively towards philosophy. To the three-volume circulating-library novel of the ordinary stamp she is merciless in her sarcasm. One of her most pithy articles of this time, or rather later, its date being 1856, is directed against "Silly Novels by Lady Novelists." "These," she says, "consist of the frothy, the prosy, the pious, or the pedantic. But it is a mixture of all these — a composite order of feminine fatuity — that produces the largest class of such novels, which we shall distinguish as the *mind and millinery* species. We had imagined that destitute women turned novelists, as they turned governesses, because they had no other 'ladylike' means of getting their bread. Empty writing was excused by an empty stomach, and twaddle was consecrated by tears. . . . It is clear that they write in elegant boudoirs, with violet-colored ink and a ruby pen; that they must be entirely indifferent to publishers' accounts; and inexperienced in every form of poverty except poverty of brains."

After finding fault with what she sarcastically calls the *white neck-cloth* species of novel, "a sort of medical sweetmeat for Low Church young ladies," she adds, "The real drama of Evangelicalism, and it has abundance of fine drama for any one who has genius enough to discern and reproduce it, lies among the middle and lower classes. Why can we not have pictures of religious life among the industrial classes in England, as interesting as Mrs. Stowe's pictures of religious life among the negroes?"

She who asked that question was herself destined, a few years later, to answer her own demand in most triumphant fashion. Already here and there we find hints and suggestions of the vein that was to be so fully worked out in 'Scenes of Clerical Life' and 'Adam Bede.' Her intimate knowledge of English country life, and the hold it had on her imagination, every now and then eats its way to the surface of her writings, and stands out amongst its surrounding matter with a certain unmistakable native force. After censuring the lack of reality with which peasant life is commonly treated in art, she makes the following apposite remarks, suggested by her own experience: "The notion that peasants are joyous, that the typical moment to represent a man in a smock-frock is when he is cracking a joke and showing a row of sound teeth, that cottage matrons are usually buxom, and village children necessarily rosy and merry, are prejudices difficult to dislodge from the artistic mind which looks for its subjects into literature instead of life. The painter is still under the influence of idyllic literature, which has always expressed the imagination of the town-bred rather than the truth of rustic life. Idyllic ploughmen are jocund when they drive their team afield; idyllic shepherds make bashful love under hawthorn bushes; idyllic villagers dance in the chequered shade, and refresh themselves not immoderately with spicy nut-brown ale. But no one who has seen much of actual ploughmen thinks them jocund, no one who is well acquainted with the English peasantry can pronounce them merry. The slow gaze, in which no sense of beauty beams, no humor twinkles; the slow utterance, and the heavy slouching walk, remind one rather of that melancholy animal the camel, than of the sturdy countryman, with striped stockings, red waistcoat, and hat aside, who represents the traditional English peasant. Observe a company of haymakers 'When you see them at a distance tossing up the forkfuls of hay in the golden light, while the wagon creeps slowly with its increasing burden over the meadow, and the bright green space which tells of work done gets larger and larger, you pronounce the scene 'smiling,' and you think these companions in labor must be as bright and cheerful as the picture to which they give animation. Approach nearer and you will find haymaking time is a time for joking, especially if there are women among the laborers; but the coarse laugh that bursts out every now and then, and expresses the triumphant taunt, is as far as possible from your conception of idyllic merriment. That delicious effervescence of the mind which we call fun has no equivalent for the northern peasant, except tipsy revelry; the only realm of fancy and imagination for the English clown exists at the bottom of the third quart pot.

"The conventional countryman of the stage, who picks up pocket-books and never looks into them, and who is too simple even to know that honesty has its opposite, represents the still lingering mistake, that an unintelligible dialect is a guarantee for ingenuousness, and that slouching shoulders indicate an upright disposition. It is quite sure that a thresher is likely to be innocent of any adroit arithmetical cheating, but he is not the less likely to carry home his master's corn in his shoes and pocket; a reaper is not given to writing begging letters, but he is quite capable of cajoling the dairy-maid into filling his small beer bottle with ale. The selfish instincts are not subdued by the sight of buttercups, nor is integrity in the least established by that classic rural occupation, sheep-washing. To make men moral something more is requisite than to turn them out to grass."

Every one must see that this is the essay-writing of a novelist rather than of a moral philosopher. The touches are put on with the vigor of a Velasquez, Balzac, or Flaubert, or that most terrible writer of the modern French school of fiction, the author of 'Le Sabot Rouge,' never described peasant life with more downright veracity. In the eyes of Miss Evans this quality of veracity is the most needful of all for the artist. Because "a picture of human life, such as a great artist can give, surprises even the trivial and the selfish into that attention to what is apart from themselves, which may be called the raw material of sentiment." For "art is the nearest thing to life; it is a mode of amplifying experience and extending our contract with our fellow-men beyond the bounds of our personal lot. All the more sacred is the task of the artist when he undertakes to paint the life of the People. Falsification here is far more pernicious than in the more artificial aspects of life. It is not so very serious that we should have false ideas about evanescent fashions — about the manners and conversation of beaux and duchesses; but it *is* serious that our sympathy with the perennial joys and struggles, the toil, the tragedy, and the humor in the life of our more heavily laden fellow-men should be perverted, and turned towards a false object instead of a true one."

George Eliot afterwards faithfully adhered to the canons fixed by the critic. Whether this consciousness of a moral purpose was altogether a gain to her art may be more fitly discussed in connection with the analysis of her works of fiction. It is only needful to point out here how close and binding she wished to make the union between ethics and æsthetics.

Almost identical views concerning fundamental laws of Art are discussed in an equally terse, vigorous, and pictorial manner in an article called 'Realism in Art: Recent German Fiction.' This article, however, is not by George Eliot, but by George Henry Lewes. It was published in October, 1858, and appeared after their joint sojourn in Germany during the spring and summer of that year. I think that if one carefully compares 'Realism in Art' with George Eliot's other articles, there appears something like a marriage of their respective styles in this paper. It seems probable that Lewes, with his flexible adaptiveness, had come under the influence of George Eliot's powerful intellect, and that many of the views he expresses here at the same time render George Eliot's, as they frequently appear, identical with hers. In the article in question the manner as well as the matter has a certain suggestion of the novelist's style. For example, she frequently indicates the quality of human speech by its resemblance to musical sounds. She is fond of speaking of "the *staccato* tones of a voice," "an *adagio* of utter indifference," and in the above-mentioned essay there are such expressions as the "stately *largo*" of good German prose. Again, in the article in question, we find the following satirical remarks about the slovenly prose of the generality of German writers: "To be gentlemen of somewhat slow, sluggish minds is perhaps their misfortune; but to be writers deplorably deficient in the first principles of composition is assuredly their fault. Some men pasture on platitudes, as oxen upon meadow-grass; they are at home on a dead-level of common-place, and do not desire to be irradiated by a felicity of expression." And in another passage to the same effect the author says sarcastically, "Graces are gifts: it can no more be required of a professor that he should write with felicity than that he should charm all beholders with his personal appearance; but literature requires that he should write intelligibly and carefully, as society requires that he should wash his face and button his waistcoat." Some of these strictures are very similar in spirit to what George Eliot had said in her review of Heinrich Heine, published in 1856, where, complaining of the general cumbrousness of German writers, she makes the following cutting remark: "A German comedy is like a German sentence: you see no reason in its structure why it should ever come to an end, and you accept the conclusion as an arrangement of Providence rather than of the author."

A passage in this article, which exactly tallies with George Eliot's general remarks on Art, must not be omitted here. "Art is a representation of Reality — a Representation, inasmuch as it is not the thing itself, but only represents it, must necessarily be limited by the nature of its medium. . . . Realism is thus the basis of all Art, and its antithesis is not Idealism but Falsism. . To misrepresent the forms of ordinary life is no less an offence than to misrepresent the forms of ideal life: a pug-nosed Apollo, or Jupiter in a great-coat, would not be more truly shocking to an artistic mind than are those senseless falsifications of Nature into which incompetence is led under the pretence of 'beautifying' Nature. Either give us true peasants or leave them untouched; either paint no drapery at all, or paint it with the utmost fidelity; either keep your people silent, or make them speak the idiom of their class."

Among German novelists (or rather writers of short stories), Paul Heyse is one of the few who is singled out for special praise in this review. And it is curious that there should be a tale by this eminent author called 'The Lonely Ones' (which also appeared in 1858), in which an incident occurs forcibly recalling the catastrophe of Grandcourt's death in 'Daniel Deronda'. the incident — although unskilfully introduced — of a Neapolitan fisherman whose momentary murderous hesitation to rescue his drowning friend ends in lifelong remorse for his death.

What makes the article in question particularly interesting are the allusions to the German tour, which give it an almost biographical interest. As has been mentioned already, Mr. Lewes and George Eliot were travelling in Germany in the spring of 1858, and in a letter to a friend she writes: "Then we had a delicious journey to Salzburg, and from thence through the Salz-Kammergut to Vienna, from Vienna to Prague, and from Prague to Dresden, where we spent our last six weeks in quiet work and quiet worship of the Madonna." And in his essay on Art Mr. G. H. Lewes alludes to the most priceless art-treasure Dresden contains, "Raphael's marvellous picture, the Madonna di San Sisto," as furnishing the most perfect illustration of what he means by Realism and Idealism. Speaking of the child Jesus he says: "In the never-to-be-forgotten divine babe, we have at once the intensest realism of presentation with the highest idealism of conception: the attitude is at once grand, easy, and natural; the face is that of a child, but the child is divine: in those eyes and in that brow there is an indefinable something which, greater than the expression of the angels, grander than that of pope or saint, is to all who see it a perfect *truth;* we feel that humanity in its highest conceivable form is before us, and that to transcend such a form would be to lose sight of the *human* nature there represented." A similar passage occurs in 'The Mill on the Floss,' where Philip Wakem says: "The greatest of painters only once painted a mysteriously divine child; he couldn't have told how he did it, and we can't tell why we feel it to be divine."

Enough has probably been quoted from George Eliot's articles to give the reader some idea of her views on art. But they are so rich in happy aphorisms, originality of illustration, and raciness of epithet that they not only deserve attentive study because they were the first fruits of the mind that afterwards gave to the world such noble and perfect works as 'The Mill on the Floss' and 'Silas Marner,' but are well worth attention for their own sake. Indeed, nothing in George Eliot's fictions excels the style of these papers. And what a clear, incisive, masterly style it was! Her prose in those days had a swiftness of movement, an epigrammatic felicity, and a brilliancy of antithesis which we look for in vain in the over-elaborate sentences and somewhat ponderous wit of 'Theophrastus Such.'

A very vapid paper on 'Weimar and its Celebrities,' April 1859, which a writer in the *Academy* attributes to the same hand, I know not on what authority, does not possess a single attribute that we are in the habit of associating with the writings of George Eliot. That an author who, by that time, had already produced some of her very finest work, namely, the 'Scenes of Clerical Life' and 'Adam Bede,' should have been responsible simultaneously for the trite common-places ventilated in this article is simply incredible. It is true that Homer is sometimes found nodding, and the right-hand of the greatest master may forget its cunning, but would George Eliot in her most abject moments have been capable of penning such a sentence as this in connection with Goethe?- "Would not Fredricka of Lili have been a more genial companion than Christina Vulpius for that great poet of whom his native land is so justly proud?" It is not worth while to point out other platitudes such as flow spontaneously from the facile pen of a penny-a-liner; but the consistent misspelling of every name may be alluded to in passing. Thus we read "Lily" for "Lely," "Zetter" for "Zelter," "Quintus Filein" for "Fixlein," "Einsedel" for "Einsiedel," etc. etc. This in itself would furnish no conclusive argument, supposing George Eliot to have been on the Continent and out of the way of correcting proofs. But as it happened she was in England in April 1859, and it is, therefore, on all grounds impossible that this worthless production should be hers.

Perhaps her two most noteworthy articles are the one called 'Evangelical Teaching,' published in 1855, and the other on 'Worldliness and Other-Worldliness,' which appeared in 1857. This happy phrase, by the way, was first used by Coleridge, who says, "As there is a worldliness or the too much of this life, so there is another *worldliness* or rather *other worldliness* equally hateful and selfish with *this worldliness.*" These articles are curious because they seem to occupy a midway position between George Eliot's earliest and latest phase of religious belief. But at this period she still felt the recoil from the pressure of a narrowing dogmatism too freshly not to launch back at it some of the most stinging shafts from the armory of her satire. Not Heine himself, in his trenchant sallies, surpasses the irony with which some of her pages are bristling. To ignore this stage in George Eliot's mental development would be to lose one of the connecting links in her history: a history by no means smooth and uneventful, as sometimes superficially represented, but full of strong contrasts, abrupt transitions, outward and inward changes sympathetically charged with all the meaning of this transitional time. Two extracts from the above-mentioned articles will amply testify to what has just been said.

"Given a man with a moderate intellect, a moral standard not higher than the average, some rhetorical affluence and great glibness of speech, what is the career in which, without the aid of birth or money, he may most easily attain power and reputation in English society? Where is that Goshen of intellectual mediocrity in which a smattering of science and learning will pass for profound instruction, where platitudes will be accepted as wisdom, bigoted narrowness as holy zeal, unctuous egoism as God-given piety? Let such a man become an evangelical preacher; he will then find it possible to reconcile small ability with great ambition, superficial knowledge with the prestige of erudition, a middling morale with a high reputation for sanctity. Let him shun practical extremes, and be ultra only in what is purely theoretic. Let him be stringent on predestination, but latitudinarian on fasting; unflinching in insisting on the eternity of punishment, but diffident of curtailing the substantial comforts of time; ardent and imaginative on the pre-millennial advent of Christ, but cold and cautious towards every other infringement of the *status quo*. Let him fish for souls, not with the bait of inconvenient singularity, but with the drag-net of comfortable conformity. Let him be hard and literal in his interpretation only when he wants to hurl texts at the heads of unbelievers and adversaries, but when the letter of the Scriptures presses too closely on the genteel Christianity of the nineteenth century, let him use his spiritualizing alembic and disperse it into impalpable ether. Let him preach less of Christ than of Antichrist; let him be less definite in showing what sin is than in showing who is the Man of Sin; less expansive on the blessedness of faith than on the accursedness of infidelity. Above all, let him set up as an interpreter of prophecy, rival 'Moore's Almanack' in the prediction of political events, tickling the interest of hearers who are but moderately spiritual by showing how the Holy Spirit has dictated problems and charades for their benefit; and how, if they are ingenious enough to solve these, they may have their Christian graces nourished by learning precisely to whom they may point as 'the horn that had eyes,' 'the lying prophet,' and the 'unclean spirits.' In this way he will draw men to him by the strong cords of their passions, made reason-proof by being baptized with the name of piety. In this way he may gain a metropolitan pulpit; the avenues to his church will be as crowded as the passages to the opera; he has but to print his prophetic sermons, and bind them in lilac and gold, and they will adorn the drawing-room table of all evangelical ladies, who will regard as a sort of pious 'light reading' the demonstration that the prophecy of the locusts, whose sting is in their tail, is fulfilled in the fact of the

Turkish commander having taken a horse's tail for his standard, and that the French are the very frogs predicted in the Revelations."

Even more scathing than this onslaught on a certain type of the popular evangelical preacher, is the paper on the poet Young, one of the wittiest things from George Eliot's pen, wherein she castigates with all her powers of sarcasm and ridicule that class of believers who cannot vilify this life sufficiently in order to make sure of the next, and who, in the care of their own souls, are careless of the world's need. Her analysis of the 'Night Thoughts' remains one of the most brilliant criticisms of its kind. Young's contempt for this earth, of all of us, and his exaltation of the starry worlds above, especially provoke his reviewer's wrath. This frame of mind was always repulsive to George Eliot, who could never sufficiently insist on the need of man's concentrating his love and energy on the life around him. She never felt much toleration for that form of aspiration that would soar to some shadowy infinite beyond the circle of human fellowship. One of the most epigrammatic passages in this article is where she says of Young, "No man can be better fitted for an Established Church. He personifies completely her nice balance of temporalities and spiritualities. He is equally impressed with the momentousness of death and of burial fees; he languishes at once for immortal life and for 'livings;' he has a fervid attachment to patrons in general, but on the whole prefers the Almighty. He will teach, with something more than official conviction, the nothingness of earthly things; and he will feel something more than private disgust, if his meritorious efforts in directing men's attention to another world are not rewarded by substantial preferment in this. His secular man believes in cambric bands and silk stockings as characteristic attire for 'an ornament of religion and virtue;' he hopes courtiers will never forget to copy Sir Robert Walpole; and writes begging letters to the king's mistress. His spiritual man recognizes no motives more familiar than Golgotha and 'the skies;' it walks in graveyards, or soars among the stars. . . . If it were not for the prospect of immortality, he considers it would be wise and agreeable to be indecent, or to murder one's father; and, heaven apart, it would be extremely irrational in any man not to be a knave. Man, he thinks, is a compound of the angel and the brute; the brute is to be humbled by being reminded of its 'relation to the stars,' and frightened into moderation by the contemplation of death-beds and skulls; the angel is to be developed by vituperating this world and exalting the next, and by this double process you get the Christian — 'the highest style of man.' With all this our new-made divine is an unmistakable poet. To a clay compounded chiefly of the worldling and the rhetorician there is added a real spark of Promethean fire. He will one day clothe his apostrophes and objurgations, his astronomical religion and his charnel-house morality, in lasting verse, which will stand, like a Juggernaut made of gold and jewels, at once magnificent and repulsive: for this divine is Edward Young, the future author of the 'Night Thoughts.'"

It has seemed appropriate to quote thus largely from these essays, because, never having been reprinted, they are to all intents and purposes inaccessible to the general reader. Yet they contain much that should not willingly be consigned to the dust and cobwebs, among which obsolete magazines usually sink into oblivion. They may as well be specified here according to their dates. 'Carlyle's Life of Sterling,' January 1852; 'Woman in France: Madame de Sablé,' October 1854; 'Evangelical Teaching: Dr. Cumming,' October 1855; 'German Wit: Heinrich Heine,' January 1856; 'Silly Novels by Lady Novelists,' October 1856; 'The Natural History of German Life,' July 1856; and 'Worldliness and Other-Worldliness: the Poet Young,' January 1857.

Miss Evans's main employment on the *Westminster Review* was, however, editorial. She used to write a considerable portion of the summary of contemporary literature at the end of each number. But her co-operation as sub-editor ceased about the close of 1853, when she left Dr. Chapman's house, and went to live in apartments in a small house in Cambridge Terrace, Hyde Park. Marian Evans was not entirely dependent at this time on the proceeds of her literary work, her father having settled the sum of 80*l*. to 100*l*. a year on her for life, the capital of which, however, did not belong to her. She was very generous with her money; and although her earnings at this time were not considerable, they were partly spent on her poor relations.

CHAPTER VI.

GEORGE HENRY LEWES.

MEANWHILE, these literary labors were pleasantly diversified by frequent visits to her friends at Rosehill and elsewhere. In October 1852, she stayed with Mr. and Mrs. George Combe at Edinburgh, and on her way back was the guest of Harriet Martineau, at her delightfully situated house in Ambleside. Her acquaintance with Mr. Herbert Spencer had ripened into a cordial friendship. They met constantly both in London and in the country, and their intercourse was a source of mutual intellectual enjoyment and profit. As must already have become evident, it is erroneous to suppose that he had any share in the formation of her mind: for as Mr. Herbert Spencer said, in a letter to the *Daily News*, "Our friendship did not commence until 1851 . . . when she was already distinguished by that breadth of culture, and universality of power, which have since made her known to all the world."

In a letter to Miss Phelps, George Eliot touches on this rumor, after alluding in an unmistakable manner to another great contemporary: "I never — to answer one of your questions quite directly — I never had any personal acquaintance with" (naming a prominent Positivist), "never saw him to my knowledge, except in the House of Commons; and though I have studied his books, especially his 'Logic' and 'Political Economy,' with much benefit, I have no consciousness of their having made any marked epoch in my life.

"Of Mr. ——'s friendship I have had the honor and advantage for twenty years, but I believe that every main bias of my mind had been taken before I knew him. Like the rest of his readers, I am, of course, indebted to him for much enlargement and clarifying of thought."

But there was another acquaintance which Miss Evans made during the first year of her residence in the Strand, destined to affect the whole future tenor of her life — the acquaintance of Mr. George Henry Lewes, then, like her, a contributor to the *Westminster Review*.

George Henry Lewes was Marian's senior by two years, having been born in London on the 18th of April, 1817. He was educated at Greenwich in a school once possessing a high reputation for thoroughly "grounding" its pupils in a knowledge of the classics. When his education was so far finished, he was placed as clerk in a merchant's office. This kind of occupation proving very distasteful, he turned medical student for a time. Very early in life he was attracted towards philosophy, for at the age of nineteen we find him attending the weekly meetings of a small club, in the habit of discussing metaphysical problems in the parlor of a tavern in Red Lion Square, Holborn. This club, from which the one in 'Daniel Deronda' is supposed to have borrowed many of its features, was the point of junction for a most heterogeneous company. Here, amicably seated round the fire, a speculative tailor would hob and nob with some medical student deep in anatomy; a second-hand bookseller having devoured the literature on his shelves, ventilated their contents for the general benefit; and a discursive American mystic was listened to in turn with a Jewish journeyman watchmaker deeply imbued with Spinozism. It is impossible not to connect this Jew, named Cohen, and described as "a man of astonishing subtilty and logical force, no less than of sweet personal worth," with the Mordecai of the novel just mentioned. However wide the after divergencies, here evidently lies the germ. The weak eyes and chest, the grave and gentle demeanor, the whole ideality of character, correspond. In some respects G. H. Lewes was the "Daniel Deronda" to this "Mordecai." For he not only loved but venerated his "great calm intellect." "An immense pity," says Mr. Lewes, "a fervid indignation, filled me as I came away from his attics in one of the Holborn courts, where I had seen him in the pinching poverty of his home, with his German wife and two little black-eyed children."

To this pure-spirited suffering watchmaker, Lewes owed his

first acquaintance with Spinoza. A certain passage, casually cited by Cohen, awakened an eager thirst for more in the youth. The desire to possess himself of Spinoza's works, still in the odor of pestilential heresy, haunted him like a passion. For he himself, then "suffering the social persecution which embitters any departure from accepted creeds," felt in defiant sympathy with all outcasts. On a dreary November evening, the coveted volumes were at length discovered on the dingy shelves of a second-hand bookseller. By the flaring gaslight, young Lewes, with a beating heart, read on the back of a small brown quarto those thrilling words, 'Spinoza: Opera Posthuma!' He was poor in those days, and the price of the volume was twenty shillings, but he would gladly have sacrificed his last sixpence to secure it. Having paid his money with feverish delight, he hurried home in triumph, and immediately set to work on a translation of the 'Ethics,' which, however, he was too impatient to finish.

This little incident is well worth dwelling upon not only as being the first introduction of a notable thinker to philosophy, but as showing the eager impulsive nature of the man. The study of Spinoza led to his publishing an article on his life and works in the *Westminster Review* of 1843, almost the first account of the great Hebrew philosopher which appeared in this country. This article, afterwards incorporated in the 'Biographical History of Philosophy,' formed the nucleus, I believe, of that "admirable piece of synthetic criticism and exposition," as Mr. Frederic Harrison calls it; a work which, according to him, has influenced the thought of the present generation almost more than any single book except Mr. Mill's 'Logic.'

Before the appearance of either article or 'History of Philosophy,' Mr. Lewes went to Germany, and devoted himself to the study of its language and literature, just brought into fashion by Carlyle. Returning to England in 1839, he became one of the most prolific journalists of the day. Witty, brilliant, and many-sided, he seemed pre-eminently fitted by nature for a press-writer and *littérateur*. His versatility was so amazing, that a clever talker once said of him: "Lewes can do everything in the world but paint; and he could do that, too, after a week's study." At this time, besides assisting in the editorship of the *Classical Museum*, he wrote for the *Morning Chronicle*, the *Athenæum*, the *Edinburgh*, *Foreign Quarterly*, *British Quarterly*, *Blackwood*, *Fraser*, and the *Westminster Review*. After publishing 'A Biographical History of Philosophy,' through Mr. Knight's 'Weekly Volumes' in 1846, he wrote two novels, 'Ranthorpe,' and 'Rose, Blanche, and Violet,' which successively appeared in 1847 and 1848 But fiction was not his *forte*, these two productions being singularly crude and immature as compared with his excellent philosophical work. Some jokes in the papers about "rant" killed what little life there was in 'Ranthorpe.' Nevertheless, Charlotte Bronte, who had some correspondence with Mr. Lewes about 1847, actually wrote about it as follows. "In reading 'Ranthorpe,' I have read a new book, not a reprint, not a reflection of any other book, but a *new book*." Another great writer, Edgar Poe, admired it no less, for he says of the work: "I have lately read it with deep interest, and derived great *consolation* from it also. It relates to the career of a literary man, and gives a just view of the true aims and the true dignity of the literary character."

'The Spanish Drama,' 'The Life of Maximilian Robespierre, with extracts from his unpublished correspondence;' 'The Noble Heart: a Tragedy;' all followed in close succession from the same inexhaustible pen. The last, it was said, proved also a tragedy to the publishers. But not content with writing dramas, Mr. Lewes was also ambitious of the fame of an actor, the theatre having always possessed a strong fascination for him. Already as a child he had haunted the theatres, and now, while delivering a lecture at the Philosophical Institution in Edinburgh, he shocked its staid *habitués* not a little by immediately afterwards appearing on the stage in the character of Shylock: so many, and seemingly incompatible, were Lewes's pursuits. But this extreme mobility of mind, this intellectual tripping from subject to subject, retarded the growth of his popularity. The present mechanical subdivision of labor has most unfortunately also affected the judgment passed on literary and artistic products. Let a man once have written a novel typical of the manners and ways of a certain class of English society, or painted a picture with certain peculiar effects of sea or landscape, or composed a poem affecting the very trick and language of some bygone mediæval singer, he will be doomed, to the end of his days, to do the same thing over and over again, *ad nauseam*. Nothing can well be more deadening to any vigorous mental life, and Mr. Lewes set a fine example of intellectual disinterestedness in sacrificing immediate success to the free play of a most variously endowed nature.

The public too was a gainer by this. For the 'Life of Goethe' could not have been made the rich, comprehensive, many-sided biography it is, had Mr. Lewes himself not tried his hand at such a variety of subjects. This life, begun in 1845, the result partly of his sojourn in Germany, did not appear in print until 1855. Ultimately destined to a great and lasting success, the MS. of the 'Life of Goethe' was ignominiously sent from one publisher to another, until at last Mr. David Nutt, of the Strand, showed his acumen by giving it to the reading world.

Some years before the publication of this biography, Mr. Lewes had also been one of the founders of that able but unsuccessful weekly, the *Leader*, of which he was the literary editor from 1849 to 1854. Many of his articles on Auguste Comte were originally written for this paper, and afterwards collected into a volume for Bohn's series. Indeed, after Mr. John Stuart Mill, he is to be regarded as the earliest exponent of Positivism in England. He not only considered the '*Cours de Philosophie Positive*' the greatest work of the century, but believed it would " form one of the mighty landmarks in the history of opinion. No one before M. Comte," he says, " ever dreamed of treating social problems otherwise than upon theological or metaphysical methods. He first showed how possible, nay, how imperative, it was that social questions should be treated on the same footing with all other scientific questions. This being his object, he was forced to detect the law of mental evolution before he could advance. This law is the law of historical progression." But while Mr. Lewes, with his talent for succinct exposition, helped more than any other Englishman to disseminate the principles of Comte's philosophy in this country, he was at the same time violently opposed to his '*Politique Positive*,' with its schemes of social reorganization.

Even so slight a survey as this must show the astonishing discursiveness of Mr. Lewes's intellect. By the time he was thirty he had already tried his hand at criticism, fiction, biography, the drama, and philosophy. He had enlarged his experience of human nature by foreign travel; he had addressed audiences from the lecturer's platform; he had enjoyed the perilous sweets of editing a newspaper; he had even, it is said, played the harlequin in a company of strolling actors. Indeed, Mr. Thackeray was once heard to say that it would not surprise him to meet Lewes in Piccadilly, riding on a white elephant; whilst another wit likened him to the Wandering Jew, as you could never tell where he was going to turn up, or what he was going to do next.

In this discursiveness of intellect he more nearly resembled the Encyclopedists of the eighteenth century than the men of his own time. Indeed, his personal appearance, temperament, manners, general tone of thought, seemed rather to be those of a highly accomplished foreigner than of an Englishman. He was a lightly built, fragile man, with bushy curly hair, and a general shagginess of beard and eyebrow not unsuggestive of a Skye terrier. For the rest, he had a prominent mouth and gray, deeply set eyes under an ample, finely proportioned forehead. Volatile by nature, somewhat wild and lawless in his talk, he in turn delighted and shocked his friends by the gayety, recklessness, and genial *abandon* of his manners and conversation. His companionship was singularly stimulating, for the commonest topic served him as a starting-point for the lucid development of some pet philosophical theory. In this gift of making abstruse problems intelligible, and difficult things easy, he had some resemblance to the late W. K. Clifford, with his magical faculty of illuminating the most abstruse subjects by his vivid directness of exposition.

As Lewes's life was so soon to be closely united to that of Marian Evans, this cursory sketch of his career will not seem inappropriate. At the time they met at Dr. Chapman's house,

Mr. Lewes, who had married early in life, found his conjugal relations irretrievably spoiled. How far the blame of this might attach to one side or to the other does not concern us here. Enough that in the intercourse with a woman of such astonishing intellect, varied acquirements, and rare sympathy, Mr. Lewes discovered a community of ideas and a moral support that had been sadly lacking to his existence hitherto.

In many ways these two natures, so opposite in character, disposition, and tone of mind, who, from such different starting-points had reached the same standpoint, seemed to need each other for the final fruition and utmost development of what was best in each. A crisis was now impending in Marian's life. She was called upon to make her private judgment a law unto herself, and to shape her actions, not according to the recognized moral standard of her country, but in harmony with her own convictions of right and wrong. From a girl, it appears, she had held independent views about marriage, strongly advocating the German divorce laws. On the appearance of 'Jane Eyre,' when every one was talking of this book and praising the exemplary conduct of Jane in her famous interview with Rochester, Marian Evans, then only four-and-twenty, remarked to a friend that in his position she considered him justified in contracting a fresh marriage. And in an article on Madame Sablé, written as early as 1854, there is this significant passage in reference to the "laxity of opinion and practice with regard to the marriage-tie in France." "Heaven forbid," she writes, "that we should enter on a defence of French morals, most of all in relation to marriage! But it is undeniable that unions formed in the maturity of thought and feeling, and grounded only on inherent fitness and mutual attraction, tended to bring women into more intelligent sympathy with man, and to heighten and complicate their share in the political drama. The quiescence and security of the conjugal relation are, doubtless, favorable to the manifestation of the highest qualities by persons who have already attained a high standard of culture, but rarely foster a passion sufficient to rouse all the faculties to aid in winning or retaining its beloved object — to convert indolence into activity, indifference into ardent partisanship, dulness into perspicuity."

Such a union, formed in the full maturity of thought and feeling, was now contracted by Marian Evans and George Henry Lewes. Legal union, however, there could be none, for though virtually separated from his wife, Mr. Lewes could not get a divorce. Too little has as yet transpired concerning this important step to indicate more than the bare outline of events. Enough that Mr. Lewes appears to have written a letter in which, after a full explanation of his circumstances, he used all his powers of persuasion to win Miss Evans for his life-long companion; that she consented, after having satisfied her conscience that in reality she was not injuring the claims of others; and that henceforth she bore Mr. Lewes's name, and became his wife in every sense but the legal one.

This proceeding caused the utmost consternation amongst her acquaintances, especially amongst her friends at Rosehill. The former intimate and affectionate intercourse with Mrs. Bray and her sister was only gradually restored, and only after they had come to realize how perfectly her own conscience had been consulted and satisfied in the matter. Miss Hennell, who had already entered on the scheme of religious doctrine which ever since she has been setting forth in her printed works, "swerved nothing from her own principles that the maintenance of a conventional form of marriage (re-moulded to the demands of the present age) is essentially attached to all religion, and pre-eminently so to the religion of the future."

In thus defying public opinion, and forming a connection in opposition to the laws of society, George Eliot must have undergone some trials and sufferings peculiarly painful to one so shrinkingly sensitive as herself. Conscious of no wrong-doing, enjoying the rare happiness of completest intellectual fellowship in the man she loved, the step she had taken made a gap between her kindred and herself which could not but gall her clinging, womanly nature. To some of her early companions, indeed, who had always felt a certain awe at the imposing gravity of her manners, this dereliction from what appeared to them the path of duty was almost as startling and unexpected as if they had seen the heavens falling down.

How far the individual can ever be justified in following the dictates of his private judgment, in opposition to the laws and prevalent opinions of his time and country, must remain a question no less difficult than delicate of decision. It is precisely the point where the highest natures and the lowest sometimes apparently meet; since to act in opposition to custom may be due to the loftiest motives — may be the spiritual exaltation of the reformer, braving social ostracism for the sake of an idea, or may spring, on the other hand, from purely rebellious promptings of an anti-social egoism, which recognizes no law higher than that of personal gratification. At the same time, it seems that no progress could well be made in the evolution of society without these departures on the part of individuals from the well-beaten tracks, for even the failures help eventually towards a fuller recognition of what is beneficial and possible of attainment. Mary Wollstonecraft, Shelley, George Sand, the New England Transcendentalists, with their communistic experiment at Brook Farm, all more or less strove to be path-finders to a better and happier state of society. George Eliot, however, hardly belonged to this order of mind. Circumstances prompted her to disregard one of the most binding laws of society, yet, while she considered herself justified in doing so, her sympathies were, on the whole, more enlisted in the state of things as they are than as they might be. It is certainly curious that the woman, who in her own life had followed such an independent course, severing herself in many ways from her past with all its traditional sanctities, should yet so often inculcate the very opposite teaching in her works — should inculcate an almost slavish adherence to whatever surroundings, beliefs, and family ties a human being may be born to.

I need only add here that Mr. Lewes and Marian went to Germany soon after forming this union, which, only ending by death, gave to each what had hitherto been lacking in their lives. Many marriages solemnized in a church, and ushered in with all the ostentation of *trousseau*, bridesmaids, and wedding breakfast, are indeed less essentially such in all the deeper human aspects which this relation implies, than the one contracted in this informal manner. Indeed, to those who saw them together, it seemed as if they could never be apart. Yet, while so entirely at one, each respected the other's individuality, his own, at the same time, gaining in strength by the contact. Mr. Lewes's mercurial disposition now assumed a stability greatly enhancing his brilliant talents, and for the first time facilitating that concentration of intellect so necessary for the production of really lasting philosophic work. On the other hand, George Eliot's still dormant faculties were roused and stimulated to the utmost by the man to whom this union with her formed the most memorable year of his life. By his enthusiastic belief in her he gave her the only thing she wanted — a thorough belief in herself. Indeed, he was more than a husband: he was, as an intimate friend once pithily remarked, a very mother to her. Tenderly watching over her delicate health, cheering the grave tenor of her thoughts by his inexhaustible buoyancy, jealously shielding her from every adverse breath of criticism, Mr. Lewes in a manner created the spiritual atmosphere in which George Eliot could best put forth all the flowers and fruits of her genius.

In joining her life with that of Mr. Lewes, the care of his three children devolved upon George Eliot, who henceforth showed them the undeviating love and tenderness of a mother. One of the sons had gone out to Natal as a young man, and contracted a fatal disease, which, complicated with some accident, resulted in an untimely death. He returned home a hopeless invalid, and his tedious illness was cheered by the affectionate tendance of her who had for so many years acted a mother's part towards him.

CHAPTER VII.

SCENES OF CLERICAL LIFE.

As has already been mentioned, Mr. Lewes and Marian went to Germany in 1854, dividing the year between Berlin, Munich, and Weimar. In the latter pleasant little Saxon city, on which the mighty influence of Goethe seemed still visibly resting, as the reflection of the sun lingers in the sky long after the sun himself has set, Lewes partly re-wrote his 'Life of Goethe.' Here must have been spent many delightful days, wandering in Goethe's track, exploring the beautiful neighborhood, and enjoying some of the most cultivated society in Germany. Several articles on German life and literature, afterwards published in the *Westminster Review*, were probably written at this time. The translation of Spinoza's 'Ethics' by George Eliot was also executed in the same year. Mr. Lewes, alluding to it in 'Goethe's Life,' says, in a foot-note, "It may interest some readers to learn that Spinoza will ere long appear in English, edited by the writer of these lines." This was a delusive promise, since the translation has not yet made its appearance. But surely its publication would now be warmly welcomed.

The time, however, was approaching when George Eliot was at last to discover where her real mastery lay. And this is the way, as the story goes, that she discovered it. They had returned from the Continent and were settled again in London, both actively engaged in literature. But literature, unless in certain cases of triumphant popularity, is perhaps the worst paid of all work. Mr. Lewes and George Eliot were not too well off. The former, infinite in resources, having himself tried every form of literature in turn, could not fail to notice the matchless power of observation, and the memory matching it in power, of the future novelist. One day an idea struck him. "My dear," he said, "I think you could write a capital story." Shortly afterwards there was some dinner engagement, but as he was preparing to go out, she said, "I won't go out this evening, and when you come in don't disturb me. I shall be very busy." And this was how the 'Scenes of Clerical Life' came first to be written! On being shown a portion of the first tale, 'Amos Barton,' Mr. Lewes was fairly amazed.

Stories are usually fabricated after the event; but, if not true, they often truly paint a situation. And the general testimony of friends seems to agree that it was Mr. Lewes who first incited the gifted woman, of whose great powers he was best able to form a judgment, to express herself in that species of literature which would afford the fullest scope to the creative and dramatic faculties which she so eminently possessed. Here, however, his influence ended. He helped to reveal George Eliot to herself, and after that there was little left for him to do. But this gift of stimulating another by sympathetic insight and critical appreciation is itself of priceless value. When Schiller died, Goethe said, " The half of my existence is gone from me." A terrible word to utter for one so great. But never again, he knew, would he meet with the same complete comprehension, and, lacking that, his genius itself seemed less his own than before.

There is an impression abroad that Mr. Lewes, if anything, did some injury to George Eliot from a literary point of view; that the nature of his pursuits led her to adopt too technical and pedantic a phraseology in her novels. But this idea is unjust to both. In comparing her earliest with her latest style, it is clear that from the first she was apt to cull her illustrations from the physical sciences, thereby showing how much these studies had become part of herself. Indeed, she was far more liable to introduce these scientific modes of expression than Mr. Lewes, as may be easily seen by comparing his 'Life of Goethe,' partly re-written in 1854, with some of her essays of the same date. As to her matter, it is curious how much of it was drawn from the earliest sources of memory — from that life of her childhood to which she may sometimes have turned yearningly as to a long-lost Paradise. Most of her works might, indeed, not inaptly be called 'Looking Backward' They are a half-pathetic, half-humorous, but entirely tender revivification of the "days that are no more." No one, however intimate, could really intermeddle with the workings of a genius drawing its happiest inspiration from the earliest experiences of its own individual past.

Nothing is more characteristic of this obvious tendency than the first of the 'Scenes of Clerical Life,' 'The Sad Fortunes of the Rev. Amos Barton.' At Chilvers Coton the curious in such matters may still see the identical church where the incumbent of Shepperton used to preach sermons shrewdly compounded of High Church doctrines and Low

Church evangelicalism, not forgetting to note "its little flight of steps with their wooden rail running up the outer wall, and leading to the school-children's gallery." There they may still see the little churchyard, though they may look in vain for the "slim black figure" of the Rev. Amos, "as it flits past the pale gravestones," in "the silver light that falls aslant on church and tomb." And among the tombs there is one, a handsome substantial monument, overshadowed by a yew-tree, on which there is this inscription:—

HERE LIES,
WAITING THE SUMMONS OF THE ARCHANGEL'S TRUMPET,
ALL THAT WAS MORTAL OF
THE BELOVED WIFE OF THE
REV. JOHN GWYTHER, B A.,
CURATE OF THIS PARISH,
NOV. 4TH, 1836,
AGED THIRTY-FOUR YEARS,
LEAVING A HUSBAND AND SEVEN CHILDREN.

This Emma Gwyther is none other than the beautiful Milly, the wife of Amos, so touchingly described by George Eliot, whose mother, Mrs. Evans, was her intimate friend. George Eliot would be in her teens when she heard the story of this sweet woman: heard the circumstantial details of her struggles to make the two ends of a ridiculously small income meet the yearly expenses: heard her mother, no doubt (in the words of Mrs. Hackit) blame her weak forbearance in tolerating the presence in her house of the luxurious and exacting countess, who, having ingratiated herself with the gullible Amos by her talk of the "livings" she would get him, gave much scandal in the neighborhood: heard of the pathetic death-bed, when, worn by care and toil, the gentle life ebbed quietly away, leaving a life-long void in her husband's heart and home. All this was the talk of the neighborhood when George Eliot was a girl; and her extraordinary memory allowed nothing to escape.

On the completion of 'Amos Barton,' Mr. Lewes, who, as

already mentioned, was a contributor to 'Maga,' sent the MS. to the editor, the late Mr. John Blackwood, as the work of an anonymous friend. This was in the autumn of 1856. The other scenes of 'Clerical Life' were then unwritten, but the editor was informed that the story submitted to his approval formed one of a series. Though his judgment was favorable, he begged to see some of the other tales before accepting this, freely making some criticisms on the plot and studies of character in 'Amos Barton.' This, however, disheartened the author, whose peculiar diffidence had only been overcome by Mr. Lewes's hearty commendation. When the editor had been made aware of the injurious effect of his objections, he hastened to efface it by accepting the tale without further delay. It appeared soon afterwards in *Blackwood's Magazine* for January 1857, where it occupied the first place. This story, by some considered as fine as anything the novelist ever wrote, came to an end in the next number. 'Mr. Gilfil's Love-Story' and 'Janet's Repentance' were written in quick succession, and the series was completed in November of the same year.

Although there was nothing sufficiently sensational in these 'Scenes' to arrest the attention of that great public which must be roused by something new and startling, literary judges were not slow to discern the powerful realism with which the author had drawn these uncompromising studies from life. After the appearance of 'Amos Barton,' Mr. Blackwood wrote to the anonymous author: "It is a long time since I have read anything so fresh, so humorous, and so touching. The style is capital, conveying so much in so few words." Soon afterwards he began another letter: "My dear Amos, I forget whether I told you or Lewes that I had shown part of the MS. to Thackeray. He was staying with me, and having been out at dinner, came in about eleven o'clock, when I had just finished reading it. I said to him, 'Do you know that I think I have lighted upon a new author, who is uncommonly like a first-class passenger.' I showed him a page or two, I think the passage where the curate returns home and Milly is first introduced. He would not pronounce whether it came up to my ideas, but remarked afterwards that he would have liked to have read more, which I thought a good sign."

Dickens, after the publication of the 'Scenes,' sent a letter to the unknown writer through the editor, warmly expressing the admiration he felt for them. But he was strongly of opinion from the first that they must have been written by a woman. In the meanwhile the tales were reprinted in a collected form, and they were so successful that the editor, writing to Mr. Lewes at the end of January 1858, when the book had hardly been out a month, was able to say, "George Eliot has fairly achieved a literary reputation among judges, and the public must follow, although it may take time." And in a letter to George Eliot herself, he wrote in February: "You will recollect, when we proposed to reprint, my impression was that the series had not lasted long enough in the magazine to give you a hold on the general public, although long enough to make your literary reputation. Unless in exceptional cases, a very long time often elapses between the two stages of reputation — the literary and the public. Your progress will be *sure*, if not so quick as we could wish."

While the sketches were being re-issued in book-form, Messrs. Blackwood informed its author that they saw good cause for making a large increase in the forthcoming reprint, and their anticipations were fully justified by its success. All sorts of rumors were abroad as to the real author of these clerical tales. Misled by a hint, calculated to throw him off the real scent, Mr. Blackwood was at first under the impression that they were the work of a clergyman, and this may perhaps have been the origin of a belief which lingered till quite recently, that George Eliot was the daughter of a clergyman, a statement made by several of the leading daily papers after her death. Abandoning the idea of the clergyman, Mr. Blackwood next fixed upon a very different sort of person, to wit, Professor Owen, whom he suspected owing to the similarity of hand-writing and the scientific knowledge so exceptional in a novelist. No less funny was the supposition held by others of Lord Lytton — who more than once hoaxed the public under a new literary disguise — having at last surpassed himself in the sterling excellence of these tales. Now that Bulwer has gone the way of all fashions, it seems incredible that the most obtuse and slow-witted of critics should have mistaken for a moment his high-flown sentimental style for the new author's terse, vigorous, and simple prose.

It was impossible, however, for an author to remain a mere nameless abstraction. An appellation of some kind became an imperative necessity, and, during the passage of 'Mr. Gilfil's Love-Story' through the press, the pseudonym of "George Eliot" — a name destined to become so justly renowned — was finally assumed.

The 'Scenes of Clerical Life' were to George Eliot's future works what a bold, spirited sketch is to a carefully elaborated picture. All the qualities that distinguished her genius may be discovered in this, her first essay in fiction. With all Miss Austen's matchless faculty for painting common-place characters, George Eliot has that other nobler faculty of showing what tragedy, pathos, and humor may be lying in the experience of a human soul "that looks out through dull gray eyes, and that speaks in a voice of quite ordinary tones." While depicting some common-place detail of every-day life, she has the power to make her reader realize its close relation to the universal life. She never gives you the mere dry bones and fragments of existence as represented in some particular section of society, but always manages to keep before the mind the invisible links connecting it with the world at large. In 'Mr. Gilfil's Love-Story' there is a passage as beautiful as any in her works, and fully illustrating this attitude of her mind. It is where Tina, finding herself deceived in Captain Wybrow, gives way to her passionate grief in solitude.

"While this poor little heart was being bruised with a weight too heavy for it, Nature was holding on her calm inexorable way, in unmoved and terrible beauty. The stars were rushing in their eternal courses; the tides swelled to the level of the last expectant weed; the sun was making brilliant day to busy nations on the other side of the swift earth. The stream of human thought and deed was hurrying and broadening onward. The astronomer was at his telescope; the great ships were laboring over the waves; the toiling eagerness of commerce, the fierce spirit of revolution, were only ebbing in brief rest; and sleepless statesmen were dreading the possible crisis of the morrow. What were our little Tina and her trouble in this mighty torrent, rushing from one awful unknown to another? Lighter than the smallest centre of quivering life in the water-drop, hidden and uncared for as the pulse of anguish in the breast of the tiniest bird that has fluttered down to its nest with the long-sought food, and has found the nest torn and empty."

There is rather more incident in this story of Mr. Gilfil than in either of the two other 'Scenes of Clerical Life.' In 'Amos Barton' the narrative is of the simplest, as has already been indicated; and the elements from which 'Janet's Repentance' is composed are as free from any complex entanglement of plot. The author usually describes the most ordinary circumstances of English life, but the powerful rendering of the human emotions which spring from them takes a most vivid hold of the imagination: 'Mr. Gilfil's Love-Story,' however, seems a little Italian romance dropped on English soil.

It is, in brief, the narration of how Sir Christopher Cheverel and his wife, during their residence at Milan, took pity on a little orphan girl, " whose large dark eyes shone from out her queer little face like the precious stones in a grotesque image carved in old ivory." Caterina, or Tina as she is called, taken back to Cheverel Manor, grew up under the care of the Baronet's wife, to whom she became endeared by her exceptional musical talent. Sir Christopher had no children, but had chosen his nephew, Captain Wybrow, for his heir, and planned a marriage between him and Miss Assher, the handsome and accomplished owner of a pretty estate. Another marriage, on which he has equally set his heart, is that between his ward Maynard Gilfil, an open-eyed manly young fellow destined for the Church, and the mellow-voiced, large-eyed Tina, for whom he has long nursed an undeclared passion. But alas, for the futility of human plans! Tina, to whom the elegant Anthony Wybrow has been secretly professing love, suffers tortures of jealousy when he and Miss Assher, to whom he has dutifully become engaged, come on a visit to Cheverel Manor. The treacherous Captain, to lull the suspicions of his betrothed, insinuates that poor Miss Sarti entertains a hopeless passion for him, which puts the poor girl, who gets an inkling of this double-dealing, into a frenzy of indignation. In this state she possesses herself of a dagger, and as she is going to meet the Captain by appointment, dreams of plunging the weapon in the traitor's heart. But on reaching the appointed spot, she beholds the false lover stretched motionless on the ground already — having suddenly died of heart disease. Tina's anguish is indescribable: she gives the alarm to the household, but stung by remorse for a contemplated revenge of which her tender-hearted nature was utterly incapable, she flies unperceived from the premises at night. Being searched for in vain, she is suspected of having committed suicide. After some days of almost unbearable suspense, news is brought that Tina is lying ill at the cottage of a former maid in the household. With reviving hopes her anxious lover rides to the farm, sees the half-stunned, unhappy girl, and, after a while, manages to remove her to his sister's house. She gradually recovers under Mrs. Heron's gentle tendance, and one day a child's accidental striking of a deep bass note on the harpsichord suddenly revives her old passionate delight in music. And 'the soul that was born anew to music was born anew to love.' After a while Tina agrees to become Mr. Gilfil's wife, who has been given the living at Shepperton, where a happy future seems in store for the Vicar. "But the delicate plant had been too deeply bruised, and in the struggle to put forth a blossom it died.

"Tina died, and Maynard Gilfil's love went with her into deep silence forevermore."

Besides this sympathy with the homeliest characters and situations, or, more properly speaking, springing from it, there already runs through these three tales the delicious vein of humor irradiating George Eliot's otherwise sombre pictures of life with sudden flashes of mirth as of sunlight trembling above dark waters. In this depth and richness of humor George Eliot not only takes precedence of all other distinguished women, but she stands among them without a rival. Hers is that thoughtful outlook on life, that infinite depth of observation which, taking note of the inconsistencies and the blunders, the self-delusions and "fantastic pranks" of her fellow-men, finds the source of laughter very near to tears, never going out of her way for the eccentric and peculiar in human nature, seeing that human nature itself appears to her as the epitome of all incongruity. It is this breath of conception and unerringness of vision piercing through the external and accidental to the core of man's mixed nature which give certain of her creations something of the life-like complexity of Shakespeare's.

Her power of rendering the idiom and manners of peasants, artisans, and paupers, of calling up before us the very gestures and phrases of parsons, country practitioners, and other varieties of inhabitants of our provincial towns and rural districts, already manifests itself fully in these clerical stories. Here we find such types as Mr. Dempster, the unscrupulous, brutal, drunken lawyer; Mr. Pilgrim, the tall, heavy, rough-mannered, and spluttering doctor, profusely addicted to bleeding and blistering his patients; Mr. Gilfil, the eccentric vicar, with a tender love-story hidden beneath his rugged exterior; the large-hearted, unfortunate Janet, rescued from moral ruin by Mr. Tryan, the ascetic evangelical clergyman, whose character, the author remarks, might have been found sadly wanting in perfection by feeble and fastidious minds, but, as she adds, "The blessed work of helping the world forward happily does not wait to be done by perfect men; and I should imagine that neither Luther nor John Bunyan, for example, would have satisfied the modern demand for an ideal hero, who believes nothing but what is true, feels nothing but what is exalted, and does nothing but what is graceful. The real heroes of God's making are quite different: they have their natural heritage of love and conscience, which they drew in with their mother's milk; they know one or two of those deep spiritual truths which are only to be won by long wrestling with their own sins and their own sorrows; they have earned faith and strength so far as they have done genuine work, but the rest is dry, barren theory, blank prejudice, vague hearsay."

George Eliot's early acquaintance with many types of the clerical character, and her sympathy with the religious life in all its manifestations, was never more fully shown than in these 'Scenes.' In 'Janet's Repentance' we already discover one of George Eliot's favorite psychological studies — the awakening of a morally mixed nature to a new, a spiritual life. This work of regeneration Mr. Tryan performs for Janet, Felix Holt for Esther, and Daniel Deronda for Gwendolen. Her protest against the application of too lofty a moral standard in judging of our fellow-creatures, her championship of the "mongrel, ungainly dogs who are nobody's pets," is another of the prominent qualities of her genius fully expressed in this firstling work, being, indeed, at the root of her humorous conception of life. One of the finest bits of humor in the present volume is the scene in 'Amos Barton,' which occurs at the workhouse, euphemistically called the "College." Mr. Barton, having just finished his address to the paupers, is thus accosted by Mr. Spratt, " a small-featured, small-statured man, with a remarkable power of language, mitigated by hesitation, who piqued himself on expressing unexceptionable sentiments in unexceptionable language on all occasions.

"'Mr. Barton, sir — aw — aw — excuse my trespassing on your time — aw — to beg that you will administer a rebuke to this boy; he is — aw — aw — most inveterate in ill-behavior during service-time.'

" The inveterate culprit was a boy of seven, vainly contending against 'candles' at his nose by feeble sniffing. But no sooner had Mr. Spratt uttered his impeachment than Mrs. Fodge rushed forward, and placed herself between Mr. Barton and the accused.

"'That's *my* child, Muster Barton,' she exclaimed, further manifesting her maternal instincts by applying her apron to her offspring's nose. 'He's aly's a-findin' faut wi' him, and a-poundin' him for nothin.' Let him goo an' eat his roost goose as is a-smellin' up in our noses while we're a-swallering them greasy broth, an' let my boy alooan.'

" Mr. Spratt's small eyes flashed, and he was in danger of uttering sentiments not unexceptionable before the clergyman; but Mr. Barton, foreseeing that a prolongation of this episode would not be to edification, said 'Silence!' in his severest tones.

" 'Let me hear no abuse. Your boy is not likely to behave

well, if you set him the example of being saucy.' Then stooping down to Master Fodge, and taking him by the shoulder, ' Do you like being beaten ? '

" ' No — a.'

" ' Then what a silly boy you are to be naughty. If you were not naughty, you would n't be beaten. But if you are naughty, God will be angry, as well as Mr. Spratt; and God can burn you forever. That will be worse than being beaten.'

"Master Fodge's countenance was neither affirmative nor negative of this proposition.

" ' But,' continued Mr. Barton, ' if you will be a good boy, God will love you, and you will grow up to be a good man. Now, let me hear next Thursday that you have been a good boy.'

"Master Fodge had no distinct vision of the benefit that would accrue to him from this change of courses."

CHAPTER VIII.

ADAM BEDE.

RARELY has a novelist come to his task with such a far-reaching culture, such an intellectual grasp, as George Eliot. We have seen her girlhood occupied with an extraordinary variety of studies; we have seen her plunged in abstruse metaphysical speculations; we have seen her translating some of the most laborious philosophical investigations of German thinkers; we have seen her again translating from the Latin the ' Ethics ' of Spinoza; and, finally, we have seen her attracting, and attracted by, some of the leaders in science, philosophy, and literature.

Compared with such qualifications who among novelists could compete ? What could a Dickens, or a Thackeray himself, throw into the opposing scale ? Lewes, indeed, was a match for her in variety of attainments, but he had made several attempts at fiction, and the attempts had proved failures. When at last, in the maturity of her powers, George Eliot produced 'Adam Bede,' she produced a novel in which the amplest results of knowledge and meditation were so happily blended with instinctive insight into life and character, and the rarest dramatic imagination, as to stamp it immediately as one of the great triumphs and masterpieces in the world of fiction.

It is worth noticing that in 'Adam Bede' George Eliot fulfils to the utmost the demands which she had been theoretically advocating in her essays. In some of these she had not only eloquently enforced the importance of a truthful adherence to nature, but had pointed out how the artist is thus in the very vanguard of social and political reforms; as in familiarizing the imagination with the real condition of the people, he did much towards creating that sympathy with their wants, their trials, and their sufferings, which would eventually effect external changes in harmony with this better understanding. Such had been her teaching. And in Dickens she had recognized the one great novelist who, in certain respects, had painted the lower orders with unerring truthfulness. His "Oliver Twists," his "Nancys," his "Joes," were terrible and pathetic pictures of the forlorn outcasts haunting our London streets. And if, as George Eliot says, Dickens had been able to " give us their psychological character, their conception of life and their emotions, with the same truth as their idiom and manners, his books would be the greatest contribution Art has ever made to the awakening of social sympathies." Now George Eliot absolutely does what Dickens aimed at doing. She not merely seizes the outward and accidental traits of her characters: she pierces with unerring vision to the very core of their nature, and enables us to realize the peculiarly subtle relations between character and circumstance. Her primary object is to excite our sympathy with the most ordinary aspects of human life, with the people that one may meet any day in the fields, the workshops, and the homes of England. Her most vivid creations are not exceptional beings, not men or women pre-eminently conspicuous for sublime heroism of character or magnificent mental endowments, but work-a-day folk,

> "Not too fine or good
> For human nature's daily food."

To this conscientious fidelity of observation and anxious endeavor to report the truth and nothing but the truth, as of a witness in a court of justice, are owing that life-like vividness with which the scenery and people in 'Adam Bede' seem projected on the reader's imagination. The story, indeed, is so intensely realistic as to have given rise to the idea that it is entirely founded on fact. That there is such a substratum is hardly a matter of doubt, and there have been various publications all tending to prove that the chief characters in 'Adam Bede' were not only very faithful copies of living people, but of people closely connected with its author. To some extent this is incontrovertible. But, on the other hand, there is a likelihood of the fictitious events having in their turn been grafted on to actual personages and occurrences, till the whole has become so fused together as to lead some persons to the firm conviction that Dinah Morris is absolutely identical with Mrs. Elizabeth Evans, the Derbyshire Methodist. Such a supposition would help to reconcile the conflicting statements respectively made by the great novelist and the writers of two curious little books entitled 'Seth Bede, the Methody, his Life and Labors,' chiefly written by himself, and 'George Eliot in Derbyshire,' by Guy Roslyn.

From these brochures one gathers that Hayslope, where the rustic drama of 'Adam Bede' unfolds itself, is the village of Ellaston, not far from Ashbourne in Staffordshire. This village is so little altered that the traveller may still see the sign-board of the "Donnithorne Arms," and the red brick hall, only with windows no longer unpatched. Samuel, William, and Robert Evans (the father of the novelist) were born in this place, and began life as carpenters, as their father before them. Samuel Evans became a zealous Methodist, and was rather laughed at by his family in consequence, for he says, "My elder brothers often tried to tease me; they entertained High Church principles. They told me what great blunders I made in preaching and prayer; that I had more zeal than knowledge." In this, as in other respects, he is the prototype of Seth, as Adam resembles Robert Evans, one of the more secular elder brothers, only that in real life it was Samuel who married Elizabeth, the Dinah Morris of fiction.

Much has been written about this Elizabeth Evans (the aunt of George Eliot, already spoken of): indeed, her life was one of such rare devotion to an ideal cause, that even such imperfect fragments of it as have been committed to writing by herself or her friends are of considerable interest. Elizabeth was born at Newbold in Leicestershire, and left her father's house when little more than fourteen years old. She joined the Methodists in 1797, after which she had entirely done with the pleasures of the world and all her old companions. "I saw it my duty," she says, "to leave off all my superfluities of dress; hence I pulled off all my bunches, cut off my curls, left off my lace, and in this I found an unspeakable pleasure. I saw I could make a better use of my time and money than to follow the fashions of a vain world." While still a beautiful young girl, attired in a Quaker dress and bonnet, she used to walk across those bleak Derbyshire hills, looking so strangely mournful in their treeless nudity, with their bare stone fences gray against a grayer sky. Here she trudged from village to village, gathering the poor about her, and pouring forth words of such earnest conviction that, as she says, "Many were brought to the Lord." The points of resemblance between her career and that of Dinah Morris cannot fail to strike the reader, even their phraseology being often singularly alike, as when Mrs. Evans writes in the short account of what she calls her "unprofitable life": "I saw it my duty to be wholly devoted to God, and to be set apart for the Master's use;" while Dinah says: "My life is too short, and God's work is too great for me to think of making a home for myself in this world." It must be borne in mind, however, that these similarities of expression are natural enough when one considers that Dinah is a type of the same old-fashioned kind of Methodism to which Mrs. Evans belonged. What is perhaps stranger is, that the account given by George Eliot of her various meetings with her aunt, Mrs. Elizabeth Evans, should differ considerably from what the latter herself remembered or has stated about them. Shortly after the appearance of 'Adam Bede,' attention had been publicly called to the identity of the heroine of fiction with the Methodist preacher. This conviction was so strong in Wirksworth, that a number of friends placed a memorial tablet in the Methodist chapel at Wirksworth with the following inscription:

ERECTED BY GRATEFUL FRIENDS,

In Memory of

MRS. ELIZABETH EVANS,

(KNOWN TO THE WORLD AS "DINAH BEDE")
WHO DURING MANY YEARS PROCLAIMED ALIKE IN THE
OPEN AIR, THE SANCTUARY, AND FROM HOUSE
TO HOUSE,
THE LOVE OF CHRIST:

SHE DIED IN THE LORD, MAY 9TH, 1849, AGED 74 YEARS

In order to give a correct notion of the amount of truth in her novel, George Eliot wrote in the following terms to her friend Miss Hennell on the 7th of October, 1859: "I should like, while the subject is vividly present with me, to tell you more exactly than I have ever yet done, *what* I knew of my aunt, Elizabeth Evans. My father, you know, lived in Warwickshire all my life with him, having finally left Staffordshire first, and then Derbyshire, six or seven years before he married my mother. There was hardly any intercourse between my father's family, resident in Derbyshire and Staffordshire, and our family — few and far between visits of (to my childish feeling) strange uncles and aunts and cousins from my father's far-off native county, and once a journey of my own, as a little child, with my father and mother, to see my uncle William (a rich builder) in Staffordshire — but *not* my uncle and aunt Samuel, so far as I can recall the dim outline of things — are what I remember of northerly relatives in my childhood.

"But when I was seventeen or more — after my sister was married, and I was mistress of the house — my father took a journey into Derbyshire, in which, visiting my uncle and aunt Samuel, who were very poor, and lived in a humble cottage at Wirksworth, he found my aunt in a very delicate state of health after a serious illness, and, to do her bodily good, he persuaded her to return with him, telling her that *I* should be very, very happy to have her with me for a few weeks. I was then strongly under the influence of evangelical belief, and earnestly endeavoring to shape this anomalous English-Christian life of ours into some consistency with the spirit and simple verbal tenor of the New Testament. I *was* delighted to see my aunt. Although I had only heard her spoken of as a strange person, given to a fanatical vehemence of exhortation in private as well as public, I believed that I should find sympathy between us. She was then an old woman — above sixty — and, I believe, had for a good many years given up preaching. A tiny little woman, with bright, small dark eyes, and hair that had been black, I imagine, but was now gray — a pretty woman in her youth, but of a totally different physical type from Dinah. The difference — as you will believe — was not *simply* physical; no difference is. She was a woman of strong natural excitability, which I know, from the description I have heard my father and half-sister give, prevented her from the exercise of discretion under the promptings of her zeal. But this vehemence was now subdued by age and sickness; she was very gentle and quiet in her manners, very loving, and (what she must have been from the very first) a truly religious soul, in whom the love of God and love of man were fused together. There was nothing rightly distinctive in her religious conversation. I had had much intercourse with pious dissenters before; the only freshness I found in her talk came from the fact that she had been the greater part of her life a Wesleyan, and though *she left the society when women were no longer allowed to preach*, and joined the New Wesleyans, she retained the character of thought that belongs to the genuine old Wesleyan. I had never talked with a Wesleyan before, and we used to have little debates about predestination, for I was then a strong Calvinist. Here her superiority came out, and I remember now, with loving admiration, one thing which at the time I disapproved; it was not strictly a consequence of her Arminian belief, and at first sight might seem opposed to it, yet it came from the spirit of love which clings to the bad logic of Arminianism. When my uncle came to fetch her, after she had been with us a fortnight or three weeks, he was speaking of a deceased minister once greatly respected, who, from the action of trouble upon him, had taken to small tippling, though otherwise not culpable. 'But I hope the good man's in heaven for all that,' said my uncle. 'Oh yes,' said my aunt, with a deep inward groan of joyful conviction, 'Mr. A.'s in heaven, that's sure.' This was at the time an offence to my stern, ascetic, hard views — how beautiful it is to me now!

"As to my aunt's conversation, it is a fact that the only two things of any interest I remember in our lonely sittings and walks are her telling me one sunny afternoon how she had, with another pious woman, visited an unhappy girl in prison, stayed with her all night, and gone with her to execution; and one or two accounts of supposed miracles in which she believed, among the rest, *the face with the crown of thorns seen in the glass*. In her account of the prison scenes I remember no word she uttered; I only remember her tone and manner, and the deep feeling I had under the recital. Of the girl she knew nothing, I believe, or told me nothing, but that she was a common, coarse girl, convicted of child-murder. The incident lay in my mind for years on years, as a dead germ, apparently, till time had made my mind a nidus in which it could fructify; it then turned out to be the germ of 'Adam Bede.'

"I saw my aunt twice after this. Once I spent a day and night with my father in the Wirksworth cottage, sleeping with my aunt, I remember. Our interview was less interesting than in the former time; I think I was less simply devoted to religious ideas And once again she came with my uncle to see me, when father and I were living at Foleshill; *then* there was some pain, for I had given up the form of Christian belief, and was in a crude state of free-thinking. She stayed about three or four days, I think. This is all I remember distinctly, as matter I could write down, of my dear aunt, whom I really loved. You see how she suggested 'Dinah;' but it is not possible you should see, as I do, how entirely her individuality differed from 'Dinah's.' How curious it seems to me that people should think 'Dinah's' sermon, prayers, and speeches were *copied*, when they were written with hot tears as they surged up in my own mind!

"As to my indebtedness to facts of local and personal history of a small kind connected with Staffordshire and Derbyshire, you may imagine of what kind that is, when I tell you that I never remained in either of those counties more than a few days together, and of only two such visits have I more than a shadowy, interrupted recollection. The details which I know as facts, and have made use of for my picture, were gathered from such imperfect allusion and narrative as I heard from my father in his occasional talk about old times.

"As to my aunt's children or grandchildren saying, if they *did* say, that 'Dinah' is a good portrait of my aunt, that is simply the vague, easily satisfied notion imperfectly instructed people always have of portraits. It is not surprising that simple men and women, without pretension to enlightened discrimination, should think a generic resemblance constitutes a portrait, when we see the great public, so accustomed to be delighted with *mis*-representations of life and character, which they accept as representations, that they are scandalized when art makes a nearer approach to truth.

"Perhaps I am doing a superfluous thing in writing all this to you, but I am prompted to do it by the feeling that in future years 'Adam Bede,' and all that concerns it, may have become a dim portion of the past, and that I may not be able to recall so much of the truth as I have now told you."

Nothing could prove more conclusively how powerful was the impression which 'Adam Bede' created than this controversy concerning the amount of truth which its characters contained. But, as hinted before, it seems very likely that some of the doings and sayings of the fictitious personages should have been attributed, almost unconsciously, to the real people whom they resembled. How quick is the popular imagination in effecting these transformations came only quite recently under my notice, when some English travellers, while visiting Château d'If, were taken by the guide in perfect good faith to see the actual dungeon where Monte Cristo was imprisoned! Similarly, one would think that the moving sermon preached by Dinah on the Green at Hayslope had been afterwards erroneously ascribed to Mrs. Elizabeth Evans. But an account recently published in the *Century Magazine* by one who had long known the Evanses of Wirksworth, seems irreconcilable with such a supposition. According to this writer it would appear that besides the visits to her aunt at Wirksworth, of which George Eliot speaks in the letter just quoted, there was one other of which no mention is made. This visit, which she paid her cousin, Mr. Samuel Evans, occurred in 1842, when she remained a week at his house in Wirksworth. The aunt and niece were in the habit of seeing each other every day for several hours at this time. They usually met at the house of one of the married daughters of Mrs. Elizabeth Evans, holding long conversations while sitting by themselves in the parlor. "These secret conversations," says the writer of the article, "excited some curiosity in the family, and one day one of the daughters said, 'Mother, I can't think what thee and Mary Ann have got to talk about so much.' To which Mrs Evans replied: 'Well, my dear, I don't know what she wants, but she gets me to tell her all about my life and my religious experience, and she puts it all down in a little book. I can't make out what she wants it for.'" After her departure, Mrs. Evans is reported to have said to her daughter, "Oh dear, Mary Ann has got one thing I did not mean her to take away, and that is the notes of the first sermon I preached at Ellaston Green." According to the same authority, Marian Evans took notes of everything people said in her hearing: no matter who was speaking, down it went into the note-book, which seemed never out of her hand; and these notes she is said to have transcribed every night before going to bed. Yet this habit was foreign to her whole character, and the friends who knew her most intimately in youth and later life never remember seeing her resort to such a practice. Be that as it may, there can be no doubt that the novelist very freely used many of the circumstances connected with her aunt's remarkable career. How closely she adhered to nature is shown by the fact that in Mrs. Poyser and Bartle Massey she retained the actual names of the characters portrayed, as they happened to be both dead. Bartle Massey, the village cynic, had been the schoolmaster of her father, Robert Evans. How accurately the latter, together with all his surroundings, was described is shown by the following anecdote. On its first appearance 'Adam Bede' was read aloud to an old man, an intimate associate of Robert Evans in his Staffordshire days. This man knew nothing concerning either author or subject beforehand, and his astonishment was boundless on recognizing so many friends and incidents of his own youth portrayed with unerring fidelity. He sat up half the night listening to the story in breathless excitement, now and then slapping his knee as he exclaimed, "'That's Robert, that's Robert to the life."

Although Wirksworth is not the locality described in 'Adam Bede,' it contains features recalling that quaint little market-town, where over the door of one of the old-fashioned houses may be read the name made illustrious by the inimitable Mrs. Poyser. In the neighborhood, too, are "Arkwright's mills there at Cromford," casually alluded to by Adam Bede; and should the tourist happen to enter one of the cottages of gray stone, with blue-washed door and window-frames, he may still alight on specimens of Methodism, as devout as Seth Bede, eloquently expounding the latest political event by some prophecy of Daniel or Ezekiel. In short, one breathes the atmosphere in which such characters as Dinah and Seth actually lived and had their being. This uncompromising Realism, so far from detracting, only enhances the genius of this powerful novel. A thousand writers might have got hold of these identical materials: a George Eliot alone could have cast these materials into the mould of 'Adam Bede.' Let any one glance at the account of their religious experiences, as given by Elizabeth or Samuel Evans, and he will realize all the more strongly how great was the genius of her who transfused these rambling, common-place effusions into such an artistic whole. I have entered so minutely into this question of the likeness between the actual characters and those in the novel purely on account of the biographical interest attaching to it. In judging of 'Adam Bede' as a work of art these facts possess next to no importance. If we could trace the characters in any one of Shakespeare's plays to human beings actually connected with the poet, we should consider such a discovery immensely valuable as throwing new light on his own life, though it would hardly affect our critical estimate of the drama itself.

So much has been said already about the characters in 'Adam Bede' in connection with the real people they resemble, that little need be added here about them. Dinah Morris — the youthful preacher, whose eloquence is but the natural, almost involuntary manifestation in words, of a beautiful soul, whose spring of love is so abundant that it overflows the narrow limits of private affection, and blesses multitudes of toiling, suffering men and women with its wealth of pity, hope, and sympathy — was a new creation in the world of fiction. Some writer has pointed out a certain analogy between the sweet Derbyshire Methodist and the gentle pietist whose confessions form a very curious chapter of 'Wilhelm Meister.' But the two characters are too dissimilar for comparison. The German heroine is a dreamy, passive, introspective nature, feeling much but doing little; whereas the English preacher does not inquire too curiously into the mysteries of her faith, but moved by the spirit of its teaching goes about actively, participating in the lives of others by her rousing words and her acts of charity. Only a woman would or could have described just such a woman as this: a woman whose heart is centred in an impersonal ideal instead of in any individual object of love; whereas a man's heroine always has her existence rooted in some personal affection or passion, whether for parent or lover, child or husband. This makes Dinah less romantically interesting than Hetty Sorrel, the beautiful, kittenlike, self-involved creature with whom she is so happily contrasted. George Eliot never drew a more living figure than this of Hetty, hiding such a hard little heart under that soft dimpling beauty of hers. Again, I think that only a woman would have depicted just such a Hetty as this. The personal charms of this young girl are drawn in words that have the glow of life itself; yet while intensely conscious of her beauty, we are kept aware all the time that, to use one of the famous Mrs. Poyser's epigrammatic sayings, Hetty is "no better nor a cherry wi' a hard stone inside it." George Eliot is never dazzled or led away by her own bewitching creation as a man would have been. There is a certain pitilessness in her analysis of Hetty's shallow, frivolous little soul, almost as if she were saying — See here, what stuff this beauty which you adore is made of in reality! To quote her own subtle, far-reaching interpretation of beauty· "Hetty's face had a language that transcended her feelings. There are faces which nature charges with a meaning and pathos not belonging to the simple human soul that flutters beneath them, but speaking the joys and sorrows of foregone generations; eyes that tell of deep love which doubtless has been and is somewhere, but not paired with these eyes, perhaps paired with pale eyes that can say nothing, just as a national language may be instinct with poetry unfelt by the lips that use it."

The sensation created by 'Adam Bede' was shown in other ways besides the claim of some to have discovered the original characters of this striking novel. The curiosity of the public was naturally much exercised as to who the unknown author could possibly be, who had so suddenly leaped into fame. And now there comes on the scene an individual who does not claim to be the living model of one of the characters portrayed, but to be the author of the book himself. And the name of this person was Liggins!

While the 'Scenes of Clerical Life' were yet appearing in *Blackwood's Magazine* the inhabitants of Nuneaton and its neighborhood were considerably perplexed and excited to find well-known places and persons touched off to the life. In Amos Barton they recognized the incumbent of Coton Church, in Mr. Pilgrim a medical man familiar to every child in the town, and indeed in every one of the characters an equally unmistakable portrait. Clearly no one but a fellow-townsman could have hit off these wonderful likenesses. Literary talent not being too abundant, their choice of an author was limited. The only man who by any stretch of imagination seemed to have the making of a man of letters in him was this above-mentioned Liggins. To have studied at Cambridge, gallantly run through a fortune, and be in very needy circumstances, were exactly the qualifications to be expected in a man of genius. Further evidence seeming unnecessary, the real authorship of the 'Scenes' was now revealed in an Isle of Man paper. At first the reputed author gently denied the impeachment, but on the appearance of 'Adam Bede' he succumbed to the temptation. To be fêted at dinner parties as a successful author, and to have a subscription set on foot by enthusiastic lady-admirers and fellow-townsmen, in whose eyes he was a sadly unrequited genius, proved irresistible. A local clergyman even wrote to the *Times* stating Liggins to be the real surname of "George Eliot"! The latter wrote, of course, denying the statement, and challenging the pretender to produce some specimen of his writing in the style of 'Adam Bede.' But the confidence of the Nuneaton public in their hero Liggins was not to be so easily shaken. Two dissenting ministers from Coventry went over to Attleborough to call upon the "great author," and to find out if he really did write 'Adam Bede.' Liggins evaded their questions, indirectly admitting that he did; but when they asked him point blank, "Liggins, tell us, *did* you write 'Adam Bede'?" he said, "If I didn't, the devil did!" and that was all they could get out of him. Another clergyman was much less sceptical, assuring every one that he was positive as to Liggins being the author, as he had seen the MS. of 'Adam Bede' in his hands. To this day there lives in the Isle of Man a certain venerable old gentleman who has never lost his faith in Liggins, but, when George Eliot is mentioned, gravely shakes his head, implying that there is more in the name than meets the eye of the superficial observer. But a heavy retribution befell the poor pseudo-author at last, for when his false pretences to favor were fully manifest he fell into utter neglect and poverty, ending his days in the workhouse.

This foolish misrepresentation hastened the disclosure of George Eliot's real personality and name, which occurred on the publication of 'The Mill on the Floss.' Shortly before that, Mr. Blackwood, who had long entertained the wish to know the author of the 'Scenes of Clerical Life' and of 'Adam Bede,' was invited by Lewes to meet him at last. No one was present at the dinner-table besides Mr. Lewes, Marian, and Mr. Blackwood himself. The dinner was an extremely pleasant one, but when it was over, the guest could not help expressing his regret that George Eliot himself should not have been present. "Here he is," said Lewes, introducing the quiet, low-spoken lady who had presided at table, not without enjoyment at the sensation he produced as the astonished publisher shook hands with his contributor.

CHAPTER IX.

THE MILL ON THE FLOSS.

WHILE the public had been trying to discover who the mysterious George Eliot could possibly be, one person there was who immediately penetrated the disguise, and felt positive as to the identity of the author. On reading the 'Scenes' and especially 'Adam Bede,' he was convinced that no one but a member of his own family could have written these stories. He recognized incidents, touches, a saying here or there, just the things that no one outside his own home could by any chance have come upon. But George Eliot's brother kept this discovery closely locked within his own breast. He trembled lest any one else should discover the secret, fearing the outcry of neighbors who might not always feel that the author had represented them in colors sufficiently flattering.

When 'The Mill on the Floss' appeared, however, the veil was lifted, and people heard that George Eliot had once been a Miss Marian Evans, who came from the neighborhood of Nuneaton in Warwickshire. To her brother Isaac alone this was no news, as he had detected his sister in the first of the 'Scenes.' The child-life of Tom and Maggie Tulliver was in many respects an autobiography; and no biographer can ever hope to describe the early history of George Eliot as she herself has done in 'The Mill on the Floss.' How many joys and griefs of those happy careless days must have been recalled to her brother — those days when little Mary Ann had sat poring over Daniel Defoe's 'History of the Devil' — or sought refuge in the attic at Griff House, after a quarrel with him: "This attic was Maggie's favorite retreat on a wet day, when the weather was not too cold; here she fretted out all her ill-humors, and talked aloud to the worm-eaten floors and the worm-eaten shelves, and the dark rafters festooned with cobwebs; and here she kept a Fetish which she punished for all her misfortunes. This was the trunk of a large wooden doll, which once stared with the roundest of eyes above the reddest of cheeks, but was now entirely defaced by a long career of vicarious suffering. Three nails driven into the head commemorated as many crises in Maggie's nine years of earthly struggle, that luxury of vengeance having been suggested to her by the picture of Jael destroying Sisera in the old Bible."

Again, at some fields' distance from their old home there had been a "Round Pool" called "The Moat," "almost a perfect round, framed in with willows and tall reeds, so that the water was only to be seen when you got close to the brink. This was a favorite resort of Isaac and Mary Ann, as also of Tom and his sister when they went fishing together, and "Maggie thought it probable that the small fish would come to her hook and large ones to Tom's." The "Red Deeps," too, where Maggie loved to walk in June, when the "dog-roses were in their glory," and where she lived through many phases of her shifting inner life, was in the same vicinity, and at one time a beloved haunt of the future novelist.

But although some of the spots mentioned in 'The Mill on the Floss' have been easily identified as connected with George Eliot's early home, the scenery of that novel is mainly laid in Lincolnshire. St. Oggs, with "its red-fluted roofs and broad warehouse gables," is the ancient town of Gainsborough. The Floss is a tidal river like the Trent, and in each case the spring-tide, rushing up the river with its terrific wave and flooding the land for miles round, is known as the Eagre, a name not a little descriptive of the thing itself.

'The Mill on the Floss' (a title adopted by the author at the suggestion of Mr. Blackwood in preference to 'Sister Maggie') is the most poetical of George Eliot's novels. The great Floss, hurrying between green pastures to the sea, gives a unity of its own to this story, which opens to the roar of waters, the weltering waters which accompany it at the close. It forms the elemental background which rounds the little lives of the ill-starred family group nurtured on its banks. The childhood of Tom and Maggie Tulliver is inextricably blended with this swift river, the traditions of which have been to them as fairy tales; its haunting presence is more or less with them throughout their chequered existence; and when pride and passion, when shame and sorrow, have divided the brother and sister, pursued as by some tragic fate, the Floss seems to rise in sympathy, and submerges them in its mighty waters to unite them once more "in an embrace never to be parted." It cannot fail to strike the reader that in almost every one of George Eliot's novels there occurs a death by drowning: as in the instance of Thias Bede, of Dunstan Cass, of Henleigh Grandcourt, and nearly in that of Tito. This may be accounted for by the fact that as a child the novelist became acquainted with the sudden death of a near relative who had accidentally fallen into a stream: an incident which sunk deeply into her retentive mind.

Fate plays a very conspicuous part in this as in most of George Eliot's novels. But it is not the Fate of the Greeks, it is not a power that affects human existence from without: it rather lies at the root of it, more or less shaping that existence according to obscure inherited tendencies, and in the collision between character and circumstance, between passion and law, potent only in proportion as the individual finally issues conquered or a conqueror from the struggle of life. This action of character on circumstance and of circumstance on character is an ever-recurring *motif* with George Eliot. We constantly see adverse circumstances modifying and moulding the lives of the actors in her stories. She has hardly, if ever, therefore drawn a hero or heroine, for these, instead of yielding, make circumstances yield to them. Dorothea and Lydgate, in abandoning their striving after the highest kind of life; Tito in invariably yielding to the most pleasurable prompting of the moment; Gwendolen in being mainly influenced by circumstances acting on her, without her reacting on them, are all types of this kind.

Maggie belongs, on the whole, to the same type. She, too, is what Goethe calls a problematic nature, a nature which, along with vast possibilities and lofty aspirations, lacks a certain fixity of purpose, and drifting helplessly from one extreme to another, is shattered almost as soon as it has put out of port. In Maggie's case this evil springs from the very fulness of her nature; from the acuteness of an imagination which the many-sidedness of life attracts by turns in the most opposite directions. Tom, on the other hand, with his narrow practical understanding, entirely concentrated on the business in hand, swerves neither to right nor left, because he may be said to resemble a horse with blinkers, in that he sees only the road straight ahead. Maggie, with all her palpable weaknesses and startling inconsistencies, is the most adorable of George Eliot's women. In all poetry and fiction there is no child more delicious than the "little wench" with her loving heart and dreamy ways, her rash impulses and wild regrets, her fine susceptibilities and fiery jets of temper — in a word, her singularly fresh and vital nature. The same charm pervades every phase of her life. In her case the child, if I may so far modify Wordsworth's famous saying, is eminently the mother of the woman.

Profoundly affectionate by nature, and sympathizing as she does with her father in his calamity, she cannot help rebelling at the sordid narrowness of her daily life, passionately craving for a wider field wherein to develop her inborn faculties. In this state of yearning and wild unrest, her accidental reading of Thomas à Kempis forms a crisis in her life, by bringing about a spiritual awakening in which Christianity, for the first time, becomes a living truth to her. Intense as she is, Maggie now throws all the ardor of her nature into renunciation and self-conquest. She seeks her highest satisfaction in abnegation of all personal desire, and in entire devotion to others. In her young asceticism she relinquishes a world of which she is ignorant, stifling every impulse, however innocent, that seems opposed to her new faith.

But Maggie has more actual affinity with poets and artists than with saints and martyrs. Her soul thrills like a finely touched instrument to the beauty of the world around her, and though she doubts whether there may not even be a sinfulness in the indulgence of this enjoyment, yet the summer flowers and the summer sunshine put her scruples to flight. And then, when, through the intervention of Philip Wakem, the enchantments of romance and poetry are brought within her reach, the glory of the world again lays hold of her imagination, and a fresh conflict is begun in her soul. Thus she drifts from one state into another most opposed to it, and to an outside observer, such as Tom, her abrupt transitions are a sign that she is utterly wanting in moral stamina.

Not only Tom, but many eminent critics, who have descanted with fond partiality on Maggie's early life, seem to be shocked by that part of her story in which she allows herself to fall passionately in love with such an ordinary specimen of manhood as Stephen Guest. The author has even been accused of violating the truth of Nature, inasmuch as such a high-minded woman as Maggie could never have inclined to so vulgar, so commonplace a man as her lover. Others, while not questioning the truth of the character, find fault with the poor heroine herself, whom they pronounce an ineffective nature revealing its innate unsoundness by the crowning error of an abject passion for so poor a creature as the dandy of St. Oggs. This contention only proves the singular vitality of the character itself, and nothing is more psychologically true in George Eliot's studies of character than this love of the high-souled heroine for a man who has no corresponding fineness of fibre in his nature, his attraction lying entirely in the magnetism of mutual passion. This vitality places Maggie Tulliver by the side of the Juliets, the Mignons, the Consuelos, the Becky Sharps, and other airy inheritors of immortality. It is curious that Mr. Swinburne, in view of such a character as this, or, indeed, bearing in mind a Silas Marner, a Dolly Winthrop, a Tito, and other intrinsically living reproductions of human nature, should describe George Eliot's as intellectually constructed characters in contrast to Charlotte Brontë's creations, the former, according to him, being the result of intellect, the latter of genius. If ever character came simply dropped out of the mould of Nature it is that of Maggie. His assumption, that 'The Mill on the Floss' can in any sense have been suggested by, or partially based upon, Mrs. Gaskell's story of 'The Moorland Cottage,' seems equally baseless. There is certainly the identity of name in the heroines, and some resemblance of situation as regards portions of the story, but both the name and the situation are sufficiently common not to excite astonishment at such a coincidence. Had George Eliot really known of this tale — a tale feebly executed at the best — she would obviously have altered the name so as not to make her obligation too patent to the world. As it is, she was not a little astonished and even indignant, on accidentally seeing this opinion stated in some review, and positively denied ever having seen the story in question.

Indeed, when one knows how this story grew out of her own experience, how its earlier portions especially are a record of her own and her brother's childhood — how even Mrs. Glegg and Mrs. Pullet were only too faithfully done from the aunts of real life, one need not go far afield to seek for its origin. Every author usually writes one book, which he might more or less justly entitle 'My Confessions,' into which he pours an intimate part of his life under a thin disguise of fiction, a book invariably exciting a unique kind of interest in the reader be he conscious or not of the presence of this autobiographical element. Fielding's 'Amelia,' Thackeray's 'Pendennis,' Dickens's 'David Copperfield,' Charlotte Brontë's 'Villette,' are cases in point. 'The Mill on the Floss' is a work of similar nature. Maggie Tulliver is George Eliot herself, but only one side, one portion, one phase of George Eliot's many-sided, vastly complex nature. It is George Eliot's inner life in childhood and youth as it appeared to her own consciousness. We recognize in it her mental acuteness, her clinging affectionateness, her ambition, her outlook beyond the present, her religious and moral preoccupations; even her genius is not so much omitted as left in an undeveloped, rudimentary state. While her make-believe stories, her thirst for knowledge, her spiritual wrestlings, and the passionate response of her soul to high thinking, noble music, and the beautiful in all its forms, show that the making of genius was there in germ. Much in the same manner Gœthe was fond of partitioning his nature, and of giving only the weaker side to his fictitious representatives. Conscious in himself of fluctuations of purpose which he only got the better of by his indomitable will, he usually endowed these characters with his more impulsive, pliant self, as manifested in Werther, in Tasso, in Edward of the 'Elective Affinities.' In this sense also Maggie Tulliver resembles George Eliot. She is her potential self, such as she might have been had there not been counterbalancing tendencies of unusual force, sufficient to hold in check all erratic impulses contrary to the main direction of her life.

While tempted to dwell largely on Maggie Tulliver, the central figure of 'The Mill on the Floss,' it would be very unfair to slur over the other admirably drawn characters of this novel. Her brother Tom, already repeatedly alluded to, is in every sense the counterpart of "Sister Maggie." Hard and narrow-minded he was from a boy, "particularly clear and positive on one point, namely, that he would punish everybody who deserved it: why, he wouldn't have minded being punished himself, if he deserved it; but, then, he never *did* deserve it." This strikes the key-note of a character whose stern inflexibility, combined with much practical insight and dogged persistence of effort, is at the same time dignified by a high, if somewhat narrow, sense of family honor. Conventional respectability, in fact, is Tom Tulliver's religion. He is not in any sense bad, or mean, or sordid; he is only so circumscribed in his perspective faculties that he has no standard by which to measure thoughts or feelings that transcend his own very limited conception of life.

Both by his good and his bad qualities, by his excellences and his negations, Tom Tulliver proves himself what he is — a genuine sprig of the Dodson family, a chip of the old block! And the Dodson sisters are, in their way, among the most amazingly living portraitures that George Eliot ever achieved. Realism in art can go no further in this direction. These women, if present in the flesh, would not be so distinctively vivid as when beheld through the transfixing medium of George Eliot's genius. For here we have the personages, with all their quaintnesses, their eccentricities, their odd, old-fashioned twists and ways — only observed by fragments in actual life — successfully brought to a focus for the delight and amusement of generations of readers. There is nothing grotesque, nothing exaggerated, in these humorous figures. The comic effect is not produced, as is often the case with the inventions of Dickens, by some set peculiarity of manner or trick of speech, more in the spirit of caricature. On the contrary, it is by a strict adherence to the just mean of nature, by a conscientious care not to overstep her probabilities, that we owe these matchless types of English provincial life. And the genuine humor of these types verges on the pathetic, in that the infinitely little of their lives is so magnified by them out of all proportion to its real importance. Mrs. Glegg, with her dictatorial ways, her small economies, her anxiety to make a handsome figure in her will, and her invariable reference to what was "the way in our family," as a criterion of right behavior on all occasions: Mrs. Pullet, the wife of the well-to-do yeoman-farmer, bent on proving her gentility and wealth by the delicacy of her health, and the quantity of doctor's stuff she can afford to imbibe: Mrs. Tulliver, the good, muddle-headed woman, whose husband "picked her from her sisters o' purpose, 'cause she was a bit weak, like," and for whom the climax of misery in bankruptcy is the loss of her china and table linen: these, as well as the henpecked Mr. Glegg, and the old-maidish Mr. Pullet, are worthy pendants to Mrs. Poyser and Dolly Winthrop.

Whether too great a predominance may not be given to the narrow, trivial views of these people, with their prosaic respectability, is a nice question, which one is inclined to answer in the negative on reading such a conjugal scene as that between Mr. and Mrs. Glegg, after the latter's quarrel with Mr. Tulliver:

"It was a hard case that a vigorous mood for quarrelling, so highly capable of using any opportunity, should not meet with a single remark from Mr. Glegg on which to exercise itself. But by-and-by it appeared that his silence would answer the purpose, for he heard himself apostrophized at last in that tone peculiar to the wife of one's bosom.

"'Well, Mr. Glegg! It's a poor return I get for making you the wife I've made you all these years. If this is the way I'm to be treated, I'd better ha' known it before my poor father died, and then when I'd wanted a home, I should ha' gone elsewhere — as the choice was offered me.'

"Mr. Glegg paused from his porridge and looked up, not with any new amazement, but simply with that quiet, habitual wonder with which we regard constant mysteries.

"'Why, Mrs. G., what have I done now?'

"'Done now, Mr. Glegg? *done now?* . . . I'm sorry for you.'

"Not seeing his way to any pertinent answer, Mr. Glegg reverted to his porridge.

"'There's husbands in the world,' continued Mrs. Glegg, after a pause, 'as 'ud have known how to do something different to siding with everybody else against their own wives. Perhaps I'm wrong, and you can teach me better. But I've allays heard as it's the husband's place to stand by the wife, instead of rejoicing and triumphing when folks insult her.'

"'Now what call have you to say that?' said Mr. Glegg, rather warmly, for, though a kind man, he was not as meek as Moses. 'When did I rejoice or triumph over you?'

"'There's ways o' doing things worse than speaking out plain, Mr. Glegg. I'd sooner you'd tell me to my face as you make light of me, than try to make as everybody's in the right but me, and come to your breakfast in the morning, as I've hardly slept an hour this night, and sulk at me as if I was the dirt under your feet.'

"'Sulk at you?' said Mr. Glegg, in a tone of angry facetiousness. 'You're like a tipsy man as thinks everybody's had too much but himself.'

"'Don't lower yourself with using coarse language to *me*, Mr. Glegg! It makes you look very small, though you can't see yourself,' said Mrs Glegg, in a tone of energetic compassion. 'A man in your place should set an example, and talk more sensible.'"

After a good deal of sparring in the same tone, Mr. Glegg at last bursts forth: "'Did ever anybody hear the like i' this parish? A woman with everything provided for her, and allowed to keep her own money the same as if it was settled on her, and with a gig new stuffed and lined at no end o' expense, and provided for when I die beyond anything she could expect . . . to go on i' this way, biting and snapping like a mad dog! It's beyond everything, as God A'mighty should ha' made women *so*.' (These last words were uttered in a tone of sorrowful agitation. Mr. Glegg pushed his tea from him, and tapped the table with both his hands.)

"'Well, Mr. Glegg! if those are your feelings, it's best they should be known,' said Mrs. Glegg, taking off her napkin, and folding it in an excited manner. 'But if you talk o' my being provided for beyond what I could expect, I beg leave to tell you as I'd a right to expect a many things as I don't find. And as to my being like a mad dog, it's well if you're not cried shame on by the country for your treatment of me, for it's what I can't bear, and I won't bear.' . . .

"Here Mrs. Glegg's voice intimated that she was going to cry, and, breaking off from speech, she rang the bell violently.

"'Sally,' she said, rising from her chair, and speaking in rather a choked voice, 'light a fire up-stairs, and put the blinds down. Mr. Glegg, you'll please order what you like for dinner. I shall have gruel.'"

Equally well drawn in their way, though belonging to a different class of character, are Maggie's cousin, the lovely, gentle, and refined Lucy; Philip Wakem, whose physical malformation is compensated by exceptional culture and nobility of nature; Mr. Tulliver, the headstrong, violent, but withal generous, father of Maggie, and his sister Mrs. Moss, whose motherliness and carelessness of appearances form a striking foil to the Dodson sisters. Indeed, 'The Mill on the Floss' is so rich in minor characters that it is impossible to do more than mention such capital sketches as that of Bob Jakin and his dog Mumps, or of Luke, the head miller, who has no opinion of reading, considering that "There's fools enoo — an' rogues enoo — wiout lookin' i' books for 'em."

The distinguishing feature of this novel, however, lies not so much in its wealth of portraiture or freshness of humor as in a certain passionate glow of youth, which emanates from the heroine, and seems to warm the story through and through. For passion, pathos, and poetic beauty of description, 'The Mill on the Floss' is certainly unique among George Eliot's works.

CHAPTER X.

SILAS MARNER.

'THE Mill on the Floss,' which appeared in 1860, fully established George Eliot's popularity with the public. In the same year she published anonymously, in *Blackwood's Magazine*, a short story called 'The Lifted Veil.' This tale is curious as differing considerably from her general style, having a certain mystical turn, which perhaps recommended it more especially to the admiration of Bulwer Lytton; but, indeed, it attracted general attention. In the meanwhile the relations between author and publisher became more and more friendly; the latter's critical acumen and sound judgment being highly esteemed by George Eliot. "He judged well of writing," she remarked, "because he had learned to judge well of men and things, not merely through quickness of observation and insight, but with the illumination of a heart in the right place."

This was the most productive period of George Eliot's life. In three successive years she published 'Adam Bede,' 'The Mill on the Floss,' and 'Silas Marner,' the last story appearing in 1861. When the amount of thought, observation, and wisdom concentrated in these novels is taken into consideration, it must be admitted that her mental energy was truly astonishing. But it was the accumulated experience of her whole past, the first abundant math borne by the spring-tide of life which was garnered up in these three remarkable works. Afterwards, when she came to write her next book, 'Romola,' she turned to entirely fresh fields of inspiration; indeed, already at this date her mind was occupied with the idea of an Italian novel of the time of Savonarola.

In the meanwhile she produced her most finished work. She wrote 'Silas Marner, the Weaver of Raveloe.' I call 'Silas Marner' her most finished work, not only because of the symmetry with which each part is adjusted in relation to the whole, nor because of the absence of those partly satirical, partly moral reflections with which George Eliot usually accompanies the action of her stories, but chiefly on account of the simple pathos of the central motive into which all the different incidents and characters naturally converge. How homely are the elements from which this work of art is constructed, and how matchless the result!

Nothing but the story of a humble weaver belonging to a small dissenting community which assembled in Lantern Yard, somewhere in the back streets of a manufacturing town; of a faithless love and a false friend, and the loss of trust in all things human or divine. Nothing but the story of a lone, bewildered man, shut out from his kind, concentrating every balked passion into one — the all-engrossing passion for gold. And then the sudden disappearance of the hoard from its accustomed hiding-place, and in its stead the startling apparition of a golden-haired little child, found one snowy winter's night sleeping on the floor in front of the glimmering hearth. And the gradual re-awakening of love in the heart of the solitary man, a love "drawing his hope and joy continually onward beyond the money," and once more bringing him into sympathetic relations with his fellow-men.

"In old days," says the story, "there were angels who came and took men by the hand and led them away from the city of destruction. We see no white-winged angels now. But yet men are led away from threatening destruction; a hand is put into theirs, which leads them forth gently towards a calm and bright land, so that they look no more backward, and the hand may be a little child's."

Curiously enough, I came quite recently upon a story which in its leading features very closely resembles this tale of the 'Weaver of Raveloe.' It is called 'Jermola the Potter,' and is considered the masterpiece of J. I. Kraszewski, the Polish novelist, author of at least one hundred and fifty works in different branches of literature. 'Jermola,' the most popular of them all, has been translated into French, Dutch, and German. It gives an extraordinarily vivid picture of peasant life in a remote Polish village, and not only of peasant life, but of the manners and habits of the landed proprietor, the Jew, the artisan, and the yeoman, in a community whose modes of life have undergone but little modification since the Middle Ages.

These pictures, though not elaborated with anything like the minute care of George Eliot's descriptions of English country life, yet from their extreme simplicity produce a most powerful impression on the reader.

The story, in brief, is that of Jermola, the body servant of a Polish nobleman in Volhynia, whom he has served with rare devotion during the greater part of his life. Left almost a beggar at his master's death, without a single human tie, all he can get for years of faithful service is a tumble-down, forsaken old inn, where he manages to keep body and soul together in a dismantled room that but partly shelters him from the inclemency of the weather. Hopeless, aimless, loveless, he grows old before his time, and the passing of the days affects him hardly more than it does a stone. But one evening, as he is sitting in front of a scanty fire repeating the Lord's Prayer, the cry as of a little child startles him from his devotion. Going to look what can be the meaning of such unusual sounds, he soon discovers an infant in linen swaddling-clothes wailing under an old oak-tree. He takes the foundling home, and from that moment a new life enters the old man's breast. He is rejuvenated by twenty years. He is kept in a constant flutter of hope, fear, and activity. A kind-hearted woman, called the Kozaczicha, tenders him her services, but he is so jealous of any one but himself doing aught for the child, that he checks her advances, and by hook or by crook obtains a goat from an extortionate Jew, by the help of which he rears the boy satisfactorily. Then, wishing to make a livelihood for the child's sake, he inclines at first to the craft of the weaver, but finally turns potter in his old age. Love sharpening his wits, he plies quite a thriving trade in time, and the beautiful boy brings him into more friendly relations with his neighbors. But one day, when Radionek, who has learned Jermola's trade, is about twelve years old, the real parents appear and claim him as their own. They had never dared to acknowledge their marriage till the father, who had threatened to disinherit his son in such an event, had departed this life. Now, having nothing more to fear, they want to have their child back, and to bring him up as befits their station in life. Jermola suffers a deadly anguish at this separation;

the boy, too, is in despair, for he clings fondly to the old man who has reared him with more than a father's love. But the parents insisting on their legal rights, Radionek is at last carried off to their house in town, to be turned into a gentleman, being only grudgingly allowed to see Jermola from time to time. The boy pines, however, for the dear familiar presence of his foster-father, and the free outdoor life, and at last, after some years of misery, he appears one day suddenly in Jermola's hut, who has given up his pottery in order to be secretly near the child he is afraid to go and see. The piteous entreaties of Radionek, and the sight of his now sickly countenance, induce the old man to flee into the pathless forests, where the two may escape unseen, and reach some distant part of the country to take up their old pleasant life once more. But the hardships and fatigues of the journey are too much for the boy's enfeebled health, and just as they come within sight of human dwellings, he is seized with a fever which cuts his young life short, leaving Jermola nearly crazy with anguish. Long afterwards a little decrepit old man was to be seen by churchgoers sitting near a grave, whom the children mocked by calling the "bony little man," because he seemed to consist of nothing but bones.

Such is the bare outline of a story whose main idea, that of the redemption of a human soul from cold, petrifying isolation, by means of a little child, is unquestionably the same as in 'Silas Marner.' Other incidents, such as that of the peasant woman who initiates Jermola into the mysteries of baby management, and the disclosure of the real parents after a lapse of years, wanting to have their child back, suggest parallel passages in the English book. But coincidences of this kind are, after all, natural enough, considering that the circle of human feeling and action is limited, and that in all ages and countries like conditions must give rise to much the same sequence of events. It is therefore most likely that George Eliot never saw, and possibly never even heard of, 'Jermola the Potter.'

The monotonous tone in the narrative of this Polish novel is in strong contrast, it may be observed, to George Eliot's vivid and varied treatment of her subject. This monotony, however, suits the local coloring of 'Jermola,' by suggesting the idea of the league-long expanse of ancient forests whose sombre solitudes encompass with a mysterious awe the little temporary dwellings of men. But if the foreign story surpasses 'Silas Marner' in tragic pathos, the latter far excels it in the masterly handling of character and dialogue, in the underlying breadth of thought, and, above all, in the precious salt of its humor.

Indeed, for humor, for sheer force, for intense realism, George Eliot, in the immortal scene at the "Rainbow," may be said to rival Shakespeare. Her farriers, her butchers, her wheelwrights, her tailors, have the same startling vitality, the same unmistakable accents of nature, the same distinctive yet unforced individuality, free from either exaggeration or caricature. How delicious is the description of the party assembled in the kitchen of that inn, whose landlord — a strong advocate for compromising whatever differences of opinion may arise between his customers, as beings "all alike in need of liquor" — clinches all arguments by his favorite phrase — "You're both right and you're both wrong, as I say." How admirably comic are these villagers, invariably beginning their nightly sittings by a solemn silence, in which one and all puff away at their pipes, staring at the fire "as if a bet were depending on the first man who winked." And when they begin at last, how rich is the flavor of that talk, given with an unerring precision that forthwith makes one acquainted with the crass ignorance and shrewdness, the mother-wit and superstition, so oddly jumbled together in the villager's mind. What sublime absence of all knowledge of his native land is shown by the veteran parish clerk, Mr. Macey, in speaking of a person from another county which apparently could not be so very different "from this country, for he brought a fine breed o' sheep with him, so there must be pastures there, and everything reasonable." Yet the same man can put down youthful presumption pretty sharply, as when he remarks: "There's allays two 'pinions; there's the 'pinion a man has o' himsen, and there's the 'pinion other folks have on him. There'd be two 'pinions about a cracked bell, if the bell could hear itself."

Dolly Winthrop, the wife of the jolly wheelwright who makes one of the company at the "Rainbow," is no less admirable. She is not cut after any particular pattern or type of human nature, but has a distinctive individuality, and is full of a freshness and unexpectedness which sets foregone conclusions at defiance. A notable woman, with a boundless appetite for work, so that, rising at half-past four, she has "a bit o' time to spare most days, for when one gets up betimes i' the morning the clock seems to stan' still tow'rt ten, afore it's time to go about the victual." Yet with all this energy she is not shrewish, but a calm, grave woman, in much request in sick-rooms or wherever there is trouble. She is good-looking, too, and of a comfortable temper, being patiently tolerant of her husband's jokes, "considering that 'men would be so,' and viewing the stronger sex 'in the light of animals whom it pleased Heaven to make troublesome like bulls or turkey-cocks.'"

Her vague idea, shared indeed by Silas, that he has quite another faith from herself, as coming from another part of the country, gives a vivid idea of remote rural life, as well as her own dim, semi-pagan but thoroughly reverential religious feelings, prompting her always to speak of the Divinity in the plural, as when she says to Marner: "I've looked for help in the right quarter, and give myself up to Them as we must all give ourselves up to at the last; and if we 'n done our part, it is n't to be believed as Them as are above us 'ull be worse nor we are, and come short o' Theirn."

The humor shown in these scenes and characters, or, more properly speaking, George Eliot's humor in general, belongs to the highest order, the same as Shakespeare's. It is based on the essential elements of human nature itself, on the pathetic incongruities of which that "quintessence of dust," man, is made up, instead of finding the comic in the purely accidental or external circumstances of life, as is the case with such humorists as Rabelais and Dickens. These latter might find a good subject for their comic vein in seeing the Venus of Milo's broken nose, which a mischievous urchin had again stuck on the wrong side upwards — a sight to send the ordinary spectator into fits of laughter. But the genuine humorist sees something in that feature itself, as nature shaped it, to excite his facetiousness. In 'A Minor Prophet' some lines occur in which a somewhat similar view of the genuine source of humor is pithily put:

> "My yearnings fail
> To reach that high apocalyptic mount
> Which shows in bird's-eye view a perfect world,
> Or enter warmly into other joys
> Than those of faulty, struggling human kind
> That strain upon my soul's too feeble wing
> Ends in ignoble floundering I fall
> Into short-sighted pity for the men
> Who, living in those perfect future times,
> Will not know half the dear imperfect things
> That move my smiles and tears — will never know
> The fine old incongruities that raise
> My friendly laugh; the innocent conceits
> That like a needless eyeglass or black patch
> Give those who wear them harmless happiness;
> The twists and cracks in our poor earthenware,
> That touch me to more conscious fellowship
> (I am not myself the finest Parian)
> With my coevals"

Again, in her essay on 'Heinrich Heine,' George Eliot thus defines the difference between humor and wit: "Humor is of earlier growth than wit, and it is in accordance with this earlier growth that it has more affinity with the poetic tendencies, while wit is more nearly allied to the ratiocinative intellect. Humor draws its materials from situations and characteristics; wit seizes on unexpected and complex relations. . . . It is only the ingenuity, condensation, and instantaneousness which lift some witticisms from reasoning into wit; they are reasoning raised to its highest power. On the other hand, humor, in its higher forms and in proportion as it associates itself with the sympathetic emotions, continually passes into poetry: nearly all great modern humorists may be called prose poets."

The quality which distinguishes George Eliot's humor may be said to characterize her treatment of human nature generally. In her delineations of life she carefully eschews the anomalous or exceptional, pointing out repeatedly that she would not, if she could, be the writer, however brilliant, who dwells by preference on the moral or intellectual attributes which mark off his hero from the crowd instead of on those which he has in common with average humanity. Nowhere perhaps in her works do we find this tendency so strikingly illustrated as in the one now under consideration; for here we have the study of a human being who, by stress of circumstances, develops into a most abnormal specimen of mankind, yet who is brought back to normal conditions and to wholesome relations with his fellow-men by such a natural process as the re-awakening of benumbed sympathies through his love for the little foundling child. The scene where he finds that child has only been touched on in a passing allusion, yet there is no more powerfully drawn situation in any of her novels than that where Silas, with the child in his arms, goes out into the dark night, and, guided by the little footprints in the virgin snow, discovers the dead mother, Godfrey Cass's opium-eating wife, lying with "her head sunk low in the furze and half covered with the shaken snow." There is a picture of this subject by the young and singularly gifted artist, the late Oliver Madox Brown, more generally known as a novelist, which is one of the few pictorial interpretations that seem to completely project on the canvas a visible embodiment of the spirit of the original. The pale, emaciated weaver, staring with big, short-sighted eyes at the body of the unconscious young woman stretched on the ground, clutching the lusty, struggling child with one arm, while with the other he holds a lantern which throws a feeble gleam on the snow — is realized with exceptional intensity.

The exquisite picture of Eppie's childhood, the dance she leads her soft-hearted foster-father, are things to read, not to describe, unless one could quote whole pages of this delightful idyl, which for gracious charm and limpid purity of description recalls those pearls among prose-poems, George Sand's 'François le Champi' and 'La Mare au Diable.'

CHAPTER XI.

ROMOLA.

'ROMOLA' marks a new departure in George Eliot's literary career. From the present she turned to the past, from the native to the foreign, from the domestic to the historical. Yet in thus shifting her subject-matter, she did not alter the strongly pronounced tendencies underlying her earlier novels; there was more of spontaneous, humorous description of life in the latter, whereas in 'Romola' the ethical teaching which forms so prominent a feature of George Eliot's art, though the same in essence, was more distinctly wrought out. Touching on this very point, she observes in a letter to an American correspondent: "It is perhaps less irrelevant to say, apropos of a distinction you seem to make between my earlier and later works, that though I trust there is some growth in my appreciation of others and in my self-distrust, there has been no change in the point of view from which I regard our life since I wrote my first fiction, the 'Scenes of Clerical Life.' Any apparent change of spirit must be due to something of which I am unconscious. The principles which are at the root of my effort to paint Dinah Morris are equally at the root of my effort to paint Mordecai."

The first section of 'Romola' appeared in the *Cornhill Magazine* for the summer of 1862, and, running its course in that popular periodical, was finished in the summer of the following year. Mr. Lewes, in a letter written from 16 Blandford Square, July 5, 1862, to some old friends of George Eliot, makes the following remarks in reference to this new form of publication: "My main object in persuading her to consent to serial publication was not the unheard-of magnificence of the offer, but the advantage to such a work of being read slowly and deliberately, instead of being galloped through in three volumes. I think it quite unique, and so will the public when it gets over the first feeling of surprise and disappointment at the book not being English, and like its predecessor." And some time afterwards he wrote to the same friends: "Marian lives entirely in the fifteenth century, and is much cheered every now and then by hearing indirectly how her book is appreciated by the higher class of minds, and some of the highest; though it is not, and cannot be popular. In Florence we hear they are wild with delight and surprise at such a work being executed by a foreigner; as if an Italian had ever done anything of the kind!"

Before writing 'Romola' George Eliot had spent six weeks in Florence in order to familiarize herself with the manners and conversation of its inhabitants, and yet she hardly caught the trick of Italian speech, and for some time afterwards she hung back from beginning her story, as her characters not only refused to speak Italian to her, but would not speak at all, as we can well imagine Mrs. Poyser, Bartle Massey, and Maggie to have done. These recalcitrant spirits were at last brought to order, and she succeeded so well, especially in her delineation of the lower classes, that they have been recognized by Italians as true to the life.

It should, however, be mentioned that the greatest modern Italian, Giuseppe Mazzini, found fault with the handling, and, indeed, with the introduction into this novel of the great figure of Savonarola. He considered that it compared unfavorably with 'Adam Bede,' a novel he genuinely admired, all but the marriage of Adam with Dinah Morris, which, he said, shocked his feelings, not having any conception that the taste of the novel-reading public demands a happy ending, whatever may have been the previous course of the three volumes. Another illustrious man, D. G. Rossetti, whose judgment on such a subject carries peculiar weight, considered George Eliot to have been much less successful in 'Romola' than in her novels of English country life. He did not think that the tone and color of Italian life in the fifteenth century were caught with that intuitive perception of a bygone age characteristic of a Walter Scott or a Meinhold. The Florentine contemporaries of "Fra Girolamo" seemed to him Nineteenth Century men and women dressed up in the costume of the Fifteenth. The book, to use his expression, was not "native."

It is a majestic book, however: the most grandly planned of

George Eliot's novels. It has a certain architectural dignity of structure, quite in keeping with its Italian nationality, a quality, by the way, entirely absent from the three later novels. The impressive historical background is not unlike one of Mr. Irving's magnificently wrought Italian stage-effects, rich in movement and color, yet helping to throw the chief figures into greater relief. The erudition shown in this work; the vast yet minute acquaintance with the habits of thought, the manners, the very talk of the Florentines of that day are truly surprising; but perhaps the very fact of that erudition being so perceptible shows that the material has not been absolutely vitalized. The amount of labor George Eliot expended on 'Romola' was so great that it was the book which, she remarked to a friend, "she began a young woman and ended an old one." The deep impression her works had made upon the public mind heightened her natural conscientiousness, and her gratitude for the confidence with which each fresh contribution from her pen was received, increased her anxiety to wield her influence for the highest ends.

But her gratitude to the public by no means extended to the critics. She recoiled from them with the instinctive shrinking of the sensitive plant. These interpreters between author and public were in her eyes a most superfluous modern institution: though at one time she herself had not scorned to sit in the critic's seat. It is well known that G. H. Lewes acted as a kind of moral screen protecting her from every gust or breath of criticism that was not entirely genial. One lady, after reading 'The Mill on the Floss,' had written off in the heat of the moment, and, with the freedom of old friendship, while expressing the warmest admiration for the beauty of the first two volumes, she had ventured to find fault with part of the third. This letter was returned by Lewes, who begged her at the same time never to write again in this strain to George Eliot, to whom he had not ventured to show it for fear it should too painfully affect her. In a letter to the American lady already mentioned, George Eliot, after referring to this habit of Mr. Lewes, says: "In this way I get confirmed in my impression that the criticism of any new writing is shifting and untrustworthy. I hardly think that any critic can have so keen a sense of the shortcomings in my works as that I groan under in the course of writing them, and I cannot imagine any edification coming to an author from a sort of reviewing which consists in attributing to him or her unexpressed opinions, and in imagining circumstances which may be alleged as petty private motives for the treatment of subjects which ought to be of general human interest. . . . I have been led into this rather superfluous sort of remark by the mention of a rule which seemed to require explanation."

And again on another occasion to the same effect: "But do not expect criticism from me. I hate 'sitting in the seat of judgment,' and I would rather impress the public generally with the sense that they may get the best result from a book without necessarily forming an 'opinion' about it, than I would rush into stating opinions of my own. The floods of nonsense printed in the form of critical opinions seem to me a chief curse of our times — a chief obstacle to true culture."

In spite of these severe strictures on the critics and their opinions, an "opinion" must now be given about 'Romola.' This novel may really be judged from two entirely different points of view, possibly from others besides, but, as it appears to me, from two. One may consider it as an historical work, with its moving pageants, its civic broils, its church festivals, its religious revival, its fickle populace, now siding with the Pope, and now with the would-be reformer of the Papacy. Or again one may regard the conjugal relations between Romola and Tito, the slow spiritual growth of the one, and the swifter moral disintegration of the other, as one of the subtlest studies in psychology in literature.

To turn to the scenic details which form a considerable element of this historical picture, I have already hinted that they are not without a taint of cumbrousness and pedantry. The author seems to move somewhat heavily under her weight of learning, and we miss that splendid natural swiftness and ease of movement which Shakespeare, Goethe, and Hugo know how to impart to their crowds and spectacular effects. If, instead of the people, one examines the man who dominated the people, the large, massive, imposing figure of Savonarola, one must admit that the character is very powerfully and faithfully executed but not produced at one throw. He does not take the imagination by storm as he would have done had Carlyle been at his fashioning. With an epithet or two, with a sharp, incisive phrase, the latter would have conjured the great Dominican from his grave, and we should have seen him, or believed at least that we saw him, as he was in the flesh when his impassioned voice resounded through the Duomo, swaying the hearts of the Florentine people with the force of a great conviction. That he stands out thus tangibly in 'Romola' it would be futile to assert: nevertheless, he is a noble, powerful study, although one has laboriously to gather into one's mind the somewhat mechanical descriptions which help to portray his individuality. The idea underlying the working out of this grand character is the same which Goethe had once proposed to himself in his projected, but unfortunately never executed, drama of 'Mahomet.' It is that of a man of moral genius, who, in solitude and obscurity, has conceived some new, profounder aspect of religious truth, and who, stirred by a sublime devotion, now goes forth among men to bless and regenerate them by teaching them this higher life. But in his contact with the multitude, in his efforts at influencing it, the prophet or preacher is in his turn influenced. If he fails to move by the loftiest means, he will gradually resort to the lower in order to effect his purpose. The purity of his spirit is tarnished, ambition has crept in where holiness reigned, and his perfect rectitude of purpose will be sacrificed so that he may but rule.

Such are the opposing tendencies co-existing in Savonarola's mixed but lofty nature. For "that dissidence between inward reality and outward seeming was not the Christian simplicity after which he had striven through years of his youth and prime, and which he had preached as a chief fruit of the Divine life. In the heat and stress of the day, with cheeks burning, with shouts ringing in the ears, who is so blest as to remember the yearnings he had in the cool and silent morning, and know that he has not belied them?" And again: "It was the habit of Savonarola's mind to conceive great things, and to feel that he was the man to do them. Iniquity should be brought low; the cause of justice, purity, and love should triumph, and it should triumph by his voice, by his work, by his blood. In moments of ecstatic contemplation, doubtless, the sense of self melted in the sense of the Unspeakable, and in that part of his experience lay the elements of genuine self-abasement; but in the presence of his fellow-men for whom he was to act, pre-eminence seemed a necessary condition of life." But, as George Eliot says, " Power rose against him, not because of his sins, but because of his greatness; not because he sought to deceive the world, but because he sought to make it noble. And through that greatness of his he endured a double agony; not only the reviling, and the torture, and the death-throe, but the agony of sinking from the vision of glorious achievement into that deep shadow where he could only say, 'I count as nothing: darkness encompasses me; yet the light I saw was the true light.'"

But after all, in George Eliot's story the chief interest attaching to "Fra Girolamo" consists in his influence on Romola's spiritual growth. This may possibly be a blemish; yet in most novels the fictitious characters eclipse the historical ones. The effect produced by the high-souled Romola is not unlike that of an antique statue, at once splendidly beautiful and imposingly cold. By the side of Tito she reminds one of the pure whiteness of marble sculpture as contrasted with the rich glowing sensuousness of a Venetian picture.

It is difficult to analyze why the proud, loving, single-hearted Romola, who has something of the fierceness and impetuosity of the old "Bardo blood" in her, should leave this impression of coldness; for in spite of her acts of magnanimity and self-devotion, such, curiously enough, is the case. Perhaps in this instance George Eliot modelled the character too much according to a philosophical conception instead of projecting it, complete in its incompleteness, as it might have come from the hand of Nature. Another objection sometimes brought forward, of Romola having but little resemblance to an Italian woman of the fifteenth century, seems to me less relevant. The lofty dignity, the pride, the intense adhesion to family traditions, were, on the contrary, very marked attributes of a high national type during the period of Italian supremacy. In fact, the character is not without hints and suggestions of such a woman as Vittoria Colonna, while its didactic tendency slightly recalls "those awful women of Italy who held professorial chairs, and were great in civil and canon law." In one sense Romola is a true child of the Renaissance. Brought up by her father, the enthusiastic old scholar, in pagan ideas, she had remained aloof from Roman Catholic beliefs and superstitions, and even when transformed by the mighty influence of Savonarola into a devoted *Piagnone*, her attitude always remains more or less that of a Protestant, unwilling to surrender the right of private judgment to the Church.

The clash of character when a woman like Romola finds herself chained in a life-long bond to such a nature as Tito's — the beautiful, wily, insinuating Greek — is wrought out with wonderful skill and matchless subtlety of analysis. Indeed, Tito is not only one of George Eliot's most original creations, he is a unique character in fiction. Novelists, as a rule, only depict the full-blown villain or traitor, their virtuous and wicked people being separated from each other by a hard and fast line much like the goats and sheep. They continually treat character as something permanent and unchangeable, whereas to George Eliot it presents itself as an organism flexible by nature, subject to change under varying conditions, liable on the one hand to disease and deterioration, but on the other hand no less capable of being rehabilitated, refined, or ennobled. This is one of the most distinctive notes of George Eliot's art, and gives a quickening, fructifying quality to her moral teaching. But it is an artistic no less than a moral gain, sharpening the interest felt in the evolution of her fictitious personages. For this reason Tito, the creature of circumstances, is perhaps the most striking of all her characters in the eyes of the psychologist. We seem to see the very pulse of the human machine laid bare, to see the corroding effect of self-indulgence and dread of pain on a nature not intrinsically wicked, to see at last how, little by little, weakness has led to falsehood, and falsehood to infamy. And yet this creature, who, under our eyes, gradually hardens into crime, is one so richly dowered with rare gifts of person and mind, that in spite of his moral degeneracy, he fascinates the reader no less than the men and women supposed to come into actual contact with him. His beauty is described with the same life-like intensity as Hetty's: the warm glow of color in his perfectly moulded face, with its dark curls and long agate-like eyes; his sunny brightness of look, the velvet softness of a manner with which he ingratiates himself with young and old, and the airy buoyancy of his whole gracious being, are as vividly portrayed as the quick talent to which everything comes natural, the abundant good-humor, the acuteness of a polished intellect, whose sharp edge will, at need, cut relentlessly through every tissue of sentiment.

From Melema's first uneasy debate with himself, when, in his splendid, unsoiled youth, he enters Florence a shipwrecked stranger — a debate, that is, as to whether he is bound to go in search of Baldassare, who has been as a father to him — to the moment when his already blunted conscience absolves him from such a search, and again, on to that supreme crisis when, suddenly face to face with his benefactor, he denies him, and so is inevitably urged from one act of baseness and cruelty to another still blacker — we have unfolded before us, by an unshrinking analyzer of human nature, what might not inappropriately be called "A Soul's Tragedy." The wonderful art in the working out of this character is shown in the fact that one has no positive impression of Tito's innate badness, but, on the contrary, feels as if, after his first lapses from truth and goodness, there is still a possibility of his reforming, if only his soft, pleasure-loving nature were not driven on, almost in spite of himself, by his shuddering dread of shame or suffering in any form. "For," writes George Eliot, "Tito was experiencing that inexorable law of human souls, that we prepare ourselves for sudden deeds by the reiterated choice of good or evil which gradually determines character."

The description of the married life of Romola and Tito is unsurpassed in George Eliot's novels for subtlety and depth of insight: notably the young wife's fond striving after complete inner harmony, her first, faint, unavowed sense of something wanting, her instinctive efforts to keep fast hold of her love and trust, and her violent, irrevocable recoil on the discovery of Tito's first faithless action. Perhaps there is something cold, almost stern, in Romola's loathing alienation from her husband, and the instantaneous death of her passionate love. One cannot quite hinder the impression that a softer woman might have forgiven and won from him a confession of his wrong-doing; a confession which would have averted the committal of his worst and basest deeds. Indeed, it is Tito's awe of his grand, noble wife, and his dread of her judgment, which first of all incite him to prevarication and lies.

It is curious to compare George Sand's theory of love, in this instance, with George Eliot's. In 'Leon Leoni,' and in many of her novels besides, the Frenchwoman seems to imply that for a woman to love once is to love always, and that there is nothing so base, or mean, or cruel, but she will forgive the man on whom she has placed her affections. In the story mentioned above she has worked out this idea to an extent which, in many of its details, is simply revolting. Love is there described as a magnetic attraction, unresisted and irresistible, to which the heroine absolutely surrenders pride, reason, and conscience. Just the opposite kind of love is that which we find portrayed in 'Romola': it is a love identical with the fullest belief in the truth and goodness of the beloved object, so that at the first realization of moral obliquity the repulsion created extinguishes that love, although there is no outward severance of the marriage bond.

This great novel closes with these significant words, which Romola addresses to Lillo, Tito's child, but not her own:

"And so, my Lillo, if you mean to act nobly, and seek to know the best things God has put within reach of man, you must learn to fix your mind on that end, and not on what will happen to you because of it. And remember, if you were to choose something lower, and make it the rule of your life to seek your own pleasure and escape from what is disagreeable, calamity might come just the same; and it would be calamity falling on a base mind, which is the one form of sorrow that has no balm in it, and that may well make a man say, 'It would have been better for me if I had never been born!'"

CHAPTER XII.

HER POEMS.

FEW are the external events to be now recorded of George Eliot's life. The publication of her successive works forms the chief landmarks. But the year 1865 is distinguished by circumstances of some importance. In this year Mr. Lewes, after assisting to found the *Fortnightly Review*, assumed its editorship; and among the contributions to the first number of the new Review was a short article from the pen of George Eliot on Mr. Lecky's important work 'The Influence of Rationalism.'

In the course of the same year Mr. and Mrs. Lewes moved from 16 Blanford Square to the Priory, a commodious house in North Bank, St. John's Wood, which has come to be intimately associated with the memory of George Eliot. Here, in the pleasant dwelling-rooms decorated by Owen Jones, might be met, at her Sunday afternoon receptions, some of the most eminent men in literature, art, and science. For the rest, her life flowed on its even tenor, its routine being rigidly regulated. The morning till lunch time was invariably devoted to writing: in the afternoon she either went out for a quiet drive of about two hours, or she took a walk with Lewes in Regent's Park. There the strange-looking couple — she with a certain weird, sibylline air, he not unlike some unkempt Polish refugee of vivacious manners — might be seen, swinging their arms, as they hurried along at a pace as rapid and eager as their talk. Besides these walks, George Eliot's chief recreation consisted in frequenting concerts and picture galleries. To music she was passionately devoted, hardly ever failing to attend at the Saturday afternoon concerts at St. James's Hall, besides frequenting various musical réunions, such as the following extract from one of her letters will show: "The other night we went to hear the Bach choir — a society of ladies and gentlemen got together by Jenny Lind, who sings in the middle of them, her husband acting as conductor. It is pretty to see people who might be nothing but simply fashionables taking pains to sing fine music in tune and time, with more or less success. One of the baritones we know is a G——, who used to be a swell guardsman, and has happily taken to good courses while still quite young. Another is a handsome young G——, not of the unsatisfactory Co., but of the R—— G—— kin. A soprano is Mrs. P——, wife of the Queen's Secretary, General P——, the granddaughter of Earl Grey, and just like him in the face — and so on. These people of 'high' birth are certainly reforming themselves a little."

She likewise never omitted to visit the "Exhibition of Old Masters" at Burlington House. To most people few things exercise so great a strain on their mental and physical powers of endurance as the inspection of a picture gallery, with its incessant appeal to the most concentrated attention Yet, in spite of physical weakness, George Eliot possessed such inexhaustible mental energy that she could go on, hour after hour, looking with the same unflagging interest at whatever possessed any claim to attention, tiring out even vigorous men that were in her company. In her works the allusions to art are much less frequent than to music; but from a few hints here and there, it is possible to form some idea of her taste, one very significant passage in 'Adam Bede' showing her peculiar love of Dutch paintings, and her readiness to turn without shrinking "from cloud-borne angels, from prophets, sibyls, and heroic warriors, to an old woman bending over her flower-pot, or eating her solitary dinner, while the noonday light, softened perhaps by a screen of leaves, falls on her mob-cap, and just touches the rim of her spinning-wheel and her stone jug, and all those cheap common things which are the precious necessaries of life to her."

Another favorite resort of George Eliot's was the Zoological Gardens. She went there a great deal to study the animals, and was particularly fond of the "poor dear ratel" that used to turn somersaults. In fact, her knowledge of, and sympathy with, animals was as remarkable as that which she showed for human nature. Thus she astonished a gentleman farmer by drawing attention to the fine points of his horses. Her intimate acquaintance with the dog comes out in a thousand touches in her novels, and her humorous appreciation of little pigs led her to watch them attentively, and to pick out some particular favorite in every litter. In her country rambles, too, she was fond of turning over stones to inspect the minute insect life teeming in moist, dark places; and she was as interested as Lewes himself in the creatures, frogs, etc., he kept for scientific purposes, and which would sometimes, like the frog in the fairy tale, surprise the household by suddenly making their entrance into the dining-room. Her liking for the "poor brutes," as she calls them, had its origin no doubt in the same source of profound pity which she feels for "the twists and cracks" of imperfect human beings.

Her evenings were usually passed at home, and spent in reading, or in playing and singing; but she and Lewes used to go to the theatre on any occasion of special interest, as when Salvini appeared in 'Othello,' a performance attended repeatedly by both with enthusiastic delight. Otherwise they rarely left home, seldom visiting at other people's houses, although they made an exception in the case of a favored few.

They were both fond of travelling, and, whenever it was possible, would take trips to the Continent, or seek some quiet English rural retreat away from the sleepless tumult of London. "For," says Lewes incidentally in a letter, "Mrs. Lewes never seems at home except under a broad sweep of sky and the *greenth* of the uplands round her." So we find them frequently contriving a change of scene; and the visits to foreign countries, the pleasant sauntering on long summer days through Continental towns, "dozing round old cathedrals," formed delightful episodes in George Eliot's strenuously active life. The residence in Germany in 1854, and again in 1858, has already been alluded to. Now, in the year 1865, they paid a short visit to France, in the course of which they saw Normandy, Brittany, and Touraine, returning much refreshed at the beginning of the autumn. Two years afterwards they went to Spain, a country that must have possessed a peculiar interest for both; for in 1846 Lewes had published a charming, if one-sided, little book on 'The Spanish Drama,' with especial reference to Lope de Vega and Calderon; and in 1864, only a year after the appearance of 'Romola,' George Eliot produced the first draught of 'The Spanish Gypsy.' On becoming personally acquainted with this land of "old romance," however, her impressions were so far modified and deepened that she re-wrote and amplified her poem, which was not published till 1868.

The subject of the gypsies was probably suggested to George Eliot by her own memorable adventure in childhood, which thus became the germ of a very impressive poem. Be that as it may, it is worth noticing that the conception of 'The Spanish Gypsy' should have followed so closely on the completion of the Italian novel, both being foreign subjects, belonging to much the same period of history. In both the novelist has departed from her habitual track, seeking for "pastures new" in a foreign soil. After inculcating on the artist the desirability of giving "the loving pains of a life to the faithful representation of commonplace things," she remarks in 'Adam Bede' that "there are few prophets in the world, few sublimely beautiful women, few heroes," and that we cannot afford to give all our love and reverence to such rarities. But having followed this rule, and given the most marvellously truthful delineations of her fellow-men as they are ordinarily to be met with, she now also felt prompted to draw the exceptional types of human character, the rare prophets, and the sublime heroes.

To her friend Miss Simcox, George Eliot one day mentioned a plan of giving "the world an ideal portrait of an actual character in history, whom she did not name, but to whom she alluded as an object of possible reverence unmingled with disappointment." This idea was never carried out, but at any rate Dinah Morris, Savonarola, Zarca, and Mordecai are all exceptional beings — beings engrossed by an impersonal aim, having the spiritual or national regeneration of their fellow-men for its object. Dinah and Savonarola are more of the nature of prophets; Zarca and Mordecai of that of patriots. Among these the fair Methodist preacher, whose yearning piety is only a more sublimated love of her kind, is the most vividly realized; while Mordecai, the patriot of an ideal country, is but the abstraction of a man, entirely wanting in that indefinable solidity of presentation which gives a life of its own to the creations of art.

On the whole, Zarca, the gypsy chief, is perhaps the most vividly drawn of George Eliot's purely ideal characters — characters which never have the flesh-and-blood reality of her Mrs. Poysers, her Silas Marners, and her dear little Totties and Eppies. Yet there is an unmistakable grandeur and power of invention in the heroic figure of Zarca, although, in spite of this power, we miss the convincing stamp of reality in him, and not only in him, but more or less in all the characters of 'The Spanish Gypsy.' George Eliot's feeling for the extraordinary and romantic was very subordinate to that which she entertained for the more familiar aspects of our life. For, although she here chose one of the most romantic of periods and localities, the Spain of Ferdinand and Isabella, with the mingled horror and magnificence of its national traditions, she does not really succeed in resuscitating the spirit which animated those devout, cruel, fanatical, but ultra-picturesque times. The Castilian noble, the Jewish astrologer, Zarca, and the Spanish Inquisitor, even the bright, gloriously conceived Fedalma herself, think and speak too much like sublimated modern positivists. For example, would, could, or should any gypsy of the fifteenth century have expressed himself in the following terms :

> "Oh, it is a faith
> Taught by no priest, but by this beating heart:
> Faith to each other : the fidelity
> Of fellow-wanderers in a desert place,
> Who share the same dire thirst, and therefore share
> The scanty water: the fidelity
> Of men whose pulses leap with kindred fire,
> Who in the flash of eyes, the clasp of hands,
> The speech that even in lying tells the truth
> Of heritage inevitable as birth,
> Nay, in the silent bodily presence feel
> The mystic stirring of a common life
> Which makes the many one: fidelity
> To the consecrating oath our sponsor Fate
> Made through our infant breath when we were born
> The fellow-heirs of that small island, Life,
> Where we must dig and sow and reap with brothers.

> Fear thou that oath, my daughter—nay, not fear,
> But love it; for the sanctity of oaths
> Lies not in lightning that avenges them,
> But in the injury wrought by broken bonds
> And in the garnered good of human trust."

The poetic mode of treatment corresponds to the exalted theme of 'The Spanish Gypsy,' a subject certainly fitted for drama or romance rather than for the novel, properly so called. Nothing could apparently be better adapted for the purposes of a noble historical poem than the conception of a great man such as Zarca, whose aim is nothing less than the fusion of the scattered, wandering, lawless gypsy tribes into one nation, with common traditions and a common country · the romantic incident of the discovery of his lost daughter in the affianced bride of Silva, Duke of Bedmar: the supreme conflict in Fedalma's breast between love and duty, her renunciation of happiness in order to cast in her lot with that of her outcast people: Silva's frantic grief, his desertion of his country, his religion, and all his solemn responsibilities to turn gypsy for Fedalma's sake, and having done so, his agony of remorse on seeing the fortress committed to his trust taken by the gypsies he has joined, his dearest friends massacred, his nearest of kin, Isidor, the inquisitor, hanged before his very eyes, a sight so maddening that, hardly conscious of his act, he slays Zarca, and so divides himself forever, by an impassable gulf, from the woman for whose sake he had turned apostate.

Clearly a subject containing the highest capabilities, and, if great thoughts constituted a great poem, this should be one of the greatest. But with all its high merits, its sentiments imbued with rare moral grandeur, its felicitous descriptions, the work lacks that best and incommunicable gift which comes by nature to the poet. Here, as in her novels, we find George Eliot's instinctive insight into the primary passions of the human heart, her wide sympathy and piercing keenness of vision; but her thoughts, instead of being naturally winged with melody, seem mechanically welded into song. This applies to all her poetic work, although some of it, especially 'The Legend of Jubal,' reaches a much higher degree of metrical and rhythmical excellence. But although George

Eliot's poems cannot be considered on a par with her prose, they possess a distinctive interest, and should be carefully studied by all lovers of her genius, as affording a more intimate insight into the working of her own mind. Nowhere do we perceive so clearly as here the profound sadness of her view of life; nowhere does she so emphatically reiterate the stern lesson of the duty of resignation and self-sacrifice; or that other doctrine that the individual is bound absolutely to subordinate his personal happiness to the social good, that he has no rights save the right of fulfilling his obligations to his age, his country, and his family. This idea is perhaps more completely incorporated in Fedalma than in any other of her characters — Fedalma, who seems so bountifully endowed with the fullest measure of beauty, love, and happiness, that her renunciation may be the more absolute. She who in her young joy suddenly knows herself as "an aged sorrow," exclaiming:

> "I will not take a heaven
> Haunted by shrieks of far-off misery.
> This deed and I have ripened with the hours:
> It is a part of me — a wakened thought
> That, rising like a giant, masters me,
> And grows into a doom. O mother life,
> That seemed to nourish me so tenderly,
> Even in the womb you vowed me to the fire,
> Hung on my soul the burden of men's hopes,
> And pledged me to redeem! — I'll pay the debt.
> You gave me strength that I should pour it all
> Into this anguish. I can never shrink
> Back into bliss — my heart has grown too big
> With things that might be."

This sacrifice is the completer for being without hope; for not counting "on aught but being faithful;" for resting satisfied in such a sublime conviction as —

> "The grandest death, to die in vain — for love
> Greater than sways the forces of the world."

Limit forbids me dwell longer on this poem, which contains infinite matter for discussion, yet some of the single passages are so full of fine thoughts felicitously expressed that it would be unfair not to allude to them. Such a specimen as this exposition of the eternal dualism between the Hellenic and the Christian ideals, of which Heine was the original and incomparable expounder, should not be left unnoted:

> "Forevermore
> With grander resurrection than was feigned
> Of Attila's fierce Huns, the soul of Greece
> Conquers the bulk of Persia. The maimed form
> Of calmly joyous beauty, marble-limbed,
> Yet breathing with the thought that shaped its limbs,
> Looks mild reproach from out its opened grave
> At creeds of terror, and the vine-wreathed god
> Fronts the pierced Image with the crown of thorns"

And again how full of deep mysterious suggestion is this line —

> "Speech is but broken light upon the depth
> Of the unspoken."

And this grand saying —

> "What times are little? To the sentinel
> That hour is regal when he mounts on guard"

Quotations of this kind might be indefinitely multiplied; while showing that exaltation of thought properly belonging to poetry, they at the same time indubitably prove to the delicately attuned ear the absence of that subtle intuitive music, that "linked sweetness" of sound and sense which is the birthright of poets. If an intimate and profound acquaintance with the laws and structure of metre could bestow this quality, which appertain to the elemental, George Eliot's verse ought to have achieved the highest success. For in mere technical knowledge concerning rhyme, assonance, alliteration, and the manipulation of blank verse according to the most cunning distribution of pauses, she could hold her own with the foremost contemporary poets, being no doubt far more versed than either Shelley or Byron in the laws governing these matters.

How incalculable she felt the poet's influence to be, and how fain she would have had him wield this influence only for the loftiest ends, is well shown in a beautiful letter, hitherto unpublished, now possessing an added pathos as addressed to one who has but lately departed, at the very time when his rare poetic gifts were beginning to be more widely recognized. James Thomson, the author of 'The City of Dreadful Night,' a poem which appeared first in the pages of the *National Reformer*, with the signature of "B. V.," was thus addressed by George Eliot:

"DEAR POET,—I cannot rest satisfied without telling you that my mind responds with admiration to the distinct vision and grand utterance in the poem which you have been so good as to send me.

"Also, I trust that an intellect informed by so much passionate energy as yours will soon give us more heroic strains, with a wider embrace of human fellowship, such as will be to the laborers of the world what the Odes of Tyrtæus were to the Spartans, thrilling them with the sublimity of the social order and the courage of resistance to all that would dissolve it. To accept life and write much fine poetry, is to take a very large share in the quantum of human good, and seems to draw with it necessarily some recognition, affectionate, and even joyful, of the manifold willing labors which have made such a lot possible."

These words are of peculiar interest, because, although the writer of them is almost as much of a pessimist as its recipient, they are so with a difference. The pessimism of 'The City of Dreadful Night,' in its blank hopelessness, paralyzes the inmost nerve of life by isolating the individual in cold obstruction. Whereas George Eliot, while recognizing to the utmost "the burthen of a world, where even the sunshine has a heart of care," insists the more on the fact that this common suffering binds man more indissolubly to man; that so far from justifying him in ending his life "when he will," the groaning and travailing generations exact that he should stand firm at his post, regardless of personal consideration or requital, so long only as he can help towards making the fate of his fellow-mortals less heavy for them to bear. In fact, the one is a theory of life, the other a disease of the soul.

The same stoic view, in a different form, finds expression in this answer to a dear friend's query: "I cannot quite agree that it is hard to see what has been the good of your life. It seems to me very clear that you have been a good of a kind that would have been sorely missed by those who have been nearest to you, and also by some who are more distant. And it is this kind of good which must reconcile us to life, and not any answer to the question, 'What would the universe have been without me?' The point one has to care for is, 'Are A, B, and C the better for me?' And there are several letters of the alphabet that could not have easily spared you in the past, and that can still less spare you in the present."

This lesson of resignation, which is enforced more and more stringently in her writings, is again dwelt upon with peculiar emphasis in the interesting dramatic sketch entitled 'Armgart.' The problem here is not unlike that in 'Silas Marner.' It is that of an individual, in exceptional circumstances, brought back to the average condition of humanity; but whereas Silas, having sunk below the common standard, is once more united to his fellow-men by love, the magnificently endowed Armgart, who seems something apart and above the crowd, is reduced to the level of the undistinguished million by the loss of her peerless voice. 'Armgart' is the single instance, excepting, perhaps, the Princess Halm-Eberstein, where George Eliot has attempted to depict the woman-artist, to whom life's highest object consists in fame —

> "The benignant strength of one, transformed
> To joy of many."

But in the intoxicating flush of success, the singer, who has refused the love of *one* for that "sense transcendent which can taste the joy of swaying multitudes," loses her glorious gift, and so sinks irretrievably to a "drudge among the crowd." In the first delirium of despair she longs to put an end to herself, "sooner than bear the yoke of thwarted life;" but is painfully startled from her defiant mood by the indignant query of Walpurga, her humble cousin —

> "Where is the rebel's right for you alone?
> Noble rebellion lifts a common load,
> But what is he who flings his own load off
> And leaves his fellows toiling? Rebel's right?

Say rather the deserter's. Oh, you smiled
From your clear height on all the million lots
Which yet you brand as abject"

It may seem singular that having once, in 'Armgart,' drawn a woman of the highest artistic aims and ambitions, George Eliot should imply that what is most valuable in her is not the exceptional gift, but rather that part of her nature which she shares with ordinary humanity. This is, however, one of her leading beliefs, and strongly contrasts her, as a teacher, with Carlyle. To the author of 'Hero Worship' the promiscuous mass — moiling and toiling as factory hands and artisans, as miners and laborers — only represents so much raw material, from which is produced that final result and last triumph of the combination of human forces — the great statesman, great warrior, great poet, and so forth. To George Eliot, on the contrary — and this is the democratic side of her nature — it is the multitude, so charily treated by destiny, which claims deepest sympathy and tenderest compassion; so that all greatness, in her eyes, is not a privilege, but a debt, which entails on its possessor a more strenuous effort, a completer devotion to the service of average humanity.

CHAPTER XIII.

FELIX HOLT AND MIDDLEMARCH.

In 'Felix Holt,' which was published in 1866, George Eliot returned once more to her own peculiar field, where she stands supreme and unrivalled — the novel of English provincial life. This work, which, however, is not equal to her earlier or later fictions, yet possesses a double interest for us. It is the only one of her writings from which its author's political views may be inferred, if we exclude a paper published in *Blackwood's Magazine* in January 1868, which, indeed, seems to be part of the novel, seeing that it is entitled "Address to Working Men, by Felix Holt." The paper contains, in a more direct and concise form, precisely the same general views as regards the principles of government which were previously enunciated through Felix the Radical. It was an appeal to the operative classes who had been only recently enfranchised by the Reform Bill. Its advice is mainly to the effect that genuine political and social improvements to be durable must be the result of inward change rather than of outward legislation. The writer insists on the futility of the belief that beneficial political changes can be effected by revolutionary measures. She points out the necessity of a just discrimination between what is curable in the body politic and what has to be endured. She dwells once again, with solemn insistence, on the "aged sorrow," the inheritance of evil transmitted from generation to generation, an evil too intimately entwined with the complex conditions of society to be violently uprooted, but only to be gradually eradicated by the persistent cultivation of knowledge, industry, judgment, sobriety, and patience.

"This is only one example," she says, "of the law by which human lives are linked together; another example of what we complain of when we point to our pauperism, to the brutal ignorance of multitudes among our fellow-countrymen, to the weight of taxation laid on us by blamable wars, to the wasteful channels made for the public money, to the expense and trouble of getting justice, and call these the effects of bad rule. This is the law that we all bear the yoke of; the law of no man's making, and which no man can undo. Everybody now sees an example of it in the case of Ireland. We who are living now are sufferers by the wrong-doing of those who lived before us; we are sufferers by each other's wrong-doing; and the children who come after us will be sufferers from the same causes."

To remedy this long-standing wrong-doing and suffering, so argues Felix Holt, is not in the power of any one measure, class, or period. It would be childish folly to expect any Reform Bill to possess the magical property whereby a sudden social transformation could be accomplished. On the contrary, abrupt transitions should be shunned as dangerous to order and law, which alone are certain to insure a steady collective progress; the only means to this end consisting in the general spread of education, to secure which, at least for his children, the working-man should spare no pains. Without knowledge, the writer continues, no political measures will be of any benefit, ignorance with or without vote always of necessity engendering vice and misery. But, guided by a fuller knowledge, the working classes would be able to discern what sort of men they should choose for their representatives, and instead of electing " platform swaggerers, who bring us nothing but the ocean to make our broth with," they would confide the chief power to the hands of the truly wise, those who know how to regulate life "according to the truest principles mankind is in possession of."

The "Felix Holt" of the story is described by George Eliot as shaping his actions much according to the ideas which are here theoretically expressed. His knowledge and aptitude would enable him to choose what is considered a higher calling. But he scorns the vulgar ambition called "getting on in the world;" his sense of fellowship prompting him to remain a simple artisan that he may exert an elevating influence on the class to which he belongs. Class differences, so argues this Radical-Conservative, being inherent in the constitution of society, it becomes something of a desertion to withdraw what abilities one may have from the medium where they are urgently needed, in order to join, for the sake of selfish aims, some other body of men where they may be superfluous.

The other distinctive feature of 'Felix Holt' consists in its elaborate construction, ranking it, so to speak, amongst sensational novels. As a rule, George Eliot's stories have little or no plot, the incidents seeming not so much invented by the writer for the sake of producing an effective work, as to be the natural result of the friction between character and circumstance. This simplicity of narrative belongs, no doubt, to the highest class of novel, the class to which 'The Vicar of Wakefield,' 'Waverley,' and 'Vanity Fair' belong. In 'Felix Holt,' however, the intricate network of incident in which the characters seem to be enmeshed is not unlike the modern French art of story-telling, with its fertility of invention, as is also the strangely repellent intrigue which forms the nucleus of the whole. All the elements which go to make up a thrilling narrative — such as a dubious inheritance, the disappearance of the rightful claimant, a wife's guilty secret, the involvements of the most desperate human fates in a perplexing coil through sin and error — are interwoven in this story of 'Felix Holt the Radical.'

Though ingeniously invented, the different incidents seem not so much naturally to have grown the one from the other as to be constructed with too conscious a seeking for effect. There is something forced, uneasy, and inadequate in the laborious contrivance of fitting one set of events on to another, and the machinery of the disputed Transome claim is so involved that the reader never masters the "ins" and "outs" of that baffling mystery. Still, the groundwork of the story is deeply impressive: its interest is, notwithstanding the complex ramification of events, concentrated with much power upon a small group of personages, such as Mrs. Transome, her son Harold, the little dissenting minister, Rufus Lyon, Esther, and Felix Holt. Here, as elsewhere, the novelist reveals the potent qualities of her genius. Not only does this story contain such genuine humorous portraiture as the lachrymose Mrs. Holt, and the delightfully quaint Job Tudge, but it is also enriched by some descriptions of rural scenery and of homely existence in remote country districts as admirable as any to be found in her writings. Rufus Lyon is a worthy addition to that long gallery of clerical portraits which are among the triumphs of George Eliot's art. This "singular-looking apostle of the meeting in Skipper's Lane" — with his rare purity of heart, his unworldliness, his zeal in the cause of dissent, his restless argumentative spirit, and the moving memories of romance and passion hidden beneath the odd, quaint *physique* of the little minister encased in rusty black — is among the most loving and lovable of characters, and recalls more particularly that passage in the poem entitled 'A Minor Prophet,' which I cannot but think one of the author's finest, the passage beginning —

> "The pathos exquisite of lovely minds
> Hid in harsh forms — not penetrating them
> Like fire divine within a common bush
> Which glows transfigured by the heavenly guest,

> So that men put their shoes off, but encaged
> Like a sweet child within some thick-walled cell,
> Who leaps and fails to hold the window-bars,
> But having shown a little dimpled hand,
> Is visited thenceforth by tender hearts
> Whose eyes keep watch about the prison walls."

Esther, on the other hand, is one of those fortunate beings whose lovely mind is lodged in a form of corresponding loveliness. This charming Esther, though not originally without her feminine vanities and worldly desires, is one of those characters dear to George Eliot's heart, who renounce the allurements of an easy pleasurable existence for the higher satisfactions of a noble love or a nobler ideal. It is curious to notice that Eppie, Esther, Fedalma, and Daniel Deronda are all children who have been reared in ignorance of their real parentage, and that to all of them there comes a day when a more or less difficult decision has to be made, when for good or evil they have to choose, once for all, between two conflicting claims. Like Eppie, Esther rejects the advantages of birth and fortune, and elects to share the hard but dignified life of the high-minded Felix. But this decision in her case shows even higher moral worth, because by nature she is so keenly susceptible to the delicate refinements and graceful elegancies which are the natural accompaniment of rank and wealth.

The most curious feature of this book consists, perhaps, in its original treatment of illicit passion. Novelists, as a rule, when handling this subject, depict its fascinations in brilliant contrast to the sufferings and terrors which follow in its train. But George Eliot contents herself with showing us the reverse side of the medal. Youth has faded, joy is dead, love has turned to loathing, yet memory, like a relentless fury, pursues the gray-haired Mrs. Transome, who hides within her breast such a heavy load of shame and dread. The power and intensity with which this character of the haughty, stern, yet inwardly quailing woman is drawn are unsurpassed in their way, and there is tragic horror in the recoil of her finest sensibilities from the vulgar, mean, self-complacent lawyer, too thick-skinned ever to know that in his own person he is a daily judgment on her whose life has been made hideous for his sake. Never more impressively than here does the novelist enforce her teaching that the deed follows the doer, being imbued with an incalculable vitality of its own, shaping all after life, and subduing to its guise the nature that is in bondage to it. Like those fabled dragon's teeth planted by Cadmus, which sprung up again as armed men, spreading discord and ruin, so a man's evil actions seem endowed with independent volition, and their consequences extend far beyond the individual life where they originated.

If 'Felix Holt' is the most intricately constructed of George Eliot's novels, 'Middlemarch,' which appeared five years afterwards, is, on the other hand, a story without a plot. In fact, it seems hardly appropriate to call it a novel. Like Hogarth's serial pictures representing the successive stages in their progress through life of certain typical characters, so in this book there is unrolled before us, not so much the history of any particular individual, as a whole phase of society portrayed with as daring and uncompromising a fidelity to Nature as that of Hogarth himself. In 'Middlemarch,' English provincial life in the first half of the nineteenth century is indelibly fixed in words "holding a universe impalpable" for the apprehension and delight of the furthest generations of English-speaking nations. Here, as in some kind of panorama, sections of a community and groups of character pass before the mind's eye. To dwell on the separate, strongly individualized figures which constitute this great crowd would be impossible within the present limits. But from the county people such as the Brookes and Chettams, to respectable middle-class families of the Vincy and Garth type, down to the low, avaricious, harpy-tribes of the Waules and Featherstones, every unit of this complex social agglomeration is described with a life-like vividness truly amazing, when the number and variety of the characters especially are considered. I know not where else in literature to look for a work which leaves such a strong impression on the reader's mind of the intertexture of human lives. Seen thus in perspective, each separate individuality, with its specialized consciousness, is yet as indissolubly connected with the collective life as that of the indistinguishable zoöphyte which is but a sentient speck necessarily moved by the same vital agency which stirs the entire organism.

Among the figures which stand out most prominently from the crowded background are Dorothea, Lydgate, Casaubon, Rosamond Vincy, Ladislaw, Bulstrode, Caleb, and Mary Garth. Dorothea belongs to that stately type of womanhood, such as Romola and Fedalma, a type which seems to be specifically George Eliot's own, and which has perhaps more in common with such Greek ideals as Antigone and Iphigenia, than with more modern heroines. But Dorothea, however lofty her aspirations, has not the Christian heroism of Romola, or the antique devotion of Fedalma. She is one of those problematic natures already spoken of; ill-adjusted to her circumstances, and never quite adjusting circumstances to herself. It is true that her high aims and glorious possibilities are partially stifled by a social medium where there seems no demand for them: still the resolute soul usually finds some way in which to work out its destiny.

"Many 'Theresas,'" says George Eliot, "have been born who found for themselves no epic life wherein there was a constant unfolding of far-resonant action; perhaps only a life of mistakes, the offspring of a certain spiritual grandeur ill-matched with the meanness of opportunity; perhaps a tragic failure which found no sacred poet, and sank unwept into oblivion. With dim lights and tangled circumstance they tried to shape their thought and deed in noble agreement; but, after all, to common eyes, their struggles seemed mere inconsistency and formlessness; for these later-born 'Theresas' were helped by no coherent social faith and order which could perform the function of knowledge for the ardently willing soul.

"Some have felt that these blundering lives are due to the inconvenient indefiniteness with which the Supreme Power has fashioned the natures of women; if there were one level of feminine incompetence as strict as the ability to count three and no more, the social lot of woman might be treated with scientific certitude. Meanwhile the indefiniteness remains, and the limits of variation are really much wider than any one would imagine from the sameness of women's coiffure, and the favorite love-stories in prose and verse."

Such a life of mistakes is that of the beautiful Dorothea,

the ill-starred wife of Casaubon. In his way the character of Casaubon is as great a triumph as that of Tito himself. The novelist seems to have crept into the inmost recesses of that uneasy consciousness, to have probed the most sensitive spots of that diseased vanity, and to lay bare before our eyes the dull labor of a brain whose ideas are still-born. In an article by Mr. Myers it is stated, however incredible it may sound, that an undiscriminating friend once condoled with George Eliot on the melancholy experience which, from her knowledge of Lewes, had taught her to depict the gloomy character of Casaubon, whereas, in fact, there could not be a more striking contrast than that between the pedant groping amid dim fragments of knowledge, and the vivacious *littérateur* and thinker with his singular mental energy and grasp of thought. On the novelist's laughingly assuring him that such was by no means the case, "From whom, then," persisted he, "did you draw 'Casaubon'?" With a humorous solemnity, which was quite in earnest, she pointed to her own heart. She confessed, on the other hand, having found the character of Rosamond Vincy difficult to sustain, such complacency of egoism, as has been pointed out, being alien to her own habit of mind. But she laid no claim to any such natural magnanimity as could avert Casaubon's temptations of jealous vanity, and bitter resentment.

If there is any character in whom one may possibly trace some suggestions of Lewes, it is in the versatile, brilliant, talented Ladislaw, who held, that while genius must have the utmost play for its spontaneity, it may await with confidence "those messages from the universe which summon it to its peculiar work, only placing itself in an attitude of receptivity towards all sublime chances." But however charming, the impression Ladislaw produces is that of a somewhat shallow, frothy character, so that he seems almost as ill-fitted for Dorothea as the dreary Casaubon himself. Indeed, the heroine's second marriage seems almost as much a failure as the stultifying union of Lydgate with Rosamond Vincy, and has altogether a more saddening effect than the tragic death of Maggie which is how much less pitiful than that death in life of the fashionable doctor whose best aims and vital purposes have been killed by his wife

Much might be said of Bulstrode, the sanctimonious hypocrite, who is yet not altogether a hypocrite, but has a vein of something resembling goodness running through his crafty character; of Farebrother, the lax, amiable, genuinely honorable vicar of St. Botolph's; of Mrs. Cadwallader, the glib-tongued, witty, meddling rector's wife, a kind of Mrs. Poyser of high life; of Caleb Garth, whose devotion to work is a religion, and whose likeness to Mr. Robert Evans has already been pointed out; of the whole-hearted, sensible Mary, and of many other supremely vivid characters, whom to do justice to would carry us too far.

'Middlemarch' is the only work of George Eliot's, I believe, in which there is a distinct indication of her attitude towards the aspirations and clearly formulated demands of the women of the nineteenth century. Her many sarcastic allusions to the stereotyped theory about woman's sphere show on which side her sympathies were enlisted. On the whole, she was more partial to the educational movement than to that other agitation which aims at securing the political enfranchisement of women. How sincerely she had the first at heart is shown by the donation of 50*l*. "From the author of 'Romola,'" when Girton College was first started. And in a letter to a young lady who studied there, and in whose career she was much interested, she says, "the prosperity of Girton is very satisfactory." Among her most intimate friends, too, were some of the ladies who had initiated and organized the Women's Suffrage movement. Likewise writing to Miss Phelps, she alludes to the Woman's Lectureship in Boston, and remarks concerning the new University: "An office that may make a new precedent in social advance, and which is at the very least an experiment that ought to be tried. America is the seed-ground and nursery of new ideals, where they can grow in a larger, freer air than ours."

In 1871, the year when 'Middlemarch' was appearing in parts, George Eliot spent part of the spring and summer months at Shottermill, a quaint Hampshire village situated amid a landscape that unites beauties of the most varied kind. Here we may imagine her and Mr. Lewes, after their day's work was done, either seeking the vast stretch of heath and common only bounded by the horizon, or strolling through the deep-sunk lanes, or finding a soothing repose in "places of nestling green for poets made." They had rented Brookbank, an old-fashioned cottage with tiled roof and lattice-paned windows, belonging to Mrs. Gilchrist, the widow of the distinguished biographer of William Blake.

The description of Mrs. Meyrick's house in 'Daniel Deronda' "where the narrow spaces of wall held a world-history in scenes and heads," may have been suggested by her present abode, rich in original drawings by Blake, and valuable prints, and George Eliot writes: "If I ever steal anything in my life, I think it will be the two little Sir Joshuas over the drawing-room mantelpiece." At this time she and Mr. Lewes also found intense interest in reading the 'Life of Blake.' Some correspondence, kindly placed at my disposal by Mrs. Gilchrist, passed between this lady and the Leweses in connection with the letting of the house, giving interesting glimpses into the domesticities of the latter. Their habits here, as in London, were of clock-work regularity, household arrangements being expected to run on wheels. "Everything," writes George Eliot, "goes on slowly at Shottermill, and the mode of narration is that typified in 'This is the house that Jack built.' But there is an exquisite stillness in the sunshine and a sense of distance from London hurry, which encourages the growth of patience.

"Mrs. G——'s" (their one servant) "pace is proportionate to the other slownesses, but she impresses me as a worthy person, and her cooking — indeed, all her attendance on us — is of satisfactory quality. But we find the awkwardness of having only one person in the house, as well as the advantage (this latter being quietude). The butcher does not bring the meat, everybody grudges selling new milk, eggs are scarce, and an expedition we made yesterday in search of fowls showed us nothing more hopeful than some chickens six weeks old, which the good woman observed were sometimes 'eaten by the gentry with asparagus.' Those eccentric people, the gentry!

"But have we not been reading about the siege of Paris all the winter, and shall we complain while we get excellent bread and butter and many etceteras? . . . Mrs. S—— kindly sent us a dish of asparagus, which we ate (without the skinny chicken) and had a feast.

"You will imagine that we are as fond of eating as Friar Tuck—I am enlarging so on our commissariat. But you will also infer that we have no great evils to complain of, since I make so much of the small."

George Eliot rarely went out in the daytime during her stay at Shottermill, but in the course of her rambles she would sometimes visit such cottagers in remote places as were not likely to know who she was. She used also to go and see a farmer's wife living at a short distance from Brookbank, with whom she would freely chat about the growth of fruits and vegetables and the quality of butter, much to the astonishment of the simple farm people. Speaking of her recollection of the great novelist to an American lady by whom these facts are recorded, the old countrywoman remarked: "It were wonderful, just wonderful, the sight o' green peas that I sent down to that gentleman and lady every week."

After the lapse of a few months spent in this sweet rural retreat, George Eliot again writes to Mrs. Gilchrist: "I did not imagine that I should ever be so fond of the place as I am now. The departure of the bitter winds, some improvement in my health, and the gradual revelation of fresh and fresh beauties in the scenery, especially under a hopeful sky such as we have sometimes had—all these conditions have made me love our little world here, and wish not to quit it until we can settle in our London home. I have the regret of thinking that it was my original indifference about it (I hardly ever like things until they are familiar) that hindered us from securing the cottage until the end of September."

George Eliot's conscientiousness and precision in the small affairs of life are exemplified in her last note to Mrs. Gilchrist: "After Mr. Lewes had written to you, I was made aware that a small dessert or bread-and-butter dish had been broken. That arch-sinner, the cat, was credited with the guilt. I am assured by Mrs. G—— that nothing else has been injured during her reign, and Mrs. L—— confirmed the statement to me yesterday. I wish I could replace the unfortunate dish. . . . This note, of course, needs no answer, and it is intended simply to make me a clean breast about the crockery."

About this time George Eliot was very much out of health: indeed, both she and Lewes repeatedly speak of themselves as "two nervous, dyspeptic creatures, two ailing, susceptible bodies," to whom slight inconveniences are injurious and upsetting. Although it was hot summer weather, Mrs. Lewes suffered much from cold, sitting always with artificial heat to her feet. One broiling day in August, after she had left Brookbank, and taken another place in the neighborhood, an acquaintance happening to call on her, found her sitting in the garden writing, as was her wont, her head merely shaded by a deodora, on the lawn. Being expostulated with by her visitor for her imprudence in exposing herself to the full blaze of the midday sun, she replied, "Oh, I like it! To-day is the first time I have felt warm this summer."

They led a most secluded life, George Eliot being at this time engaged with the continuation of 'Middlemarch;' and Lewes, alluding to their solitary habits, writes at this date: " Work goes on smoothly away from all friendly interruptions. Lord Houghton says that it is incomprehensible how we can live in such Simeon Stylites fashion, as we often do, all alone — but the fact is we never *are* alone when alone. And I sometimes marvel how it is I have contrived to get through so much work living in London. It's true I'm a London child." Occasionally, however, they would go and see Tennyson, whose house is only three miles from Shottermill, but the road being all uphill made the ride a little tedious and uncomfortable, especially to George Eliot who had not got over her old nervousness. The man who used to drive them on these occasions was so much struck by this that he told the lady who has recorded these details in the *Century Magazine:* "Withal her being such a mighty clever body, she were very nervous in a carriage — allays wanted to go on a smooth road, and seemed dreadful feared of being thrown out." On one of these occasional meetings with Tennyson, the poet got involved in a conversation with the novelist concerning evolution and such weighty questions. They had been walking together in close argument, and as the Poet-Laureate bade George Eliot farewell, he called to her, already making her way down the hill, " Well, good-by, you and your molecules ! " And she, looking back, said in her deep low voice (which always got lower when she was at all roused), " I am quite content with my molecules."

The country all around Shottermill with its breezy uplands, its pine-clad hills, its undulating tracts of land purpled with heath in the autumn, became more and more endeared to George Eliot, who, indeed, liked it better than any scenery in England. Here she could enjoy to the full that " sense of standing on a round world," which, she writes to Mrs. Gilchrist who had used the phrase, " was precisely what she most cared for amongst out-of-door delights." Some years afterwards we find her and Mr. Lewes permanently taking a house not far off, at Witley in Surrey, which has the same kind of beautiful open scenery. Writing from her town residence about it to her old friend Mrs. Bray, George Eliot says: " We, too, are thinking of a new settling down, for we have bought a house in Surrey about four miles from Godalming on a gravelly hill among the pine-trees, but with neighbors to give us a sense of security. Our present idea is that we shall part with this house and give up London except for occasional visits. We shall be on the same line of railway with some good friends at Weybridge and Guildford."

CHAPTER XIV.

DANIEL DERONDA.

' DANIEL DERONDA,' which appeared five years after ' Middlemarch,' occupies a place apart among George Eliot's novels. In the spirit which animates it, it has perhaps the closest affinity with ' The Spanish Gypsy.' Speaking of this work to a young friend of Jewish extraction (in whose career George Eliot felt keen interest), she expressed surprise at the amazement which her choice of a subject had created. "I wrote about the Jews," she remarked, "because I consider them a fine old race who have done great things for humanity. I feel the same admiration for them as I do for the Florentines. Only lately I have heard to my great satisfaction that an influential member of the Jewish community is going to start an emigration to Palestine. You will also be glad to learn that Helmholtz is a Jew."

These observations are valuable as affording a key to the leading motive of 'Daniel Deronda.' Mordecai's ardent desire to found a new national state in Palestine is not simply the author's dramatic realization of the feeling of an enthusiast, but expresses her own very definite sentiments on the subject. The Jewish apostle is, in fact, more or less the mouthpiece of George Eliot's own opinions on Judaism. For so great a master in the art of creating character, this type of the loftiest kind of man is curiously unreal. Mordecai delivers himself of the most eloquent and exalted views and sentiments, yet his own personality remains so vague and nebulous that it has no power of kindling the imagination. Mordecai is meant for a Jewish Mazzini. Within his consciousness he harbors the future of a people. He feels himself destined to become the savior of his race; yet he does not convince us of his greatness. He convinces us no more than he does the mixed company at the "Hand and Banner," which listens with pitying incredulity to his passionate harangues. Nevertheless the first and final test of the religious teacher or of the social reformer is the magnetic force with which his own intense beliefs become binding on the consciences of others, if only of a few. It is true Mordecai secures one disciple — the man destined to translate his thought into action, Daniel Deronda, as shadowy, as puppet-like, as lifeless as Ezra Mordecai Cohen himself. These two men, of whom the one is the spiritual leader and the other the hero destined to realize his aspirations, are probably the two most unsuccessful of George Eliot's vast gallery of characters. They are the representatives of an idea, but the idea has never been made flesh. A succinct expression of it may be gathered from the following passage:

"Which among the chief of the Gentile nations has not an ignorant multitude? They scorn our people's ignorant observance; but the most accursed ignorance is that which has no observance — sunk to the cunning greed of the fox, to which all law is no more than a trap or the cry of the worrying hound. There is a degradation deep down below the memory that has withered into superstition. For the multitude of the ignorant on three continents who observe our rites and make the confession of the Divine Unity the Lord of Judaism is not dead. Revive the organic centre: let the unity of Israel which has made the growth and form of its religion be an outward reality. Looking towards a land and a polity, our dispersed people in all the ends of the earth may share the dignity of a national life which has a voice among the peoples of the East and the West; which will plant the wisdom and skill of our race, so that it may be, as of old, a medium of transmission and understanding. Let that come to pass, and the living warmth will spread to the weak extremities of Israel, and superstition will vanish, not in the lawlessness of the renegade, but in the illumination of great facts which widen feeling, and make all knowledge alive as the young offspring of beloved memories."

This notion that the Jews should return to Palestine in a body, and once more constitute themselves into a distinct nation, is curiously repugnant to modern feelings. As repugnant as that other doctrine, which is also implied in the book, that Jewish separateness should be still further insured by strictly adhering to their own race in marriage — at least Mirah, the most faultless of George Eliot's heroines, whose character expresses the noblest side of Judaism, "is a Jewess who will not accept any one but a Jew."

Mirah Lapidoth and the Princess Halm-Eberstein, Deronda's mother, are drawn with the obvious purpose of contrasting two types of Jewish women. Whereas the latter, strictly brought up in the belief and most minute observances of her Hebrew father, breaks away from the "bondage of having been born a Jew," from which she wishes to relieve her son by parting from him in infancy, Mirah, brought up in disregard, "even in dislike of her Jewish origin," clings with inviolable tenacity to the memory of that origin and to the fellowship of her people. The author leaves one in little doubt as to which side her own sympathies incline towards. She is not so much the artist here, impartially portraying different kinds of characters, as the special pleader proclaiming that one set of motives are righteous, just, and praiseworthy, as well as that the others are mischievous and reprehensible.

This seems carrying the principle of nationality to an extreme, if not pernicious length. If there were never any breaking up of old forms of society, any fresh blending of nationalities and races, we should soon reduce Europe to another China. This unwavering faithfulness to the traditions of the past may become a curse to the living. A rigidity as unnatural as it is dangerous would be the result of too tenacious a clinging to inherited memories. For if this doctrine were strictly carried out, such a country as America, where there is a slow amalgamation of many allied and even heterogeneous races into a new nation, would practically become impossible. Indeed, George Eliot does not absolutely hold these views. She considers them necessary at present in order to act as a drag to the too rapid transformations of society. In the most interesting paper of 'Theophrastus Such,' that called 'The Modern Hep! Hep! Hep!' she remarks: "The tendency of things is towards quicker or slower fusion of races. It is impossible to arrest this tendency; all we can do is to moderate its course so as to hinder it from degrading the moral status of societies by a too rapid effacement of those national traditions and customs which are the language of the national genius — the deep suckers of healthy sentiment. Such moderating and guidance of inevitable movement is worthy of all effort."

Considering that George Eliot was convinced of this modern tendency towards fusion, it is all the more singular that she should, in 'Daniel Deronda,' have laid such stress on the reconstruction, after the lapse of centuries, of a Jewish state; singular, when one considers that many of the most eminent Jews, so far from aspiring towards such an event, hardly seem to have contemplated it as a desirable or possible prospect. The sympathies of Spinoza, the Mendelssohns,

Rahel, Meyerbeer, Heine, and many others, are not distinctively Jewish but humanitarian. And the grandest, as well as truest thing that has been uttered about them is that saying of Heine's: "The country of the Jews is the ideal, is God."

Indeed, to have a true conception of Jewish nature and character, of its brilliant lights and deep shadows, of its pathos, depth, sublimity, degradation, and wit; of its infinite resource and boundless capacity for suffering — one must go to Heine and not to 'Daniel Deronda.' In 'Jehuda-ben-Halevy' Heine expresses the love and longing of a Jewish heart for Jerusalem in accents of such piercing intensity that compared with it "Mordecai's" fervid desire fades into mere abstract rhetoric.

Nature and experience were the principal sources of George Eliot's inspiration. And though she knew a great deal about the Jews, her experience had not become sufficiently incorporated with her consciousness. Otherwise, instead of portraying such tame models of perfection as Deronda and Mirah, she would have so mixed her colors as to give us that subtle involvement of motive and tendency — as of cross-currents in the sea — which we find in the characters of nature's making and in her own finest creations, such as Maggie, Silas Marner, Dorothea Casaubon, and others.

In turning to the English portion of the story there is at once greater play of spontaneity in the people depicted. Grandcourt, Gascoigne, Rex, Mrs. Davilow, Sir Hugh Mallinger, and especially Gwendolen, show all the old cunning in the psychological rendering of human nature. Curiously enough, this novel consists of two perfectly distinct narratives; the only point of junction being Daniel Deronda himself, who, as a Jew by birth and an English gentleman by education, stands related to both sets of circumstances. The influence he exerts on the spiritual development of Gwendolen seems indeed the true *motif* of the story. Otherwise there is no intrinsic connection between the group of people clustering round Mordecai, and that of which Gwendolen is the centre: unless it be that the author wished to show the greater intensity of aim and higher moral worth of the

Jews as contrasted with these purposeless, worldly, unideal Christians of the nineteenth century.

Compared with the immaculate Mirah, Gwendolen Harleth is a very naughty, spoiled, imperfect specimen of maidenhood. But she has life in her; and one speculates as to what she will say and do next, as if she were a person among one's acquaintances. On that account most readers of 'Daniel Deronda' find their interest engrossed by the fate of Gwendolen, and the conjugal relations between her and Grandcourt. This is so much the case, that one suspects her to have been the first idea of the story. She is at any rate its most attractive feature. In Gwendolen, George Eliot once remarked, she had wished to draw a girl of the period. Fascinating, accomplished, of siren-like beauty, she has every outward grace combined with a singular inward vacuity. The deeper aspects of life are undreamed of in her philosophy. Her religion consists in a vague awe of the unknown and invisible, and her ambition in the acquisition of rank, wealth, and personal distinction. She is selfish, vain, frivolous, worldly, domineering, yet not without sudden impulses of generosity, and jets of affection. Something there is in her of Undine before she had a soul — something of a gay, vivacious, unfeeling sprite, who recks nothing of human love or of human misery, but looks down with utter indifference on the poor humdrum mortals around her, whom she inspires at once with fear and fondness: something, also, of the "princess in exile, who in time of famine was to have her breakfast-roll made of the finest bolted flour from the seven thin ears of wheat, and in a general decampment was to have her silver fork kept out of the baggage."

How this bewitching creature, whose "iridescence of character" makes her a psychological problem, is gradually brought to accept Henleigh Grandcourt, in spite of the promise she has given to Lydia Glasher (his discarded victim), and her own fleeting presentiments, is described with an analytical subtlety unsurpassed in George Eliot's works. So, indeed, is the whole episode of the married life of Grandcourt. This territorial magnate, who possesses every worldly advantage that Gwendolen desired, is worthy, as a study of character, to be placed beside that of Casaubon himself. Gwendolen's girlish type of egoism, which loves to be the centre of admiration, here meets with that far other deadlier form of an "exorbitant egoism," conspicuous for its intense obstinacy and tenacity of rule, "in proportion as the varied susceptibilities of younger years are stripped away." This cold, negative nature lies with a kind of withering blight on the susceptible Gwendolen. Roused from the complacent dreams of girlhood by the realities of her married life, shrinking in helpless repulsion from the husband whom she meant to manage, and who holds her as in a vice, the unhappy woman has nothing to cling to in this terrible inward collapse of her happiness, but the man, who, from the first moment when his eye arrests hers at the gaming table at Leubronn, becomes, as it were, a conscience visibly incarnate to her. This incident, which is told in the first chapter of the novel, recalls a sketch by Dante Rossetti, where Mary Magdalene, in the flush of joyous life, is held by the Saviour's gaze, and in a sudden revulsion from her old life, breaks away from companions that would fain hold her back, with a passionate movement towards the Man of Sorrow. This impressive conception may have unconsciously suggested a somewhat similar situation to the novelist, for that George Eliot was acquainted with this drawing is shown by the following letter addressed in 1870 to Dante Rossetti:

"I have had time now to dwell on the photographs. I am especially grateful to you for giving me the head marked June 1861: it is exquisite. But I am glad to possess every one of them. The subject of the Magdalene rises in interest for me, the more I look at it. I hope you will keep in the picture an equally passionate type for her. Perhaps you will indulge me with a little talk about the modifications you intend to introduce."

The relation of Deronda to Gwendolen is of a Christlike nature. He is her only moral hold in the fearful temptations that assail her now and again under the intolerable irritations of her married life, temptations which grow more urgent when Grandcourt leads his wife captive, after his fashion, in a yacht on the Mediterranean. For "the intensest form of hatred is that rooted in fear, which compels to silence, and drives vehemence into a constructive vindictiveness, an imaginary annihilation of the detested object, something like the hidden rites of vengeance, with which the persecuted have made a dark vent for their rage, and soothed their suffering into numbness. Such hidden rites went on in the secrecy of Gwendolen's mind, but not with soothing effect — rather with the effect of a struggling terror. Side by side with dread of her husband had grown the self-dread which urged her to flee from the pursuing images wrought by her pent-up impulse."

The evil wish at last finds fulfilment, the murderous thought is outwardly realized. And though death is not eventually the result of the criminal desire, it yet seems to the unhappy wife as if it had a determining power in bringing about the catastrophe. But it is precisely this remorse which is the redeeming quality of her nature, and awakens a new life within her. In this quickening of the moral consciousness through guilt we are reminded, although in a different manner, of a similar process, full of pregnant suggestions, described in Nathaniel Hawthorne's 'Transformation.' It will be remembered that Donatello leads a purely instinctive, that is to say, animal, existence, till the commission of a crime awakens the dormant conscience, and a soul is born in the throes of anguish and remorse.

'In Daniel Deronda' there is an entire absence of that rich, genial humor which seemed spontaneously to bubble up and overflow her earlier works. Whether George Eliot's conception of the Jews as a peculiarly serious race had any share in bringing about that result, it is difficult to say. At any rate, in one of her essays she remarks that, "The history and literature of the ancient Hebrews gives the idea of a people who went about their business and pleasure as gravely as a society of beavers." Certainly Mordecai, Deronda, and Mirah are preternaturally solemn; even the Cohen family are not presented with any of those comic touches one would have looked for in this great humorist; only in the boy Jacob there are gleams of drollery such as in this description of him by Hans Meyrick. "He treats me with the easiest familiarity, and seems in general to look at me as a second-hand Christian commodity, likely to come down in price; remarking on my disadvantages with a frankness which seems to imply some thoughts of future purchase. It is pretty, though, to see the change in him if Mirah happens to come in. He turns child suddenly — his age usually strikes one as being like the Israelitish garments in the desert, perhaps near forty, yet with an air of recent production."

A certain subdued vein of humor is not entirely absent from the portraiture of the Meyrick family, a delightful group, who "had their little oddities, streaks of eccentricity from the mother's blood as well as the father's, their minds being like mediæval houses with unexpected recesses and openings from this into that, flights of steps, and sudden outlooks. But on the whole, instead of the old humor, we find in 'Daniel Deronda' a polished irony and epigrammatic sarcasm, which were afterwards still more fully developed in the 'Impressions of Theophrastus Such.'

Soon after the publication of this novel, we find the following allusion to it in one of George Eliot's letters to Mrs. Bray. "I don't know what you refer to in the *Jewish World*. Perhaps the report of Dr. Hermann Adler's lecture on 'Deronda' to the Jewish working-men, given in the *Times*. Probably the Dr. Adler whom you saw is Dr. Hermann's father, still living as Chief Rabbi. I have had some delightful communications from Jews and Jewesses, both at home and abroad. Part of the Club scene in 'D. D.,' is flying about in the Hebrew tongue through the various Hebrew newspapers, which have been copying the 'Maga,' in which the translation was first sent to me three months ago. The Jews naturally are not indifferent to themselves."

This Club scene gave rise at the time to quite a controversy. It could not fail to be identified with that other club of philosophers out at elbows so vividly described by G. H. Lewes in the *Fortnightly Review* of 1866. Nor was it possible not to detect an affinity between the Jew Cohen, the poor consumptive journeyman watchmaker, with his weak voice and his great calm intellect, and Ezra Mordecai Cohen, in precisely similar conditions; the difference being that the one is penetrated by the philosophical idea of Spinozism, and the other by the political idea of reconstituting a Jewish State in Palestine. This difference of mental bias, no doubt, forms a contrast between the two characters, without, however, invalidating the surmise that the fictitious enthusiast may have been originally suggested by the noble figure of the living Jew. Be that as it may, Lewes often took the opportunity in conversation of "pointing out that no such resemblance existed, Cohen being a keen dialectician and a highly impressive man, but without any specifically Jewish enthusiasm."

When she undertook to write about the Jews, George Eliot was deeply versed in Hebrew literature, ancient and modern. She had taught herself Hebrew when translating the *Leben Jesu*, and this knowledge now stood her in good stead. She was also familiar with the splendid utterances of Jehuda-ben-Halevy; with the visionary speculations of the Cabbalists, and with the brilliant Jewish writers of the Hispano-Arabic epoch. She had read portions of the Talmud, and remarked one day in conversation that Spinoza had really got something from the Cabbala. On her friend humbly suggesting that by ordinary accounts it appeared to be awful nonsense, she said "that it nevertheless contained fine ideas, like Plato and the Old Testament, which, however, people took in the lump, being accustomed to them."

CHAPTER XV.

LAST YEARS.

'DANIEL DERONDA' is the last great imaginative work with which George Eliot was destined to enrich the world. It came out in small volumes, the appearance of each fresh number being hailed as a literary event. In allusion to an author's feeling on the conclusion of a weighty task, George Eliot remarks in one of her letters : " As to the great novel which remains to be written, I must tell you that I never believe in future books. . . . Always after finishing a book I have a period of despair that I can never again produce anything worth giving to the world. The responsibility of the writer grows heavier and heavier — does it not? — as the world grows older, and the voices of the dead more numerous. It is difficult to believe, until the germ of some new work grows into imperious activity within one, that it is possible to make a really needed contribution to the poetry of the world — I mean possible to one's self to do it."

This singular diffidence, arising from a sense of the tremendous responsibility which her position entailed, was one of the most noticeable characteristics of this great woman, and struck every one who came in contact with her. Her conscientiousness made her even painfully anxious to enter sympathetically into the needs of every person who approached her, so as to make her speech a permanently fruitful influence in her hearer's life. Such an interview, for example, as that between Goethe and Heine — where the younger poet, after thinking all the way what fine things to say to Goethe, was so disconcerted by the awe-inspiring presence of the master, that he could find nothing better to say than that the plums on the road-side between Jena and Weimar were remarkably good — would have been impossible with one so eager always to give of her best.

This deep seriousness of nature made her Sunday afternoon receptions, which became more and more fashionable as time went on, something of a tax to one who preferred the intimate converse of a few to that more superficially brilliant talk which a promiscuous gathering brings with it. Among the distinguished visitors to be met more or less frequently at the Priory may be mentioned Mr. Herbert Spencer, Professor Huxley, Mr. Frederic Harrison, Professor Beesly, Dr. and Mrs. Congreve, Madame Bodichon, Lord Houghton, M. Tourguénief, Mr. Ralston, Sir Theodore and Lady Martin (better known as Helen Faucit), Mr. Burton of the National Gallery, Mr. George Howard and his wife, Mr. C. G. Leland, Mr. Moncure Conway, Mr. Justin McCarthy, Dr. Hueffer, Mr. and Mrs. Buxton Forman, Mr. F. Myers, Mr. Sully, Mr. Du Maurier, Mr. and Mrs. Mark Pattison, Mr. and Mrs. Clifford, Lady Castletown and her daughters, Mr. and Mrs. Burne Jones, Mr. John Everett Millais, Mr. Robert Browning, and Mr. Tennyson.

Persons of celebrity were not the only ones, however, that were made welcome at the Priory. The liveliest sympathy was shown by both host and hostess in many young people as yet struggling in obscurity, but in whom they delighted to recognize the promise of some future excellence. If a young man were pursuing some original scientific inquiry, or striking out a new vein of speculation, in all London there was none likely to enter with such zest into his ideas as G. H. Lewes. His generous appreciation of intellectual gifts is well shown in the following lines to Professor W. K. Clifford:

"Few things have given us more pleasure than the intimation in your note that you had a *fiancée*. May she be the central happiness and motive force of your career, and, by satisfying the affections, leave your *rare* intellect free to work out its glorious destiny. For, if you don't become a glory to your age and time, it will be a sin and a shame. Nature does n't often send forth such gifted sons, and when she does, Society usually cripples them. Nothing but marriage — a happy marriage — has seemed to Mrs. Lewes and myself wanting to your future."

On the Sunday afternoon receptions just mentioned, G. H. Lewes acted, so to speak, as a social cement. His vivacity, his ready tact, the fascination of his manners, diffused that general sense of ease and *abandon* so requisite to foster an harmonious flow of conversation. He was inimitable as a *raconteur*, and Thackeray, Trollope, and Arthur Helps were fond of quoting some of the stories which he would dramatize in the telling. One of the images which, on these occasions, recurs oftenest to George Eliot's friends, is that of the frail-looking woman who would sit with her chair drawn close to the fire, and whose winning womanliness of bearing and manners struck every one who had the privilege of an introduction to her. Her long, pale face, with its strongly marked features, was less rugged in the mature prime of life than in youth, the inner meanings of her nature having worked themselves more and more to the surface, the mouth, with its benignant suavity of expression, especially softening the too prominent under-lip and massive jaw. Her abundant hair, untinged with gray, whose smooth bands made a kind of frame to the face, was covered by a lace or muslin cap, with lappets of rich point or Valenciennes lace fastened under her chin. Her gray-blue eyes, under noticeable eyelashes, expressed the same acute sensitiveness as her long, thin, beautifully shaped hands. She had a pleasant laugh and smile, her voice being low, distinct, and intensely sympathetic in quality: it was contralto in singing, but she seldom sang or played before more than one or two friends. Though her conversation was perfectly easy, each sentence was as finished, as perfectly formed, as the style of her published works. Indeed, she laid great stress on the value of correct speaking and clearness of enunciation; and in 'Theophrastus Such' she laments "the general ambition to speak every language except our mother English, which persons 'of style' are not ashamed of corrupting with slang, false foreign equivalents, and a pronunciation that crushes out all color from the vowels, and jams them between jostling consonants."

Besides M. D'Albert's Genevese portrait of George Eliot, we have a drawing by Mr. Burton, and another by Mr. Lawrence, the latter taken soon after the publication of 'Adam Bede.' In criticising the latter likeness, a keen observer of human nature remarked that it conveyed no indication of the infinite depth of her observant eye, nor of that cold, subtle, and unconscious cruelty of expression which might occasionally be detected there. George Eliot had an unconquerable aversion to her likeness being taken: once, however, in 1860, she was photographed for the sake of her "dear sisters" at Rosehill. But she seems to have repented of this weakness, for, after the lapse of years, she writes: "Mr. Lewes has just come to me after reading your letter, and says, 'For God's sake tell her not to have the photograph reproduced!' and I had nearly forgotten to say that the fading is what I desired. I should not like this image to be perpetuated. It needs the friendly eyes that regret to see it fade, and must not be recalled into emphatic black and white for indifferent gazers. Pray let it vanish."

Those who knew George Eliot were even more struck by the force of her entire personality than by her writings. Sympathetic, witty, or learned in turn, her conversation deeply impressed her hearers, being enriched by such felicities of expression as: "The best lesson of tolerance we have to learn is to tolerate intolerance." In answer to a friend's surprise that a clever man should allow himself to be contradicted by a stupid one, without dropping down on him, she remarked: "He is very liable to drop down as a baked apple would." And of a very plain acquaintance she said: "He has the most dreadful kind of ugliness one can be afflicted with, because it takes on the semblance of beauty."

Poetry, music, and art naturally absorbed much attention at the Priory. Here Mr. Tennyson has been known to read 'Maud' aloud to his friends: Mr. Browning expatiated on the most recondite metrical rules: and Rossetti sent presents of poems and photographs. In the following unpublished letters George Eliot thanks the latter for his valued gifts —
"We returned only the night before last from a two months' journey to the Continent, and among the parcels awaiting me I found your generous gift. I am very grateful to you both as giver and poet.

"In cutting the leaves, while my head is still swimming from the journey, I have not resisted the temptation to read many things as they ought not to be read — hurriedly. But even in this way I have received a stronger impression than any fresh poems have for a long while given me, that to read once is a reason for reading again. The sonnets towards 'The House of Life' attract me peculiarly. I feel about them as I do about a new cahier of music which I have been 'trying' here and there with the delightful conviction that I have a great deal to become acquainted with and to like better and better." And again, in acknowledgment of some photographs: "The 'Hamlet' seems to me perfectly intelligible, and altogether admirable in conception, except in the type of the man's head. I feel sure that 'Hamlet' had a square anterior lobe.

"Mr. Lewes says, this conception of yours makes him long to be an actor who has 'Hamlet' for one of his parts, that he might carry out this scene according to your idea.

"One is always liable to mistake prejudices for sufficient inductions, about types of head and face, as well as about all other things. I have some impressions — perhaps only prejudices dependent on the narrowness of my experience — about forms of eyebrow and their relation to passionate expression. It is possible that such a supposed relation has a real anatomical basis. But in many particulars facial expression is like the expression of hand-writing: the relations are too subtle and intricate to be detected, and only shallowness is confident."

George Eliot read but little contemporary fiction, being usually absorbed in the study of some particular subject. "For my own spiritual good I need all other sort of reading," she says, "more than I need fiction. I know nothing of contemporary English novelists with the exception of ——, and a few of ——'s works. My constant groan is that I must leave so much of the greatest writing which the centuries have sifted for me unread for want of time." For the same reason, on being recommended by a literary friend to read Walt Whitman, she hesitated on the ground of his not containing anything spiritually needful for her, but, having been induced to take him up, she changed her opinion and admitted that he *did* contain what was "good for her soul." As to lighter reading, she was fond of books of travel, pronouncing "'The Voyage of the Challenger' a splendid book." Among foreign novelists she was very partial to Henry Gréville, and speaks of 'Les Koumiassine' as a pleasant story.

Persons who were privileged enough to be admitted to the intimacy of George Eliot and Mr. Lewes could not fail to be impressed by the immense admiration which they had for one another. Lewes's tenderness, always on the watch lest the great writer, with her delicately poised health, should over-exert herself, had something of doglike fidelity. On the other hand, in spite of George Eliot's habitually retiring manner, if any one ever engaged on the opposite side of an argument to that maintained by the brilliant *savant*, in taking his part, she usually had the best of it, although in the most gentle and feminine way.

Although there was entire oneness of feeling between them, there was no unanimity of opinion. George Eliot had the highest regard for Lewes's opinions, but held to her own. One of the chief subjects of difference consisted in their attitude towards Christianity: whereas he was its uncompromising opponent, she had the greatest sympathy with its various manifestations from Roman Catholic asceticism to Evangelical austerity and Methodist fervor. Her reverence for every form of worship in which mankind has more or less consciously embodied its sense of the mystery of all "this unintelligible world" increased with the years. She was deeply penetrated by that tendency of the Positivist spirit which recognizes the beneficial element in every form of religion, and sees the close, nay indissoluble, connection between the faith of former generations and the ideal of our own. She herself found ample scope for the needs and aspirations of her spiritual nature in the religion of humanity. As has already been repeatedly pointed out, there runs through all her works the same persistent teaching of "the Infinite Nature of Duty." And with Comte she refers "the obligations of duty, as well as all sentiments of devotion, to a concrete object, at once ideal and real; the Human Race, conceived as a continuous whole, including the past, the present, and the future."

Though George Eliot drew many of her ideas of moral cultivation from the doctrines of Comte's *Philosophie Positive*, she was not a Positivist in the strict sense of the word. Her mind was far too creative by nature to give an unqualified adhesion to such a system as Comte's. Indeed, her devotion to the idea of mankind, conceived as a collective whole, is not so much characteristic of Positivists as of the greatest modern minds, minds such as Lessing, Bentham, Shelley, Mill, Mazzini, and Victor Hugo. Inasmuch as Comte co-ordinated these ideas into a consistent doctrine, George Eliot found herself greatly attracted to his system; and Mr. Beesly, after an acquaintance of eighteen years, considered himself justified in stating that her powerful intellect had accepted the teaching of Auguste Comte, and that she looked forward to the reorganization of belief on the lines which he had laid down. Still her adherence, like that of G. H. Lewes, was only partial, and applied mainly to his philosophy, and not to his scheme of social policy. She went farther than the latter, however, in her concurrence. For Mr. Lewes, speaking of the *Politique Positive* in his 'History of Philosophy,' admits that his antagonistic attitude had been considerably modified on learning from the remark of one very dear to him, "to regard it as an Utopia, presenting hypotheses rather than doctrines — suggestions for future inquiries rather than dogmas for adepts."

On the whole, although George Eliot did not agree with Comte's later theories concerning the reconstruction of society, she regarded them with sympathy "as the efforts of an individual to anticipate the work of future generations." This sympathy with the general Positivist movement she showed by subscribing regularly to Positivist objects, especially to the fund of the Central Organization presided over by M. Laffitte, but she invariably refused all membership with the Positivist community. In conversation with an old and valued friend, she also repeatedly expressed her objection to much in Comte's later speculations, saying on one occasion, "I cannot submit my intellect or my soul to the guidance of Comte." The fact is that, although George Eliot was greatly influenced by the leading Positivist ideas, her mind was too original not to work out her own individual conception of life.

What this conception is has been already indicated, so far as space would permit, in the discussion of her successive works. Perhaps in the course of time her moralizing analytical tendency encroached too much on the purely artistic faculty. Her eminently dramatic genius — which enabled her to realize characters the most varied and opposite in type, somewhat in the manner of Shakespeare — became hampered by theories and abstract views of life. This was especially shown in her latest work 'The Impressions of Theophrastus Such,' a series of essays chiefly satirizing the weaknesses and vanities of the literary class In these unattractive "impressions" the wit is often labored, and does not play "beneficently round the changing facets of egotism, absurdity, and vice, as the sunshine over the rippling sea or the dewy meadows." Its cutting irony and incisive ridicule are no longer tempered by the

k

humorous laugh, but have the corrosive quality of some acrid chemical substance.

One of the papers, however, that entitled 'Debasing the Moral Currency,' expresses a strongly marked characteristic of George Eliot's mind. It is a pithy protest against the tendency of the present generation to turn the grandest deeds and noblest works of art into food for laughter. For she hated nothing so much as mockery and ridicule of what other people reverenced, often remarking that those who considered themselves freest from superstitious fancies were the most intolerant. She carried this feeling to such a pitch that she even disliked a book like 'Alice in Wonderland' because it laughed at the things which children had had a kind of belief in. In censuring this vicious habit of burlesquing the things that ought to be regarded with awe and admiration, she remarks, "Let a greedy buffoonery debase all historic beauty, majesty, and pathos, and the more you heap up the desecrated symbols, the greater will be the lack of the ennobling emotions which subdue the tyranny of suffering, and make ambition one with virtue."

'Looking Backward' is the only paper in 'Theophrastus Such' quite free from cynicism. It contains, under a slightly veiled form, pathetically tender reminiscences of her own early life. This volume, not published till May 1879, was written before the incalculable loss which befell George Eliot in the autumn of the preceding year.

After spending the summer of 1878 in the pleasant retirement of Witley, Lewes and George Eliot returned to London. A severe cold taken by Lewes proved the forerunner of a serious disorder, and, after a short illness, this bright, many-sided, indefatigable thinker passed away in his sixty-second year. He had frequently said to his friends that the most desirable end of a well-spent life was a painless death; and although his own could not be called painless, his sufferings were at least of short duration. Concerning the suffering and anguish of her who was left behind to mourn him, one may most fitly say, in her own words, that "for the first sharp pangs there is no comfort — whatever goodness may surround us, darkness and silence still hang about our pain." In her case, also, the "clinging companionship with the dead" was gradually linked with her living affections, and she found alleviation for her sorrow in resuming those habits of continuous mental occupation which had become second nature with her. In a letter addressed to a friend, who, only a few short months afterwards, suffered a like heavy bereavement, there breathes the spirit in which George Eliot bore her own sorrow: "I understand it all. . . . There is but one refuge — the having much to do. You have the mother's duties. Not that these can yet make your life other than a burden to be patiently borne. Nothing can, except the gradual adaptation of your soul to the new conditions. . . . It is among my most cherished memories that I knew your husband, and from the first delighted in him. . . . All blessing — and even the sorrow that is a form of love has a heart of blessing — is tenderly wished for you."

On seeing this lady for the first time after their mutual loss, George Eliot asked her eagerly: "Do the children help? Does it make any difference?" Some help there was for the widowed heart of this sorrowing woman in throwing herself, with all her energies, into the work which Lewes had left unfinished at his death, and preparing it for publication, with the help of an expert. Another subject which occupied her thoughts at this time was the foundation of the "George Henry Lewes Studentship," in order to commemorate the name of one who had done so much to distinguish himself in the varied fields of literature, science, and philosophy. The value of the studentship is slightly under 200*l.* a year. It is worth noticing that persons of both sexes are received as candidates. The object of the endowment is to encourage the prosecution of original research in physiology, a science to whose study Lewes had devoted himself most assiduously for many years. Writing of this matter to a young lady, one of the Girton students, George Eliot says: "I know . . . will be glad to hear also that both in England and Germany the type, or scheme, on which the studentship is arranged has been regarded with satisfaction, as likely to be a useful model."

Amid such preoccupations, and the preparation of 'Theophrastus Such' for the press, the months passed on, and

George Eliot was beginning to see her friends again, when one day she not only took the world, but her intimate circle by surprise, by her marriage with Mr. John Walter Cross, on the 6th of May, 1880. The acquaintance with this gentleman, dating from the year 1867, had long ago grown into the warmest friendship, and his boundless devotion to the great woman whose society was to him as his daily bread, no doubt induced her to take a step which could not fail to startle even those who loved her the most. But George Eliot's was a nature that needed some one especially to love. And though that precious companionship, at once stimulating and sympathetic, which she had so long enjoyed, was taken from her, she could still find comfort during the remainder of her life in the love, the appreciation, and the tender care which were proffered to her by Mr. Cross. Unfortunately her life was not destined to be prolonged.

Although seeming fairly well at this date, George Eliot's health, always delicate, had probably received a shock, from which it never recovered. Only six months before her marriage three eminent medical men were attending her for a painful disease. However, there seemed still a prospect of happiness for her when she and Mr. Cross went for a tour in Italy, settling, on their return, at her favorite country house at Witley. In the autumn they once more made their home in London, at Mr. Cross's town house at 4 Cheyne Walk, Chelsea, and Mrs. Cross, who was again beginning to receive her friends, seemed, to all appearances, well and happy, with a prospect of domestic love and unimpaired mental activity stretching out before her. But it was not to be. On Friday, the 17th of December, George Eliot attended a representation of the 'Agamemnon,' in Greek, by Oxford undergraduates, and was so stirred by the grand words of her favorite Æschylus, that she was contemplating a fresh perusal of the Greek dramatists with her husband. On the following day she went to the Saturday popular concert, and on returning home played through some of the music she had been hearing. Her fatal cold was probably caught on that occasion, for, although she received her friends, according to custom, on the Sunday afternoon, she felt indisposed in the evening, and on the following day an affection of the larynx necessitated medical advice. There seemed no cause for alarm at first, till on Wednesday it was unexpectedly discovered that inflammation had arisen in the heart, and that no hope of recovery remained. Before midnight of the 22nd of December, 1880, George Eliot, who died at precisely the same age as Lewes, had passed quietly and painlessly away; and on Christmas Eve the announcement of her death was received with general grief. She was buried by the side of George Henry Lewes, in the cemetery at Highgate.

George Eliot's career has been habitually described as uniform and uneventful. In reality nothing is more misleading. On the contrary, her life, from its rising to its setting, describes an astonishingly wide orbit. If one turns back in imagination from the little Staffordshire village whence her father sprang, to the simple rural surroundings of her own youth, and traces her history to the moment when a crowd of mourners, consisting of the most distinguished men and women in England, followed her to the grave, one cannot help realizing how truly eventful was the life of her who now joined in spirit the

> "Choir invisible
> Of those immortal dead who live again
> In minds made better by their presence: live
> In pulses stirred to generosity,
> In deeds of daring rectitude, in scorn
> For miserable aims that end in self,
> In thoughts sublime that pierce the night like stars,
> And with their mild persistence urge man's search
> To vaster issues."

ROMOLA.

PROEM.

More than three centuries and a half ago, in the mid-springtime of 1492, we are sure that the angel of the dawn, as he travelled with broad slow wing from the Levant to the Pillars of Hercules, and from the summits of the Caucasus across all the snowy Alpine ridges to the dark nakedness of the Western Isles, saw nearly the same outline of firm land and unstable sea—saw the same great mountain shadows on the same valleys as he has seen to-day—saw olive mounts, and pine forests, and the broad plains green with young corn or rain-freshened grass—saw the domes and spires of cities rising by the river-sides or mingled with the sedge-like masts on the many-curved seacoast, in the same spots where they rise to-day. And as the faint light of his course pierced into the dwellings of men, it fell, as now, on the rosy warmth of nestling children; on the haggard waking of sorrow and sickness; on the hasty uprising of the hard-handed laborer; and on the late sleep of the night-student, who had been questioning the stars or the sages, or his own soul, for that hidden knowledge which would break through the barrier of man's brief life, and show its dark path, that seemed to bend nowhither, to be an arc in an immeasurable circle of light and glory. The great river-courses which have shaped the lives of men have hardly changed; and those other streams, the life-currents that ebb and flow in human hearts, pulsate to the same great needs, the same great loves and terrors. As our thought follows close in the slow wake of the dawn, we are impressed with the broad sameness of the human lot, which never alters in the main headings of its history—hunger and labor, seed-time and harvest, love and death.

Even if, instead of following the dim daybreak, our imagination pauses on a certain historical spot and awaits the fuller morning, we may see a world-famous city, which has hardly changed its outline since the days of Columbus, seeming to stand as an almost unviolated symbol, amidst the flux of human things, to remind us that we still resemble the men of the past more than we differ from them, as the great mechanical principles on which those domes and towers were raised must make a likeness in human building that will be broader and deeper than all possible change. And doubtless, if the spirit of a Florentine citizen, whose eyes were closed for the last time while Columbus was still waiting and arguing for the three poor vessels with which he was to set sail from the port of Palos, could return from the shades and pause where our thought is pausing, he would believe that there must still be fellowship and understanding for him among the inheritors of his birthplace.

Let us suppose that such a Shade has been permitted to revisit the glimpses of the golden morning, and is standing once more on the famous hill of San Miniato, which overlooks Florence from the south.

The Spirit is clothed in his habit as he lived: the folds of his well-lined black silk garment or *lucco* hang in grave unbroken lines from neck to ankle; his plain cloth cap, with its *becchetto*, or long hanging strip of drapery, to serve as a scarf in case of need, surmounts a penetrating face, not, perhaps, very handsome, but with a firm, well-cut mouth, kept distinctly human by a close-shaven lip and chin. It is a face charged with memories of a keen and various life passed below there on the banks of the gleaming river; and as he looks at the scene before him, the sense of familiarity is so much stronger than the perception of change, that he thinks it might be possible to descend once more amongst the streets, and take up that busy life where he left it. For it is not only the mountains and the westward-bending river that he recognizes; not only the dark sides of Mount Morello opposite to him, and the long valley of the Arno that seems to stretch its gray low-tufted luxuriance to the far-off ridges of Carrara; and the steep height of Fiesole, with its crown of monastic walls and cypresses; and all the green and gray slopes sprinkled with villas which he can name as he looks at them. He sees other familiar objects much closer to his daily walks. For though he misses the seventy or more towers that once surmounted the walls, and encircled the city as with a regal diadem, his eyes will not dwell on that blank; they are drawn irresistibly to the unique tower springing, like a tall flower-stem drawn toward the sun, from the square turreted mass of the Old Palace in the very heart of the city—the tower that looks none the worse for the four centuries that have passed since he used to walk under it. The great dome, too, greatest in the world, which, in his early boyhood, had been only a daring thought in the mind of a small, quick-eyed man—there it raises its large curves still, eclipsing the hills. And the well-known bell-towers—Giotto's, with its distant hint of rich color, and the graceful-spired Badia, and the rest—he looked at them all from the shoulder of his nurse.

"Surely," he thinks, "Florence can still ring her bells with the solemn hammer-sound that used to beat on the hearts of her citizens and strike out the fire there. And here, on the right, stands the long dark mass of Santa Croce, where we buried our famous dead, laying the laurel on their cold brows and fanning them with the breath of praise and of banners. But Santa Croce had no spire then: we Florentines were too full of great building projects to carry them all out in stone and marble; we had our frescoes and our shrines to pay for, not to speak of rapacious condottieri, bribed royalty, and purchased territories, and our façades and spires must needs wait. But what architect can the Frati Minori[1] have employed to build that spire for them? If it had been built in my day, Filippo Brunelleschi or Michelozzo would have devised something of another fashion than that—something worthy to crown the church of Arnolfo."

At this the Spirit, with a sigh, lets his eyes travel on to the city walls, and now he dwells on the change there with wonder at these modern times. Why have five out of the eleven convenient gates been closed? And why, above all, should the towers have been levelled that were once a glory and de-

[1] The Franciscans.

fence? Is the world become so peaceful, then, and do Florentines dwell in such harmony, that there are no longer conspiracies to bring ambitious exiles home again with armed bands at their back? These are difficult questions: it is easier and pleasanter to recognize the old than to account for the new. And there flows Arno, with its bridges just where they used to be—the Ponte Vecchio, least like other bridges in the world, laden with the same quaint shops where our Spirit remembers lingering a little on his way perhaps to look at the progress of that great palace which Messer Luca Pitti had set a-building with huge stones got from the Hill of Bogoli[1] close behind, or perhaps to transact a little business with the cloth-dressers in Oltrarno. The exorbitant line of the Pitti roof is hidden from San Miniato; but the yearning of the old Florentine is not to see Messer Luca's too-ambitious palace which he built unto himself; it is to be down among those narrow streets and busy humming Piazze where he inherited the eager life of his fathers. Is not the anxious voting with black and white beans still going on down there? Who are the priori in these months, eating soberly regulated official dinners in the Palazzo Vecchio, with removes of tripe and boiled partridges, seasoned by practical jokes against the ill-fated butt among those potent signors? Are not the significant banners still hung from the windows—still distributed with decent pomp under Orcagna's Loggia every two months?

Life had its zest for the old Florentine when he, too, trod the marble steps and shared in those dignities. His politics had an area as wide as his trade, which stretched from Syria to Britain, but they had also the passionate intensity, and the detailed practical interest, which could belong only to a narrow scene of corporate action; only to the members of a community shut in close by the hills and by walls of six miles' circuit, where men knew each other as they passed in the street, set their eyes every day on the memorials of their commonwealth, and were conscious of having not simply the right to vote, but the chance of being voted for. He loved his honors and his gains, the business of his counting-house, of his guild, of the public council-chamber; he loved his enmities

[1] Now Boboli.

too, and fingered the white bean which was to keep a hated name out of the *borsa* with more complacency than if it had been a golden florin. He loved to strengthen his family by a good alliance, and went home with a triumphant light in his eyes after concluding a satisfactory marriage for his son or daughter under his favorite loggia in the evening cool; he loved his game at chess under that same loggia, and his biting jest, and even his coarse joke, as not beneath the dignity of a man eligible for the highest magistracy. He had gained an insight into all sorts of affairs at home and abroad: he had been of the "Ten" who managed the war department, of the "Eight" who attended to home discipline, of the Priori or Signori who were the heads of the executive government; he had even risen to the supreme office of Gonfaloniere; he had made one in embassies to the Pope and to the Venetians; and he had been commissary to the hired army of the Republic, directing the inglorious bloodless battles in which no man died of brave breast wounds—*virtuosi colpi*—but only of casual falls and tramplings. And in this way he had learned to distrust men without bitterness; looking on life mainly as a game of skill, but not dead to traditions of heroism and cleanhanded honor. For the human soul is hospitable, and will entertain conflicting sentiments and contradictory opinions with much impartiality. It was his pride, besides, that he was duly tinctured with the learning of his age, and judged not altogether with the vulgar, but in harmony with the ancients: he, too, in his prime, had been eager for the most correct manuscripts, and had paid many florins for antique vases and for disinterred busts of the ancient immortals—some, perhaps, *truncis naribus*, wanting as to the nose, but not the less authentic; and in his old age he had made haste to look at the first sheets of that fine Homer which was among the early glories of the Florentine press. But he had not, for all that, neglected to hang up a waxen image or double of himself under the protection of the Madonna Annunziata, or to do penance for his sins in large gifts to the shrines of saints whose lives had not been modelled on the study of the classics; he had not even neglected making liberal bequests toward buildings for the Frati, against whom he had levelled many a jest.

For the Unseen Powers were mighty. Who knew—who was sure—that there was *any* name given to them behind which there was no angry force to be appeased, no intercessory pity to be won? Were not gems medicinal, though they only pressed the finger? Were not all things charged with occult virtues? Lucretius might be right—he was an ancient, and a great poet; Luigi Pulci, too, who was suspected of not believing anything from the roof upward (*dal tetto in su*), had very much the air of being right over the supper-table, when the wine and jests were circulating fast, though he was only a poet in the vulgar tongue. There were even learned personages who maintained that Aristotle, wisest of men (unless, indeed, Plato were wiser?), was a thoroughly irreligious philosopher; and a liberal scholar must entertain all speculations. But the negatives might, after all, prove false; nay, seemed manifestly false, as the circling hours swept past him, and turned round with graver faces. For had not the world become Christian? Had he not been baptized in San Giovanni, where the dome is awful with the symbols of coming judgment, and where the altar bears a crucified Image disturbing to perfect complacency in oneself and the world? Our resuscitated Spirit was not a pagan philosopher, nor a philosophizing pagan poet, but a man of the fifteenth century, inheriting its strange web of belief and unbelief; of Epicurean levity and fetichistic dread; of pedantic impossible ethics uttered by rote, and crude passions acted out with childish impulsiveness; of inclination toward a self-indulgent paganism, and inevitable subjection to that human conscience which, in the unrest of a new growth, was filling the air with strange prophecies and presentiments.

He had smiled, perhaps, and shaken his head dubiously, as he heard simple folk talk of a Pope Angelico, who was to come by and by and bring in a new order of things, to purify the Church from simony, and the lives of the clergy from scandal —a state of affairs too different from what existed under Innocent the Eighth for a shrewd merchant and politician to regard the prospect as worthy of entering into his calculations. But he felt the evils of the time, nevertheless; for he was a man of public spirit, and public spirit can never be wholly immoral, since its essence is care for a common good. That very Quaresima or Lent of 1492 in which he died, still in his erect old age, he had listened in San Lorenzo, not without a mixture of satisfaction, to the preaching of a Dominican Friar, named Girolamo Savonarola, who denounced with a rare boldness the worldliness and vicious habits of the clergy, and insisted on the duty of Christian men not to live for their own ease when wrong was triumphing in high places, and not to spend their wealth in outward pomp even in the churches, when their fellow-citizens were suffering from want and sickness. The Frate carried his doctrine rather too far for elderly ears; yet it was a memorable thing to see a preacher move his audience to such a pitch that the women even took off their ornaments, and delivered them up to be sold for the benefit of the needy.

"He was a noteworthy man, that Prior of San Marco," thinks our Spirit; "somewhat arrogant and extreme, perhaps, especially in his denunciations of speedy vengeance. Ah, *Iddio non paga il Sabato*¹—the wages of men's sins often linger in their payment, and I myself saw much established wickedness of long-standing prosperity. But a Frate Predicatore who wanted to move the people—how could he be moderate? He might have been a little less defiant and curt, though, to Lorenzo de' Medici, whose family had been the very makers of San Marco: was that quarrel ever made up? And our Lorenzo himself, with the dim outward eyes and the subtle inward vision, did he get over that illness at Careggi? It was but a sad, uneasy-looking face that he would carry out of the world which had given him so much, and there were strong suspicions that his handsome son would play the part of Rehoboam. How has it all turned out? Which party is likely to be banished and have its houses sacked just now? Is there any successor of the incomparable Lorenzo, to whom the great Turk is so gracious as to send over presents of rare animals, rare relics, rare manuscripts, or fugitive enemies, suited to the tastes of a Christian Magnifico who is at once lettered and devout—and also slightly vindictive? And what famous scholar is dictating the Latin letters of the Republic—what

¹ "God does not pay on a Saturday."

fiery philosopher is lecturing on Dante in the Duomo, and going home to write bitter invectives against the father and mother of the bad critic who may have found fault with his classical spelling? Are our wiser heads leaning toward alliance with the Pope and the Regno,[1] or are they rather inclining their ears to the orators of France and of Milan?

"There is knowledge of these things to be had in the streets below, on the beloved *marmi* in front of the churches, and under the sheltering Loggie, where surely our citizens have still their gossip and debates, their bitter and merry jests as of old. For are not the well-remembered buildings all there? The changes have not been so great in those uncounted years. I will go down and hear—I will tread the familiar pavement, and hear once again the speech of Florentines."

Go not down, good Spirit! for the changes are great and the speech of Florentines would sound as a riddle in your ears. Or, if you go, mingle with no politicians on the *marmi*, or elsewhere; ask no questions about trade in the Calimara; confuse yourself with no inquiries into scholarship, official or monastic. Only look at the sunlight and shadows on the grand walls that were built solidly, and have endured in their grandeur; look at the faces of the little children, making another sunlight amid the shadows of age; look, if you will, into the churches, and hear the same chants, see the same images as of old—the images of willing anguish for a great end, of beneficent love and ascending glory; see upturned living faces, and lips moving to the old prayers for help. These things have not changed. The sunlight and shadows bring their old beauty and waken the old heart-strains at morning, noon, and eventide; the little children are still the symbol of the eternal marriage between love and duty, and men still yearn for the reign of peace and righteousness—still own *that* life to be the highest which is a conscious voluntary sacrifice. For the Pope Angelico is not come yet.

[1] The name given to Naples by way of distinction among the Italian States.

BOOK I.

CHAPTER I.

THE SHIPWRECKED STRANGER.

THE Loggia de' Cerchi stood in the heart of old Florence, within a labyrinth of narrow streets behind the Badia, now rarely threaded by the stranger, unless in a dubious search for a certain severely simple door-place, bearing this inscription:

QUI NACQUE IL DIVINO POETA.

To the ear of Dante, the same streets rang with the shout and clash of fierce battle between rival families; but in the fifteenth century, they were only noisy with the unhistorical quarrels and broad jests of wool-carders in the cloth-producing quarters of San Martino and Garbo.

Under this loggia, in the early morning of the 9th of April, 1492, two men had their eyes fixed on each other: one was stooping slightly, and looking downward with the scrutiny of curiosity; the other, lying on the pavement, was looking upward with the startled gaze of a suddenly awakened dreamer.

The standing figure was the first to speak. He was a gray-haired, broad-shouldered man, of the type which, in Tuscan phrase, is moulded with the fist and polished with the pickaxe; but the self-important gravity which had written itself out in the deep lines about his brow and mouth seemed intended to correct any contemptuous inferences from the hasty workmanship which Nature had bestowed on his exterior. He had deposited a large well-filled bag, made of skins, on the pavement, and before him hung a pedler's basket, garnished partly with small woman's-ware, such as thread and pins, and partly with fragments of glass, which had probably been taken in exchange for those commodities.

"Young man," he said, pointing to a ring on the finger of the reclining figure, "when your chin has got a stiffer crop on it, you'll know better than to take your nap in street corners with a ring like that on your forefinger. By the Holy 'vangels! if it had been anybody but me standing over you two minutes ago—but Bratti Ferravecchi is not the man to steal. The cat couldn't eat her mouse if she didn't catch it alive, and Bratti couldn't relish gain if it had no taste of a bargain. Why, young man, one San Giovanni, three years ago, the Saint sent a dead body in my way—a blind beggar, with his cap well lined with pieces—but, if you'll believe me, my stomach turned against the money I'd never bargained for, till it came into my head that San Giovanni owed me the pieces for what I spend yearly at the Festa; besides, I buried the body and paid for a mass—and so I saw it was a fair bargain. But how comes a young man like you, with the face of Messer San Michele, to be sleeping on a stone bed with the wind for a curtain?"

The deep guttural sounds of the speaker were scarcely intelligible to the newly waked, bewildered listener, but he understood the action of pointing to his ring: he looked down at it, and, with a half-automatic obedience to the warning, took it off and thrust it within his doublet, rising at the same time and stretching himself.

"Your tunic and hose match ill with that jewel, young man," said Bratti, deliberately. "Anybody might say the saints had sent *you* a dead body; but if you took the jewels, I hope you buried him—and you can afford a mass or two for him into the bargain."

Something like a painful thrill appeared to dart through the frame of the listener, and arrest the careless stretching of his arms and chest. For an instant he turned on Bratti with a sharp frown; but he immediately recovered an air of indifference, took off the red Levantine cap which hung like a great purse over his left ear, pushed back his long dark-brown curls, and glancing at his dress, said, smilingly—

"You speak truth, friend: my garments are as weather-stained as an old sail, and they are not old either, only, like an old sail, they have had a sprinkling of the sea as well as the rain. The fact is, I'm a stranger in Florence, and when I came in footsore last night, I preferred flinging myself in a corner of this hospitable porch to hunting any longer for a chance hostelry, which might turn out to be a nest of bloodsuckers of more sorts than one."

"A stranger, in good sooth," said Bratti, "for the words come all melting out of your throat, so that a Christian and a Florentine can't tell a hook from a hanger. But you're not from Genoa? More likely from Venice, by the cut of your clothes?"

"At this present moment," said the stranger, smiling, "it is of less importance where I come from than where I can go to for a mouthful of breakfast. This city of yours turns a grim look on me just here: can you show me the way to a more lively quarter, where I can get a meal and a lodging?"

"That I can," said Bratti, "and it is your good fortune, young man, that I have happened to be walking in from Rovezzano this morning, and turned out of my way to Mercato Vecchio to say an Ave at the Badia. That, I say, is your good fortune. But it remains to be seen what is *my* profit in the matter. Nothing for nothing, young man. If I show you the way to Mercato Vecchio, you'll swear by your patron saint to let me have the bidding for that stained suit of yours, when you set up a better—as doubtless you will."

"Agreed, by San Niccolò," said the other, laughing. "But now let us set off to this said Mercato, for I feel the want of a better lining to this doublet of mine which you are coveting."

"Coveting? Nay," said Bratti, heaving his bag on his back and setting out. But he broke off in his reply, and burst out in loud, harsh tones, not unlike the creaking and grating of a cart-wheel: "*Chi abbaratta—baratta—b'ratta—chi abbaratta, cenci e vetri—b'ratta ferri vecchi?*"[1]

"It's worth but little," he said presently, relapsing into his conversational tone. "Hose and altogether, your clothes are worth but little. Still, if you've a mind to set yourself up

[1] "Who wants to exchange rags, broken glass, or old iron?"

with a lute worth more than any new one, or with a sword that's been worn by a Ridolfi, or with a paternoster of the best mode, I could let you have a great bargain, by making an allowance for the clothes; for, simple as I stand here, I've got the best-furnished shop in the Ferravecchi, and it's close by the Mercato. The Virgin be praised! it's not a pumpkin I carry on my shoulders. But I don't stay caged in my shop all day: I've got a wife and a raven to stay at home and mind the stock. *Chi abbaratta—baratta—b'ratta?* . . . And now, young man, where do you come from, and what's your business in Florence?"

"I thought you liked nothing that came to you without a bargain," said the stranger. "You've offered me nothing yet in exchange for that information."

"Well, well; a Florentine doesn't mind bidding a fair price for news: it stays the stomach a little though he may win no hose by it. If I take you to the prettiest damsel in the Mercato to get a cup of milk—that will be a fair bargain."

"Nay; I can find her myself, if she be really in the Mercato; for pretty heads are apt to look forth of doors and windows. No, no. Besides, a sharp trader, like you, ought to know that he who bids for nuts and news may chance to find them hollow."

"Ah! young man," said Bratti, with a sideway glance of some admiration, "you were not born of a Sunday—the salt-shops were open when you came into the world. You're not a Hebrew, eh?—come from Spain or Naples, eh? Let me tell you the Frati Minori are trying to make Florence as hot as Spain for those dogs of hell that want to get all the profit of usury to themselves and leave none for Christians; and when you walk the Calimara with a piece of yellow cloth in your cap, it will spoil your beauty more than a sword-cut across that smooth olive cheek of yours.—*Abbaratta, baratta—chi abbaratta?*—I tell you, young man, gray cloth is against yellow cloth; and there's as much gray cloth in Florence as would make a gown and cowl for the Duomo, and there's not so much yellow cloth as would make hose for Saint Christopher —blessed be his name, and send me a sight of him this day! —*Abbaratta, baratta, b'ratta—chi abbaratta?*"

"All that is very amusing information you are parting with for nothing," said the stranger, rather scornfully; "but it happens not to concern me. I am no Hebrew."

"See, now!" said Bratti, triumphantly; "I've made a good bargain with mere words. I've made you tell me something, young man, though you're as hard to hold as a lamprey. San Giovanni be praised! a blind Florentine is a match for two one-eyed men. But here we are in the Mercato."

They had now emerged from the narrow streets into a broad piazza, known to the elder Florentine writers as the Mercato Vecchio, or the Old Market. This piazza, though it had been the scene of a provision-market from time immemorial, and may, perhaps, says fond imagination, be the very spot to which the Fesulean ancestors of the Florentines descended from their high fastness to traffic with the rustic population of the valley, had not been shunned as a place of residence by Florentine wealth. In the early decades of the fifteenth century, which was now near its end, the Medici and other powerful families of the *popolani grassi*, or commercial nobility, had their houses there, not perhaps finding their ears much offended by the loud roar of mingled dialects, or their eyes much shocked by the butchers' stalls, which the old poet Antonio Pucci accounts a chief glory, or *dignità*, of a market that, in his esteem, eclipsed the markets of all the earth beside. But the glory of mutton and veal (well attested to be the flesh of the right animals; for were not the skins, with the heads attached, duly displayed, according to the decree of the Signoria?) was just now wanting to the Mercato, the time of Lent not being yet over. The proud corporation, or "Art," of butchers was in abeyance, and it was the great harvest-time of the market-gardeners, the cheesemongers, the venders of macaroni, corn, eggs, milk, and dried fruits: a change which was apt to make the women's voices predominant in the chorus. But in all seasons there was the experimental ringing of pots and pans, the chinking of the money-changers, the tempting offers of cheapness at the old-clothes stalls, the challenges of the dicers, the vaunting of new linens and woollens, of excellent wooden-ware, kettles, and frying-pans; there was the choking of the narrow inlets with mules and carts, together with much uncomplimentary remonstrance in terms remarkably identical with the insults in use by the gentler sex of the present day, under the same embrowning and heating circumstances. Ladies and gentlemen, who came to market, looked on at a larger amount of amateur fighting than could easily be seen in these later times, and beheld more revolting rags, beggary, and rascaldom than modern householders could well picture to themselves. As the day wore on, the hideous drama of the gaming-house might be seen here by any chance open-air spectator—the quivering eagerness, the blank despair, the sobs, the blasphemy, and the blows:—

> "E vedesi chi perde con gran soffi,
> E bestemmiar colla mano alla mascella,
> E ricever e dar di molti ingoffi."

But still there was the relief of prettier sights: there were brood-rabbits, not less innocent and astonished than those of our own period; there were doves and singing birds to be bought as presents for the children; there were even kittens for sale, and here and there a handsome *gattuccio*, or "Tom," with the highest character for mousing; and, better than all, there were young softly rounded cheeks and bright eyes, freshened by the start from the far-off castello[1] at daybreak, not to speak of older faces with the unfading charm of honest good-will in them, such as are never quite wanting in scenes of human industry. And high on a pillar in the centre of the place—a venerable pillar, fetched from the Church of San Giovanni—stood Donatello's stone statue of Plenty, with a fountain near it, where, says old Pucci, the good wives of the market freshened their utensils, and their throats also; not because they were unable to buy wine, but because they wished to save the money for their husbands.

But on this particular morning a sudden change seemed to have come over the face of the market. The *deschi*, or stalls, were indeed partly dressed with their various commodities, and already there were purchasers assembled, on the alert to secure the finest, freshest vegetables and the most unexceptionable butter. But when Bratti and his companion entered

[1] Walled village.

the piazza, it appeared that some common preoccupation had for the moment distracted the attention both of buyers and sellers from their proper business. Most of the traders had turned their backs on their goods, and had joined the knots of talkers who were concentrating themselves at different points in the piazza. A vender of old clothes, in the act of hanging out a pair of long hose, had distractedly hung them round his neck in his eagerness to join the nearest group; an oratorical cheesemonger, with a piece of cheese in one hand and a knife in the other, was incautiously making notes of his emphatic pauses on that excellent specimen of *marzolino;* and elderly market-women, with their egg-baskets in a dangerously oblique position, contributed a wailing fugue of invocation.

In this general distraction, the Florentine boys, who were never wanting in any street scene, and were of an especially mischievous sort—as who should say, very sour crabs indeed —saw a great opportunity. Some made a rush at the nuts and dried figs, others preferred the farinaceous delicacies at the cooked provision stalls—delicacies to which certain four-footed dogs also, who had learned to take kindly to Lenten fare, applied a discriminating nostril, and then disappeared with much rapidity under the nearest shelter; while the mules, not without some kicking and plunging among impeding baskets, were stretching their muzzles toward the aromatic green-meat.

"Diavolo!" said Bratti, as he and his companion came, quite unnoticed, upon the noisy scene; "the Mercato is gone as mad as if the most Holy Father had excommunicated us again. I must know what this is. But never fear: it seems a thousand years to you till you see the pretty Tessa, and get your cup of milk; but keep hold of me, and I'll hold to my bargain. Remember, I'm to have the first bid for your suit; specially for the hose, which, with all their stains, are the best *panno di garbo*—as good as ruined, though, with mud and weather stains."

"Olà, Monna Trecca," Bratti proceeded, turning toward an old woman on the outside of the nearest group, who for the moment had suspended her wail to listen, and shouting close in her ear: "Here are the mules upsetting all your bunches of parsley: is the world coming to an end, then?"

"Monna Trecca" (equivalent to "Dame Greengrocer") turned round at this unexpected trumpeting in her right ear, with a half-fierce, half-bewildered look, first at the speaker, then at her disarranged commodities, and then at the speaker again.

"A bad Easter and a bad year to you, and may you die by the sword!" she burst out, rushing toward her stall, but directing this first volley of her wrath against Bratti, who, without heeding the malediction, quietly slipped into her place, within hearing of the narrative which had been absorbing her attention; making a sign at the same time to the younger stranger to keep near him.

"I tell you I saw it myself," said a fat man with a bunch of newly purchased leeks in his hand. "I was in Santa Maria Novella, and saw it myself. The woman started up and threw out her arms, and cried out and said she saw a big bull with fiery horns coming down on the church to crush it. I saw it myself."

"Saw what, Goro?" said a man of slim figure, whose eye twinkled rather roguishly. He wore a close jerkin, a skullcap lodged carelessly over his left ear as if it had fallen there by chance, a delicate linen apron tucked up on one side, and a razor stuck in his belt. "Saw the bull or only the woman?"

"Why, the woman, to be sure; but it's all one, *mi pare;* it doesn't alter the meaning—*va!*" answered the fat man, with some contempt.

"Meaning? no, no; that's clear enough," said several voices at once, and then followed a confusion of tongues, in which "Lights shooting over San Lorenzo for three nights together"—"Thunder in the clear starlight"—"Lantern of the Duomo struck with the sword of St. Michael"—"*Palle*"[1] —"All smashed"—"Lions tearing each other to pieces"— "Ah! and they might well"—"*Boto*[2] *caduto in Santissima Nunziata!*"—"Died like the best of Christians"—"God will have pardoned him"—were often-repeated phrases, which shot

---

[1] Arms of the Medici

[2] A votive image of Lorenzo, in wax, hung up in the Church of the Annunziata, supposed to have fallen at the time of his death. *Boto* is popular Tuscan for *Voto*.

across each other like storm-driven hailstones, each speaker feeling rather the necessity of utterance than of finding a listener. Perhaps the only silent members of the group were Bratti, who, as a newcomer, was busy in mentally piecing together the flying fragments of information; the man of the razor; and a thin-lipped, eager-looking personage in spectacles, wearing a pen-and-ink case at his belt.

"*Ebbene*, Nello," said Bratti, skirting the group till he was within hearing of the barber. "It appears the Magnifico is dead—rest his soul!—and the price of wax will rise?"

"Even as you say," answered Nello; and then added, with an air of extra gravity, but with marvellous rapidity, "and his waxen image in the Nunziata fell at the same moment, they say; or at some other time, whenever it pleases the Frati Serviti, who know best. And several cows and women have had still-born calves this Quaresima; and for the bad eggs that have been broken since the Carnival, nobody has counted them. Ah! a great man—a great politician—a greater poet than Dante. And yet the cupola didn't fall, only the lantern. *Che miracolo!*"

A sharp and lengthened "Pst!" was suddenly heard darting across the pelting storm of gutturals. It came from the pale man in spectacles, and had the effect he intended; for the noise ceased, and all eyes in the group were fixed on him with a look of expectation.

"'Tis well said you Florentines are blind," he began, in an incisive high voice. "It appears to me, you need nothing but a diet of hay to make cattle of you. What! do you think the death of Lorenzo is the scourge God has prepared for Florence? Go! you are sparrows chattering praise over the dead hawk. What! a man who was trying to slip a noose over every neck in the Republic that he might tighten it at his pleasure! You like that; you like to have the election of your magistrates turned into closet-work, and no man to use the rights of a citizen unless he is a Medicean. That is what is meant by qualification now: *netto di specchio*[1] no longer means that a man pays his dues to the Republic: it means

[1] The phrase used to express the absence of disqualification—*i e*, the not being entered as a debtor in the public book (*specchio*).

that he'll wink at robbery of the people's money—at robbery of their daughters' dowries; that he'll play the chamberer and the philosopher by turns—listen to bawdy songs at the Carnival and cry 'Bellissimi!'—and listen to sacred lauds and cry again 'Bellissimi!' But this is what you love: you grumble and raise a riot over your *quattrini bianchi*" (white farthings); "but you take no notice when the public treasury has got a hole in the bottom for the gold to run into Lorenzo's drains. You like to pay for footmen to walk before and behind one of your citizens, that he may be affable and condescending to you. 'See, what a tall Pisan we keep,' say you, 'to march before him with the drawn sword flashing in our eyes!—and yet Lorenzo smiles at us. What goodness!' And you think the death of a man, who would soon have saddled and bridled you as the Sforza has saddled and bridled Milan— you think his death is the scourge God is warning you of by portents. I tell you there is another sort of scourge in the air."

"Nay, nay, Ser Cioni, keep astride your politics, and never mount your prophecy; politics is the better horse," said Nello. "But if you talk of portents, what portent can be greater than a pious notary? Balaam's ass was nothing to it."

"Ay, but a notary out of work, with his ink-bottle dry," said another bystander, very much out at elbows. "Better don a cowl at once, Ser Cioni; everybody will believe in your fasting."

The notary turned and left the group with a look of indignant contempt, disclosing, as he did so, the sallow but mild face of a short man who had been standing behind him, and whose bent shoulders told of some sedentary occupation.

"By San Giovanni, though," said the fat purchaser of leeks with the air of a person rather shaken in his theories, "I am not sure there isn't some truth in what Ser Cioni says. For I know I have good reason to find fault with the *quattrini bianchi* myself. Grumble, did he say? Suffocation! I should think we do grumble; and, let anybody say the word, I'll turn out into the piazza with the readiest, sooner than have our money altered in our hands as if the magistracy were so many necromancers. And it's true Lorenzo might have hindered such work if he would—and for the bull with the flaming horns, why, as Ser Cioni says, there may be many meanings to it, for the matter of that; it may have more to do with the taxes than we think. For when God above sends a sign, it's not to be supposed he'd have only one meaning."

"Spoken like an oracle, Goro!" said the barber. "Why, when we poor mortals can pack two or three meanings into one sentence, it were mere blasphemy not to believe that your miraculous bull means everything that any man in Florence likes it to mean."

"Thou art pleased to scoff, Nello," said the sallow, round-shouldered man, no longer eclipsed by the notary, "but it is not the less true that every revelation, whether by visions, dreams, portents, or the written word, has many meanings, which it is given to the illuminated only to unfold."

"Assuredly," answered Nello. "Haven't I been to hear the Frate in San Lorenzo? But then, I've been to hear Fra Menico in the Duomo too; and according to him, your Fra Girolamo, with his visions and interpretations, is running after the wind of Mongibello, and those who follow him are like to have the fate of certain swine that ran headlong into the sea—or some hotter place. With San Domenico roaring *è vero* in one ear, and San Francisco screaming *è falso* in the other, what is a poor barber to do—unless he were illuminated? But it's plain our Goro here is beginning to be illuminated, for he already sees that the bull with the flaming horns means first himself, and secondly all the other aggrieved taxpayers of Florence, who are determined to gore the magistracy on the first opportunity."

"Goro is a fool!" said a bass voice, with a note that dropped like the sound of a great bell in the midst of much tinkling. "Let him carry home his leeks and shake his flanks over his wool-beating. He'll mend matters more that way than by showing his tun-shaped body in the piazza, as if everybody might measure his grievances by the size of his paunch. The burdens that harm him most are his heavy carcass and his idleness."

The speaker had joined the group only in time to hear the conclusion of Nello's speech, but he was one of those figures for whom all the world instinctively makes way, as it would for a battering-ram. He was not much above the middle height, but the impression of enormous force which was conveyed by his capacious chest and brawny arms bared to the shoulder, was deepened by the keen sense and quiet resolution expressed in his glance and in every furrow of his cheek and brow. He had often been an unconscious model to Domenico Ghirlandajo, when that great painter was making the walls of the churches reflect the life of Florence, and translating pale aerial traditions into the deep color and strong lines of the faces he knew. The naturally dark tint of his skin was additionally bronzed by the same powdery deposit that gave a polished black surface to his leathern apron: a deposit which habit had probably made a necessary condition of perfect ease, for it was not washed off with punctilious regularity.

Goro turned his fat cheek and glassy eye on the frank speaker with a look of deprecation rather than of resentment.

"Why, Niccolò," he said in an injured tone, "I've heard you sing to another tune than that, often enough, when you've been laying down the law at San Gallo on a festa. I've heard you say yourself, that a man wasn't a mill-wheel, to be on the grind, grind, as long as he was driven, and then stick in his place without stirring when the water was low. And you're as fond of your vote as any man in Florence—ay, and I've heard you say, if Lorenzo——"

"Yes, yes," said Niccolò. "Don't you be bringing up my speeches again after you've swallowed them, and handing them about as if they were none the worse. I vote and I speak when there's any use in it: if there's hot metal on the anvil, I lose no time before I strike; but I don't spend good hours in tinkling on cold iron, or in standing on the pavement as thou dost, Goro, with snout upward, like a pig under an oak-tree. And as for Lorenzo—dead and gone before his time—he was a man who had an eye for curious ironwork; and if anybody says he wanted to make himself a tyrant, I say '*Sia;* I'll not deny which way the wind blows when every man can see the weathercock.' But that only means that Lorenzo was a crested hawk, and there are plenty of hawks without crests whose claws and beaks are as good for tearing. Though if there was any chance of a real reform, so that Marzocco[1] might shake his mane and roar again, instead of dipping his head to lick the feet of anybody that will mount and ride him, I'd strike a good blow for it."

"And that reform is not far off, Niccolò," said the sallow, mild-faced man, seizing his opportunity like a missionary among the too light-minded heathens; "for a time of tribulation is coming, and the scourge is at hand. And when the Church is purged of cardinals and prelates who traffic in her inheritance that their hands may be full to pay the price of blood and to satisfy their own lusts, the State will be purged too—and Florence will be purged of men who love to see avarice and lechery under the red hat and the mitre because it gives them the screen of a more hellish vice than their own."

"Ay, as Goro's broad body would be a screen for my narrow person in case of missiles," said Nello; "but if that excellent screen happened to fall, I were stifled under it, surely enough. That is no bad image of thine, Nanni—or, rather, of the Frate's; for I fancy there is no room in the small cup of thy understanding for any other liquor than what he pours into it."

"And it were well for thee, Nello," replied Nanni, "if thou couldst empty thyself of thy scoffs and thy jests, and take in that liquor too. The warning is ringing in the ears of all men: and it's no new story; for the Abbot Joachim prophesied of the coming time three hundred years ago, and now Fra Girolamo has got the message afresh. He has seen it in a vision, even as the prophets of old: he has seen the sword hanging from the sky."

"Ay, and thou wilt see it thyself, Nanni, if thou wilt stare upward long enough," said Niccolò; "for that pitiable tailor's work of thine makes thy noddle so overhang thy legs, that thy eyeballs can see naught above the stitching-board but the roof of thy own skull."

The honest tailor bore the jest without bitterness, bent on convincing his hearers of his doctrine rather than of his dig-

[1] The stone Lion, emblem of the Republic.

nity. But Niccolò gave him no opportunity for replying; for he turned away to the pursuit of his market business, probably considering further dialogue as a tinkling on cold iron.

"*Ebbene*," said the man with the hose round his neck, who had lately migrated from another knot of talkers, "they are safest who cross themselves and jest at nobody. Do you know that the Magnifico sent for the Frate at the last, and couldn't die without his blessing?"

"Was it so—in truth?" said several voices. "Yes, yes—God will have pardoned him." "He died like the best of Christians." "Never took his eyes from the holy crucifix."

"And the Frate will have given him his blessing?"

"Well, I know no more," said he of the hosen; "only Guccio there met a footman going back to Careggi, and he told him the Frate had been sent for yesternight, after the Magnifico had confessed and had the holy sacraments."

"It's likely enough the Frate will tell the people something about it in his sermon this morning; is it not true, Nanni?" said Goro. "What do you think?"

But Nanni had already turned his back on Goro, and the group was rapidly thinning; some being stirred by the impulse to go and hear "new things" from the Frate ("new things" were the nectar of Florentines); others by the sense that it was time to attend to their private business. In this general movement, Bratti got close to the barber and said,—

"Nello, you've a ready tongue of your own, and are used to worming secrets out of people when you've once got them well lathered. I picked up a stranger this morning as I was coming in from Rovezzano, and I can spell him out no better than I can the letters on that scarf I bought from the French cavalier. It isn't my wits are at fault,—I want no man to help me tell peas from paternosters,—but when you come to foreign fashions, a fool may happen to know more than a wise man."

"Ay, thou hast the wisdom of Midas, who could turn rags and rusty nails into gold, even as thou dost," said Nello, "and he had also something of the ass about him. But where is thy bird of strange plumage?"

Bratti was looking round, with an air of disappointment.

"Diavolo!" he said, with some vexation. "The bird's flown. It's true he was hungry, and I forgot him. But we shall find him in the Mercato, within scent of bread and savors, I'll answer for him."

"Let us make the round of the Mercato, then," said Nello.

"It isn't his feathers that puzzle me," continued Bratti, as they pushed their way together. "There isn't much in the way of cut and cloth on this side the Holy Sepulchre that can puzzle a Florentine."

"Or frighten him either," said Nello, "after he has seen an Englander or a German."

"No, no," said Bratti, cordially; "one may never lose sight of the Cupola and yet know the world, I hope. Besides, this stranger's clothes are good Italian merchandise, and the hose he wears were dyed in Ognissanti before ever they were dyed with salt water, as he says. But the riddle about him is——"

Here Bratti's explanation was interrupted by some jostling as they reached one of the entrances of the piazza, and before he could resume it they had caught sight of the enigmatical object they were in search of.

CHAPTER II.

BREAKFAST FOR LOVE.

AFTER Bratti had joined the knot of talkers, the young stranger, hopeless of learning what was the cause of the general agitation, and not much caring to know what was probably of little interest to any but born Florentines, soon became tired of waiting for Bratti's escort; and chose to stroll round the piazza, looking out for some vender of eatables who might happen to have less than the average curiosity about public news. But as if at the suggestion of a sudden thought, he thrust his hand into a purse or wallet that hung at his waist, and explored it again and again with a look of frustration.

"Not an obolus, by Jupiter!" he murmured, in a language

which was not Tuscan or even Italian. "I thought I had one poor piece left. I must get my breakfast for love, then!"

He had not gone many steps farther before it seemed likely that he had found a quarter of the market where that medium of exchange might not be rejected.

In a corner, away from any group of talkers, two mules were standing, well adorned with red tassels and collars. One of them carried wooden milk-vessels, the other a pair of panniers filled with herbs and salads. Resting her elbow on the neck of the mule that carried the milk, there leaned a young girl, apparently not more than sixteen, with a red hood surrounding her face, which was all the more baby-like in its prettiness from the entire concealment of her hair. The poor child, perhaps, was weary after her labor in the morning twilight in preparation for her walk to market from some castello three or four miles off, for she seemed to have gone to sleep in that half-standing, half-leaning posture. Nevertheless, our stranger had no compunction in awaking her; but the means he chose were so gentle, that it seemed to the damsel in her dream as if a little sprig of thyme had touched her lips while she was stooping to gather the herbs. The dream was broken, however, for she opened her blue baby-eyes, and started up with astonishment and confusion to see the young stranger standing close before her. She heard him speaking to her in a voice which seemed so strange and soft, that even if she had been more collected she would have taken it for granted that he said something hopelessly unintelligible to her, and her first movement was to turn her head a little away, and lift up a corner of her green serge mantle as a screen. He repeated his words,—

"Forgive me, pretty one, for awaking you. I'm dying with hunger, and the scent of milk makes breakfast seem more desirable than ever."

He had chosen the words "*muoio di fame*," because he knew they would be familiar to her ears; and he had uttered them playfully, with the intonation of a mendicant. This time he was understood; the corner of the mantle was dropped, and in a few moments a large cup of fragrant milk was held out to him. He paid no further compliments before raising it to his lips, and while he was drinking, the little maiden found courage to look up at the long dark curls of this singular-voiced stranger, who had asked for food in the tones of a beggar, but who, though his clothes were much damaged, was unlike any beggar she had ever seen.

While this process of survey was going on, there was another current of feeling that carried her hand into a bag which hung by the side of the mule, and when the stranger set down his cup, he saw a large piece of bread held out toward him, and caught a glance of the blue eyes that seemed intended as an encouragement to him to take this additional gift.

"But perhaps that is your own breakfast," he said. "No, I have had enough without payment. A thousand thanks, my gentle one."

There was no rejoinder in words; but the piece of bread was pushed a little nearer to him, as if in impatience at his refusal; and as the long dark eyes of the stranger rested on the baby-face, it seemed to be gathering more and more courage to look up and meet them.

"Ah, then, if I must take the bread," he said, laying his hand on it, "I shall get bolder still, and beg for another kiss to make the bread sweeter."

His speech was getting wonderfully intelligible, in spite of the strange voice, which had at first almost seemed a thing to make her cross herself. She blushed deeply, and lifted up a corner of her mantle to her mouth again. But just as the too presumptuous stranger was leaning forward, and had his fingers on the arm that held up the screening mantle, he was startled by a harsh voice close upon his ear.

"Who are *you*—with a murrain to you? No honest buyer, I'll warrant, but a hanger-on of the dicers—or something worse. Go! dance off, and find fitter company, or I'll give you a tune to a little quicker time than you'll like."

The young stranger drew back and looked at the speaker with a glance provokingly free from alarm and deprecation, and his slight expression of saucy amusement broke into a broad beaming smile as he surveyed the figure of his threatener. She was a stout but brawny woman, with a man's jerkin slipped over her green serge gamurra or gown, and the peaked hood of some departed mantle fastened round her sunburned face, which, under all its coarseness and premature wrinkles, showed a half-sad, half-ludicrous maternal resemblance to the tender baby-face of the little maiden—the sort of resemblance which often seems a more croaking, shudder-creating prophecy than that of the death's-head.

There was something irresistibly propitiating in that bright young smile, but Monna Ghita was not a woman to betray any weakness, and she went on speaking, apparently with heightened exasperation.

"Yes, yes, you can grin as well as other monkeys in cap and jerkin. You're a minstrel or a mountebank, I'll be sworn; you look for all the world as silly as a tumbler when he's been upside down and has got on his heels again. And what fool's tricks hast thou been after, Tessa?" she added, turning to her daughter, whose frightened face was more inviting to abuse. "Giving away the milk and victuals, it seems; ay, ay, thou'dst carry water in thy ears for any idle vagabond that didn't like to stoop for it, thou silly staring rabbit! Turn thy back, and lift the herbs out of the panniers, else I'll make thee say a few Aves without counting."

"Nay, Madonna," said the stranger, with a pleading smile, "don't be angry with your pretty Tessa for taking pity on a hungry traveller, who found himself unexpectedly without a quattrino. Your handsome face looks so well when it frowns, that I long to see it illuminated by a smile."

"*Va via!* I know what paste you are made of. You may tickle me with that straw a good long while before I shall laugh, I can tell you. Get along, with a bad Easter! else I'll make a beauty-spot or two on that face of yours that shall spoil your kissing on this side Advent."

As Monna Ghita lifted her formidable talons by way of complying with the first and last requisite of eloquence, Bratti, who had come up a minute or two before, had been saying to his companion, "What think you of this pretty parrot, Nello? Doesn't his tongue smack of Venice?"

"Nay, Bratti," said the barber in an undertone, "thy wisdom hath much of the ass in it, as I told thee just now; especially about the ears. This stranger is a Greek, else I'm not the barber who has had the sole and exclusive shaving of the excellent Demetrio, and drawn more than one sorry tooth from his learned jaw. And this youth might be taken to have come straight from Olympus—at least when he has had a touch of my razor."

"*Orsù!* Monna Ghita!" continued Nello, not sorry to see some sport; "what has happened to cause such a thunderstorm? Has this young stranger been misbehaving himself?"

"By San Giovanni!" said the cautious Bratti, who had not shaken off his original suspicions concerning the shabbily clad possessor of jewels, "he did right to run away from *me*, if he meant to get into mischief. I can swear that I found him under the Loggia de' Cerchi, with a ring on his finger such as I've seen worn by Bernardo Rucellai himself. Not another rusty nail's worth do I know about him."

"The fact is," said Nello, eying the stranger good-humoredly, "this *bello giovane* has been a little too presumptuous in admiring the charms of Monna Ghita, and has attempted to kiss her while her daughter's back is turned; for I observe that the pretty Tessa is too busy to look this way at present. Was it not so, Messer?" Nello concluded, in a tone of courtesy.

"You have divined the offence like a soothsayer," said the stranger, laughingly. "Only that I had not the good fortune to find Monna Ghita here at first. I begged a cup of milk from her daughter, and had accepted this gift of bread, for which I was making a humble offering of gratitude, before I had the higher pleasure of being face to face with these riper charms which I was perhaps too bold in admiring."

"*Va, va!* be off, every one of you, and stay in purgatory till I pay to get you out, will you?" said Monna Ghita, fiercely, elbowing Nello, and leading forward her mule so as to compel the stranger to jump aside. "Tessa, thou simpleton, bring forward thy mule a bit. the cart will be upon us."

As Tessa turned to take the mule's bridle, she cast one timid glance at the stranger, who was now moving with Nello out of the way of an approaching market-cart; and the glance was just long enough to seize the beckoning movement of his hand, which indicated that he had been watching for this opportunity of an adieu.

"*Ebbene,*" said Bratti, raising his voice to speak across the cart; "I leave you with Nello, young man, for there's no pushing my bag and basket any farther, and I have business at home. But you'll remember our bargain, because if you found Tessa without me, it was not my fault. Nello will show you my shop in the Ferravecchi, and I'll not turn my back on you."

"A thousand thanks, friend!" said the stranger, laughing, and then turned away with Nello up the narrow street which led most directly to the Piazza del Duomo.

CHAPTER III.

THE BARBER'S SHOP.

"To tell you the truth," said the young stranger to Nello, as they got a little clearer of the entangled vehicles and mules, "I am not sorry to be handed over by that patron of mine to one who has a less barbarous accent, and a less enigmatical business. Is it a common thing among you Florentines for an itinerant trafficker in broken glass and rags to talk of a shop where he sells lutes and swords?"

"Common? No: our Bratti is not a common man. He has a theory, and lives up to it, which is more than I can say for any philosopher I have the honor of shaving," answered Nello, whose loquacity, like an over-full bottle, could never pour forth a small dose. "Bratti means to extract the utmost possible amount of pleasure, that is to say, of hard bargaining, out of this life; winding it up with a bargain for the easiest possible passage through purgatory, by giving Holy Church his winnings when the game is over. He has had his will made to that effect on the cheapest terms a notary could be got for. But I have often said to him, 'Bratti, thy bargain is a limping one, and thou art on the lame side of it. Does it not make thee a little sad to look at the pictures of the

Paradiso? Thou wilt never be able there to chaffer for rags and rusty nails: the saints and angels want neither pins nor tinder; and except with San Bartolommeo, who carries his skin about in an inconvenient manner, I see no chance of thy making a bargain for second-hand clothing.' But God pardon me," added Nello, changing his tone, and crossing himself, "this light talk ill beseems a morning when Lorenzo lies dead, and the Muses are tearing their hair—always a painful thought to a barber; and you yourself, Messere, are probably under a cloud, for when a man of your speech and presence takes up with so sorry a night's lodging, it argues some misfortune to have befallen him."

"What Lorenzo is that whose death you speak of?" said the stranger, appearing to have dwelt with too anxious an interest on this point to have noticed the indirect inquiry that followed it.

"What Lorenzo? There is but one Lorenzo, I imagine, whose death could throw the Mercato into an uproar, set the lantern of the Duomo leaping in desperation, and cause the lions of the Republic to feel under an immediate necessity to devour one another. I mean Lorenzo de' Medici, the Pericles of our Athens—if I may make such a comparison in the ear of a Greek."

"Why not?" said the other, laughingly, "for I doubt whether Athens, even in the days of Pericles, could have produced so learned a barber."

"Yes, yes; I thought I could not be mistaken," said the rapid Nello, "else I have shaved the venerable Demetrio Calcondila to little purpose; but pardon me, I am lost in wonder: your Italian is better than his, though he has been in Italy forty years—better even than that of the accomplished Marullo, who may be said to have married the Italic Muse in more senses than one, since he has married our learned and lovely Alessandra Scala."

"It will lighten your wonder to know that I come of a Greek stock planted in Italian soil much longer than the mulberry-trees which have taken so kindly to it. I was born at Bari, and my—I mean, I was brought up by an Italian—and, in fact, I am a Greek very much as your peaches are Persian.

The Greek dye was subdued in me, I suppose, till I had been dipped over again by long abode and much travel in the land of gods and heroes. And, to confess something of my private affairs to you, this same Greek dye, with a few ancient gems I have about me, is the only fortune shipwreck has left me. But—when the towers fall, you know it is an ill business for the small nest-builders—the death of your Pericles makes me wish I had rather turned my steps toward Rome, as I should have done but for a fallacious Minerva in the shape of an Augustinian monk. 'At Rome,' he said, 'you will be lost in a crowd of hungry scholars, but at Florence every corner is penetrated by the sunshine of Lorenzo's patronage: Florence is the best market in Italy for such commodities as yours.'"

"*Gnaffè*, and so it will remain, I hope," said Nello. "Lorenzo was not the only patron and judge of learning in our city —Heaven forbid! Because he was a large melon, every other Florentine is not a pumpkin, I suppose. Have we not Bernardo Rucellai, and Alamanno Rinuccini, and plenty more? And if you want to be informed on such matters, I, Nello, am your man. It seems to me a thousand years till I can be of service to a *bel erudito* like yourself. And, first of all, in the matter of your hair. That beard, my fine young man, must be parted with, were it as dear to you as the nymph of your dreams. Here at Florence, we love not to see a man with his nose projecting over a cascade of hair. But, remember, you will have passed the Rubicon, when once you have been shaven: if you repent, and let your beard grow after it has acquired stoutness by a struggle with the razor, your mouth will by and by show no longer what Messer Angelo calls the divine prerogative of lips, but will appear like a dark cavern fringed with horrent brambles."

"That is a terrible prophecy," said the Greek, "especially if your Florentine maidens are many of them as pretty as the little Tessa I stole a kiss from this morning."

"Tessa? she is a rough-handed contadina. you will rise into the favor of dames who bring no scent of the mule-stables with them. But to that end, you must not have the air of a *sgherro*, or a man of evil repute: you must look like a courtier, and a scholar of the more polished sort, such as our

Pietro Crinito—like one who sins among well-bred, well-fed people, and not one who sucks down vile *vino di sotto* in a chance tavern."

"With all my heart," said the stranger. "If the Florentine Graces demand it, I am willing to give up this small matter of my beard, but——"

"Yes, yes," interrupted Nello. "I know what you would say. It is the *bella zazzera*—the hyacinthine locks, you do not choose to part with; and there is no need. Just a little pruning—ecco!—and you will look not unlike the illustrious prince Pico di Mirandola in his prime. And here we are in good time in the Piazza San Giovanni, and at the door of my shop. But you are pausing, I see. naturally, you want to look at our wonder of the world, our Duomo, our Santa Maria del Fiore. Well, well, a mere glance, but I beseech you to leave a closer survey till you have been shaved: I am quivering with the inspiration of my art even to the very edge of my razor. Ah, then, come round this way."

The mercurial barber seized the arm of the stranger, and led him to a point, on the south side of the piazza, from which he could see at once the huge dark shell of the cupola, the slender soaring grace of Giotto's campanile, and the quaint octagon of San Giovanni in front of them, showing its unique gates of storied bronze, which still bore the somewhat dimmed glory of their original gilding. The inlaid marbles were then fresher in their pink, and white, and purple, than they are now, when the winters of four centuries have turned their white to the rich ochre of well-mellowed meerschaum; the façade of the cathedral did not stand ignominious in faded stucco, but had upon it the magnificent promise of the half-completed marble inlaying and statued niches, which Giotto had devised a hundred and fifty years before; and as the campanile in all its harmonious variety of color and form led the eyes upward, high into the clear air of this April morning, it seemed a prophetic symbol, telling that human life must somehow and some time shape itself into accord with that pure aspiring beauty.

But this was not the impression it appeared to produce on the Greek. His eyes were irresistibly led upward, but as he stood with his arms folded and his curls falling backward, there was a slight touch of scorn on his lip, and when his eyes fell again they glanced round with a scanning coolness which was rather piquing to Nello's Florentine spirit.

"Well, my fine young man," he said, with some impatience, "you seem to make as little of our Cathedral as if you were the Angel Gabriel come straight from Paradise. I should like to know if you have ever seen finer work than our Giotto's tower, or any cupola that would not look a mere mushroom by the side of Brunelleschi's there, or any marbles finer or more cunningly wrought than these that our Signoria got from far-off quarries, at a price that would buy a dukedom. Come, now, have you ever seen anything to equal them?"

"If you asked me that question with a scimitar at my throat, after the Turkish fashion, or even your own razor," said the young Greek, smiling gayly, and moving on toward the gates of the Baptistery, "I dare say you might get a confession of the true faith from me. But with my throat free from peril, I venture to tell you that your buildings smack too much of Christian barbarism for my taste. I have a shuddering sense of what there is inside—hideous smoked Madonnas; fleshless saints in mosaic, staring down idiotic astonishment and rebuke from the apse; skin-clad skeletons hanging on crosses, or stuck all over with arrows, or stretched on gridirons; women and monks with heads aside in perpetual lamentation. I have seen enough of those wry-necked favorites of heaven at Constantinople. But what is this bronze door rough with imagery? These women's figures seem moulded in a different spirit from those starved and staring saints I spoke of: these heads in high relief speak of a human mind within them, instead of looking like an index to perpetual spasms and colic."

"Yes, yes," said Nello, with some triumph. "I think we shall show you by and by that our Florentine art is not in a state of barbarism. These gates, my fine young man, were moulded half a century ago, by our Lorenzo Ghiberti, when he counted hardly so many years as you do."

"Ah, I remember," said the stranger, turning away, like one whose appetite for contemplation was soon satisfied. "I have heard that your Tuscan sculptors and painters have been studying the antique a little. But with monks for models, and the legends of mad hermits and martyrs for subjects, the vision of Olympus itself would be of small use to them."

"I understand," said Nello, with a significant shrug, as they walked along. "You are of the same mind as Michele Marullo, ay, and as Angelo Poliziano himself, in spite of his canonicate, when he relaxes himself a little in my shop after his lectures, and talks of the gods awaking from their long sleep and making the woods and streams vital once more. But he rails against the Roman scholars who want to make us all talk Latin again: 'My ears,' he says, 'are sufficiently flayed by the barbarisms of the learned, and if the vulgar are to talk Latin I would as soon have been in Florence the day they took to beating all the kettles in the city because the bells were not enough to stay the wrath of the saints.' Ah, Messer Greco, if you want to know the flavor of our scholarship, you must frequent my shop: it is the focus of Florentine intellect, and in that sense the navel of the earth—as my great predecessor, Burchiello, said of *his* shop, on the more frivolous pretension that his street of the Calimara was the centre of our city. And here we are at the sign of 'Apollo and the Razor.' Apollo, you see, is bestowing the razor on the Triptolemus of our craft, the first reaper of beards, the sublime *Anonimo*, whose mysterious identity is indicated by a shadowy hand."

"I see thou hast had custom already, Sandro," continued Nello, addressing a solemn-looking dark-eyed youth, who made way for them on the threshold. "And now make all clear for this signor to sit down. And prepare the finest-scented lather, for he has a learned and a handsome chin."

"You have a pleasant little adytum there, I see," said the stranger, looking through a latticed screen which divided the shop from a room of about equal size, opening into a still smaller walled enclosure, where a few bays and laurels surrounded a stone Hermes. "I suppose your conclave of *eruditi* meets there?"

"There, and not less in my shop," said Nello, leading the way into the inner room, in which were some benches, a table, with one book in manuscript and one printed in capitals lying open upon it, a lute, a few oil-sketches, and a model or two of hands and ancient masks. "For my shop is a no less fitting haunt of the Muses, as you will acknowledge when you feel the sudden illumination of understanding and the serene vigor of inspiration that will come to you with a clear chin. Ah! you can make that lute discourse, I perceive. I, too, have some skill that way, though the serenata is useless when daylight discloses a visage like mine, looking no fresher than an apple that has stood the winter. But look at that sketch: it is a fancy of Piero di Cosimo's, a strange freakish painter, who says he saw it by long looking at a mouldy wall."

The sketch Nello pointed to represented three masks—one a drunken laughing Satyr, another a sorrowing Magdalen, and the third, which lay between them, the rigid, cold face of a Stoic: the masks rested obliquely on the lap of a little child, whose cherub features rose above them with something of the supernal promise in the gaze which painters had by that time learned to give to the Divine Infant.

"A symbolical picture, I see," said the young Greek, touching the lute while he spoke, so as to bring out a slight musical murmur. "The child, perhaps, is the Golden Age, wanting neither worship nor philosophy And the Golden Age can always come back as long as men are born in the form of babies, and don't come into the world in cassock or furred mantle. Or, the child may mean the wise philosophy of Epicurus, removed alike from the gross, the sad, and the severe."

"Ah! everybody has his own interpretation for that picture," said Nello; "and if you ask Piero himself what he meant by it, he says his pictures are an appendix which Messer Domeneddio has been pleased to make to the universe, and if any man is in doubt what they mean, he had better inquire of Holy Church. He has been asked to paint a picture after the sketch, but he puts his fingers to his ears and shakes his head at that; the fancy is past, he says—a strange animal, our Piero. But now all is ready for your initiation into the mysteries of the razor.

"Mysteries they may well be called," continued the barber, with rising spirits at the prospect of a long monologue, as he imprisoned the young Greek in the shroud-like shaving-cloth; "mysteries of Minerva and the Graces. I get the flower of men's thoughts, because I seize them in the first moment after shaving. (Ah! you wince a little at the lather; it tickles the outlying limits of the nose, I admit.) And that is what makes the peculiar fitness of a barber's shop to become a resort of wit and learning. For, look now at a druggist's shop: there is a dull conclave at the sign of 'The Moor,' that pretends to rival mine; but what sort of inspiration, I beseech you, can be got from the scent of nauseous vegetable decoctions?—to say nothing of the fact that you no sooner pass the threshold than you see a doctor of physic, like a gigantic spider disguised in fur and scarlet, waiting for his prey; or even see him blocking up the doorway seated on a bony hack, inspecting saliva. (Your chin a little elevated, if it please you: contemplate that angel who is blowing the trumpet at you from the ceiling. I had it painted expressly for the regulation of my clients' chins.) Besides, your druggist, who herborizes and decocts, is a man of prejudices: he has poisoned people according to a system, and is obliged to stand up for his system to justify the consequences. Now a barber can be dispassionate; the only thing he necessarily stands by is the razor, always providing he is not an author. That was the flaw in my great predecessor Burchiello: he was a poet, and had consequently a prejudice about his own poetry. I have escaped that; I saw very early that authorship is a narrowing business, in conflict with the liberal art of the razor, which demands an impartial affection for all men's chins. Ecco, Messer! the outline of your chin and lip is as clear as a maiden's: and now fix your mind on a knotty question—ask yourself whether you are bound to spell Virgil with an *i* or an *e*, and say if you do not feel an unwonted clearness on the point. Only, if you decide for the *i*, keep it to yourself till your fortune is made, for the *e* hath the stronger following in Florence. Ah! I think I see a gleam of still quicker wit in your eye. I have it on the authority of our young Niccolò Macchiavelli, himself keen enough to discern *il pelo nell' uovo*, as we say, and a great lover of delicate shaving, though his beard is hardly of two years' date, that no sooner do the hairs begin to push themselves, than he perceives a certain grossness of apprehension creeping over him."

"Suppose you let me look at myself," said the stranger, laughing. "The happy effect on my intellect is perhaps obstructed by a little doubt as to the effect of my appearance."

"Behold yourself in this mirror, then; it is a Venetian mirror from Murano, the true *nosce teipsum*, as I have named it, compared with which the finest mirror of steel or silver is mere darkness. See now, how by diligent shaving, the nether region of your face may preserve its human outline, instead of presenting no distinction from the physiognomy of a bearded owl or a Barbary ape. I have seen men whose beards have so invaded their cheeks, that one might have pitied them as the victims of a sad, brutalizing chastisement befitting our Dante's Inferno, if they had not seemed to strut with a strange triumph in their extravagant hairiness."

"It seems to me," said the Greek, still looking into the mirror, "that you have taken away some of my capital with your razor—I mean a year or two of age which might have won me more ready credit for my learning. Under the inspection of a patron whose vision has grown somewhat dim, I shall have a perilous resemblance to a maiden of eighteen in the disguise of hose and jerkin."

"Not at all," said Nello, proceeding to clip the too extravagant curls, "your proportions are not those of a maiden. And for your age, I myself remember seeing Angelo Poliziano begin his lectures on the Latin language when he had a younger beard than yours; and between ourselves, his juvenile ugliness was not less signal than his precocious scholarship. Whereas you—no, no, your age is not against you; but between ourselves, let me hint to you that your being a Greek, though it be only an Apulian Greek, is not in your favor. Certain of our scholars hold that your Greek learning is but a wayside degenerate plant until it has been transplanted into Italian brains, and that now there is such a plentiful crop of the superior quality, your native teachers are mere propagators of degeneracy. Ecco! your curls are now of the right proportion to neck and shoulders; rise, Messer, and I will free you from the encumbrance of this cloth. *Gnaffè!* I almost advise you to retain the faded jerkin and hose a little longer; they give you the air of a fallen prince."

"But the question is," said the young Greek, leaning against the high back of a chair, and returning Nello's contemplative admiration with a look of inquiring anxiety; "the question is, in what quarter I am to carry my princely air, so as to rise from the said fallen condition. If your Florentine patrons of learning share this scholarly hostility to the Greeks, I see not how your city can be a hospitable refuge for me, as you seemed to say just now."

"*Pian piano*—not so fast," said Nello, sticking his thumbs into his belt and nodding to Sandro to restore order. "I will not conceal from you that there is a prejudice against Greeks among us; and though, as a barber unsnared by authorship, I share no prejudices, I must admit that the Greeks are not always such pretty youngsters as yourself: their erudition is often of an uncombed, unmannerly aspect, and incrusted with a barbarous utterance of Italian, that makes their converse hardly more euphonious than that of a Tedesco in a state of vinous loquacity. And then, again, excuse me—we Florentines have liberal ideas about speech, and consider that an instrument which can flatter and promise so cleverly as the tongue, must have been partly made for those purposes; and that truth is a riddle for eyes and wit to discover, which it were a mere spoiling of sport for the tongue to betray. Still we have our limits beyond which we call dissimulation treachery. But it is said of the Greeks that their honesty begins at what is the hanging-point with us, and that since the old Furies went to sleep, your Christian Greek is of so easy a conscience that he would make a stepping-stone of his father's corpse."

The flush on the stranger's face indicated what seemed so natural a movement of resentment, that the good-natured Nello hastened to atone for his want of reticence.

"Be not offended, *bel giovane;* I am but repeating what I hear in my shop; as you may perceive, my eloquence is simply the cream which I skim off my clients' talk. Heaven forbid I should fetter my impartiality by entertaining an opinion. And for that same scholarly objection to the Greeks," added

Nello, in a more mocking tone, and with a significant grimace, "the fact is, you are heretics, Messer; jealousy has nothing to do with it: if you would just change your opinion about leaven, and alter your Doxology a little, our Italian scholars would think it a thousand years till they could give up their chairs to you. Yes, yes; it is chiefly religious scruple, and partly also the authority of a great classic,—Juvenal, is it not? He, I gather, had his bile as much stirred by the swarm of Greeks as our Messer Angelo, who is fond of quoting some passage about their incorrigible impudence—*audacia perdita.*"

"Pooh! the passage is a compliment," said the Greek, who had recovered himself, and seemed wise enough to take the matter gayly,—

"'Ingenium velox, audacia perdita, sermo
Promptus, et Isæo torrentior.'

A rapid intellect and ready eloquence may carry off a little impudence."

"Assuredly," said Nello. "And since, as I see, you know Latin literature as well as Greek, you will not fall into the mistake of Giovanni Argiropulo, who ran full tilt against Cicero, and pronounced him all but a pumpkin-head. For, let me give you one bit of advice, young man—trust a barber who has shaved the best chins, and kept his eyes and ears open for twenty years—oil your tongue well when you talk of the ancient Latin writers, and give it an extra dip when you talk of the modern. A wise Greek may win favor among us; witness our excellent Demetrio, who is loved by many, and not hated immoderately even by the most renowned scholars."

"I discern the wisdom of your advice so clearly," said the Greek, with the bright smile which was continually lighting up the fine form and color of his young face, "that I will ask you for a little more. Who now, for example, would be the most likely patron for me? Is there a son of Lorenzo who inherits his tastes? Or is there any other wealthy Florentine specially addicted to purchasing antique gems? I have a fine Cleopatra cut in sardonyx, and one or two other intaglios and cameos, both curious and beautiful, worthy of being added to the cabinet of a prince. Happily, I had taken the precaution of fastening them within the lining of my doublet before I set out on my voyage. Moreover, I should like to raise a small sum for my present need on this ring of mine" (here he took out the ring and replaced it on his finger), "if you could recommend me to any honest trafficker."

"Let us see, let us see," said Nello, perusing the floor, and walking up and down the length of his shop. "This is no time to apply to Piero de' Medici, though he has the will to make such purchases if he could always spare the money; but I think it is another sort of Cleopatra that he covets most. . . . Yes, yes, I have it. What you want is a man of wealth, and influence, and scholarly tastes—not one of your learned porcupines, bristling all over with critical tests, but one whose Greek and Latin are of a comfortable laxity. And that man is Bartolommeo Scala, the secretary of our Republic. He came to Florence as a poor adventurer himself—a miller's son —a ' branny monster,' as he has been nicknamed by our honey-lipped Poliziano, who agrees with him as well as my teeth agree with lemon-juice. And, by the by, that may be a reason why the secretary may be the more ready to do a good turn to a strange scholar. For, between you and me, *bel giovane*—trust a barber who has shaved the best scholars—friendliness is much such a steed as Ser Benghi's: it will hardly show much alacrity unless it has got the thistle of hatred under its tail. However, the secretary is a man who'll keep his word to you, even to the halving of a fennel-seed; and he is not unlikely to buy some of your gems."

"But how am I to get at this great man?" said the Greek, rather impatiently.

"I was coming to that," said Nello. "Just now everybody of any public importance will be full of Lorenzo's death, and a stranger may find it difficult to get any notice. But in the mean time, I could take you to a man who, if he has a mind, can help you to a chance of a favorable interview with Scala sooner than anybody else in Florence—worth seeing for his own sake too, to say nothing of his collections, or of his daughter Romola, who is as fair as the Florentine lily before it got quarrelsome and turned red."

"But if this father of the beautiful Romola makes collections, why should he not like to buy some of my gems himself?"

Nello shrugged his shoulders. "For two good reasons—want of sight to look at the gems, and want of money to pay for them. Our old Bardo de' Bardi is so blind that he can see no more of his daughter than, as he says, a glimmering of something bright when she comes very near him: doubtless her golden hair, which, as Messer Luigi Pulci says of his Meridiana's, '*raggia come stella per sereno.*' Ah! here come some clients of mine, and I shouldn't wonder if one of them could serve your turn about that ring."

CHAPTER IV.

FIRST IMPRESSIONS.

"GOOD-DAY, Messer Domenico," said Nello to the foremost of the two visitors who entered the shop, while he nodded silently to the other. "You come as opportunely as cheese on macaroni. Ah! you are in haste—wish to be shaved without delay—ecco! And this is a morning when every one has grave matter on his mind. Florence orphaned—the very pivot of Italy snatched away—heaven itself at a loss what to do next. *Oimè!* Well, well; the sun is nevertheless travelling on toward dinner-time again; and as I was saying, you come like cheese ready grated. For this young stranger was wishing for an honorable trader who would advance him a sum on a certain ring of value, and if I had counted every goldsmith and money-lender in Florence on my fingers, I couldn't have found a better name than Menico Cennini. Besides, he hath other ware in which you deal—Greek learning, and young eyes—a double implement which you printers are always in need of."

The grave elderly man, son of that Bernardo Cennini who, twenty years before, having heard of the new process of printing carried on by Germans, had cast his own types in

Florence, remained necessarily in lathered silence and passivity while Nello showered this talk in his ears, but turned a slow sideway gaze on the stranger.

"This fine young man has unlimited Greek, Latin, or Italian at your service," continued Nello, fond of interpreting by very ample paraphrase. "He is as great a wonder of juvenile learning as Francesco Filelfo or our own incomparable Poliziano. A second Guarino, too, for he has had the misfortune to be shipwrecked, and has doubtless lost a store of precious manuscripts that might have contributed some correctness even to your correct editions, Domenico. Fortunately, he has rescued a few gems of rare value. His name is—you said your name, Messer, was——?"

"Tito Melema," said the stranger, slipping the ring from his finger, and presenting it to Cennini, whom Nello, not less rapid with his razor than with his tongue, had now released from the shaving-cloth.

Meanwhile the man who had entered the shop in company with the goldsmith—a tall figure, about fifty, with a short trimmed beard, wearing an old felt hat and a threadbare mantle—had kept his eye fixed on the Greek, and now said abruptly,—

"Young man, I am painting a picture of Sinon deceiving old Priam, and I should be glad of your face for my Sinon, if you'd give me a sitting."

Tito Melema started and looked round with a pale astonishment in his face as if at a sudden accusation; but Nello left him no time to feel at a loss for an answer: "Piero," said the barber, "thou art the most extraordinary compound of humors and fancies ever packed into a human skin. What trick wilt thou play with the fine visage of this young scholar to make it suit thy traitor? Ask him rather to turn his eyes upward, and thou mayst make a Saint Sebastian of him that will draw troops of devout women; or, if thou art in a classical vein, put myrtle about his curls and make him a young Bacchus, or say rather a Phœbus Apollo, for his face is as warm and bright as a summer morning; it made me his friend in the space of a 'credo.'"

"Ay, Nello," said the painter, speaking with abrupt pauses;

"and if thy tongue can leave off its everlasting chirping long enough for thy understanding to consider the matter, thou mayst see that thou hast just shown the reason why the face of Messere will suit my traitor. A perfect traitor should have a face which vice can write no marks on—lips that will lie with a dimpled smile—eyes of such agate-like brightness and depth that no infamy can dull them—cheeks that will rise from a murder and not look haggard. I say not this young man is a traitor: I mean, he has a face that would make him the more perfect traitor if he had the heart of one, which is saying neither more nor less than that he has a beautiful face, informed with rich young blood, that will be nourished enough by food, and keep its color without much help of virtue. He may have the heart of a hero along with it; I aver nothing to the contrary. Ask Domenico there if the lapidaries can always tell a gem by the sight alone. And now I'm going to put the tow in my ears, for thy chatter and the bells together are more than I can endure: so say no more to me, but trim my beard."

With these last words Piero (called "di Cosimo," from his master, Cosimo Rosselli) drew out two bits of tow, stuffed them in his ears, and placed himself in the chair before Nello, who shrugged his shoulders and cast a grimacing look of intelligence at the Greek as much as to say, "A whimsical fellow, you perceive! Everybody holds his speeches as mere jokes."

Tito, who had stood transfixed, with his long dark eyes resting on the unknown man who had addressed him so equivocally, seemed recalled to his self-command by Piero's change of position, and apparently satisfied with his explanation, was again giving his attention to Cennini, who presently said,—

"This is a curious and valuable ring, young man. This intaglio of the fish with the crested serpent above it, in the black stratum of the onyx, or rather nicolo, is well shown by the surrounding blue of the upper stratum. The ring has, doubtless, a history?" added Cennini, looking up keenly at the young stranger.

"Yes, indeed," said Tito, meeting the scrutiny very frankly. "The ring was found in Sicily, and I have understood from those who busy themselves with gems and sigils, that both the stone and intaglio are of virtue to make the wearer fortunate, especially at sea, and also to restore to him whatever he may have lost. But," he continued, smiling, "though I have worn it constantly since I quitted Greece, it has not made me altogether fortunate at sea, you perceive, unless I am to count escape from drowning as a sufficient proof of its virtue. It remains to be seen whether my lost chest will come to light; but to lose no chance of such a result, Messer, I will pray you only to hold the ring for a short space as pledge for a small sum far beneath its value, and I will redeem it as soon as I can dispose of certain other gems which are secured within my doublet, or indeed as soon as I can earn something by any scholarly employment, if I may be so fortunate as to meet with such."

"That may be seen, young man, if you will come with me," said Cennini. "My brother Pietro, who is a better judge of scholarship than I, will perhaps be able to supply you with a task that may test your capabilities. Meanwhile, take back your ring until I can hand you the necessary florins, and, if it please you, come along with me."

"Yes, yes," said Nello, "go with Messer Domenico, you cannot go in better company; he was born under the constellation that gives a man skill, riches, and integrity, whatever that constellation may be, which is of the less consequence because babies can't choose their own horoscopes, and, indeed, if they could, there might be an inconvenient rush of babies at particular epochs. Besides, our Phœnix, the incomparable Pico, has shown that your horoscopes are all a nonsensical dream—which is the less troublesome opinion. *Addio! bel giovane!* don't forget to come back to me."

"No fear of that," said Tito, beckoning a farewell, as he turned round his bright face at the door. "You are to do me a great service:—that is the most positive security for your seeing me again."

"Say what thou wilt, Piero," said Nello, as the young stranger disappeared, "I shall never look at such an outside as that without taking it as a sign of a lovable nature. Why, thou wilt say next that Lionardo, whom thou art always raving about, ought to have made his Judas as beautiful as St.

John! But thou art as deaf as the top of Mount Morello with that accursed tow in thy ears. Well, well: I'll get a little more of this young man's history from him before I take him to Bardo Bardi."

CHAPTER V.

THE BLIND SCHOLAR AND HIS DAUGHTER.

The Via de' Bardi, a street noted in the history of Florence, lies in Oltrarno, or that portion of the city which clothes the southern bank of the river. It extends from the Ponte Vecchio to the Piazza de' Mozzi at the head of the Ponte alle Grazie; its right-hand line of houses and walls being backed by the rather steep ascent which in the fifteenth century was known as the hill of Bogoli, the famous stone-quarry whence the city got its pavement—of dangerously unstable consistence when penetrated by rains; its left-hand buildings flanking the river and making on their northern side a length of quaint, irregularly pierced façade, of which the waters give a softened loving reflection as the sun begins to decline toward the western heights. But quaint as these buildings are, some of them seem to the historical memory a too modern substitute for the famous houses of the Bardi family destroyed by popular rage in the middle of the fourteenth century.

They were a proud and energetic stock, these Bardi; conspicuous among those who clutched the sword in the earliest world-famous quarrels of Florentines with Florentines, when the narrow streets were darkened with the high towers of the nobles, and when the old tutelar god Mars, as he saw the gutters reddened with neighbors' blood, might well have smiled at the centuries of lip-service paid to his rival, the Baptist. But the Bardi hands were of the sort that not only clutch the sword-hilt with vigor, but love the more delicate pleasure of fingering minted metal: they were matched, too, with true Florentine eyes, capable of discerning that power was to be won by other means than by rending and riving, and by the middle of the fourteenth century we find them risen from their original condition of *popolani* to be possessors, by purchase, of lands and strongholds, and the feudal dignity of Counts of Vernio, disturbing to the jealousy of their republican fellow-citizens. These lordly purchases are explained by our seeing the Bardi disastrously signalized only a few years later as standing in the very front of European commerce—the Christian Rothschilds of that time—undertaking to furnish specie for the wars of our Edward the Third, and having revenues "in kind" made over to them; especially in wool, most precious of freights for Florentine galleys. Their august debtor left them with an august deficit, and alarmed Sicilian creditors made a too sudden demand for the payment of deposits, causing a ruinous shock to the credit of the Bardi and of associated houses, which was felt as a commercial calamity along all the coasts of the Mediterranean. But, like more modern bankrupts, they did not, for all that, hide their heads in humiliation; on the contrary, they seemed to have held them higher than ever, and to have been among the most arrogant of those grandees who, under certain noteworthy circumstances, open to all who will read the honest pages of Giovanni Villani, drew upon themselves the exasperation of the armed people in 1343. The Bardi, who had made themselves fast in their street between the two bridges, kept these narrow inlets, like panthers at bay, against the oncoming gonfalons of the people, and were only made to give way by an assault from the hill behind them. Their houses by the river, to the number of twenty-two (*palagi e case grandi*), were sacked and burned, and many among the chief of those who bore the Bardi name were driven from the city. But an old Florentine family was many-rooted, and we find the Bardi maintaining importance and rising again and again to the surface of Florentine affairs in a more or less creditable manner, implying an untold family history that would have included even more vicissitudes and contrasts of dignity and disgrace, of wealth and poverty, than are usually seen on the background of wide kinship.[1]

[1] A sign that such contrasts were peculiarly frequent in Florence is the fact that Saint Antonine, Prior of San Marco, and afterward archbishop, in the first half of this fifteenth century, founded the society of Buonuomini di San Martino (Good Men of St. Martin) with the main

But the Bardi never resumed their proprietorship in the old street on the banks of the river, which in 1492 had long been associated with other names of mark, and especially with the Neri, who possessed a considerable range of houses on the side toward the hill.

In one of these Neri houses there lived, however, a descendant of the Bardi, and of that very branch which a century and a half before had become Counts of Vernio: a descendant who had inherited the old family pride and energy, the old love of pre-eminence, the old desire to leave a lasting track of his footsteps on the fast-whirling earth. But the family passions lived on in him under altered conditions: this descendant of the Bardi was not a man swift in street warfare, or one who loved to play the signor, fortifying strongholds and asserting the right to hang vassals, or a merchant and usurer of keen daring, who delighted in the generalship of wide commercial schemes: he was a man with a deep-veined hand cramped by much copying of manuscripts, who ate sparing dinners, and wore threadbare clothes, at first from choice and at last from necessity; who sat among his books and his marble fragments of the past, and saw them only by the light of those far-off younger days which still shone in his memory: he was a moneyless, blind old scholar—the Bardo de' Bardi to whom Nello, the barber, had promised to introduce the young Greek, Tito Melema.

The house in which Bardo lived was situated on the side of the street nearest the hill, and was one of those large sombre masses of stone building pierced by comparatively small windows, and surmounted by what may be called a roofed terrace or loggia, of which there are many examples still to be seen in the venerable city. Grim doors, with conspicuous scrolled hinges, having high up on each side of them a small window defended by iron bars, opened on a groined entrance-court,

---

object of succoring the *poveri vergognosi*—in other words, paupers of good family. In the records of the famous Panciatichi family we find a certain Girolamo in this century who was reduced to such a state of poverty that he was obliged to seek charity for the mere means of sustaining life, though other members of his family were enormously wealthy.

empty of everything but a massive lamp-iron suspended from the centre of the groin. A smaller grim door on the left hand admitted to the stone staircase, and the rooms on the ground floor. These last were used as a warehouse by the proprietor; so was the first floor; and both were filled with precious stores, destined to be carried, some perhaps to the banks of the Scheldt, some to the shores of Africa, some to the isles of the Ægean, or to the banks of the Euxine. Maso, the old serving-man, when he returned from the Mercato with the stock of cheap vegetables, had to make his slow way up to the second story before he reached the door of his master, Bardo, through which we are about to enter only a few mornings after Nello's conversation with the Greek.

We follow Maso across the antechamber to the door on the left hand, through which we pass as he opens it. He merely looks in and nods, while a clear young voice says, "Ah, you are come back, Maso. It is well. We have wanted nothing."

The voice came from the farther end of a long, spacious room surrounded with shelves, on which books and antiquities were arranged in scrupulous order. Here and there, on separate stands in front of the shelves, were placed a beautiful feminine torso; a headless statue, with an uplifted muscular arm wielding a bladeless sword; rounded, dimpled, infantine limbs severed from the trunk, inviting the lips to kiss the cold marble; some well-preserved Roman busts; and two or three vases from Magna Grecia. A large table in the centre was covered with antique bronze lamps and small vessels in dark pottery. The color of these objects was chiefly pale or sombre: the vellum bindings, with their deep-ridged backs, gave little relief to the marble, livid with long burial; the once splendid patch of carpet at the farther end of the room had long been worn to dimness; the dark bronzes wanted sunlight upon them to bring out their tinge of green, and the sun was not yet high enough to send gleams of brightness through the narrow windows that looked on the Via de' Bardi.

The only spot of bright color in the room was made by the hair of a tall maiden of seventeen or eighteen, who was standing before a carved *leggio*, or reading-desk, such as is often seen in the choirs of Italian churches. The hair was of a reddish gold color, enriched by an unbroken small ripple, such as may be seen in the sunset clouds on grandest autumnal evenings. It was confined by a black fillet above her small ears, from which it rippled forward again, and made a natural veil for her neck above her square-cut gown of black *rascia*, or serge. Her eyes were bent on a large volume placed before her: one long white hand rested on the reading-desk, and the other clasped the back of her father's chair.

The blind father sat with head uplifted and turned a little aside toward his daughter, as if he were looking at her. His delicate paleness, set off by the black velvet cap which surmounted his drooping white hair, made all the more perceptible the likeness between his aged features and those of the young maiden, whose cheeks were also without any tinge of the rose. There was the same refinement of brow and nostril in both, counterbalanced by a full though firm mouth and powerful chin, which gave an expression of proud tenacity and latent impetuousness: an expression carried out in the backward poise of the girl's head, and the grand line of her neck and shoulders. It was a type of face of which one could not venture to say whether it would inspire love or only that unwilling admiration which is mixed with dread: the question must be decided by the eyes, which often seemed charged with a more direct message from the soul. But the eyes of the father had long been silent, and the eyes of the daughter were bent on the Latin pages of Politian's "Miscellanea," from which she was reading aloud at the eightieth chapter, to the following effect:—

"There was a certain nymph of Thebes named Chariclo, especially dear to Pallas; and this nymph was the mother of Teiresias. But once when in the heat of summer, Pallas, in company with Chariclo, was bathing her disrobed limbs in the Heliconian Hippocrene, it happened that Teiresias coming as a hunter to quench his thirst at the same fountain, inadvertently beheld Minerva unveiled, and immediately became blind. For it is declared in the Saturnian laws, that he who beholds the gods against their will, shall atone for it by a heavy penalty. . . . When Teiresias had fallen into this calamity, Pallas, moved by the tears of Chariclo, endowed him with prophecy and length of days, and even caused his prudence and wisdom to continue after he had entered among the shades, so that an oracle spake from his tomb: and she gave him a staff, wherewith, as by a guide, he might walk without stumbling. . . . And hence, Nonnus, in the fifth book of the 'Dionysiaca,' introduces Actæon exclaiming that he calls Teiresias happy, since, without dying, and with the loss of his eyesight merely, he had beheld Minerva unveiled, and thus, though blind, could forevermore carry her image in his soul."

At this point in the reading, the daughter's hand slipped from the back of the chair and met her father's, which he had that moment uplifted; but she had not looked round, and was going on, though with a voice a little altered by some suppressed feeling, to read the Greek quotation from Nonnus, when the old man said,—

"Stay, Romola; reach me my own copy of Nonnus. It is a more correct copy than any in Poliziano's hands, for I made emendations in it which have not yet been communicated to any man. I finished it in 1477, when my sight was fast failing me."

Romola walked to the farther end of the room, with the queenly step which was the simple action of her tall, finely wrought frame, without the slightest conscious adjustment of herself.

"Is it in the right place, Romola?" asked Bardo, who was perpetually seeking the assurance that the outward fact continued to correspond with the image which lived to the minutest detail in his mind.

"Yes, father; at the west end of the room, on the third shelf from the bottom, behind the bust of Hadrian, above Apollonius Rhodius and Callimachus, and below Lucan and Silius Italicus."

As Romola said this, a fine ear would have detected in her clear voice and distinct utterance a faint suggestion of weariness struggling with habitual patience. But as she approached her father and saw his arms stretched out a little with nervous excitement to seize the volume, her hazel eyes filled with pity; she hastened to lay the book on his lap, and kneeled down by him, looking up at him as if she believed that the love in her face must surely make its way through the dark obstruction that shut out everything else. At that moment the doubtful attractiveness of Romola's face, in which pride and passion seemed to be quivering in the balance with native refinement and intelligence, was transfigured to the most lovable womanliness by mingled pity and affection; it was evident that the deepest fount of feeling within her had not yet wrought its way to the less changeful features, and only found its outlet through her eyes.

But the father, unconscious of that soft radiance, looked flushed and agitated as his hands explored the edges and back of the large book.

"The vellum is yellowed in these thirteen years, Romola."

"Yes, father," said Romola, gently; "but your letters at the back are dark and plain still—fine Roman letters; and the Greek character," she continued, laying the book open on her father's knee, "is more beautiful than that of any of your bought manuscripts."

"Assuredly, child," said Bardo, passing his finger across the page, as if he hoped to discriminate line and margin. "What hired amanuensis can be equal to the scribe who loves the words that grow under his hand, and to whom an error or indistinctness in the text is more painful than a sudden darkness or obstacle across his path? And even these mechanical printers who threaten to make learning a base and vulgar thing—even they must depend on the manuscript over which we scholars have bent with that insight into the poet's meaning which is closely akin to the *mens divinior* of the poet himself; unless they would flood the world with grammatical falsities and inexplicable anomalies that would turn the very fountain of Parnassus into a deluge of poisonous mud. But find the passage in the fifth book, to which Poliziano refers—I know it very well."

Seating herself on a low stool, close to her father's knee, Romola took the book on her lap and read the four verses containing the exclamation of Actæon.

"It is true, Romola," said Bardo, when she had finished; "it is a true conception of the poet; for what is that grosser, narrower light by which men behold merely the petty scene around them, compared with that far-stretching, lasting light which spreads over centuries of thought, and over the life of nations, and makes clear to us the minds of the immortals who have reaped the great harvest and left us to glean in their furrows? For me, Romola, even when I could see, it was with the great dead that I lived; while the living often seemed to me mere spectres—shadows dispossessed of true feeling and intelligence; and unlike those Lamiæ, to whom Poliziano, with that superficial ingenuity which I do not deny to him, compares our inquisitive Florentines, because they put on their eyes when they went abroad, and took them off when they got home again, I have returned from the converse of the streets as from a forgotten dream, and have sat down among my books, saying with Petrarca, the modern who is least unworthy to be named after the ancients, ' Libri medullitus delectant, colloquuntur, consulunt, et viva quadam nobis atque arguta familiaritate junguntur.' "

"And in one thing you are happier than your favorite Petrarca, father," said Romola, affectionately humoring the old man's disposition to dilate in this way; "for he used to look at his copy of Homer and think sadly that the Greek was a dead letter to him: so far, he had the inward blindness that you feel is worse than your outward blindness."

"True, child; for I carry within me the fruits of that fervid study which I gave to the Greek tongue under the teaching of the younger Crisolora, and Filelfo, and Argiropulo; though that great work in which I had desired to gather, as into a firm web, all the threads that my research had laboriously disentangled, and which would have been the vintage of my life, was cut off by the failure of my sight and my want of a fitting coadjutor. For the sustained zeal and unconquerable patience demanded from those who would tread the unbeaten paths of knowledge are still less reconcilable with the wandering, vagrant propensity of the feminine mind than with the feeble powers of the feminine body."

"Father," said Romola, with a sudden flush and in an injured tone, "I read anything you wish me to read; and I will look out any passages for you, and make whatever notes you want."

Bardo shook his head, and smiled with a bitter sort of pity. "As well try to be a pentathlos and perform all the five feats of the palæstra with the limbs of a nymph. Have I forgotten thy fainting in the mere search for the references I needed to explain a single passage of Callimachus?"

"But, father, it was the weight of the books, and Maso can help me; it was not want of attention and patience."

Bardo shook his head again. "It is not mere bodily organs that I want: it is the sharp edge of a young mind to pierce the way for my somewhat blunted faculties. For blindness acts like a dam, sending the streams of thought backward along the already-travelled channels and hindering the course onward. If my son had not forsaken me, deluded by debasing fanatical dreams, worthy only of an energumen whose dwelling is among tombs, I might have gone on and seen my path broadening to the end of my life; for he was a youth of great promise. . . . But it has closed in now," the old man continued, after a short pause; "it has closed in now;—all but the narrow track he has left me to tread—alone in my blindness."

Romola started from her seat, and carried away the large volume to its place again, stung too acutely by her father's last words to remain motionless as well as silent; and when she turned away from the shelf again, she remained standing at some distance from him, stretching her arms downward and clasping her fingers tightly as she looked with a sad dreariness in her young face at the lifeless objects around her—the parchment backs, the unchanging mutilated marble, the bits of obsolete bronze and clay.

Bardo, though usually susceptible to Romola's movements and eager to trace them, was now too entirely preoccupied by the pain of rankling memories to notice her departure from his side.

"Yes," he went on, "with my son to aid me, I might have had my due share in the triumphs of this century; the names of the Bardi, father and son, might have been held reverently on the lips of scholars in the ages to come; not on account of frivolous verses or philosophical treatises, which are superfluous and presumptuous attempts to imitate the inimitable, such as allure vain men like Panhormita, and from which even the admirable Poggio did not keep himself sufficiently free; but because we should have given a lamp whereby men might have studied the supreme production of the past. For why is a young man like Poliziano (who was not yet born when I was already held worthy to maintain a discussion with Thomas of Sarzana) to have a glorious memory as a commentator on the Pandects—why is Ficino, whose Latin is an offence to me, and who wanders purblind among the superstitious fancies that marked the decline at once of art, literature, and philosophy, to descend to posterity as the very high priest of Platonism, while I, who am more than their equal, have not effected anything but scattered work, which will be appropriated by other men? Why? but because my son, whom I had brought up to replenish my ripe learning with young enterprise, left me and all liberal pursuits that he might lash himself and howl at midnight with besotted friars—that he might go wandering on pilgrimages befitting men who know of no past older than the missal and the crucifix?—left me when the night was already beginning to fall on me."

In these last words the old man's voice, which had risen high in indignant protest, fell into a tone of reproach so tremulous and plaintive that Romola, turning her eyes again toward the blind aged face, felt her heart swell with forgiving pity. She seated herself by her father again, and placed her hand on his knee—too proud to obtrude consolation in words that might seem like a vindication of her own value, yet wishing to comfort him by some sign of her presence.

"Yes, Romola," said Bardo, automatically letting his left hand, with its massive prophylactic rings, fall a little too heavily on the delicate blue-veined back of the girl's right, so that she bit her lip to prevent herself from starting. "If even Florence only is to remember me, it can but be on the same ground that it will remember Niccolò Niccoli—because I forsook the vulgar pursuit of wealth in commerce that I might devote myself to collecting the precious remains of ancient art and wisdom, and leave them, after the example of the munificent Romans, for an everlasting possession to my fellow-citizens. But why do I say Florence only? If Florence remembers me, will not the world remember me? . . . Yet," added Bardo, after a short pause, his voice falling again into a saddened key, "Lorenzo's untimely death has raised a new difficulty. I had his promise—I should have had his bond—that my collection should always bear my name and should never be sold, though the harpies might clutch everything else; but there is enough for them—there is more than enough—and for thee, too, Romola, there will be enough. Besides, thou wilt marry; Bernardo reproaches me that I do not seek a fitting *parentado* for thee, and we will delay no longer, we will think about it."

"No, no, father; what could you do? besides, it is useless: wait till some one seeks me," said Romola, hastily.

"Nay, my child, that is not the paternal duty. It was not so held by the ancients, and in this respect Florentines have not degenerated from their ancestral customs."

"But I will study diligently," said Romola, her eyes dilating with anxiety. "I will become as learned as Cassandra Fedele: I will try and be as useful to you as if I had been a boy, and then perhaps some great scholar will want to marry me, and will not mind about a dowry; and he will like to come and live with you, and he will be to you in place of my brother . . . and you will not be sorry that I was a daughter."

There was a rising sob in Romola's voice as she said the last words, which touched the fatherly fibre in Bardo. He stretched his hand upward a little in search of her golden hair, and as she placed her head under his hand, he gently stroked it, leaning toward her as if his eyes discerned some glimmer there.

"Nay, Romola mia, I said not so; if I have pronounced an anathema on a degenerate and ungrateful son, I said not that I could wish thee other than the sweet daughter thou hast been to me. For what son could have tended me so gently in the frequent sickness I have had of late? And even in learning thou art not, according to thy measure, contemptible. Something perhaps were to be wished in thy capacity of attention and memory, not incompatible even with the feminine mind. But as Calcondila bore testimony, when he aided me to teach thee, thou hast a ready apprehension, and even a wide-glancing intelligence. And thou hast a man's nobility of soul: thou hast never fretted me with thy petty desires as thy mother did. It is true I have been careful to keep thee aloof from the debasing influence of thy own sex, with their sparrow-like frivolity and their enslaving superstition, except, indeed, from that of our cousin Brigida, who may well serve as a scarecrow and a warning. And though—since I agree with the divine Petrarca, when he declares, quoting the 'Aulularia' of Plautus, who again was indebted for the truth to the supreme Greek intellect, 'Optimam fœminam nullam esse, alia licet alia pejor sit'—I cannot boast that thou art entirely lifted out of that lower category to which Nature assigned thee, nor even that in erudition thou art on a par with the more learned women of this age; thou art, nevertheless—yes, Romola mia," said the old man, his pedantry again melting into tenderness, "thou art my sweet daughter, and thy voice is as the lower notes of the flute, 'dulcis, durabilis, clara, pura, secans aera et auribus sedens,' according to the choice words of Quintilian; and Bernardo tells me thou art fair, and thy hair is like the brightness of the morning, and indeed it seems to me that I discern some radiance from thee. Ah! I know how all else looks in this room, but thy form I only guess at. Thou art no longer the little woman six years old, that faded for me into darkness; thou art tall, and thy arm is but little below mine. Let us walk together."

The old man rose, and Romola, soothed by these beams of tenderness, looked happy again as she drew his arm within hers, and placed in his right hand the stick which rested at the side of his chair. While Bardo had been sitting, he had seemed hardly more than sixty: his face, though pale, had that refined texture in which wrinkles and lines are never deep; but now that he began to walk he looked as old as he really was—rather more than seventy; for his tall spare frame had the student's stoop of the shoulders, and he stepped with the undecided gait of the blind.

"No, Romola," he said, pausing against the bust of Hadrian, and passing his stick from the right to the left that he might explore the familiar outline with a "seeing hand." "There will be nothing else to preserve my memory and carry down my name as a member of the great republic of letters—nothing but my library and my collection of antiquities. And they are choice," continued Bardo, pressing the bust and speaking in a tone of insistence. "The collections of Niccolò I know were larger; but take any collection which is the work of a single man—that of the great Boccaccio even—mine will surpass it. That of Poggio was contemptible compared with mine. It will be a great gift to unborn scholars. And there is nothing else. For even if I were to yield to the wish of Aldo Manuzio when he sets up his press at Venice, and give him the aid of my annotated manuscripts, I know well what would be the result: some other scholar's name would stand on the title-page of the edition—some scholar who would have fed on my honey, and then declared in his preface that he had gathered it all himself fresh from Hymettus. Else, why have I refused the loan of many an annotated codex? why have I refused to make public any of my translations? why? but because scholarship is a system of licensed robbery, and your man in scarlet and furred robe who sits in judgment on thieves is himself a thief of the thoughts and the fame that belong to his fellows. But against that robbery Bardo de' Bardi shall struggle—though blind and forsaken, he shall struggle. I too have a right to be remembered—as great a right as Pontanus or Merula, whose names will be foremost on the lips of posterity, because they sought patronage and found it; because they had tongues that could flatter, and blood that was used to be nourished from the client's basket. I have a right to be remembered."

The old man's voice had become at once loud and tremulous, and a pink flush overspread his proud, delicately cut features, while the habitually raised attitude of his head gave the idea that behind the curtain of his blindness he saw some imaginary high tribunal to which he was appealing against the injustice of Fame.

Romola was moved with sympathetic indignation, for in her nature too there lay the same large claims, and the same spirit of struggle against their denial. She tried to calm her father by a still prouder word than his.

"Nevertheless, father, it is a great gift of the gods to be

born with a hatred and contempt of all injustice and meanness. Yours is a higher lot, never to have lied and truckled, never to have shared honors won by dishonor. There is strength in scorn, as there was in the martial fury by which men became insensible to wounds."

"It is well said, Romola. It is a Promethean word thou hast uttered," answered Bardo, after a little interval in which he had begun to lean on his stick again, and to walk on. "And I indeed am not to be pierced by the shafts of Fortune. My armor is the *œs triplex* of a clear conscience, and a mind nourished by the precepts of philosophy. 'For men,' says Epictetus, 'are disturbed not by things themselves, but by their opinions or thoughts concerning those things.' And again, 'whosoever will be free, let him not desire or dread that which is in the power of others either to deny or inflict: otherwise, he is a slave.' And of all such gifts as are dependent on the caprice of fortune or of men, I have long ago learned to say, with Horace—who, however, is too wavering in his philosophy, vacillating between the precepts of Zeno and the less worthy maxims of Epicurus, and attempting, as we say, 'duabus sellis sedere'—concerning such accidents, I say, with the pregnant brevity of the poet,—

'Sunt qui non habeant, est qui non curat habere.'

He is referring to gems, and purple, and other insignia of wealth; but I may apply his words not less justly to the tributes men pay us with their lips and their pens, which are also matters of purchase, and often with base coin. Yes, '*inanis*'—hollow, empty—is the epithet justly bestowed on Fame."

They made the tour of the room in silence after this; but Bardo's lip-born maxims were as powerless over the passion which had been moving him, as if they had been written on parchment and hung round his neck in a sealed bag; and he presently broke forth again in a new tone of insistence.

"*Inanis?* yes, if it is a lying fame; but not if it is the just meed of labor and a great purpose. I claim my right: it is not fair that the work of my brain and my hands should not be a monument to me—it is not just that my labor should bear the name of another man. It is but little to ask," the old man went on, bitterly, "that my name should be over the door—that men should own themselves debtors to the Bardi Library in Florence. They will speak coldly of me, perhaps: 'a diligent collector and transcriber,' they will say, 'and also of some critical ingenuity, but one who could hardly be conspicuous in an age so fruitful in illustrious scholars. Yet he merits our pity, for in the latter years of his life he was blind, and his only son, to whose education he had devoted his best years——' Nevertheless, my name will be remembered, and men will honor me: not with the breath of flattery, purchased by mean bribes, but because I have labored, and because my labors will remain. Debts! I know there are debts; and there is thy dowry, Romola, to be paid. But there must be enough—or, at least, there can lack but a small sum, such as the Signoria might well provide. And if Lorenzo had not died, all would have been secured and settled. But now . . ."

At this moment Maso opened the door, and advancing to his master, announced that Nello, the barber, had desired him to say, that he was come with the Greek scholar whom he had asked leave to introduce.

"It is well," said the old man. "Bring them in."

Bardo, conscious that he looked more dependent when he was walking, liked always to be seated in the presence of strangers, and Romola, without needing to be told, conducted him to his chair. She was standing by him at her full height, in quiet majestic self-possession, when the visitors entered; and the most penetrating observer would hardly have divined that this proud pale face, at the slightest touch on the fibres of affection or pity, could become passionate with tenderness, or that this woman, who imposed a certain awe on those who approached her, was in a state of girlish simplicity and ignorance concerning the world outside her father's books.

CHAPTER VI.

DAWNING HOPES.

WHEN Maso opened the door again, and ushered in the two visitors, Nello, first making a deep reverence to Romola, gently pushed Tito before him, and advanced with him toward her father.

"Messer Bardo," he said, in a more measured and respectful tone than was usual with him, "I have the honor of presenting to you the Greek scholar, who has been eager to have speech of you, not less from the report I have made to him of your learning and your priceless collections, than because of the furtherance your patronage may give him under the transient need to which he has been reduced by shipwreck. His name is Tito Melema, at your service."

Romola's astonishment could hardly have been greater if the stranger had worn a panther-skin and carried a thyrsus; for the cunning barber had said nothing of the Greek's age or appearance; and among her father's scholarly visitors, she had hardly ever seen any but middle-aged or gray-headed men. There was only one masculine face, at once youthful and beautiful, the image of which remained deeply impressed on her mind: it was that of her brother, who long years ago had taken her on his knee, kissed her, and never come back again: a fair face, with sunny hair, like her own. But the habitual attitude of her mind toward strangers—a proud self-dependence and determination to ask for nothing even by a smile—confirmed in her by her father's complaints against the world's injustice, was like a snowy embankment hemming in the rush of admiring surprise. Tito's bright face showed its rich-tinted beauty without any rivalry of color above his black *sajo* or tunic reaching to the knees. It seemed like a wreath of spring, dropped suddenly in Romola's young but wintry life, which had inherited nothing but memories—memories of a dead mother, of a lost brother, of a blind father's happier time—memories of a far-off light, love, and beauty, that lay embedded in dark mines of books, and could hardly give out their brightness again until they were kindled for her by the torch of some known joy. Nevertheless, she returned Tito's bow, made to her on entering, with the same pale proud face as ever; but, as he approached, the snow melted, and when he ventured to look toward her again, while Nello was speaking, a pink flush overspread her face, to vanish again almost immediately, as if her imperious will had recalled it. Tito's glance, on the contrary, had that gentle, beseeching admiration in it which is the most propitiating of appeals to a proud, shy woman, and is perhaps the only atonement a man can make for being too handsome. The finished fascination of his air came chiefly from the absence of demand and assumption. It was that of a fleet, soft-coated, dark-eyed animal that delights you by not bounding away in indifference from you, and unexpectedly pillows its chin on your palm, and looks up at you desiring to be stroked—as if it loved you.

"Messere, I give you welcome," said Bardo, with some condescension; "misfortune wedded to learning, and especially to Greek learning, is a letter of credit that should win the ear of every instructed Florentine; for, as you are doubtless aware, since the period when your countryman, Manuelo Crisolora, diffused the light of his teaching in the chief cities of Italy, now nearly a century ago, no man is held worthy of the name of scholar who has acquired merely the transplanted and derivative literature of the Latins; rather, such inert students are stigmatized as *opici* or barbarians according to the phrase of the Romans themselves, who frankly replenished their urns at the fountain-head. I am, as you perceive, and as Nello has doubtless forewarned you, totally blind: a calamity to which we Florentines are held especially liable, whether owing to the cold winds which rush upon us in spring from the passes of the Apennines, or to that sudden transition from the cool gloom of our houses to the dazzling brightness of our summer sun, by which the *lippi* are said to have been made so numerous among the ancient Romans; or, in fine, to some occult cause which eludes our superficial surmises. But I pray you be seated: Nello, my friend, be seated."

Bardo paused until his fine ear had assured him that the

visitors were seating themselves, and that Romola was taking her usual chair at his right hand. Then he said, —

"From what part of Greece do you come, Messere? I had thought that your unhappy country had been almost exhausted of those sons who could cherish in their minds any image of her original glory, though indeed the barbarous Sultans have of late shown themselves not indisposed to ingraft on their wild stock the precious vine which their own fierce bands have hewn down and trampled under foot. From what part of Greece do you come?"

"I sailed last from Nauplia," said Tito; "but I have resided both at Constantinople and Thessalonica, and have travelled in various parts little visited by Western Christians since the triumph of the Turkish arms. I should tell you, however, Messere, that I was not born in Greece, but at Bari. I spent the first sixteen years of my life in Southern Italy and Sicily."

While Tito was speaking, some emotion passed, like a breath on the waters, across Bardo's delicate features; he leaned forward, put out his right hand toward Romola, and turned his head as if about to speak to her; but then, correcting himself, turned away again, and said, in a subdued voice, —

"Excuse me; is it not true—you are young?"

"I am three-and-twenty," said Tito.

"Ah," said Bardo, still in a tone of subdued excitement, "and you had, doubtless, a father who cared for your early instruction—who, perhaps, was himself a scholar?"

There was a slight pause before Tito's answer came to the ear of Bardo; but for Romola and Nello it began with a slight shock that seemed to pass through him, and cause a momentary quivering of the lip; doubtless at the revival of a supremely painful remembrance.

"Yes," he replied, "at least a father by adoption. He was a Neapolitan, and of accomplished scholarship, both Latin and Greek. But," added Tito, after another slight pause, "he is lost to me—was lost on a voyage he too rashly undertook to Delos."

Bardo sank backward again, too delicate to ask another question that might probe a sorrow which he divined to be recent. Romola, who knew well what were the fibres that Tito's voice had stirred in her father, felt that this new acquaintance had with wonderful suddenness got within the barrier that lay between them and the alien world. Nello, thinking that the evident check given to the conversation offered a graceful opportunity for relieving himself from silence, said,—

"In truth, it is as clear as Venetian glass that this fine young man has had the best training; for the two Cennini have set him to work at their Greek sheets already, and it seems to me they are not men to begin cutting before they have felt the edge of their tools; they tested him well beforehand, we may be sure, and if there are two things not to be hidden—love and a cough—I say there is a third, and that is ignorance, when once a man is obliged to do something besides wagging his head. The *tonsor inequalis* is inevitably betrayed when he takes the shears in his hand; is it not true, Messer Bardo? I speak after the fashion of a barber, but, as Luigi Pulci says,—

> "'Perdonimi s'io fallo: chi m'ascolta
> Intenda il mio volgar col suo latino.'"

"Nay, my good Nello," said Bardo, with an air of friendly severity, "you are not altogether illiterate, and might doubtless have made a more respectable progress in learning if you had abstained somewhat from the *cicalata* and gossip of the street corner, to which our Florentines are excessively addicted; but still more if you had not clogged your memory with those frivolous productions of which Luigi Pulci has furnished the most peccant exemplar—a compendium of extravagances and incongruities the farthest removed from the models of a pure age, and resembling rather the *grylli* or conceits of a period when mystic meaning was held a warrant for monstrosity of form; with this difference, that while the monstrosity is retained, the mystic meaning is absent; in contemptible contrast with the great poem of Virgil, who, as I long held with Filelfo, before Landino had taken upon him to expound the same opinion, embodied the deepest lessons of philosophy in a graceful and well-knit fable. And I cannot but regard the multiplication of these babbling, lawless productions, albeit countenanced by the patronage, and in some degree the example, of Lorenzo himself, otherwise a friend to true learning, as a sign that the glorious hopes of this century are to be quenched in gloom; nay, that they have been the delusive prologue to an age worse than that of iron—the age of tinsel and gossamer, in which no thought has substance enough to be moulded into consistent and lasting form."

"Once more, pardon," said Nello, opening his palms outward, and shrugging his shoulders, "I find myself knowing so many things in good Tuscan before I have time to think of the Latin for them; and Messer Luigi's rhymes are always slipping off the lips of my customers:—that is what corrupts me. And, indeed, talking of customers, I have left my shop and my reputation too long in the custody of my slow Sandro, who does not deserve even to be called a *tonsor inequalis*, but rather to be pronounced simply a bungler in the vulgar tongue. So with your permission, Messer Bardo, I will take my leave—well understood that I am at your service whenever Maso calls upon me. It seems a thousand years till I dress and perfume the damigella's hair, which deserves to shine in the heavens as a constellation, though indeed it were a pity for it ever to go so far out of reach."

Three voices made a fugue of friendly farewells to Nello, as he retreated with a bow to Romola and a beck to Tito. The acute barber saw that the pretty youngster, who had crept into his liking by some strong magic, was well launched in Bardo's favorable regard; and satisfied that his introduction had not miscarried so far, he felt the propriety of retiring.

The little burst of wrath, called forth by Nello's unlucky quotation, had diverted Bardo's mind from the feelings which had just before been hemming in further speech, and he now addressed Tito again with his ordinary calmness.

"Ah! young man, you are happy in having been able to unite the advantages of travel with those of study, and you will be welcome among us as a bringer of fresh tidings from a land which has become sadly strange to us, except through the agents of a now restricted commerce and the reports of hasty pilgrims. For those days are in the far distance which I myself witnessed, when men like Aurispa and Guarino went out to Greece as to a storehouse, and came back laden with manuscripts which every scholar was eager to borrow—and, be it owned with shame, not always willing to restore; nay, even the days when erudite Greeks flocked to our shores for a refuge seem far off now—farther off than the on-coming of my blindness. But doubtless, young man, research after the treasures of antiquity was not alien to the purpose of your travels?"

"Assuredly not," said Tito. "On the contrary, my companion—my father—was willing to risk his life in his zeal for the discovery of inscriptions and other traces of ancient civilization."

"And I trust there is a record of his researches and their results," said Bardo, eagerly, "since they must be even more precious than those of Ciriaco, which I have diligently availed myself of, though they are not always illuminated by adequate learning."

"There *was* such a record," said Tito, "but it was lost, like everything else, in the shipwreck I suffered below Ancona. The only record left is such as remains in our—in my memory."

"You must lose no time in committing it to paper, young man," said Bardo, with growing interest. "Doubtless you remember much, if you aided in transcription; for when I was your age, words wrought themselves into my mind as if they had been fixed by the tool of the graver; wherefore I constantly marvel at the capriciousness of my daughter's memory, which grasps certain objects with tenacity, and lets fall all those minutiæ whereon depends accuracy, the very soul of scholarship. But I apprehend no such danger with you, young man, if your will has seconded the advantages of your training."

When Bardo made this reference to his daughter, Tito ventured to turn his eyes toward her, and at the accusation against her memory his face broke into its brightest smile, which was reflected as inevitably as sudden sunbeams in Romola's. Conceive the soothing delight of that smile to her! Romola had never dreamed that there was a scholar in the world who would smile at a deficiency for which she was constantly made to feel herself a culprit. It was like the dawn of a new sense to her—the sense of comradeship. They did not look away from each other immediately, as if the smile had been a stolen one; they looked and smiled with frank enjoyment.

"She is not really so cold and proud," thought Tito.

"Does *he* forget too, I wonder?" thought Romola. "Yet I hope not, else he will vex my father."

But Tito was obliged to turn away, and answer Bardo's question.

"I have had much practice in transcription," he said; "but in the case of inscriptions copied in memorable scenes, rendered doubly impressive by the sense of risk and adventure, it may have happened that my retention of written characters has been weakened. On the plain of the Eurotas, or among the gigantic stones of Mycenæ and Tyrins—especially when the fear of the Turk hovers over one like a vulture—the mind wanders, even though the hand writes faithfully what the eye dictates. But something doubtless I have retained," added Tito, with a modesty which was not false, though he was conscious that it was politic, "something that might be of service if illustrated and corrected by a wider learning than my own."

"That is well spoken, young man," said Bardo, delighted. "And I will not withhold from you such aid as I can give, if you like to communicate with me concerning your recollections. I foresee a work which will be a useful supplement to the 'Isolario' of Christoforo Buondelmonte, and which may take rank with the 'Itineraria' of Ciriaco and the admirable Ambrogio Traversari. But we must prepare ourselves for calumny, young man," Bardo went on with energy, as if the work were already growing so fast that the time of trial was near; "if your book contains novelties you will be charged with forgery; if my elucidations should clash with any principles of interpretation adopted by another scholar, our personal characters will be attacked, we shall be impeached with foul actions, you must prepare yourself to be told that your mother was a fish-woman, and that your father was a renegade priest or a hanged malefactor. I myself, for having shown error in a single preposition, had an invective written against me wherein I was taxed with treachery, fraud, indecency, and even hideous crimes. Such, my young friend—such are the flowers with which the glorious path of scholarship is strewed! But tell me, then. I have learned much concerning Byzantium and Thessalonica long ago from Demetrio Calcondila, who has but lately departed from Florence; but you, it seems, have visited less familiar scenes?"

"Yes; we made what I may call a pilgrimage full of danger, for the sake of visiting places which have almost died out of the memory of the West, for they lie away from the track of pilgrims; and my father used to say that scholars themselves hardly imagine them to have any existence out of books. He was of opinion that a new and more glorious era would open for learning when men should begin to look for their commentaries on the ancient writers in the remains of cities and temples, nay, in the paths of the rivers, and on the face of the valleys and the mountains."

"Ah!" said Bardo, fervently, "your father, then, was not a common man. Was he fortunate, may I ask? Had he many friends?" These last words were uttered in a tone charged with meaning.

"No; he made enemies—chiefly, I believe, by a certain impetuous candor; and they hindered his advancement, so that he lived in obscurity. And he would never stoop to conciliate; he could never forget an injury."

"Ah!" said Bardo again, with a long, deep intonation.

"Among our hazardous expeditions," continued Tito, willing to prevent further questions on a point so personal, "I remember with particular vividness a hastily snatched visit to Athens. Our hurry, and the double danger of being seized as prisoners by the Turks, and of our galley raising anchor before we could return, made it seem like a fevered vision of the night—the wide plain, the girdling mountains, the ruined porticos and columns, either standing far aloof, as if receding from our hurried footsteps, or else jammed in confusedly among the dwellings of Christians degraded into servitude, or among the forts and turrets of their Moslem conquerors, who have their stronghold on the Acropolis."

"You fill me with surprise," said Bardo. "Athens, then, is not utterly destroyed and swept away, as I had imagined."

"No wonder you should be under that mistake, for few even of the Greeks themselves, who live beyond the mountain boundary of Attica, know anything about the present condition of Athens, or *Setine*, as the sailors call it. I remember, as we were rounding the promontory of Sunium, the Greek pilot we had on board our Venetian galley pointed to the mighty columns that stand on the summit of the rock—the remains, as you know well, of the great temple erected to the goddess Athena, who looked down from that high shrine with triumph at her conquered rival Poseidon;—well, our Greek pilot, pointing to those columns, said, 'That was the school of the great philosopher Aristotle.' And at Athens itself, the monk who acted as our guide in the hasty view we snatched, insisted most on showing us the spot where St. Philip baptized the Ethiopian eunuch, or some such legend."

"Talk not of monks and their legends, young man!" said Bardo, interrupting Tito impetuously. "It is enough to overlay human hope and enterprise with an eternal frost to think that the ground which was trodden by philosophers and poets is crawled over by those insect-swarms of besotted fanatics or howling hypocrites."

"*Perdio*, I have no affection for them," said Tito, with a shrug; "servitude agrees well with a religion like theirs, which lies in the renunciation of all that makes life precious to other men. And they carry the yoke that befits them: their matin chant is drowned by the voice of the muezzin, who, from the gallery of the high tower on the Acropolis, calls every Mussulman to his prayers. That tower springs from the Parthenon itself; and every time we paused and directed our eyes toward it, our guide set up a wail, that a temple which had once been won from the diabolical uses of the pagans to become the temple of another virgin than Pallas—the Virgin-Mother of God —was now again perverted to the accursed ends of the Moslem. It was the sight of those walls of the Acropolis, which disclosed themselves in the distance as we leaned over the side of our galley when it was forced by contrary winds to anchor in the Piræus, that fired my father's mind with the determination to see Athens at all risks, and in spite of the sailors' warnings that if we lingered till a change of wind, they would depart without us: but, after all, it was impossible for us to venture near the Acropolis, for the sight of men eager in examining 'old stones' raised the suspicion that we were Venetian spies, and we had to hurry back to the harbor."

"We will talk more of these things," said Bardo, eagerly. "You must recall everything, to the minutest trace left in your memory. You will win the gratitude of after-times by leaving a record of the aspect Greece bore while yet the barbarians had not swept away every trace of the structures that Pausanias and Pliny described: you will take those great writers as your models, and such contribution of criticism and suggestion as my riper mind can supply shall not be wanting to you. There will be much to tell; for you have travelled, you said, in the Peloponnesus?"

"Yes; and in Bœotia also: I have rested in the groves of Helicon, and tasted of the fountain Hippocrene. But on every memorable spot in Greece conquest after conquest has set its seal, till there is a confusion of ownership even in ruins, that only close study and comparison could unravel. High over every fastness, from the plains of Lacedæmon to the straits of Thermopylæ, there towers some huge Frankish fortress, once inhabited by a French or Italian marquis, now either abandoned or held by Turkish bands."

"Stay!" cried Bardo, whose mind was now too thoroughly preoccupied by the idea of the future book to attend to Tito's further narration. "Do you think of writing in Latin or Greek? Doubtless Greek is the more ready clothing for your thoughts, and it is the nobler language. But, on the other hand, Latin is the tongue in which we shall measure ourselves with the larger and more famous number of modern rivals. And if you are less at ease in it, I will aid you—yes, I will spend on you that long-accumulated study which was to have been thrown into the channel of another work—a work in which I myself was to have had a helpmate."

Bardo paused a moment, and then added,—

"But who knows whether that work may not be executed yet? For you, too, young man, have been brought up by a father who poured into your mind all the long-gathered stream of his knowledge and experience. Our aid might be mutual."

Romola, who had watched her father's growing excitement, and divined well the invisible currents of feeling that determined every question and remark, felt herself in a glow of strange anxiety; she turned her eyes on Tito continually, to watch the impression her father's words made on him, afraid lest he should be inclined to dispel these visions of co-operation which were lighting up her father's face with a new hope. But no! He looked so bright and gentle · he must feel, as she did, that in this eagerness of blind age there was piteousness enough to call forth inexhaustible patience. How much more strongly he would feel this if he knew about her brother! A girl of eighteen imagines the feelings behind the face that has moved her with its sympathetic youth as easily as primitive people imagined the humors of the gods in fair weather: what is she to believe in, if not in this vision woven from within?

And Tito was really very far from feeling impatient. He delighted in sitting there with the sense that Romola's attention was fixed on him, and that he could occasionally look at her. He was pleased that Bardo should take an interest in him, and he did not dwell with enough seriousness on the prospect of the work in which he was to be aided to feel moved by it to anything else than that easy, good-humored acquiescence which was natural to him.

"I shall be proud and happy," he said, in answer to Bardo's last words, "if my services can be held a meet offering to the matured scholarship of Messere. But doubtless"—here he looked toward Romola—"the lovely damigella, your daughter, makes all other aid superfluous; for I have learned from Nello that she has been nourished on the highest studies from her earliest years."

"You are mistaken," said Romola; "I am by no means sufficient to my father: I have not the gifts that are necessary for scholarship."

Romola did not make this self-depreciatory statement in a tone of anxious humility, but with a proud gravity.

"Nay, my Romola," said her father, not willing that the stranger should have too low a conception of his daughter's powers; "thou art not destitute of gifts; rather, thou art endowed beyond the measure of women; but thou hast withal the woman's delicate frame, which ever craves repose and variety, and so begets a wandering imagination. My daughter"—turning to Tito—"has been very precious to me, filling up to the best of her power the place of a son. For I had once a son . . ."

Bardo checked himself: he did not wish to assume an attitude of complaint in the presence of a stranger, and he remembered that this young man, in whom he had unexpectedly become so much interested, was still a stranger, toward whom it became him rather to keep the position of a patron. His pride was roused to double activity by the fear that he had forgotten his dignity.

"But," he resumed, in his original tone of condescension, "we are departing from what I believe is to you the most important business. Nello informed me that you had certain gems which you would fain dispose of, and that you desired a passport to some man of wealth and taste who would be likely to become a purchaser."

"It is true; for, though I have obtained employment, as a corrector with the Cennini, my payment leaves little margin beyond the provision of necessaries, and would leave less but that my good friend Nello insists on my hiring a lodging from him, and saying nothing about the rent till better days."

"Nello is a good-hearted prodigal," said Bardo; "and though, with that ready ear and ready tongue of his, he is too much like the ill-famed Margites—knowing many things and knowing them all badly, as I hinted to him but now—he is nevertheless 'abnormis sapiens,' after the manner of our born Florentines. But have you the gems with you? I would willingly know what they are—yet it is useless: no, it might only deepen regret. I cannot add to my store."

"I have one or two intaglios of much beauty," said Tito, proceeding to draw from his wallet a small case.

But Romola no sooner saw the movement than she looked at him with significant gravity, and placed her finger on her lips,

"Con viso che tacendo dicea, Taci."

If Bardo were made aware that the gems were within reach, she knew well he would want a minute description of them, and it would become pain to him that they should go away from him, even if he did not insist on some device for purchasing them in spite of poverty. But she had no sooner made this sign than she felt rather guilty and ashamed at having virtually confessed a weakness of her father's to a stranger. It seemed that she was destined to a sudden confidence and familiarity with this young Greek, strangely at variance with her deep-seated pride and reserve; and this consciousness again brought the unwonted color to her cheeks.

Tito understood her look and sign, and immediately withdrew his hand from the case, saying in a careless tone, so as to make it appear that he was merely following up his last words, "But they are usually in the keeping of Messer Domenico Cennini, who has strong and safe places for these things. He estimates them as worth at least five hundred ducats."

"Ah, then they are fine intagli," said Bardo. "Five hundred ducats! Ah, more than a man's ransom!"

Tito gave a slight, almost imperceptible start, and opened his long dark eyes with questioning surprise at Bardo's blind face, as if his words—a mere phrase of common parlance, at a time when men were often being ransomed from slavery or imprisonment—had had some special meaning for him. But the next moment he looked toward Romola, as if her eyes must be her father's interpreters. She, intensely preoccupied with what related to her father, imagined that Tito was looking to her again for some guidance, and immediately spoke.

"Alessandra Scala delights in gems, you know, father; she calls them her winter flowers; and the Segretario would be almost sure to buy any gems that she wished for. Besides, he himself sets great store by rings and sigils, which he wears as a defence against pains in the joints."

"It is true," said Bardo. "Bartolommeo has overmuch confidence in the efficacy of gems—a confidence wider than what is sanctioned by Pliny, who clearly shows that he regards many beliefs of that sort as idle superstitions; though not to the utter denial of medicinal virtues in gems. Wherefore, I myself, as you observe, young man, wear certain rings, which the discreet Camillo Leonardi prescribed to me by letter when two years ago I had a certain infirmity of sudden numbness. But thou hast spoken well, Romola. I will dictate a letter to Bartolommeo, which Maso shall carry. But it were well that Messere should notify to thee what the gems are, together with the intagli they bear, as a warrant to Bartolommeo that they will be worthy of his attention."

"Nay, father," said Romola, whose dread lest a paroxysm of the collector's mania should seize her father gave her the courage to resist his proposal. "Your word will be sufficient that Messere is a scholar and has travelled much. The Segretario will need no further inducement to receive him."

"True, child," said Bardo, touched on a chord that was sure to respond. "I have no need to add proofs and arguments in confirmation of my word to Bartolommeo. And I doubt not that this young man's presence is in accord with the tones of his voice, so that, the door being once opened, he will be his own best advocate."

Bardo paused a few moments, but his silence was evidently charged with some idea that he was hesitating to express, for he once leaned forward a little as if he were going to speak, then turned his head aside toward Romola and sank backward again. At last, as if he had made up his mind, he said in a tone which might have become a prince giving the courteous signal of dismissal,—

"I am somewhat fatigued this morning, and shall prefer seeing you again to-morrow, when I shall be able to give you the secretary's answer, authorizing you to present yourself to him at some given time. But before you go"—here the old man, in spite of himself, fell into a more faltering tone—"you will perhaps permit me to touch your hand? It is long since I touched the hand of a young man."

Bardo had stretched out his aged white hand, and Tito immediately placed his dark but delicate and supple fingers within it. Bardo's cramped fingers closed over them, and he held them for a few minutes in silence. Then he said,—

"Romola, has this young man the same complexion as thy brother—fair and pale?"

"No, father," Romola answered, with determined composure, though her heart began to beat violently with mingled emotions. "The hair of Messere is dark—his complexion is dark." Inwardly she said, "Will he mind it? will it be disagreeable? No, he looks so gentle and good-natured." Then aloud again,—

"Would Messere permit my father to touch his hair and face?"

Her eyes inevitably made a timid entreating appeal while she asked this, and Tito's met them with soft brightness as he said, "Assuredly," and, leaning forward, raised Bardo's hand to his curls, with a readiness of assent which was the greater relief to her because it was unaccompanied by any sign of embarrassment.

Bardo passed his hand again and again over the long curls and grasped them a little, as if their spiral resistance made his inward vision clearer; then he passed his hand over the brow and cheek, tracing the profile with the edge of his palm and fourth finger, and letting the breadth of his hand repose on the rich oval of the cheek.

"Ah," he said, as his hand glided from the face and rested on the young man's shoulder. "He must be very unlike thy brother, Romola: and it is the better. You see no visions, I trust, my young friend?"

At this moment the door opened, and there entered unannounced a tall elderly man in a handsome black silk lucco, who, unwinding his becchetto from his neck and taking off his cap, disclosed a head as white as Bardo's. He cast a keen glance of surprise at the group before him—the young stranger leaning in that filial attitude, while Bardo's hand rested on his shoulder, and Romola sitting near with eyes dilated by anxiety and agitation. But there was an instantaneous change: Bardo let fall his hand, Tito raised himself from his stooping posture, and Romola rose to greet the visitor with an alacrity which implied all the greater intimacy because it was unaccompanied by any smile.

"Well, god-daughter," said the stately man, as he touched Romola's shoulder; "Maso said you had a visitor, but I came in nevertheless."

"It is thou, Bernardo," said Bardo. "Thou art come at a fortunate moment. This, young man," he continued, while

Tito rose and bowed, "is one of the chief citizens of Florence, Messer Bernardo del Nero, my oldest, I had almost said my only friend—whose good opinion, if you can win it, may carry you far. He is but three-and-twenty, Bernardo, yet he can doubtless tell thee much which thou wilt care to hear; for though a scholar, he has already travelled far, and looked on other things besides the manuscripts for which thou hast too light an esteem."

"Ah, a Greek, as I augur," said Bernardo, returning Tito's reverence but slightly, and surveying him with that sort of glance which seems almost to cut like fine steel. "Newly arrived in Florence, it appears. The name of Messere—or part of it, for it is doubtless a long one?"

"On the contrary," said Tito, with perfect good humor, "it is most modestly free from polysyllabic pomp. My name is Tito Melema."

"Truly?" said Bernardo, rather scornfully, as he took a seat; "I had expected it to be at least as long as the names of a city, a river, a province, and an empire all put together. We Florentines mostly use names as we do prawns, and strip them of all flourishes before we trust them to our throats.

"Well, Bardo," he continued, as if the stranger were not worth further notice, and changing his tone of sarcastic suspicion for one of sadness, "we have buried him."

"Ah!" replied Bardo, with corresponding sadness, "and a new epoch has come for Florence—a dark one, I fear. Lorenzo has left behind him an inheritance that is but like the alchemist's laboratory when the wisdom of the alchemist is gone."

"Not altogether so," said Bernardo. "Piero de' Medici has abundant intelligence; his faults are only the faults of hot blood. I love the lad—lad he will always be to me, as I have always been 'little father' to him."

"Yet all who want a new order of things are likely to conceive new hopes," said Bardo. "We shall have the old strife of parties, I fear."

"If we could have a new order of things that was something else than knocking down one coat of arms to put up another," said Bernardo. "I should be ready to say, 'I belong to no party; I am a Florentine.' But as long as parties are in question, I am a Medicean, and will be a Medicean till I die. I am of the same mind as Farinata degli Uberti: if any man asks me what is meant by siding with a party, I say, as he did, ' To wish ill or well, for the sake of past wrongs or kindnesses.'"

During this short dialogue, Tito had been standing, and now took his leave.

"But come again at the same hour to-morrow," said Bardo, graciously, before Tito left the room, "that I may give you Bartolommeo's answer."

"From what quarter of the sky has this pretty Greek youngster alighted so close to thy chair, Bardo?" said Bernardo del Nero, as the door closed. He spoke with dry emphasis, evidently intended to convey something more to Bardo than was implied by the mere words.

"He is a scholar who has been shipwrecked and has saved a few gems, for which he wants to find a purchaser. I am going to send him to Bartolommeo Scala, for thou knowest it were more prudent in me to abstain from further purchases."

Bernardo shrugged his shoulders and said, "Romola, wilt thou see if my servant is without? I ordered him to wait for me here." Then, when Romola was at a sufficient distance, he leaned forward and said to Bardo in a low, emphatic tone,—

"Remember, Bardo, thou hast a rare gem of thy own; take care no one gets it who is not likely to pay a worthy price. That pretty Greek has a lithe sleekness about him, that seems marvellously fitted for slipping easily into any nest he fixes his mind on."

Bardo was startled: the association of Tito with the image of his lost son had excluded instead of suggesting the thought of Romola. But almost immediately there seemed to be a reaction which made him grasp the warning as if it had been a hope.

"But why not, Bernardo? If the young man approved himself worthy—he is a scholar—and—and there would be no difficulty about the dowry, which always makes thee gloomy."

CHAPTER VII.

A LEARNED SQUABBLE.

BARTOLOMMEO SCALA, secretary of the Florentine Republic, on whom Tito Melema had been thus led to anchor his hopes, lived in a handsome palace close to the Porta Pinti, now known as the Casa Gherardesca. His arms—an azure ladder transverse on a golden field with the motto *Gradatim* placed over the entrance—told all comers that the miller's son held his ascent to honors by his own efforts a fact to be proclaimed without wincing. The secretary was a vain and pompous man, but he was also an honest one: he was sincerely convinced of his own merit, and could see no reason for feigning. The topmost round of his azure ladder had been reached by this time: he had held his secretaryship these twenty years—had long since made his orations on the *ringhiera*, or platform of the Old Palace, as the custom was, in the presence of princely visitors, while Marzocco, the republican lion, wore his gold crown on the occasion, and all the people cried, "Viva Messer Bartolommeo!"—had been on an embassy to Rome, and had there been made titular Senator, Apostolical Secretary, Knight of the Golden Spur; and had, eight years ago, been Gonfaloniere—last goal of the Florentine citizen's ambition. Meantime he had got richer and richer, and more and more gouty, after the manner of successful mortality; and the Knight of the Golden Spur had often to sit with helpless cushioned heel under the handsome loggia he had built for himself overlooking the spacious gardens and lawn at the back of his palace.

He was in this position on the day when he had granted the desired interview to Tito Melema. The May afternoon sun was on the flowers and the grass beyond the pleasant shade of the loggia; the too stately silk lucco was cast aside, and the light loose mantle was thrown over his tunic; his beautiful daughter, Alessandra, and her husband, the Greek soldier-poet Marullo, were seated on one side of him: on the other, two friends not oppressively illustrious, and therefore the better listeners. Yet, to say nothing of the gout, Messer Bartolommeo's felicity was far from perfect: it was embittered by the contents of certain papers that lay before him, consisting chiefly of a correspondence between himself and Politian. It was a human foible at that period (incredible as it may seem) to recite quarrels, and favor scholarly visitors with the communication of an entire and lengthy correspondence; and this was neither the first nor the second time that Scala had asked the candid opinion of his friends as to the balance of right and wrong in some half-score Latin letters between himself and Politian, all springing out of certain epigrams written in the most playful tone in the world. It was the story of a very typical and pretty quarrel, in which we are interested, because it supplied precisely that thistle of hatred necessary, according to Nello, as a stimulus to the sluggish paces of the cautious steed, Friendship.

Politian, having been a rejected pretender to the love and the hand of Scala's daughter, kept a very sharp and learned tooth in readiness against the too prosperous and presumptuous secretary, who had declined the greatest scholar of the age for a son-in-law. Scala was a meritorious public servant, and, moreover, a lucky man—naturally exasperating to an offended scholar; but then—O beautiful balance of things!—he had an itch for authorship, and was a bad writer—one of those excellent people who, sitting in gouty slippers, "penned poetical trifles" entirely for their own amusement, without any view to an audience, and, consequently, sent them to their friends in letters, which were the literary periodicals of the fifteenth century. Now Scala had abundance of friends who were ready to praise his writings: friends like Ficino and Landino—amiable browsers in the Medicean park along with himself—who found his Latin prose style elegant and masculine; and the terrible Joseph Scaliger, who was to pronounce him totally ignorant of Latinity, was at a comfortable distance in the next century. But when was the fatal coquetry inherent in superfluous authorship ever quite contented with the ready praise of friends? That critical supercilious Politian—a fellow-browser, who was far from amiable—must be made aware that the solid secretary showed, in his leisure hours, a pleasant fertility in verses, which indicated pretty clearly how much he might do in that way if he were not a man of affairs.

Ineffable moment! when the man you secretly hate sends you a Latin epigram with a false gender—hendecasyllables with a questionable elision, at least a toe too much—attempts at poetic figures which are manifest solecisms. That moment had come to Politian: the secretary had put forth his soft head from the official shell, and the terrible lurking crab was down upon him. Politian had used the freedom of a friend, and pleasantly, in the form of a Latin epigram, corrected the mistake of Scala in making the *culex* (an insect too well known on the banks of the Arno) of the inferior or feminine gender. Scala replied by a bad joke, in suitable Latin verses, referring to Politian's unsuccessful suit. Better and better. Politian found the verses very pretty and highly facetious: the more was the pity that they were seriously incorrect, and inasmuch as Scala had alleged that he had written them in imitation of a Greek epigram, Politian, being on such friendly terms, would enclose a Greek epigram of his own, on the same interesting insect—not, we may presume, out of any wish to humble Scala, but rather to instruct him; said epigram containing a lively conceit about Venus, Cupid, and the *culex*, of a kind much tasted at that period, founded partly on the zoological fact that the gnat, like Venus, was born from the waters. Scala, in reply, begged to say that his verses were never intended for a scholar with such delicate olfactories as Politian, nearest of all living men to the perfection of the ancients, and of a taste so fastidious that sturgeon itself must seem insipid to him; defended his own verses, nevertheless, though indeed they were written hastily, without correction, and intended as an agreeable distraction during the summer heat to himself and such friends as were satisfied with mediocrity, he, Scala, not being like some other people, who courted publicity through the booksellers. For the rest, he had barely enough Greek to make out the sense of the epigram so graciously sent him, to say nothing of tasting its elegances; but—the epigram was Politian's: what more need be said? Still, by way of postscript, he feared that his incomparable friend's comparison of the gnat to Venus, on account of its origin from the waters, was in many ways ticklish. On the one hand, Venus might be offended; and on the other, unless the poet intended an allusion to the doctrine of Thales, that cold and damp origin seemed doubtful to Scala in the case of a creature so fond of warmth; a fish were perhaps the better comparison, or, when the power of flying was in question, an eagle, or indeed, when the darkness was taken into consideration, a bat or an owl were a less obscure and more apposite parallel, etc. Here was a great opportunity for Politian. He was not aware, he wrote, that when he had Scala's verses placed before him, there was any question of sturgeon, but rather of frogs and gudgeons. made short work with Scala's defence of his own Latin, and mangled him terribly on the score of the stupid criticisms he had ventured on the Greek epigram kindly forwarded to him as a model. Wretched cavils, indeed! for as to the damp origin of the gnat, there was the authority of Virgil himself, who had called it the "*alumnus* of the waters"; and as to what his dear dull friend had to say about the fish, the eagle, and the rest, it was "nihil ad rem"; for because the eagle could fly higher, it by no means followed that the gnat could not fly at all, etc. He was ashamed, however, to dwell on such trivialities, and thus to swell a gnat into an elephant; but, for his own part, would only add that he had nothing deceitful or double about him, neither was he to be caught when present by the false blandishments of those who slandered him in his absence, agreeing rather with a Homeric sentiment on that head—which furnished a Greek quotation to serve as powder to his bullet.

The quarrel could not end there. The logic could hardly get worse, but the secretary got more pompously self-asserting, and the scholarly poet's temper more and more venomous. Politian had been generously willing to hold up a mirror, by which the too-inflated secretary, beholding his own likeness, might be induced to cease setting up his ignorant defences of bad Latin against ancient authorities whom the consent of centuries had placed beyond question,—unless, indeed, he had designed to sink in literature in proportion as he rose in honors, that by a sort of compensation men of letters might feel themselves his equals. In return, Politian was begged to examine Scala's writings: nowhere would he find a more devout admiration of antiquity. The secretary was ashamed of the age in which he lived, and blushed for it. *Some*, indeed, there were who wanted to have their own works praised and exalted to a level with the divine monuments of antiquity; but he, Scala, could not oblige them. And as to the honors which were offensive to the envious, they had been well earned: witness his whole life since he came in penury to Florence. The elegant scholar, in reply, was not surprised that Scala found the Age distasteful to him, since he himself was so distasteful to the Age; nay, it was with perfect accuracy that he, the elegant scholar, had called Scala a branny monster, inasmuch as he was formed from the offscourings of monsters, born amidst the refuse of a mill, and eminently worthy the long-eared office of turning the paternal millstones (*in pistrini sordibus natus et quidem pistrino dignissimus*)!

It was not without reference to Tito's appointed visit that the papers containing this correspondence were brought out to-day. Here was a new Greek scholar whose accomplishments were to be tested, and on nothing did Scala more desire a dispassionate opinion from persons of superior knowledge than on that Greek epigram of Politian's. After sufficient introductory talk concerning Tito's travels, after a survey and discussion of the gems, and an easy passage from the mention of the lamented Lorenzo's eagerness in collecting such specimens of ancient art to the subject of classical tastes and studies in general and their present condition in Florence, it was inevitable to mention Politian, a man of eminent ability, indeed, but a little too arrogant—assuming to be a Hercules, whose office it was to destroy all the literary monstrosities of the age, and writing letters to his elders without signing them, as if they were miraculous revelations that could only have one source. And after all, were not his own criticisms often questionable and his tastes perverse? He was fond of saying pungent things about the men who thought they wrote like Cicero because they ended every sentence with "esse videtur": but while he was boasting of his freedom from servile imitation, did he not fall into the other extreme, running after strange words and affected phrases? Even in his much-belauded "Miscellanea" was every point tenable? And Tito, who had just been looking into the "Miscellanea," found so much to say that was agreeable to the secretary—he would have done so from the mere disposition to please, without further motive—that he showed himself quite worthy to be made a judge in the notable correspondence concerning the *culex.* Here was the Greek epigram which Politian had doubtless thought the finest in the world, though he had pretended to believe that the "transmarini," the Greeks themselves, would make light of it: had he not been unintentionally speaking the truth in his false modesty?

Tito was ready, and scarified the epigram to Scala's content. O wise young judge! He could doubtless appreciate satire even in the vulgar tongue, and Scala—who, excellent man, not seeking publicity through the booksellers, was never unprovided with "hasty uncorrected trifles," as a sort of sherbet for a visitor on a hot day, or, if the weather were cold, why then as a cordial—had a few little matters in the shape of Sonnets, turning on well-known foibles of Politian's, which he would not like to go any further, but which would, perhaps, amuse the company.

Enough: Tito took his leave under an urgent invitation to come again. His gems were interesting; especially the agate, with the *lusus naturæ* in it—a most wonderful semblance of Cupid riding on the lion; and the "Jew's stone," with the lion-headed serpent enchased in it; both of which the secretary agreed to buy—the latter as a re-enforcement of his preventives against the gout, which gave him such severe twinges that it was plain enough how intolerable it would be if he were not well supplied with rings of rare virtue, and with an amulet worn close under the right breast. But Tito was assured that he himself was more interesting than his gems. He had won his way to the Scala Palace by the recommendation of Bardo de' Bardi, who, to be sure, was Scala's old acquaintance and a worthy scholar, in spite of his overvaluing himself a little (a frequent foible in the secretary's friends); but he must come again on the ground of his own manifest accomplishments.

The interview could hardly have ended more auspiciously for Tito, and as he walked out at the Porta Pinti that he might laugh a little at his ease over the affair of the *culex*, he felt that fortune could hardly mean to turn her back on him again at present, since she had taken him by the hand in this decided way.

CHAPTER VIII.

A FACE IN THE CROWD.

It is easy to northern people to rise early on midsummer morning, to see the dew on the grassy edge of the dusty pathway, to notice the fresh shoots among the darker green of the oak and fir in the coppice, and to look over the gate at the shorn meadow, without recollecting that it is the Nativity of St. John the Baptist.

Not so to the Florentine—still less to the Florentine of the fifteenth century: to him on that particular morning the brightness of the eastern sun on the Arno had something special in it; the ringing of the bells was articulate, and declared it to be the great summer festival of Florence, the day of San Giovanni.

San Giovanni had been the patron saint of Florence for at least eight hundred years—ever since the time when the Lombard Queen Theodolinda had commanded her subjects to do him peculiar honor; nay, says old Villani, to the best of his knowledge, ever since the days of Constantine the Great and Pope Sylvester, when the Florentines deposed their idol Mars, whom they were nevertheless careful not to treat with contumely; for while they consecrated their beautiful and noble temple to the honor of God and of the "Beato Messere Santo Giovanni," they placed old Mars respectfully on a high tower near the River Arno, finding in certain ancient memorials that he had been elected as their tutelar deity under such astral influences that if he were broken, or otherwise treated with indignity, the city would suffer great damage and mutation. But in the fifteenth century that discreet regard to the feelings of the Man-destroyer had long vanished: the god of the spear and shield had ceased to frown by the side of the Arno, and the defences of the Republic were held to lie in its craft and its coffers. For spear and shield could be hired by gold florins, and on the gold florins there had always been the image of San Giovanni.

Much good had come to Florence since the dim time of struggle between the old patron and the new: some quarrelling and bloodshed, doubtless, between Guelf and Ghibelline, between Black and White, between orthodox sons of the Church and heretic Paterini; some floods, famine, and pestilence; but still much wealth and glory. Florence had achieved conquests over walled cities once mightier than itself, and especially over hated Pisa, whose marble buildings were too high and beautiful, whose masts were too much honored on Greek and Italian coasts. The name of Florence had been growing prouder and prouder in all the courts of Europe, nay, in Africa itself, on the strength of purest gold coinage, finest dyes and textures, pre-eminent scholarship and poetic genius, and wits of the most serviceable sort for statesmanship and banking: it was a name so omnipresent that a Pope with a turn for epigram had called Florentines "the fifth element." And for this high destiny, though it might partly depend on the stars and Madonna dell' Impruneta, and certainly depended on other higher Powers less often named, the praise was greatly due to San Giovanni, whose image was on the fair gold florins.

Therefore it was fitting that the day of San Giovanni—that ancient Church festival already venerable in the days of St. Augustine—should be a day of peculiar rejoicing to Florence, and should be ushered in by a vigil duly kept in strict old Florentine fashion, with much dancing, with much street jesting, and perhaps with not a little stone-throwing and window-breaking, but emphatically with certain street sights such as could only be provided by a city which held in its service a clever Cecca, engineer and architect, valuable alike in sieges and in shows. By the help of Cecca, the very saints, surrounded with their almond-shaped glory, and floating on clouds with their joyous companionship of winged cherubs, even as they may be seen to this day in the pictures of Perugino, seemed, on the eve of San Giovanni, to have brought their piece of the heavens down into the narrow streets, and to pass slowly through them; and, more wonderful still, saints of gigantic size, with attendant angels, might be seen, not seated, but moving in a slow mysterious manner along the streets, like a procession of colossal figures come down from the high domes and tribunes of the churches. The clouds were made of good woven stuff, the saints and cherubs were unglorified mortals supported by firm bars, and those mysterious giants were really men of very steady brain, balancing themselves on stilts, and enlarged, like Greek tragedians, by huge masks and stuffed shoulders; but he was a miserably unimaginative Florentine who thought only of that—nay, somewhat impious, for in the images of sacred things was there not some of the virtue of sacred things themselves? And if, after that, there came a company of merry black demons well armed with claws and thongs, and other implements of sport, ready to perform impromptu farces of bastinadoing and clothes-tearing, why, that was the demons' way of keeping a vigil, and they, too, might have descended from the domes and the tribunes. The Tuscan mind slipped from the devout to the burlesque as readily as water round an angle; and the saints had already had their turn, had gone their way, and made their due pause before the gates of San Giovanni, to do him honor on the eve of his *festa*. And on the morrow, the great day thus ushered in, it was fitting that the tributary symbols paid to Florence by all its dependent cities, districts, and villages, whether conquered, protected, or of immemorial possession, should be offered at the shrine of San Giovanni in the old octagonal church, once the cathedral, and now the baptistery, where every Florentine had had the sign of the Cross made with the anointing chrism on his brow; that all the city, from the white-haired man to the stripling, and from the matron to the lisping child, should be clothed in its best to do honor to the great day, and see the great sight; and that again, when the sun was sloping and the streets were cool, there should be the glorious race or Corso, when the unsaddled horses, clothed in rich trappings, should run right across the city from the Porta al Prato on the northwest, through the Mercato Vecchio, to the Porta

Santa Croce on the southeast, where the richest of *Palii*, or velvet and brocade banners with silk linings and fringe of gold, such as became a city that half clothed the well-dressed world, were mounted on a triumphal car awaiting the winner or winner's owner.

And thereafter followed more dancing; nay, through the whole day, says an old chronicler at the beginning of that century, there were weddings and the grandest gatherings, with so much piping, music and song, with balls and feasts and gladness and ornament, that this earth might have been mistaken for Paradise!

In this year of 1492 it was, perhaps, a little less easy to make that mistake. Lorenzo the magnificent and subtle was dead, and an arrogant, incautious Piero was come in his room, an evil change for Florence, unless, indeed, the wise horse prefers the bad rider, as more easily thrown from the saddle; and already the regrets for Lorenzo were getting less predominant over the murmured desire for government on a broader basis, in which corruption might be arrested, and there might be that free play for everybody's jealousy and ambition which made the ideal liberty of the good old quarrelsome, struggling times, when Florence raised her great buildings, reared her own soldiers, drove out would-be tyrants at the sword's point, and was proud to keep faith at her own loss. Lorenzo was dead, Pope Innocent was dying, and a troublesome Neapolitan succession, with an intriguing, ambitious Milan, might set Italy by the ears before long: the times were likely to be difficult. Still, there was all the more reason that the Republic should keep its religious festivals.

And midsummer morning, in this year 1492, was not less bright than usual. It was betimes in the morning that the symbolic offerings to be carried in grand procession were all assembled at their starting-point in the Piazza della Signoria —that famous piazza, where stood then, and stand now, the massive turreted Palace of the People, called the Palazzo Vecchio, and the spacious Loggia, built by Orcagna—the scene of all grand State ceremonial. The sky made the fairest blue tent, and under it the bells swung so vigorously that every evil spirit with sense enough to be formidable must long since have taken his flight; windows and terraced roofs were alive with human faces; sombre stone houses were bright with hanging draperies; the boldly soaring palace tower, the yet older square tower of the Bargello, and the spire of the neighboring Badia, seemed to keep watch above; and below, on the broad polygonal flags of the piazza, was the glorious show of banners, and horses with rich trappings, and gigantic *ceri*, or tapers, that were fitly called towers—strangely aggrandized descendants of those torches by whose faint light the Church worshipped in the Catacombs. Betimes in the morning all processions had need to move under the midsummer sky of Florence, where the shelter of the narrow streets must every now and then be exchanged for the glare of wide spaces; and the sun would be high up in the heavens before the long pomp had ended its pilgrimage in the Piazza di San Giovanni.

But here, where the procession was to pause, the magnificent city, with its ingenious Cecca, had provided another tent than the sky; for the whole of the Piazza del Duomo, from the octagonal baptistery in the centre to the façade of the cathedral and the walls of the houses on the other sides of the quadrangle, was covered, at the height of forty feet or more, with blue drapery, adorned with well-stitched yellow lilies and the familiar coats of arms, while sheaves of many-colored banners drooped at fit angles under this superincumbent blue —a gorgeous rainbow-lit shelter to the waiting spectators who leaned from the windows, and made a narrow border on the pavement, and wished for the coming of the show.

One of these spectators was Tito Melema. Bright, in the midst of brightness, he sat at the window of the room above Nello's shop, his right elbow resting on the red drapery hanging from the window-sill, and his head supported in a backward position by the right hand, which pressed the curls against his ear. His face wore that bland liveliness, as far removed from excitability as from heaviness or gloom, which marks the companion popular alike amongst men and women— the companion who is never obtrusive or noisy from uneasy vanity or excessive animal spirits, and whose brow is never contracted by resentment or indignation. He showed no other change from the two months and more that had passed since his first appearance in the weather-stained tunic and hose than that added radiance of good fortune which is like the just perceptible perfecting of a flower after it has drunk a morning's sunbeams. Close behind him, ensconced in the narrow angle between his chair and the window-frame, stood the slim figure of Nello in holiday suit, and at his left the younger Cennini—Pietro, the erudite corrector of proof-sheets, not Domenico the practical. Tito was looking alternately down on the scene below, and upward at the varied knot of gazers and talkers immediately around him, some of whom had come in after witnessing the commencement of the procession in the Piazza della Signoria. Piero di Cosimo was raising a laugh among them by his grimaces and anathemas at the noise of the bells, against which no kind of ear-stuffing was a sufficient barricade, since the more he stuffed his ears the more he felt the vibration of his skull; and declaring that he would bury himself in the most solitary spot of the Valdarno on a *festa*, if he were not condemned, as a painter, to lie in wait for the secrets of color that were sometimes to be caught from the floating of banners and the chance grouping of the multitude.

Tito had just turned his laughing face away from the whimsical painter to look down at the small drama going on among the checkered border of spectators, when at the angle of the marble steps in front of the Duomo, nearly opposite Nello's shop, he saw a man's face upturned toward him, and fixing on him a gaze that seemed to have more meaning in it than the ordinary passing observation of a stranger. It was a face with tonsured head, that rose above the black mantle and white tunic of a Dominican friar—a very common sight in Florence; but the glance had something peculiar in it for Tito. There was a faint suggestion in it, certainly not of an unpleasant kind. Yet what pleasant association had he ever had with monks? None. The glance and the suggestion hardly took longer than a flash of lightning.

"Nello!" said Tito, hastily, but immediately added in a tone of disappointment, "Ah, he has turned round. It was that tall, thin friar who is going up the steps. I wanted you to tell me if you knew aught of him?"

"One of the Frati Predicatori," said Nello, carelessly;

"you don't expect me to know the private history of the crows."

"I seem to remember something about his face," said Tito. "It is an uncommon face."

"What? you thought it might be our Fra Girolamo? Too tall; and he never shows himself in that chance way."

"Besides, that loud-barking 'hound of the Lord'[1] is not in Florence just now," said Francesco Cei, the popular poet; "he has taken Piero de' Medici's hint, to carry his railing prophecies on a journey for a while."

"The Frate neither rails nor prophesies against any man," said a middle-aged personage seated at the other corner of the window; "he only prophesies against vice. If you think that an attack on your poems, Francesco, it is not the Frate's fault."

"Ah, he's gone into the Duomo now," said Tito, who had watched the figure eagerly. "No, I was not under that mistake, Nello. Your Fra Girolamo has a high nose and a large under lip. I saw him once—he is not handsome; but this man . . ."

"Truce to your descriptions!" said Cennini. "Hark! see! Here come the horsemen and the banners. That standard," he continued, laying his hand familiarly on Tito's shoulder,—"that carried on the horse with white trappings—that with the red eagle holding the green dragon between his talons, and the red lily over the eagle—is the Gonfalon of the Guelf party, and those cavaliers close round it are the chief officers of the Guelf party. That is one of our proudest banners, grumble as we may; it means the triumph of the Guelfs, which means the triumph of Florentine will, which means triumph of the popolani."

"Nay, go on, Cennini," said the middle-aged man, seated at the window, "which means triumph of the fat popolani over the lean, which again means triumph of the fattest popolano over those who are less fat."

"Cronaca, you are becoming sententious," said the printer;

---

[1] A play on the name of the Dominicans (*Domini Canes*) which was accepted by themselves, and which is pictorially represented in a fresco painted for them by Simone Memmi.

"Fra Girolamo's preaching will spoil you, and make you take life by the wrong handle. Trust me, your cornices will lose half their beauty if you begin to mingle bitterness with them; that is the *maniera Tedesca* which you used to declaim against when you came from Rome. The next palace you build we shall see you trying to put the Frate's doctrine into stone."

"That is a goodly show of cavaliers," said Tito, who had learned by this time the best way to please Florentines; "but are there not strangers among them? I see foreign costumes."

"Assuredly," said Cennini; "you see there the Orators from France, Milan, and Venice, and behind them are English and German nobles; for it is customary that all foreign visitors of distinction pay their tribute to San Giovanni in the train of that gonfalon. For my part, I think our Florentine cavaliers sit their horses as well as any of those cut-and-thrust northerners, whose wits lie in their heels and saddles: and for yon Venetian, I fancy he would feel himself more at ease on the back of a dolphin. We ought to know something of horsemanship, for we excel all Italy in the sports of the Giostra, and the money we spend on them. But you will see a finer show of our chief men by and by, Melema; my brother himself will be among the officers of the Zecca."

"The banners are the better sight," said Piero di Cosimo, forgetting the noise in his delight at the winding stream of color as the tributary standards advanced round the piazza. "The Florentine men are so-so; they make but a sorry show at this distance with their patch of sallow flesh-tint above the black garments; but those banners with their velvet, and satin, and miniver, and brocade, and their endless play of delicate light and shadow!—*Va!* your human talk and doings are a tame jest; the only passionate life is in form and color."

"Ay, Piero, if Satanasso could paint, thou wouldst sell thy soul to learn his secrets," said Nello. "But there is little likelihood of it, seeing the blessed angels themselves are such poor hands at chiaroscuro, if one may judge from their *capo-d'opera*, the Madonna Nunziata."

"There go the banners of Pisa and Arezzo," said Cennini. "Ay, Messer Pisano, it is no use for you to look sullen; you may as well carry your banner to our San Giovanni with a good grace. ' Pisans false, Florentines blind'—the second half of that proverb will hold no longer. There come the ensigns of our subject towns and signories, Melema; they will all be suspended in San Giovanni until this day next year, when they will give place to new ones."

"They are a fair sight," said Tito; "and San Giovanni will surely be as well satisfied with that produce of Italian looms as Minerva with her peplos, especially as he contents himself with so little drapery. But my eyes are less delighted with those whirling towers, which would soon make me fall from the window in sympathetic vertigo."

The "towers" of which Tito spoke were a part of the procession esteemed very glorious by the Florentine populace, and being perhaps chiefly a kind of hyperbole for the all-efficacious wax taper, were also called *ceri*. But inasmuch as hyperbole is impracticable in a real and literal fashion, these gigantic *ceri*, some of them so large as to be of necessity carried on wheels, were not solid but hollow, and had their surface made not solely of wax, but of wood and pasteboard, gilded, carved, and painted, as real sacred tapers often are, with successive circles of figures—warriors on horseback, foot-soldiers with lance and shield, dancing maidens, animals, trees and fruits, and in fine, says the old chronicler, "all things that could delight the eye and the heart"; the hollowness having the further advantage that men could stand inside these hyperbolic tapers and whirl them continually, so as to produce a phantasmagoric effect, which, considering the towers were numerous, must have been calculated to produce dizziness on a truly magnificent scale.

"*Pestilenza!*" said Piero di Cosimo, moving from the window, "those whirling circles one above the other are worse than the jangling of all the bells. Let me know when the last taper has passed."

"Nay, you will surely like to be called when the contadini come carrying their torches," said Nello; "you would not miss the country folk of the Mugello and the Casentino, of whom your favorite Lionardo would make a hundred grotesque sketches."

"No," said Piero, resolutely, "I will see nothing till the car of the Zecca comes. I have seen clowns enough holding tapers aslant, both with and without cowls, to last me for my life."

"Here it comes, then, Piero—the car of the Zecca," called out Nello, after an interval during which towers and tapers in a descending scale of size had been making their slow transit.

"*Fediddio!*" exclaimed Francesco Cei, "that is a well-tanned San Giovanni! some sturdy Romagnole beggar-man, I'll warrant. Our Signoria plays the host to all the Jewish and Christian scum that every other city shuts its gates against, and lets them fatten on us like St. Anthony's swine."

The car of the Zecca or Mint, which had just rolled into sight, was originally an immense wooden tower or *cero* adorned after the same fashion as the other tributary *ceri*, mounted on a splendid car, and drawn by two mouse-colored oxen, whose mild heads looked out from rich trappings bearing the arms of the Zecca. But the latter half of the century was getting rather ashamed of the towers with their circular or spiral paintings, which had delighted the eyes and the hearts of the other half, so that they had become a contemptuous proverb, and any ill-painted figure looking, as will sometimes happen to figures in the best ages of art, as if it had been boned for a pie, was called a *fantoccio da cero*, a tower-puppet; consequently improved taste, with Cecca to help it, had devised for the magnificent Zecca a triumphal car like a pyramidal catafalque, with ingenious wheels warranted to turn all corners easily. Round the base were living figures of saints and angels arrayed in sculpturesque fashion; and on the summit, at the height of thirty feet, well bound to an iron rod and holding an iron cross also firmly infixed, stood a living representative of St. John the Baptist, with arms and legs bare, a garment of tiger-skins about his body, and a golden nimbus fastened on his head—as the Precursor was wont to appear in the cloisters and churches, not having yet revealed himself to painters as the brown and sturdy boy who made one of the Holy Family. For where could the image of the patron saint be more fitly placed than on the symbol of the Zecca? Was not the royal prerogative of coining money the surest token that a city had won its independence? and by the blessing of San Giovanni this "beautiful sheepfold" of his had shown that token earliest among the Italian cities. Nevertheless, the annual function of representing the patron saint was not among the high prizes of public life; it was paid for with something like ten shillings, a cake weighing fourteen pounds, two bottles of wine, and a handsome supply of light eatables; the money being furnished by the magnificent Zecca, and the payment in kind being by peculiar "privilege" presented in a basket suspended on a pole from an upper window of a private house, whereupon the eidolon of the austere saint at once invigorated himself with a reasonable share of the sweets and wine, threw the remnants to the crowd, and embraced the mighty cake securely with his right arm through the remainder of his passage. This was the attitude in which the mimic San Giovanni presented himself as the tall car jerked and vibrated on its slow way round the piazza to the northern gate of the Baptistery.

"There go the Masters of the Zecca, and there is my brother —you see him, Melema?" cried Cennini, with an agreeable stirring of pride at showing a stranger what was too familiar to be remarkable to fellow-citizens. "Behind come the members of the Corporation of Calimara,[1] the dealers in foreign cloth, to which we have given our Florentine finish; men of ripe years, you see, who were matriculated before you were born; and then comes the famous Art of Money-changers."

"Many of them matriculated also to the noble art of usury before you were born," interrupted Francesco Cei, "as you may discern by a certain fitful glare of the eye and sharp curve of the nose which manifest their descent from the ancient Harpies, whose portraits you saw supporting the arms of the Zecca. Shaking off old prejudices now, such a procession as that of some four hundred passably ugly men carrying their tapers in open daylight, Diogenes-fashion, as if they were looking for a lost quattrino, would make a merry spectacle for the Feast of Fools."

"Blaspheme not against the usages of our city," said Pietro Cennini, much offended. "There are new wits who think they see things more truly because they stand on their heads to

[1] "Arte di Calimara," "arte" being, in this use of it, equivalent to corporation.

look at them, like tumblers and mountebanks, instead of keeping the attitude of rational men. Doubtless it makes little difference to Maestro Vaiano's monkeys whether they see our Donatello's statue of Judith with their heads or their tails uppermost."

"Your solemnity will allow some quarter to playful fancy, I hope," said Cei, with a shrug, "else what becomes of the ancients, whose example you scholars are bound to revere, Messer Pietro? Life was never anything but a perpetual seesaw between gravity and jest."

"Keep your jest then till your end of the pole is uppermost," said Cennini, still angry, "and that is not when the great bond of our Republic is expressing itself in ancient symbols, without which the vulgar would be conscious of nothing beyond their own petty wants of back and stomach, and never rise to the sense of community in religion and law. There has been no great people without processions, and the man who thinks himself too wise to be moved by them to anything but contempt is like the puddle that was proud of standing alone while the river rushed by."

No one said anything after this indignant burst of Cennini's till he himself spoke again.

"Hark! the trumpets of the Signoria: now comes the last stage of the show, Melema. That is our Gonfaloniere in the middle, in the starred mantle, with the sword carried before him. Twenty years ago we used to see our foreign Podestà, who was our judge in civil causes, walking on his right hand; but our Republic has been over-doctored by clever *Medici*. That is the Proposto [1] of the Priori on the left; then come the other seven Priori; then all the other magistracies and officials of our Republic. You see your patron the Segretario?"

"There is Messer Bernardo del Nero also," said Tito; "his visage is a fine and venerable one, though it has worn rather a petrifying look toward me."

"Ah," said Nello, "he is the dragon that guards the remnant of old Bardo's gold, which, I fancy, is chiefly that virgin gold that falls about the fair Romola's head and shoulders; eh, my Apollino?" he added, patting Tito's head.

[1] Spokesman or Moderator.

Tito had the youthful grace of blushing, but he had also the adroit and ready speech that prevents a blush from looking like embarrassment. He replied at once,—

"And a very Pactolus it is—a stream with golden ripples. If I were an alchemist———"

He was saved from the need for further speech by the sudden fortissimo of drums and trumpets and fifes, bursting into the breadth of the piazza in a grand storm of sound—a roar, a blast, and a whistling well befitting a city famous for its musical instruments, and reducing the members of the closest group to a state of deaf isolation.

During this interval Nello observed Tito's fingers moving in recognition of some one in the crowd below, but not seeing the direction of his glance he failed to detect the object of this greeting—the sweet round blue-eyed face under a white hood—immediately lost in the narrow border of heads, where there was a continual eclipse of round contadina cheeks by the harsh-lined features or bent shoulders of an old spadesman, and where profiles turned as sharply from north to south as weather-cocks under a shifting wind.

But when it was felt that the show was ended—when the twelve prisoners released in honor of the day, and the very *barberi* or race-horses, with the arms of their owners embroidered on their cloths, had followed up the Signoria, and been duly consecrated to San Giovanni, and every one was moving from the window—Nello, whose Florentine curiosity was of that lively canine sort which thinks no trifle too despicable for investigation, put his hand on Tito's shoulder and said,—

"What acquaintance was that you were making signals to, eh, *giovane mio?*"

"Some little contadina who probably mistook me for an acquaintance, for she had honored me with a greeting."

"Or who wished to begin an acquaintance," said Nello. "But you are bound for the Via de' Bardi and the feast of the Muses: there is no counting on you for a frolic, else we might have gone in search of adventures together in the crowd, and had some pleasant fooling in honor of San Giovanni. But your high fortune has come on you too soon: I don't mean the professor's mantle—*that* is roomy enough to hide a few stolen chickens, but—— Messer Endymion minded his manners after that singular good fortune of his; and what says our Luigi Pulci?

> " 'Da quel giorno in quà ch'amor m'accese
> Per lei son fatto e gentile e cortese ' "

"Nello, *amico mio*, thou hast an intolerable trick of making life stale by forestalling it with thy talk," said Tito, shrugging his shoulders with a look of patient resignation, which was his nearest approach to anger: "not to mention that such ill-founded babbling would be held a great offence by that same goddess whose humble worshipper you are always professing yourself."

"I will be mute," said Nello, laying his finger on his lips, with a responding shrug. "But it is only under our four eyes that I talk any folly about her."

"Pardon! you were on the verge of it just now in the hearing of others. If you want to ruin me in the minds of Bardo and his daughter——"

"Enough, enough!" said Nello. "I am an absurd old barber. It all comes from that abstinence of mine, in not making bad verses in my youth: for want of letting my folly run out that way when I was eighteen, it runs out at my tongue's end now I am at the unseemly age of fifty. But Nello has not got his head muffled for all that; he can see a buffalo in the snow. *Addio, giovane mio.*"

CHAPTER IX.

A MAN'S RANSOM.

TITO was soon down among the crowd, and, notwithstanding his indifferent reply to Nello's question about his chance acquaintance, he was not without a passing wish, as he made his way round the piazza to the Corso degli Adimari, that he might encounter the pair of blue eyes which had looked up toward him from under the square bit of white linen drapery that formed the ordinary hood of the contadina at festa time.

He was perfectly well aware that that face was Tessa's; but he had not chosen to say so. What had Nello to do with the matter? Tito had an innate love of reticence—let us say a talent for it—which acted as other impulses do, without any conscious motive, and, like all people to whom concealment is easy, he would now and then conceal something which had as little the nature of a secret as the fact that he had seen a flight of crows.

But the passing wish about the pretty Tessa was almost immediately eclipsed by the recurrent recollection of that friar whose face had some irrecoverable association for him. Why should a sickly fanatic, worn with fasting, have looked at *him* in particular, and where in all his travels could he remember encountering that face before? Folly! such vague memories hang about the mind like cobwebs, with a tickling importunity —best to sweep them away at a dash: and Tito had pleasanter occupation for his thoughts. By the time he was turning out of the Corso degli Adimari into a side street he was caring only that the sun was high, and that the procession had kept him longer than he had intended from his visit to that room in the Via de' Bardi, where his coming, he knew, was anxiously awaited. He felt the scene of his entrance beforehand: the joy beaming diffusedly in the blind face like the light in a semi-transparent lamp; the transient pink flush on Romola's face and neck, which subtracted nothing from her majesty, but only gave it the exquisite charm of womanly sensitiveness, heightened still more by what seemed the paradoxical boy-like frankness of her look and smile. They were the best comrades in the world during the hours they passed together round the blind man's chair: she was constantly appealing to Tito, and he was informing her, yet he felt himself strangely in subjection to Romola with that simplicity of hers: he felt for the first time, without defining it to himself, that loving awe in the presence of noble womanhood, which is perhaps something like the worship paid of old to a great nature-goddess, who was not all-knowing, but whose life and power were something deeper and more primordial than knowledge. They had never been alone together, and he could frame to himself no probable image of love-scenes between them: he could only fancy and wish wildly—what he knew was impossible—that Romola would some day tell him that she loved him. One day in Greece, as he was leaning over a wall in the sunshine, a little black-eyed peasant girl, who had rested her water-pot on the wall, crept gradually nearer and nearer to him, and at last shyly asked him to kiss her, putting up her round olive cheek very innocently. Tito was used to love that came in this unsought fashion. But Romola's love would never come in that way: would it ever come at all?—and yet it was that topmost apple on which he had set his mind. He was in his fresh youth—not passionate, but impressible: it was as inevitable that he should feel lovingly toward Romola as that the white irises should be reflected in the clear sunlit stream; but he had no coxcombry, and he had an intimate sense that Romola was something very much above him. Many men have felt the same before a large-eyed, simple child.

Nevertheless, Tito had had the rapid success which would have made some men presuming, or would have warranted him in thinking that there would be no great presumption in entertaining an agreeable confidence that he might one day be the husband of Romola—nay, that her father himself was not without a vision of such a future for him. His first auspicious interview with Bartolommeo Scala had proved the commencement of a growing favor on the secretary's part, and had led to an issue which would have been enough to make Tito decide on Florence as the place in which to establish himself, even if it had held no other magnet. Politian was professor of Greek as well as Latin at Florence, professorial chairs being maintained there, although the university had been removed to Pisa; but for a long time Demetrio Calcondila, one of the most eminent and respectable among the emigrant Greeks, had also held a Greek chair, simultaneously with the too-predominant Italian. Calcondila was now gone to Milan, and there was no counterpoise or rival to Politian such as was desired for him by the friends who wished him to be taught a little propriety and humility. Scala was far from being the only friend of this class, and he found several who, if they were not among those thirsty admirers of mediocrity that were glad to be refreshed with his verses in hot weather, were yet quite willing to join him in doing that moral service to Politian. It was finally agreed that Tito should be supported in a Greek chair, as Demetrio Calcondila had been by Lorenzo himself, who, being at the same time the affectionate patron of Politian, had shown by precedent that there was nothing invidious in such a measure, but only a zeal for true learning and for the instruction of the Florentine youth.

Tito was thus sailing under the fairest breeze, and besides convincing fair judges that his talents squared with his good fortune, he wore that fortune so easily and unpretentiously that no one had yet been offended by it. He was not unlikely to get into the best Florentine society: society where there was much more plate than the circle of enamelled silver in the centre of the brass dishes, and where it was not forbidden by the Signory to wear the richest brocade. For where could a handsome young scholar not be welcome when he could touch the lute and troll a gay song? That bright face, that easy smile, that liquid voice, seemed to give life a holiday aspect; just as a strain of gay music and the hoisting of colors make the workworn and the sad rather ashamed of showing themselves. Here was a professor likely to render the Greek classics amiable to the sons of great houses.

And that was not the whole of Tito's good fortune; for he had sold all his jewels, except the ring he did not choose to part with, and he was master of full five hundred gold florins.

Yet the moment when he first had this sum in his possession was the crisis of the first serious struggle his facile, good-humored nature had known. An importunate thought, of which he had till now refused to see more than the shadow as it dogged his footsteps, at last rushed upon him and grasped him: he was obliged to pause and decide whether he would surrender and obey, or whether he would give the refusal that must carry irrevocable consequences. It was in the room above Nello's shop, which Tito had now hired as a lodging, that the elder Cennini handed him the last quota of the sum on behalf of Bernardo Rucellai, the purchaser of the two most valuable gems.

" *Ecco, giovane mio!* " said the respectable printer and goldsmith, "you have now a pretty little fortune; and if you will take my advice, you will let me place your florins in a safe quarter, where they may increase and multiply, instead of slipping through your fingers for banquets and other follies which are rife among our Florentine youth. And it has been too much the fashion of scholars, especially when, like our Pietro Crinito, they think their scholarship needs to be scented and broidered, to squander with one hand till they have been fain to beg with the other. I have brought you the money, and you are free to make a wise choice or an unwise: I shall see on which side the balance dips. We Florentines hold no man a member of an Art till he has shown his skill and been matriculated; and no man is matriculated to the art of life till he has been well tempted. If you make up your mind to put your florins out to usury, you can let me know to-morrow. A scholar may marry, and should have something in readiness for the *morgen-cap*.[1] *Addio.*"

As Cennini closed the door behind him, Tito turned round with the smile dying out of his face, and fixed his eyes on the table where the florins lay. He made no other movement, but stood with his thumbs in his belt, looking down, in that transfixed state which accompanies the concentration of consciousness on some inward image.

"A man's ransom!"—who was it that had said five hundred florins was more than a man's ransom? If now, under this midday sun, on some hot coast far away, a man somewhat stricken in years—a man not without high thoughts and with the most passionate heart—a man who long years ago had rescued a little boy from a life of beggary, filth, and cruel wrong, had reared him tenderly and been to him as a father—if that man were now under this summer sun, toiling as a slave, hewing wood and drawing water, perhaps being smitten and buffeted because he was not deft and active? If he were saying to himself, "Tito will find me: he had but to carry our manuscripts and gems to Venice; he will have raised money, and will never rest till he finds me out"? If that were certain, could he, Tito, see the price of the gems lying before him, and say, "I will stay at Florence, where I am fanned by soft airs

[1] A sum given by the bridegroom to the bride the day after the marriage (*Morgengabe*).

of promised love and prosperity; I will not risk myself for his sake"? No, surely not, *if it were certain.* But nothing could be farther from certainty. The galley had been taken by a Turkish vessel on its way to Delos: *that* was known by the report of the companion galley, which had escaped. But there had been resistance, and probable bloodshed; a man had been seen falling overboard: who were the survivors, and what had befallen them amongst all the multitude of possibilities? Had not he, Tito, suffered shipwreck and narrowly escaped drowning? He had good cause for feeling the omnipresence of casualties that threatened all projects with futility. The rumor that they were pirates who had a settlement in Delos was not to be depended on, or might be nothing to the purpose. What, probably enough, would be the result if he were to quit Florence and go to Venice; get authoritative letters—yes, he knew that might be done—and set out for the Archipelago? Why, that he should be himself seized, and spend all his florins on preliminaries, and be again a destitute wanderer—with no more gems to sell.

Tito had a clearer vision of that result than of the possible moment when he might find his father again, and carry him deliverance. It would surely be an unfairness that he, in his full ripe youth, to whom life had hitherto had some of the stint and subjection of a school, should turn his back on promised love and distinction, and perhaps never be visited by that promise again. "And yet," he said to himself, "if I were certain that Baldassarre Calvo was alive, and that I could free him, by whatever exertions or perils, I would go now—now I have the money: it was useless to debate the matter before. I would go now to Bardo and Bartolommeo Scala, and tell them the whole truth." Tito did not say to himself so distinctly that if those two men had known the whole truth he was aware there would have been no alternative for him but to go in search of his benefactor, who, if alive, was the rightful owner of the gems, and whom he had always equivocally spoken of as "lost"; he did not say to himself—what he was not ignorant of—that Greeks of distinction had made sacrifices, taken voyages again and again, and sought help from crowned and mitred heads for the sake of freeing relatives from slavery to the Turks. Public opinion did not regard this as exceptional virtue.

This was his first real colloquy with himself: he had gone on following the impulses of the moment, and one of those impulses had been to conceal half the fact; he had never considered this part of his conduct long enough to face the consciousness of his motives for the concealment. What was the use of telling the whole? It was true, the thought had crossed his mind several times since he had quitted Nauplia that, after all, it was a great relief to be quit of Baldassarre, and he would have liked to know *who* it was that had fallen overboard. But such thoughts spring inevitably out of a relation that is irksome. Baldassarre was exacting, and had got stranger as he got older: he was constantly scrutinizing Tito's mind to see whether it answered to his own exaggerated expectations; and age—the age of a thick-set, heavy-browed, bald man beyond sixty, whose intensity and eagerness in the grasp of ideas have long taken the character of monotony and repetition, may be looked at from many points of view without being found attractive. Such a man stranded among new acquaintances, unless he had the philosopher's stone, would hardly find rank, youth, and beauty at his feet. The feelings that gather fervor from novelty will be of little help toward making the world a home for dimmed and faded human beings; and if there is any love of which they are not widowed, it must be the love that is rooted in memories and distils perpetually the sweet balms of fidelity and forbearing tenderness.

But surely such memories were not absent from Tito's mind? Far in the backward vista of his remembered life, when he was only seven years old, Baldassarre had rescued him from blows, had taken him to a home that seemed like opened paradise, where there was sweet food and soothing caresses, all had on Baldassarre's knee; and from that time till the hour they had parted, Tito had been the one centre of Baldassarre's fatherly cares.

And he had been docile, pliable, quick of apprehension, ready to acquire. a very bright lovely boy, a youth of even splendid grace, who seemed quite without vices, as if that beautiful form represented a vitality so exquisitely poised and balanced that it could know no uneasy desires, no unrest—a radiant presence for a lonely man to have won for himself. If he were silent when his father expected some response, still he did not look moody; if he declined some labor—why, he flung himself down with such a charming, half-smiling, half-pleading air that the pleasure of looking at him made amends to one who had watched his growth with a sense of claim and possession: the curves of Tito's mouth had ineffable good humor in them. And then, the quick talent to which everything came readily, from philosophical systems to the rhymes of a street ballad caught up at a hearing! Would any one have said that Tito had not made a rich return to his benefactor, or that his gratitude and affection would fail on any great demand?

He did not admit that his gratitude had failed; but *it was not certain* that Baldassarre was in slavery, not certain that he was living.

"Do I not owe something to myself?" said Tito, inwardly, with a slight movement of his shoulders, the first he had made since he had turned to look down at the florins. "Before I quit everything, and incur again all the risks of which I am even now weary, I must at least have a reasonable hope. Am I to spend my life in a wandering search? *I believe he is dead.* Cennini was right about my florins: I will place them in his hands to-morrow."

When, the next morning, Tito put this determination into act he had chosen his color in the game, and had given an inevitable bent to his wishes. He had made it impossible that he should not from henceforth desire it to be the truth that his father was dead; impossible that he should not be tempted to baseness rather than that the precise facts of his conduct should not remain forever concealed.

Under every guilty secret there is hidden a brood of guilty wishes, whose unwholesome infecting life is cherished by the darkness. The contaminating effect of deeds often lies less in the commission than in the consequent adjustment of our desires—the enlistment of our self-interest on the side of falsity; as, on the other hand, the purifying influence of public confession springs from the fact that by it the hope in lies is forever swept away, and the soul recovers the noble attitude of simplicity.

Besides, in this first distinct colloquy with himself the ideas which had previously been scattered and interrupted had now concentrated themselves; the little rills of selfishness had united and made a channel, so that they could never again meet with the same resistance. Hitherto Tito had left in vague indecision the question whether, with the means in his power, he would not return, and ascertain his father's fate; he had now made a definite excuse to himself for not taking that course; he had avowed to himself a choice which he would have been ashamed to avow to others, and which would have made him ashamed in the resurgent presence of his father. But the inward shame, the reflex of that outward law which the great heart of mankind makes for every individual man, a reflex which will exist even in the absence of the sympathetic impulses that need no law, but rush to the deed of fidelity and pity as inevitably as the brute mother shields her young from the attack of the hereditary enemy—that inward shame was showing its blushes in Tito's determined assertion to himself that his father was dead, or that at least search was hopeless.

CHAPTER X.

UNDER THE PLANE-TREE.

On the day of San Giovanni it was already three weeks ago that Tito had handed his florins to Cennini, and we have seen that as he set out toward the Via de' Bardi he showed all the outward signs of a mind at ease. How should it be otherwise? He never jarred with what was immediately around him, and his nature was too joyous, too unapprehensive, for the hidden and the distant to grasp him in the shape of a dread. As he turned out of the hot sunshine into the shelter of a narrow street, took off the black cloth berretta, or simple cap with upturned lappet, which just crowned his brown curls, pushing his hair and tossing his head backward to court the cooler air, there was no brand of duplicity on his brow; neither was there any stamp of candor: it was simply a finely formed, square, smooth young brow. And the slow absent glance he cast around at the upper windows of the houses had neither more dissimulation in it, nor more ingenuousness, than belongs to a youthful well-opened eyelid with its unwearied breadth of gaze; to perfectly pellucid lenses; to the undimmed dark of a rich brown iris; and to a pure cerulean-tinted angle of whiteness streaked with the delicate shadows of long eyelashes. Was it that Tito's face attracted or repelled according to the mental attitude of the observer? Was it a cipher with more than one key? The strong, unmistakable expression in his whole air and person was a negative one, and it was perfectly veracious; it declared the absence of any uneasy claim, any restless vanity, and it made the admiration that followed him as he passed among the troop of holiday-makers a thoroughly willing tribute.

For by this time the stir of the Festa was felt even in the narrowest side streets; the throng which had at one time been concentrated in the lines through which the procession had to pass was now streaming out in all directions in pursuit of a new object. Such intervals of a Festa are precisely the moments when the vaguely active animal spirits of a crowd are likely to be the most petulant and most ready to sacrifice a stray individual to the greater happiness of the greater number. As Tito entered the neighborhood of San Martino, he found the throng rather denser; and near the hostelry of the *Bertucce*, or Baboons, there was evidently some object which was arresting the passengers and forming them into a knot. It needed nothing of great interest to draw aside passengers unfreighted with a purpose, and Tito was preparing to turn aside into an adjoining street, when, amidst the loud laughter, his ear discerned a distressed childish voice crying, " Loose me! Holy Virgin, help me! " which at once determined him to push his way into the knot of gazers. He had just had time to perceive that the distressed voice came from a young contadina, whose white hood had fallen off in the struggle to get her hands free from the grasp of a man in the party-colored dress of a *cerretano*, or conjurer, who was making laughing attempts to soothe and cajole her, evidently carrying with him the amused sympathy of the spectators. These, by a persuasive variety of words signifying simpleton, for which the Florentine dialect is rich in equivalents, seemed to be arguing with the contadina against her obstinacy. At the first moment the girl's face was turned away, and he saw only her light-brown hair plaited and fastened with a long silver pin; but in the next, the struggle brought her face opposite Tito's, and he saw the baby features of Tessa, her blue eyes filled with tears, and her under lip quivering. Tessa, too, saw *him*, and through the mist of her swelling tears there beamed a sudden hope, like that in the face of a little child when, held by a stranger against its will, it sees a familiar hand stretched out.

In an instant Tito had pushed his way through the barrier of bystanders, whose curiosity made them ready to turn aside at the sudden interference of this handsome young signor, had grasped Tessa's waist, and had said, "Loose this child! What right have you to hold her against her will?"

The conjurer—a man with one of those faces in which the angles of the eye and eyebrows, of the nostrils, mouth, and sharply defined jaw, all tend upward—showed his small regular teeth in an impish but not ill-natured grin, as he let go Tessa's hands, and stretched out his own backward, shrugging his shoulders, and bending them forward a little in a half-apologetic, half-protesting manner.

"I mean the ragazza no evil in the world, Messere: ask this respectable company. I was only going to show them a few samples of my skill, in which this little damsel might have helped me the better because of her kitten face, which would have assured them of open dealing; and I had promised her a lapful of confetti as a reward. But what then? Messer has doubtless better confetti at hand, and she knows it."

A general laugh among the bystanders accompanied these last words of the conjurer, raised, probably, by the look of relief and confidence with which Tessa clung to Tito's arm, as he drew it from her waist, and placed her hand within it. She only cared about the laugh as she might have cared about the roar of wild beasts from which she was escaping, not attaching any meaning to it; but Tito, who had no sooner got her on his arm than he foresaw some embarrassment in the situation, hastened to get clear of observers who, having been despoiled of an expected amusement, were sure to re-establish the balance by jest.

"See, see, little one! here is your hood," said the conjurer, throwing the bit of white drapery over Tessa's head. "*Orsù*, bear me no malice; come back to me when Messere can spare you."

"Ah! Maestro Vaiano, she'll come back presently, as the toad said to the harrow," called out one of the spectators, seeing how Tessa started and shrank at the action of the conjurer.

Tito pushed his way vigorously toward the corner of a side street, a little vexed at this delay in his progress to the Via de' Bardi, and intending to get rid of the poor little contadina as soon as possible. The next street, too, had its passengers inclined to make holiday remarks on so unusual a pair; but they had no sooner entered it than he said, in a kind but hurried manner, "Now, little one, where were you going? Are you come by yourself to the Festa?"

"Ah, no!" said Tessa, looking frightened and distressed again; "I have lost my mother in the crowd—her and my father-in-law. They will be angry—he will beat me. It was in the crowd in San Pulinari—somebody pushed me along and I couldn't stop myself, so I got away from them. Oh, I don't know where they're gone! Please, don't leave me!"

Her eyes had been swelling with tears again, and she ended with a sob.

Tito hurried along again: the Church of the Badia was not far off. They could enter it by the cloister that opened at the back, and in the church he could talk to Tessa—perhaps leave her. No! it was an hour at which the church was not open; but they paused under the shelter of the cloister, and he said, "Have you no cousin or friend in Florence, my little Tessa, whose house you could find; or are you afraid of walking by yourself since you have been frightened by the conjurer? I am in a hurry to get to Oltrarno, but if I could take you anywhere near——"

"Oh, I *am* frightened: he was the devil—I know he was. And I don't know where to go. I have nobody: and my mother meant to have her dinner somewhere, and I don't know where. Holy Madonna! I shall be beaten."

The corners of the pouting mouth went down piteously, and the poor little bosom with the beads on it above the green serge gown heaved so, that there was no longer any help for it: a loud sob *would* come, and the big tears fell as if they were making up for lost time. Here was a situation! It would have been brutal to leave her, and Tito's nature was all gentleness. He wished at that moment that he had not been expected in the Via de' Bardi. As he saw her lifting up her holiday apron to catch the hurrying tears, he laid his hand, too, on the apron, and rubbed one of the cheeks and kissed the baby-like roundness.

"My poor little Tessa! leave off crying. Let us see what can be done. Where is your home—where do you live?"

There was no answer, but the sobs began to subside a little and the drops to fall less quickly.

"Come! I'll take you a little way, if you'll tell me where you want to go."

The apron fell, and Tessa's face began to look as contented as a cherub's budding from a cloud. The diabolical conjurer, the anger and the beating, seemed a long way off.

"I think I'll go home, if you'll take me," she said, in a half whisper, looking up at Tito with wide blue eyes, and with something sweeter than a smile—with a childlike calm.

"Come, then, little one," said Tito, in a caressing tone, putting her arm within his again. "Which way is it?"

"Beyond Peretola—where the large pear-tree is."

"Peretola? Out at which gate, pazzarella? I am a stranger, you must remember."

"Out at the Por del Prato," said Tessa, moving along with a very fast hold on Tito's arm.

He did not know all the turnings well enough to venture on an attempt at choosing the quietest streets; and besides, it occurred to him that where the passengers were most numerous there was, perhaps, the most chance of meeting with Monna Ghita and finding an end to his knight-errantship. So he made straight for Porta Rossa, and on to Ognissanti, showing his usual bright propitiatory face to the mixed observers who threw their jests at him and his little heavy-shod maiden with much liberality. Mingled with the more decent holiday-makers there were frolicsome apprentices, rather envious of his good fortune; bold-eyed women with the badge of the yellow veil; beggars who thrust forth their caps for alms, in derision at Tito's evident haste; dicers, sharpers, and loungers of the worst sort; boys whose tongues were used to wag in concert at the most brutal street games: for the streets of Florence were not always a moral spectacle in those times, and Tessa's terror at being lost in the crowd was not wholly unreasonable.

When they reached the Piazza d'Ognissanti, Tito slackened his pace; they were both heated with their hurried walk, and here was a wider space where they could take breath. They sat down on one of the stone benches which were frequent against the walls of old Florentine houses.

"Holy Virgin!" said Tessa; "I am glad we have got away from those women and boys; but I was not frightened, because you could take care of me."

"Pretty little Tessa!" said Tito, smiling at her. "What makes you feel so safe with me?"

"Because you are so beautiful—like the people going into Paradise: they are all good."

"It is a long while since you had your breakfast, Tessa," said Tito, seeing some stalls near, with fruit and sweetmeats upon them. "Are you hungry?"

"Yes, I think I am—if you will have some too."

Tito bought some apricots, and cakes, and comfits, and put them into her apron.

"Come," he said, "let us walk on to the Prato, and then perhaps you will not be afraid to go the rest of the way alone."

"But you will have some of the apricots and things," said Tessa, rising obediently and gathering up her apron as a bag for her store.

"We will see," said Tito aloud; and to himself he said, "Here is a little contadina who might inspire a better idyl than Lorenzo de' Medici's 'Nencia da Barberino,' that Nello's friends rave about; if I were only a Theocritus, or had time to cultivate the necessary experience by unseasonable walks of this sort! However, the mischief is done now: I am so late already that another half-hour will make no difference. Pretty little pigeon!"

"We have a garden and plenty of pears," said Tessa, "and two cows, besides the mules; and I'm very fond of them. But my father-in-law is a cross man: I wish my mother had not married him. I think he is wicked; he is very ugly."

"And does your mother let him beat you, poverina? You said you were afraid of being beaten."

"Ah, my mother herself scolds me; she loves my young sister better, and thinks I don't do work enough. Nobody speaks kindly to me, only the Pievano" (parish priest) "when I go to confession. And the men in the Mercato laugh at me and make fun of me. Nobody ever kissed me and spoke to me as you do; just as I talk to my little black-faced kid, because I'm very fond of it."

It seemed not to have entered Tessa's mind that there was any change in Tito's appearance since the morning he begged the milk from her, and that he looked now like a personage for whom she must summon her little stock of reverent words and signs. He had impressed her too differently from any human being who had ever come near her before, for her to make any comparison of details; she took no note of his dress; he was simply a voice and a face to her, something come from Paradise into a world where most things seemed hard and angry; and she prattled with as little restraint as if he had been an imaginary companion born of her own lovingness and the sunshine.

They had now reached the Prato, which at that time was a large open space within the walls, where the Florentine youth played at their favorite *Calcio*—a peculiar kind of football—and otherwise exercised themselves. At this midday time it was forsaken and quiet to the very gates, where a tent had been erected in preparation for the race. On the border of this wide meadow, Tito paused and said,—

"Now, Tessa, you will not be frightened if I leave you to walk the rest of the way by yourself. Addio! Shall I come and buy a cup of milk from you in the Mercato to-morrow morning, to see that you are quite safe?"

He added this question in a soothing tone, as he saw her eyes widening sorrowfully, and the corners of her mouth falling. She said nothing at first; she only opened her apron and looked down at her apricots and sweetmeats. Then she looked up at him again and said complainingly,—

"I thought you would have some, and we could sit down under a tree outside the gate, and eat them together."

"Tessa, Tessa, you little siren, you would ruin me," said Tito, laughing, and kissing both her cheeks. "I ought to have been in the Via de' Bardi long ago. No! I must go back now; you are in no danger. There—I'll take an apricot. Addio!"

He had already stepped two yards from her when he said the last word. Tessa could not have spoken; she was pale, and a great sob was rising; but she turned round as if she felt there was no hope for her, and stepped on, holding her apron so forgetfully that the apricots began to roll out on the grass.

Tito could not help looking after her, and seeing her shoulders rise to the bursting sob, and the apricots fall—could not help going after her and picking them up. It was very hard upon him: he was a long way off the Via de' Bardi, and very near to Tessa.

"See, my silly one," he said, picking up the apricots. "Come, leave off crying, I will go with you, and we'll sit down under the tree. Come, I don't like to see you cry; but you know I must go back some time."

So it came to pass that they found a great plane-tree not far outside the gates, and they sat down under it, and all the feast was spread out on Tessa's lap, she leaning with her back against the trunk of the tree, and he stretched opposite to her, resting his elbows on the rough green growth cherished by the shade, while the sunlight stole through the boughs and played about them like a winged thing. Tessa's face was all contentment again, and the taste of the apricots and sweetmeats seemed very good.

"You pretty bird!" said Tito, looking at her as she sat eying the remains of the feast with an evident mental debate about saving them, since he had said he would not have any more. "To think of any one scolding you! What sins do you tell of at confession, Tessa?"

"Oh, a great many. I am often naughty. I don't like work, and I can't help being idle, though I know I shall be beaten and scolded; and I give the mules the best fodder when nobody sees me, and then when the Madre is angry I say I didn't do it, and that makes me frightened at the devil. I think the conjurer was the devil. I am not so frightened after I've been to confession. And see, I've got a *Breve* here that a good father who came to Prato preaching this Easter blessed and gave us all." Here Tessa drew from her bosom a tiny bag carefully fastened up. "And I think the holy Madonna will take care of me; she looks as if she would; and perhaps if I wasn't idle, she wouldn't let me be beaten."

"If they are so cruel to you, Tessa, shouldn't you like to leave them, and go and live with a beautiful lady who would be kind to you, if she would have you to wait upon her?"

Tessa seemed to hold her breath for a moment or two. Then she said doubtfully, "I don't know."

"Then should you like to be *my* little servant, and live with me?" said Tito, smiling. He meant no more than to see what sort of pretty look and answer she would give.

There was a flush of joy immediately. "Will you take me with you now? Ah! I shouldn't go home and be beaten then." She paused a little while, and then added more doubtfully, "But I should like to fetch my black-faced kid."

"Yes, you must go back to your kid, my Tessa," said Tito, rising, "and I must go the other way."

"By Jupiter!" he added, as he went from under the shade of the tree, "it is not a pleasant time of day to walk from here to the Via de' Bardi; I am more inclined to lie down and sleep in this shade."

It ended so. Tito had an unconquerable aversion to anything unpleasant, even when an object very much loved and desired was on the other side of it. He had risen early; had waited; had seen sights, and had been already walking in the sun: he was inclined for a siesta, and inclined all the more because little Tessa was there, and seemed to make the air softer. He lay down on the grass again, putting his cap under his head on a green tuft by the side of Tessa. That was not quite comfortable; so he moved again, and asked Tessa to let him rest his head against her lap; and in that way he soon fell asleep. Tessa sat quiet as a dove on its nest, just venturing, when he was fast asleep, to touch the wonderful dark curls that fell backward from his ear. She was too happy to go to sleep—too happy to think that Tito would wake up, and that then he would leave her, and she must go home. It takes very little water to make a perfect pool for a tiny fish, where it will find its world and paradise all in one, and never have a presentiment of the dry bank. The fretted summer shade and stillness, and the gentle breathing of some loved life near—it would be paradise to us all, if eager thought, the strong angel with the implacable brow, had not long since closed the gates.

It really was a long while before the waking came—before the long dark eyes opened at Tessa, first with a little surprise, and then with a smile, which was soon quenched by some preoccupying thought. Tito's deeper sleep had broken into a doze, in which he felt himself in the Via de' Bardi, explaining his failure to appear at the appointed time. The clear images of that doze urged him to start up at once to a sitting posture, and as he stretched his arms and shook his cap, he said,—

"Tessa, little one, you have let me sleep too long. My hunger and the shadows together tell me that the sun has done much travel since I fell asleep. I must lose no more time. Addio," he ended, patting her cheek with one hand, and settling his cap with the other.

She said nothing, but there were signs in her face which made him speak again in as serious and as chiding a tone as he could command,—

"Now, Tessa, you must not cry. I shall be angry; I shall not love you if you cry. You must go home to your black-faced kid, or if you like you may go back to the gate and see the horses start. But I can stay with you no longer, and if you cry, I shall think you are troublesome to me."

The rising tears were checked by terror at this change in Tito's voice. Tessa turned very pale, and sat in trembling silence, with her blue eyes widened by arrested tears.

"Look now," Tito went on, soothingly, opening the wallet

that hung at his belt, "here is a pretty charm that I have had a long while—ever since I was in Sicily, a country a long way off."

His wallet had many little matters in it mingled with small coins, and he had the usual difficulty in laying his finger on the right thing. He unhooked his wallet, and turned out the contents on Tessa's lap. Among them was his onyx ring.

"Ah, my ring!" he exclaimed, slipping it on the forefinger of his right hand. "I forgot to put it on again this morning. Strange, I never missed it! See, Tessa," he added, as he spread out the smaller articles, and selected the one he was in search of. "See this pretty little pointed bit of red coral—like your goat's horn, is it not?—and here is a hole in it, so you can put it on the cord round your neck along with your *Breve*, and then the evil spirits can't hurt you: if you ever see them coming in the shadow round the corner, point this little coral horn at them, and they will run away. It is a 'buona fortuna,' and will keep you from harm when I am not with you. Come, undo the cord."

Tessa obeyed with a tranquillizing sense that life was going to be something quite new, and that Tito would be with her often. All who remember their childhood remember the strange vague sense, when some new experience came, that everything else was going to be changed, and that there would be no lapse into the old monotony. So the bit of coral was hung beside the tiny bag with the scrap of scrawled parchment in it, and Tessa felt braver.

"And now you will give me a kiss," said Tito, economizing time by speaking while he swept in the contents of the wallet and hung it at his waist again, "and look happy like a good girl, and then——"

But Tessa had obediently put forward her lips in a moment, and kissed his cheek as he hung down his head.

"Oh, you pretty pigeon!" cried Tito, laughing, pressing her round cheeks with his hands and crushing her features together so as to give them a general impartial kiss.

Then he started up and walked away, not looking round till he was ten yards from her, when he just turned and gave a parting beck. Tessa was looking after him, but he could see that she was making no signs of distress. It was enough for

Tito if she did not cry while he was present. The softness of his nature required that all sorrow should be hidden away from him.

"I wonder when Romola will kiss my cheek in that way?" thought Tito, as he walked along. It seemed a tiresome distance now, and he almost wished he had not been so soft-hearted, or so tempted to linger in the shade. No other excuse was needed to Bardo and Romola than saying simply that he had been unexpectedly hindered: he felt confident their proud delicacy would inquire no farther. He lost no time in getting to Ognissanti, and hastily taking some food there, he crossed the Arno by the Ponte alla Carraja, and made his way as directly as possible toward the Via de' Bardi.

But it was the hour when all the world who meant to be in particularly good time to see the Corso were returning from the Borghi, or villages just outside the gates, where they had dined and reposed themselves; and the thoroughfares leading to the bridges were of course the issues toward which the stream of sightseers tended. Just as Tito reached the Ponte Vecchio and the entrance of the Via de' Bardi, he was suddenly urged back toward the angle of the intersecting streets. A company on horseback, coming from the Via Guicciardini, and turning up the Via de' Bardi, had compelled the foot-passengers to recede hurriedly. Tito had been walking, as his manner was, with the thumb of his right hand resting in his belt; and as he was thus forced to pause, and was looking carelessly at the passing cavaliers, he felt a very thin cold hand laid on his. He started round, and saw the Dominican friar whose upturned face had so struck him in the morning. Seen closer, the face looked more evidently worn by sickness and not by age; and again it brought some strong but indefinite reminiscences to Tito.

"Pardon me, but—from your face and your ring"—said the friar, in a faint voice, "is not your name Tito Melema?"

"Yes," said Tito, also speaking faintly, doubly jarred by the cold touch and the mystery. He was not apprehensive or timid through his imagination, but through his sensations and perceptions he could easily be made to shrink and turn pale like a maiden.

"Then I shall fulfil my commission."

The friar put his hand under his scapulary, and drawing out a small linen bag which hung round his neck, took from it a bit of parchment, doubled and stuck firmly together with some black adhesive substance, and placed it in Tito's hand. On the outside was written in Italian, in a small but distinct character,—

"*Tito Melema, aged twenty-three, with a dark, beautiful face, long dark curls, the brightest smile, and a large onyx ring on his right forefinger.*"

Tito did not look at the friar, but tremblingly broke open the bit of parchment. Inside, the words were,—

"*I am sold for a slave: I think they are going to take me to Antioch. The gems alone will serve to ransom me.*"

Tito looked round at the friar, but could only ask a question with his eyes.

"I had it at Corinth," the friar said, speaking with difficulty, like one whose small strength had been overtaxed— "I had it from a man who was dying."

"He is dead, then?" said Tito, with a bounding of the heart.

"Not the writer. The man who gave it me was a pilgrim, like myself, to whom the writer had intrusted it, because he was journeying to Italy."

"You know the contents?"

"I do not know them, but I conjecture them. Your friend is in slavery: you will go and release him. But I am unable to talk now." The friar, whose voice had become feebler and feebler, sank down on the stone bench against the wall from which he had risen to touch Tito's hand, adding,—

"I am at San Marco; my name is Fra Luca."

CHAPTER XI.

TITO'S DILEMMA.

WHEN Fra Luca had ceased to speak, Tito still stood by him in irresolution, and it was not till, the pressure of the passengers being removed, the friar rose and walked slowly into the church of Santa Felicità that Tito also went on his way along the Via de' Bardi.

"If this monk is a Florentine," he said to himself, "if he is going to remain at Florence, everything must be disclosed." He felt that a new crisis had come, but he was not, for all that, too evidently agitated to pay his visit to Bardo, and apologize for his previous non-appearance. Tito's talent for concealment was being fast developed into something less neutral. It was still possible—perhaps it might be inevitable—for him to accept frankly the altered conditions, and avow Baldassarre's existence; but hardly without casting an unpleasant light backward on his original reticence as studied equivocation in order to avoid the fulfilment of a secretly recognized claim, to say nothing of his quiet settlement of himself and investment of his florins, when, it would be clear, his benefactor's fate had not been certified. It was at least provisionally wise to act as if nothing had happened, and for the present he would suspend decisive thought; there was all the night for meditation, and no one would know the precise moment at which he had received the letter.

So he entered the room on the second story—where Romola and her father sat among the parchment and the marble, aloof from the life of the streets on holidays as well as on common days—with a face only a little less bright than usual, from regret at appearing so late: a regret which wanted no testimony, since he had given up the sight of the Corso in order to express it; and then set himself to throw extra animation into the evening, though all the while his consciousness was at work like a machine with complex action, leaving deposits quite distinct from the line of talk; and by the time he descended the stone stairs and issued from the grim door in the starlight, his mind had really reached a new stage in its formation of a purpose.

And when, the next day, after he was free from his professorial work, he turned up the Via del Cocomero toward the convent of San Marco, his purpose was fully shaped. He was going to ascertain from Fra Luca precisely how much he conjectured of the truth, and on what grounds he conjectured it; and, further, how long he was to remain at San Marco. And on that fuller knowledge he hoped to mould a statement which would in any case save him from the necessity of quitting Florence. Tito had never had occasion to fabricate an ingenious lie before: the occasion was come now—the occasion which circumstance never fails to beget on tacit falsity; and his ingenuity was ready. For he had convinced himself that he was not bound to go in search of Baldassarre. He had once said that on a fair assurance of his father's existence and whereabout, he would unhesitatingly go after him. But, after all, *why* was he bound to go? What, looked at closely, was the end of all life but to extract the utmost sum of pleasure? And was not his own blooming life a promise of incomparably more pleasure, not for himself only, but for others, than the withered wintry life of a man who was past the time of keen enjoyment, and whose ideas had stiffened into barren rigidity? Those ideas had all been sown in the fresh soil of Tito's mind, and were lively germs there: that was the proper order of things—the order of nature, which treats all maturity as a mere nidus for youth. Baldassarre had done his work, had had his draught of life: Tito said it was *his* turn now.

And the prospect was so vague:—"I think they are going to take me to Antioch": here was a vista. After a long voyage, to spend months, perhaps years, in a search for which even now there was no guarantee that it would not prove vain. and to leave behind at starting a life of distinction and love: and to find, if he found anything, the old exacting companionship which was known by rote beforehand. Certainly the gems and therefore the florins were, in a sense, Baldassarre's: in the narrow sense by which the right of possession is determined in ordinary affairs; but in that large and more radically natural view by which the world belongs to youth and strength, they were rather his who could extract the most pleasure out of them. That, he was conscious, was not the sentiment which the complicated play of human feelings had engendered in society. The men around him would expect that he should immediately apply those florins to his benefactor's rescue. But what was the sentiment of society?—a mere tangle of anomalous traditions and opinions, which no wise man would take as a guide, except so far as his own comfort was concerned. Not that he cared for the florins save perhaps for Romola's sake: he would give up the florins readily enough. It was the joy that was due to him and was close to his lips which he felt he was not bound to thrust away from him and so travel on, thirsting. Any maxims that required a man to fling away the good that was needed to make existence sweet were only the lining of human selfishness turned outward: they were made by men who wanted others to sacrifice themselves for their sake. He would rather that Baldassarre should not suffer: he liked no one to suffer; but could any philosophy prove to him that he was bound to care for another's suffering more than for his own? To do so he must have loved Baldassarre devotedly, and he did *not* love him: was that his own fault? Gratitude! seen closely, it made no valid claim: his father's life would have been dreary without him: are we convicted of a debt to men for the pleasures they give themselves?

Having once begun to explain away Baldassarre's claim, Tito's thought showed itself as active as a virulent acid, eating its rapid way through all the tissues of sentiment. His mind was destitute of that dread which has been erroneously decried as if it were nothing higher than a man's animal care for his own skin: that awe of the Divine Nemesis which was felt by religious pagans, and, though it took a more positive form under Christianity, is still felt by the mass of mankind simply as a vague fear at anything which is called wrongdoing. Such terror of the unseen is so far above mere sensual cowardice that it will annihilate that cowardice: it is the initial recognition of a moral law restraining desire, and checks the hard bold scrutiny of imperfect thought into obligations which can never be proved to have any sanctity in the absence of feeling. "It is good," sing the old Eumenides, in Æschylus, "that fear should sit as the guardian of the soul, forcing it into wisdom—good that men should carry a threatening shadow in their hearts under the full sunshine; else, how should they learn to revere the right?" That guardianship may become needless; but only when all outward law has become needless—only when duty and love have united in one stream and made a common force.

As Tito entered the outer cloister of San Marco, and inquired for Fra Luca, there was no shadowy presentiment in his mind: he felt himself too cultured and sceptical for that: he had been nurtured in contempt for the tales of priests whose impudent lives were a proverb, and in erudite familiarity with disputes concerning the Chief Good, which had after all, he considered, left it a matter of taste. Yet fear was a strong element in Tito's nature—the fear of what he believed or saw was likely to rob him of pleasure: and he had a definite fear that Fra Luca might be the means of driving him from Florence.

"Fra Luca? ah, he is gone to Fiesole—to the Dominican monastery there. He was taken on a litter in the cool of the morning. The poor Brother is very ill. Could you leave a message for him?"

This answer was given by a *fra converso*, or lay brother, whose accent told plainly that he was a raw contadino, and whose dull glance implied no curiosity.

"Thanks; my business can wait."

Tito turned away with a sense of relief. "This friar is not likely to live," he said to himself. "I saw he was worn to a shadow. And at Fiesole there will be nothing to recall me to his mind. Besides, if he should come back, my explanation will serve as well then as now. But I wish I knew what it was that his face recalled to me."

CHAPTER XII.

THE PRIZE IS NEARLY GRASPED.

TITO walked along with a light step, for the immediate fear had vanished; the usual joyousness of his disposition reassumed its predominance, and he was going to see Romola. Yet Romola's life seemed an image of that loving, pitying devotedness, that patient endurance of irksome tasks, from which he had shrunk and excused himself. But he was not out of love with goodness, or prepared to plunge into vice: he was in his fresh youth, with soft pulses for all charm and loveliness; he had still a healthy appetite for ordinary human joys, and the poison could only work by degrees. He had sold himself to evil, but at present life seemed so nearly the same to him that he was not conscious of the bond. He meant all things to go on as they had done before, both within and without him: he meant to win golden opinions by meritorious exertion, by ingenious learning, by amiable compliance: he was not going to do anything that would throw him out of harmony with the beings he cared for. And he cared supremely for Romola; he wished to have her for his beautiful and loving wife. There might be a wealthier alliance within the ultimate reach of successful accomplishments like his, but there was no woman in all Florence like Romola. When she was near him, and looked at him with her sincere hazel eyes, he was subdued by a delicious influence as strong and inevitable as those musical vibrations which take possession of us with a rhythmic empire that no sooner ceases than we desire it to begin again.

As he trod the stone stairs, when he was still outside the door, with no one but Maso near him, the influence seemed to have begun its work by the mere nearness of anticipation.

"Welcome, Tito mio," said the old man's voice, before Tito had spoken. There was a new vigor in the voice, a new cheerfulness in the blind face, since that first interview more than two months ago. "You have brought fresh manuscript, doubtless; but since we were talking last night I have had new ideas: we must take a wider scope—we must go back upon our footsteps."

Tito, paying his homage to Romola as he advanced, went, as his custom was, straight to Bardo's chair, and put his hand in the palm that was held to receive it, placing himself on the cross-legged leather seat with scrolled ends, close to Bardo's elbow.

"Yes," he said, in his gentle way; "I have brought the new manuscript, but that can wait your pleasure. I have young limbs, you know, and can walk back up the hill without any difficulty."

He did not look at Romola as he said this, but he knew quite well that her eyes were fixed on him with delight.

"That is well said, my son." Bardo had already addressed Tito in this way once or twice of late. "And I perceive with gladness that you do not shrink from labor, without which, the poet has wisely said, life has given nothing to mortals. It is too often the 'palma sine pulvere,' the prize of glory without the dust of the race, that attracts young ambition. But what says the Greek? 'In the morning of life, work; in the mid-day, give counsel; in the evening, pray.' It is true, I might be thought to have reached that helpless evening; but not so, while I have counsel within me which is yet unspoken. For my mind, as I have often said, was shut up as by a dam, the plenteous waters lay dark and motionless; but you, my Tito, have opened a duct for them, and they rush forward with a force that surprises myself. And now, what I want is, that we should go over our preliminary ground again, with a wider scheme of comment and illustration: otherwise I may lose opportunities which I now see retrospectively, and which may never occur again. You mark what I am saying, Tito?"

He had just stooped to reach his manuscript, which had rolled down, and Bardo's jealous ear was alive to the slight movement.

Tito might have been excused for shrugging his shoulders at the prospect before him, but he was not naturally impatient; moreover, he had been bred up in that laborious erudition, at once minute and copious, which was the chief intellectual task of the age; and with Romola near, he was floated along by waves of agreeable sensation that made everything seem easy.

"Assuredly," he said; "you wish to enlarge your comments on certain passages we have cited."

"Not only so; I wish to introduce an occasional *excursus*, where we have noticed an author to whom I have given special study; for I may die too soon to achieve any separate work. And this is not a time for scholarly integrity and well-sifted learning to lie idle, when it is not only rash ignorance that we have to fear, but when there are men like Calderino, who, as Poliziano has well shown, have recourse to impudent falsities of citation to serve the ends of their vanity and secure a triumph to their own mistakes. Wherefore, my Tito, I think it not well that we should let slip the occasion that lies under our hands. And now we will turn back to the point where we have cited the passage from Thucydides, and I wish you, by way of preliminary, to go with me through all my notes on the Latin translation made by Lorenzo Valla, for which the incomparable Pope Nicholas V.—with whose personal notice I was honored while I was yet young, and when he was still Thomas of Sarzana—paid him (I say not unduly) the sum of five hundred gold scudi. But inasmuch as Valla, though otherwise of dubious fame, is held in high honor for his severe scholarship, whence the epigrammatist has jocosely said of him that since he went among the shades, Pluto himself has not dared to speak in the ancient languages, it is the more needful that his name should not be as a stamp warranting false wares; and therefore I would introduce an *excursus* on Thucydides, wherein my castigations of Valla's text may find a fitting place. My Romola, thou wilt reach the needful volumes—thou knowest them—on the fifth shelf of the cabinet."

Tito rose at the same moment with Romola, saying, "I will reach them, if you will point them out," and followed her hastily into the adjoining small room where the walls were also covered with ranges of books in perfect order.

"There they are," said Romola, pointing upward; "every book is just where it was when my father ceased to see them."

Tito stood by her without hastening to reach the books. They had never been in this room together before.

"I hope," she continued, turning her eyes full on Tito with a look of grave confidence—"I hope he will not weary you; this work makes him so happy."

"And me too, Romola—if you will only let me say, I love you—if you will only think me worth loving a little."

His speech was the softest murmur, and the dark beautiful face, nearer to hers than it had ever been before, was looking at her with beseeching tenderness.

"I do love you," murmured Romola; she looked at him with the same simple majesty as ever, but her voice had never in her life before sunk to that murmur. It seemed to them both that they were looking at each other a long while before her lips moved again; yet it was but a moment till she said, "I know *now* what it is to be happy."

The faces just met, and the dark curls mingled for an instant with the rippling gold. Quick as lightning after that, Tito set his foot on a projecting ledge of the book-shelves and reached down the needful volumes. They were both contented to be silent and separate, for that first blissful experience of mutual consciousness was all the more exquisite for being unperturbed by immediate sensation.

It had all been as rapid as the irreversible mingling of waters, for even the eager and jealous Bardo had not become impatient.

"You have the volumes, my Romola?" the old man said, as they came near him again. "And now you will get your pen ready; for, as Tito marks off the scholia we determine on extracting, it will be well for you to copy them without delay—numbering them carefully, mind, to correspond with the numbers in the text which he will write."

Romola always had some task which gave her a share in this joint work. Tito took his stand at the leggio, where he both wrote and read, and she placed herself at a table just in front of him, where she was ready to give into her father's hands anything that he might happen to want, or relieve him of a volume that he had done with. They had always been in that position since the work began, yet on this day it seemed new; it was so different now for them to be opposite each other; so different for Tito to take a book from her, as she lifted it from her father's knee. Yet there was no finesse to secure an additional look or touch. Each woman creates in her own likeness the love-tokens that are offered to her: and Romola's deep calm happiness encompassed Tito like the rich but quiet evening light which dissipates all unrest.

They had been two hours at their work, and were just desisting because of the fading light, when the door opened, and there entered a figure strangely incongruous with the current of their thoughts and with the suggestions of every object around them. It was the figure of a short stout black-eyed woman about fifty, wearing a black velvet berretta, or close cap, embroidered with pearls, under which surprisingly massive black braids surmounted the little bulging forehead, and fell in rich plaited curves over the ears, while an equally surprising carmine tint on the upper region of the fat cheeks contrasted with the surrounding sallowness. Three rows of pearls and a lower necklace of gold reposed on the horizontal cushion of her neck; the embroidered border of her trailing black velvet gown and her embroidered long-drooping sleeves of rose-colored damask, were slightly faded, but they conveyed to the initiated eye the satisfactory assurance that they were the splendid result of six months' labor by a skilled workman, and the rose-colored petticoat, with its dimmed white fringe and seed-pearl arabesques, was duly exhibited in order to suggest a similar pleasing reflection. A handsome coral rosary hung from one side of an inferential belt, which emerged into certainty with a large clasp of silver wrought in niello; and on the other side, where the belt again became inferential, hung a scarsella, or large purse, of crimson velvet, stitched with pearls. Her little fat right hand, which looked as if it had been made of paste, and had risen out of shape under partial baking, held a small book of devotions, also splendid with velvet, pearls, and silver.

The figure was already too familiar to Tito to be startling, for Monna Brigida was a frequent visitor at Bardo's, being excepted from the sentence of banishment passed on feminine triviality, on the ground of her cousinship to his dead wife and her early care for Romola, who now looked round at her with an affectionate smile, and rose to draw the leather seat to a due distance from her father's chair, that the coming gush of talk might not be too near his ear.

"*La cugina?*" said Bardo, interrogatively, detecting the short steps and the sweeping drapery.

"Yes, it is your cousin," said Monna Brigida, in an alert voice, raising her fingers smilingly at Tito, and then lifting up her face to be kissed by Romola. "Always the troublesome cousin breaking in on your wisdom," she went on, seating herself and beginning to fan herself with the white veil hanging over her arm. "Well, well; if I didn't bring you some news of the world now and then, I do believe you'd forget there

was anything in life but these mouldy ancients, who want
sprinkling with holy water, if all I hear about them is true.
Not but what the world is bad enough nowadays, for the scan-
dals that turn up under one's nose at every corner—*I* don't
want to hear and see such things, but one can't go about with
one's head in a bag; and it was only yesterday—well, well,
you needn't burst out at me, Bardo, I'm not going to tell anything; if I'm not as wise as the three kings, I know how
many legs go into one boot. But, nevertheless, Florence is a
wicked city—is it not true, Messer Tito? for you go into the
world. Not but what one must sin a little—Messer Domeneddio expects that of us, else what are the blessed sacraments for? And what I say is, we've got to reverence the
saints, and not to set ourselves up as if we could be like them,
else life would be unbearable, as it will be if things go on
after this new fashion. For what do you think? I've been
at the wedding to-day—Dianora Acciajoli's with the young
Albizzi that there has been so much talk of—and everybody
wondered at its being to-day instead of yesterday; but, *cieli!*
such a wedding as it was might have been put off till the
next Quaresima for a penance. For there was the bride looking like a white nun—not so much as a pearl about her—and
the bridegroom as solemn as San Giuseppe. It's true! And
half the people invited were *Piagnoni*—they call them *Piagnoni*[1] now, these new saints of Fra Girolamo's making. And
to think of two families like the Albizzi and the Acciajoli taking up such notions, when they could afford to wear the best!
Well, well, they invited me—but they could do no other, seeing my husband was Luca Antonio's uncle by the mother's
side—and a pretty time I had of it while we waited under the
canopy in front of the house, before they let us in. I couldn't
stand in my clothes, it seemed, without giving offence; for
there was Monna Berta, who has had worse secrets in her
time than any I could tell of myself, looking askance at me
from under her hood like a *pinzochera*,[2] and telling me to
read the Frate's book about widows, from which she had
found great guidance. Holy Madonna! it seems as if widows

[1] Funeral mourners: properly, paid mourners.
[2] A Sister of the Third Order of St. Francis: an uncloistered nun.

had nothing to do now but to buy their coffins, and think it a thousand years till they get into them, instead of enjoying themselves a little when they've got their hands free for the first time. And what do you think was the music we had, to make our dinner lively? A long discourse from Fra Domenico of San Marco, about the doctrines of their blessed Fra Girolamo —the three doctrines we are all to get by heart; and he kept marking them off on his fingers till he made my flesh creep: and the first is, Florence, or the Church—I don't know which, for first he said one and then the other—shall be scourged; but if he means the pestilence, the Signory ought to put a stop to such preaching, for it's enough to raise the swelling under one's arms with fright: but then, after that, he says Florence is to be regenerated; but what will be the good of that when we're all dead of the plague, or something else? And then, the third thing, and what he said oftenest, is, that it's all to be in our days: and he marked that off on his thumb, till he made me tremble like the very jelly before me. They had jellies, to be sure, with the arms of the Albizzi and the Acciajoli raised on them in all colors; they've not turned the world quite upside down yet. But all their talk is, that we are to go back to the old ways: for up starts Francesco Valori, that I've danced with in the Via Larga when he was a bachelor and as fond of the Medici as anybody, and he makes a speech about the old times, before the Florentines had left off crying ' Popolo ' and begun to cry ' Palle '—as if that had anything to do with a wedding!—and how we ought to keep to the rules the Signory laid down Heaven knows when, that we were not to wear this and that, and not to eat this and that—and how our manners were corrupted and we read bad books; though he can't say that of *me*———"

"Stop, cousin!" said Bardo, in his imperious tone, for he had a remark to make, and only desperate measures could arrest the rattling lengthiness of Monna Brigida's discourse. But now she gave a little start, pursed up her mouth, and looked at him with round eyes.

"Francesco Valori is not altogether wrong," Bardo went on. "Bernardo, indeed, rates him not highly, and is rather of opinion that he christens private grudges by the name of public zeal; though I must admit that my good Bernardo is too slow of belief in that unalloyed patriotism which was found in all its lustre amongst the ancients. But it is true, Tito, that our manners have degenerated somewhat from that noble frugality which, as has been well seen in the public acts of our citizens, is the parent of true magnificence. For men, as I hear, will now spend on the transient show of a Giostra sums which would suffice to found a library, and confer a lasting possession on mankind. Still, I conceive it remains true of us Florentines that we have more of that magnanimous sobriety which abhors a trivial lavishness that it may be grandly open-handed on grand occasions, than can be found in any other city of Italy; for I understand that the Neapolitan and Milanese courtiers laugh at the scarcity of our plate, and think scorn of our great families for borrowing from each other that furniture of the table at their entertainments. But in the vain laughter of folly wisdom hears half its applause."

"Laughter, indeed!" burst forth Monna Brigida again, the moment Bardo paused. "If anybody wanted to hear laughter at the wedding to-day they were disappointed, for when young Niccolò Macchiavelli tried to make a joke, and told stories out of Franco Sacchetti's book, how it was no use for the Signoria to make rules for us women, because we were cleverer than all the painters, and architects, and doctors of logic in the world, for we could make black look white, and yellow look pink, and crooked look straight, and, if anything was forbidden, we could find a new name for it—Holy Virgin! the Piagnoni looked more dismal than before, and somebody said Sacchetti's book was wicked. Well, I don't read it—they can't accuse *me* of reading anything. Save me from going to a wedding again, if that's to be the fashion; for all of us who were not Piagnoni were as comfortable as wet chickens. I was never caught in a worse trap but once before, and that was when I went to hear their precious Frate last Quaresima in San Lorenzo. Perhaps I never told you about it, Messer Tito?—it almost freezes my blood when I think of it. How he rated us poor women! and the men, too, to tell the truth, but I didn't mind that so much. He called us cows, and lumps of flesh, and wantons, and mischief-makers—and I could just bear that, for there were plenty others more fleshy and spiteful than I was, though every now and then his voice shook the very bench under me like a trumpet; but then he came to the false hair, and, O misericordia! he made a picture —I see it now—of a young woman lying a pale corpse, and us light-minded widows—of course he meant me as well as the rest, for I had my plaits on, for if one is getting old, one doesn't want to look as ugly as the Befana[1]—us widows rushing up to the corpse, like bare-pated vultures as we were, and cutting off its young dead hair to deck our old heads with. Oh, the dreams I had after that! And then he cried, and wrung his hands at us, and I cried too. And to go home, and to take off my jewels, this very clasp, and everything, and to make them into a packet, *fu tutt' uno;* and I was within a hair of sending them to the Good Men of St. Martin to give to the poor, but, by Heaven's mercy, I bethought me of going first to my confessor, Fra Cristoforo, at Santa Croce, and he told me how it was all the work of the devil, this preaching and prophesying of their Fra Girolamo, and the Dominicans were trying to turn the world upside down, and I was never to go and hear him again, else I must do penance for it; for the great preachers Fra Mariano and Fra Menico had shown how Fra Girolamo preached lies—and that was true, for I heard them both in the Duomo—and how the Pope's dream of San Francesco propping up the Church with his arms was being fulfilled still, and the Dominicans were beginning to pull it down. Well and good: I went away *con Dio*, and made myself easy. I am not going to be frightened by a Frate Predicatore again. And all I say is, I wish it hadn't been the Dominicans that poor Dino joined years ago, for then I should have been glad when I heard them say he was come back——"

"Silenzio!" said Bardo, in a loud agitated voice, while Romola half started from her chair, clasped her hands, and looked round at Tito, as if now she might appeal to him. Monna Brigida gave a little scream, and bit her lip.

[1] The name given to the grotesque black-faced figures, supposed to represent the Magi, carried about or placed in the windows on Twelfth Night, a corruption of Epifania.

"Donna!" said Bardo, again, "hear once more my will. Bring no reports about that name to this house; and thou, Romola, I forbid thee to ask. My son is dead."

Bardo's whole frame seemed vibrating with passion, and no one dared to break silence again. Monna Brigida lifted her shoulders and her hands in mute dismay; then she rose as quietly as possible, gave many significant nods to Tito and Romola, motioning to them that they were not to move, and stole out of the room like a culpable fat spaniel who has barked unseasonably.

Meanwhile, Tito's quick mind had been combining ideas with lightning-like rapidity. Bardo's son was not really dead, then, as he had supposed: he was a monk; he was "come back": and Fra Luca—yes! it was the likeness to Bardo and Romola that had made the face seem half known to him. If he were only dead at Fiesole at that moment! This importunate selfish wish inevitably thrust itself before every other thought. It was true that Bardo's rigid will was a sufficient safeguard against any intercourse between Romola and her brother; but *not* against the betrayal of what he knew to others, especially when the subject was suggested by the coupling of Romola's name with that of the very Tito Melema whose description he had carried round his neck as an index. No! nothing but Fra Luca's death could remove all danger; but his death was highly probable, and after the momentary shock of the discovery, Tito let his mind fall back in repose on that confident hope.

They had sat in silence, and in a deepening twilight, for many minutes, when Romola ventured to say,—

"Shall I light the lamp, father, and shall we go on?"

"No, my Romola, we will work no more to-night. Tito, come and sit by me here."

Tito moved from the reading-desk, and seated himself on the other side of Bardo, close to his left elbow.

"Come nearer to me, figliuola mia," said Bardo again, after a moment's pause. And Romola seated herself on a low stool and let her arm rest on her father's right knee, that he might lay his hand on her hair, as he was fond of doing.

"Tito, I never told you that I had once a son," said Bardo,

forgetting what had fallen from him in the emotion raised by their first interview. The old man had been deeply shaken, and was forced to pour out his feelings in spite of pride. "But he left me—he is dead to me. I have disowned him forever. He was a ready scholar as you are, but more fervid and impatient, and yet sometimes rapt and self-absorbed like a flame fed by some fitful source; showing a disposition from the very first to turn away his eyes from the clear lights of reason and philosophy, and to prostrate himself under the influences of a dim mysticism which eludes all rules of human duty as it eludes all argument. And so it ended. We will speak no more of him: he is dead to me. I wish his face could be blotted from that world of memory in which the distant seems to grow clearer and the near to fade."

Bardo paused, but neither Romola nor Tito dared to speak —his voice was too tremulous, the poise of his feelings too doubtful. But he presently raised his hand and found Tito's shoulder to rest it on, while he went on speaking, with an effort to be calmer.

"But *you* have come to me, Tito—not quite too late. I will lose no time in vain regret. When you are working by my side I seem to have found a son again."

The old man, preoccupied with the governing interest of his life, was only thinking of the much-meditated book which had quite thrust into the background the suggestion, raised by Bernardo del Nero's warning, of a possible marriage between Tito and Romola. But Tito could not allow the moment to pass unused.

"Will you let me be always and altogether your son? Will you let me take care of Romola—be her husband? I think she will not deny me. She has said she loves me. I know I am not equal to her in birth—in anything; but I am no longer a destitute stranger."

"Is it true, my Romola?" said Bardo, in a lower tone, an evident vibration passing through him and dissipating the saddened aspect of his features.

"Yes, father," said Romola, firmly. "I love Tito—I wish to marry him, that we may both be your children and never part."

THE PRIZE IS NEARLY GRASPED.

Tito's hand met hers in a strong clasp for the first time, while she was speaking, but their eyes were fixed anxiously on her father.

"Why should it not be?" said Bardo, as if arguing against any opposition to his assent, rather than assenting. "It would be a happiness to me; and thou, too, Romola, wouldst be the happier for it."

He stroked her long hair gently and bent toward her.

"Ah, I have been apt to forget that thou needest some other love than mine. And thou wilt be a noble wife. Bernardo thinks I shall hardly find a husband fitting for thee. And he is perhaps right. For thou art not like the herd of thy sex: thou art such a woman as the immortal poets had a vision of when they sang the lives of the heroes—tender but strong, like thy voice, which has been to me instead of the light in the years of my blindness. . . . And so thou lovest him?"

He sat upright again for a minute, and then said, in the same tone as before, "Why should it not be? I will think of it; I will talk with Bernardo."

Tito felt a disagreeable chill at this answer, for Bernardo del Nero's eyes had retained their keen suspicion whenever they looked at him, and the uneasy remembrance of Fra Luca converted all uncertainty into fear.

"Speak for me, Romola," he said pleadingly. "Messer Bernardo is sure to be against me."

"No, Tito," said Romola, "my godfather will not oppose what my father firmly wills. And it is your will that I should marry Tito—is it not true, father? Nothing has ever come to me before that I have wished for strongly: I did not think it possible that I could care so much for anything that could happen to myself."

It was a brief and simple plea; but it was the condensed story of Romola's self-repressing colorless young life, which had thrown all its passion into sympathy with aged sorrows, aged ambition, aged pride and indignation. It had never occurred to Romola that she should not speak as directly and emphatically of her love for Tito as of any other subject.

"Romola mia!" said her father fondly, pausing on the

words, "it is true thou hast never urged on me any wishes of thy own. And I have no will to resist thine; rather, my heart met Tito's entreaty at its very first utterance. Nevertheless, I must talk with Bernardo about the measures needful to be observed. For we must not act in haste, or do anything unbeseeming my name. I am poor, and held of little account by the wealthy of our family—nay, I may consider myself a lonely man—but I must nevertheless remember that generous birth has its obligations. And I would not be reproached by my fellow-citizens for rash haste in bestowing my daughter. Bartolommeo Scala gave his Alessandra to the Greek Marullo, but Marullo's lineage was well known, and Scala himself is of no extraction. I know Bernardo will hold that we must take time: he will, perhaps, reproach me with want of due forethought. Be patient, my children: you are very young."

No more could be said, and Romola's heart was perfectly satisfied. Not so Tito's. If the subtle mixture of good and evil prepares suffering for human truth and purity, there is also suffering prepared for the wrong-doer by the same mingled conditions. As Tito kissed Romola on their parting that evening, the very strength of the thrill that moved his whole being at the sense that this woman, whose beauty it was hardly possible to think of as anything but the necessary consequence of her noble nature, loved him with all the tenderness that spoke in her clear eyes, brought a strong reaction of regret that he had not kept himself free from that first deceit which had dragged him into the danger of being disgraced before her. There was a spring of bitterness mingling with that fountain of sweets. Would the death of Fra Luca arrest it? He hoped it would.

CHAPTER XIII.

THE SHADOW OF NEMESIS.

It was the lazy afternoon time on the seventh of September, more than two months after the day on which Romola and Tito had confessed their love to each other.

Tito, just descended into Nello's shop, had found the barber stretched on the bench with his cap over his eyes; one leg was drawn up, and the other had slipped toward the ground, having apparently carried with it a manuscript volume of verse, which lay with its leaves crushed. In a corner sat Sandro, playing a game at *mora* by himself, and watching the slow reply of his left fingers to the arithmetical demands of his right with solemn-eyed interest.

Treading with the gentlest step, Tito snatched up the lute, and bending over the barber, touched the strings lightly while he sang,—

>"Quant' è bella giovinezza,
>Che si fugge tuttavia!
>Chi vuol esser lieto sia,
>Di doman non c'è certezza."[1]

Nello was as easily awaked as a bird. The cap was off his eyes in an instant, and he started up.

"Ah, my Apollino! I am somewhat late with my siesta on this hot day, it seems. That comes of not going to sleep in the natural way, but taking a potion of potent poesy. Hear you, how I am beginning to match my words by the initial letter, like a Trovatore? That is one of my bad symptoms: I am sorely afraid that the good wine of my understanding is going to run off at the spigot of authorship, and I shall be left an empty cask with an odor of dregs, like many another incomparable genius of my acquaintance. What is it, my Orpheus?" here Nello stretched out his arms to their full length, and then brought them round till his hands grasped Tito's curls, and drew them out playfully. "What is it you want of your well-tamed Nello? For I perceive a coaxing sound in that soft strain of yours. Let me see the very needle's eye of your desire, as the sublime poet says, that I may thread it."

"That is but a tailor's image of your sublime poet's," said Tito, still letting his fingers fall in a light dropping way on

---

[1] "Beauteous is life in blossom!
And it fleeteth — fleeteth ever;
Whoso would be joyful — let him!
There's no surety for the morrow."
 — *Carnival Song by Lorenzo de' Medici.*

the strings. "But you have divined the reason of my affectionate impatience to see your eyes open. I want you to give me an extra touch of your art—not on my chin, no; but on the zazzera, which is as tangled as your Florentine politics. You have an adroit way of inserting your comb, which flatters the skin, and stirs the animal spirits agreeably in that region; and a little of your most delicate orange-scent would not be amiss, for I am bound to the Scala palace, and am to present myself in radiant company. The young Cardinal Giovanni de' Medici is to be there, and he brings with him a certain young Bernardo Dovizi of Bibbiena, whose wit is so rapid that I see no way of outrivalling it save by the scent of orange-blossoms."

Nello had already seized and flourished his comb, and pushed Tito gently backward into the chair, wrapping the cloth round him.

"Never talk of rivalry, bel giovane mio: Bernardo Dovizi is a keen youngster, who will never carry a net out to catch the wind; but he has something of the same sharp-muzzled look as his brother Ser Piero, the weasel that Piero de' Medici keeps at his beck to slip through small holes for him. No! you distance all rivals, and may soon touch the sky with your forefinger. They tell me you have even carried enough honey with you to sweeten the sour Messer Angelo; for he has pronounced you less of an ass than might have been expected, considering there is such a good understanding between you and the Secretary."

"And between ourselves, Nello mio, that Messer Angelo has more genius and erudition than I can find in all the other Florentine scholars put together. It may answer very well for them to cry me up now, when Poliziano is beaten down with grief, or illness, or something else; I can try a flight with such a sparrow-hawk as Pietro Crinito, but for Poliziano, he is a large-beaked eagle who would swallow me, feathers and all, and not feel any difference."

"I will not contradict your modesty there, if you will have it so; but you don't expect us clever Florentines to keep saying the same things over again every day of our lives, as we must do if we always told the truth. We cry down Dante, and we cry up Francesco Cei, just for the sake of variety; and if we cry you up as a new Poliziano, Heaven has taken care that it shall not be quite so great a lie as it might have been. And are you not a pattern of virtue in this wicked city? with your ears double-waxed against all siren invitations that would lure you from the Via de' Bardi, and the great work which is to astonish posterity?"

"Posterity in good truth, whom it will probably astonish as the universe does, by the impossibility of seeing what was the plan of it."

"Yes, something like that was being prophesied here the other day. Cristoforo Landino said that the excellent Bardo was one of those scholars who lie overthrown in their learning, like cavaliers in heavy armor, and then get angry because they are over-ridden—which pithy remark, it seems to me, was not a herb out of his own garden; for of all men, for feeding one with an empty spoon and gagging one with vain expectation by long discourse, Messer Cristoforo is the pearl. Ecco! you are perfect now." Here Nello drew away the cloth. "Impossible to add a grace more! But love is not always to be fed on learning, eh? I shall have to dress the zazzera for the betrothal before long—is it not true?"

"Perhaps," said Tito, smiling, "unless Messer Bernardo should next recommend Bardo to require that I should yoke a lion and a wild boar to the car of the Zecca before I can win my Alcestis. But I confess he is right in holding me unworthy of Romola; she is a Pleiad that may grow dim by marrying any mortal."

"*Gnaffè*, your modesty is in the right place there. Yet fate seems to have measured and chiselled you for the niche that was left empty by the old man's son, who, by the way, Cronaca was telling me, is now at San Marco. Did you know?"

A slight electric shock passed through Tito as he rose from the chair, but it was not outwardly perceptible, for he immediately stooped to pick up the fallen book, and busied his fingers with flattening the leaves, while he said,—

"No; he was at Fiesole, I thought. Are you sure he is come back to San Marco?"

"Cronaca is my authority," said Nello, with a shrug. "I

don't frequent that sanctuary, but he does. Ah," he added, taking the book from Tito's hands, "my poor Nencia da Barberino! It jars your scholarly feelings to see the pages dog's-eared. I was lulled to sleep by the well-rhymed charms of that rustic maiden—'prettier than the turnip-flower,' 'with a cheek more savory than cheese.' But to get such a well-scented notion of the contadina one must lie on velvet cushions in the Via Larga—not go to look at the Fierucoloni stumping in to the Piazza della Nunziata this evening after sundown."

"And pray who are the Fierucoloni?" said Tito, indifferently, settling his cap.

"The contadine who come from the mountains of Pistoia, and the Casentino, and Heaven knows where, to keep their vigil in the church of the Nunziata, and sell their yarn and dried mushrooms at the Fierucola,[1] as we call it. They make a queer show, with their paper lanterns, howling their hymns to the Virgin on this eve of her nativity—if you had the leisure to see them. No?—well, I have had enough of it myself, for there is wild work in the Piazza. One may happen to get a stone or two about one's ears or shins without asking for it, and I was never fond of that pressing attention. Addio."

Tito carried a little uneasiness with him on his visit, which ended earlier than he had expected, the boy-cardinal Giovanni de' Medici, youngest of red-hatted fathers, who has since presented his broad dark cheek very conspicuously to posterity as Pope Leo the Tenth, having been detained at his favorite pastime of the chase, and having failed to appear. It still wanted half an hour of sunset as he left the door of the Scala palace, with the intention of proceeding forthwith to the Via de' Bardi; but he had not gone far when, to his astonishment, he saw Romola advancing toward him along the Borgo Pinti.

She wore a thick black veil and black mantle, but it was impossible to mistake her figure and her walk; and by her side was a short stout form, which he recognized as that of Monna Brigida, in spite of the unusual plainness of her attire. Romola had not been bred up to devotional observance, and

[1] The Little Fair.

THE SHADOW OF NEMESIS. 143

the occasions on which she took the air elsewhere than under the loggia on the roof of the house were so rare and so much dwelt on beforehand, because of Bardo's dislike to be left without her, that Tito felt sure there must have been some sudden and urgent ground for an absence of which he had heard nothing the day before. She saw him through her veil and hastened her steps.

"Romola, has anything happened?" said Tito, turning to walk by her side.

She did not answer at the first moment, and Monna Brigida broke in:

"Ah, Messer Tito, you do well to turn round, for we are in haste. And is it not a misfortune?—we are obliged to go round by the walls and turn up the Via del Maglio, because of the Fair; for the contadine coming in block up the way by the Nunziata, which would have taken us to San Marco in half the time."

Tito's heart gave a great bound, and began to beat violently.

"Romola," he said, in a low tone, "are you going to San Marco?"

They were now out of the Borgo Pinti and were under the city walls, where they had wide gardens on their left hand, and all was quiet. Romola put aside her veil for the sake of breathing the air, and he could see the subdued agitation in her face.

"Yes, Tito mio," she said, looking directly at him with sad eyes. "For the first time I am doing something unknown to my father. It comforts me that I have met you, for at least I can tell *you*. But if you are going to him, it will be well for you not to say that you met me. He thinks I am only gone to my cousin, because she sent for me. I left my godfather with him: *he* knows where I am going, and why. You remember that evening when my brother's name was mentioned and my father spoke of him to you?"

"Yes," said Tito, in a low tone. There was a strange complication in his mental state. His heart sank at the probability that a great change was coming over his prospects, while at the same time his thoughts were darting over a hundred details of the course he would take when the change had come; and yet he returned Romola's gaze with a hungry sense that it might be the last time she would ever bend it on him with full unquestioning confidence.

"The *cugina* had heard that he was come back, and the evening before—the evening of San Giovanni—as I afterward found, he had been seen by our good Maso near the door of our house; but when Maso went to inquire at San Marco, Dino, that is, my brother—he was christened Bernardino, after our godfather, but now he calls himself Fra Luca—had been taken to the monastery at Fiesole, because he was ill. But this morning a message came to Maso, saying that he was come back to San Marco, and Maso went to him there. He is very ill, and he has adjured me to go and see him. I cannot refuse it, though I hold him guilty; I still remember how I loved him when I was a little girl, before I knew that he would forsake my father. And perhaps he has some word of penitence to send by me. It cost me a struggle to act in opposition to my father's feeling, which I have always held to be just. I am almost sure you will think I have chosen rightly, Tito, because I have noticed that your nature is less rigid than mine, and nothing makes you angry: it would cost you less to be forgiving; though, if you had seen your father forsaken by one to whom he had given his chief love—by one in whom he had planted his labor and his hopes—forsaken when his need was becoming greatest—even you, Tito, would find it hard to forgive."

What could he say? He was not equal to the hypocrisy of telling Romola that such offences ought not to be pardoned; and he had not the courage to utter any words of dissuasion.

"You are right, my Romola; you are always right, except in thinking too well of me."

There was really some genuineness in those last words, and Tito looked very beautiful as he uttered them, with an unusual pallor in his face, and a slight quivering of his lip. Romola, interpreting all things largely, like a mind prepossessed with high beliefs, had a tearful brightness in her eyes as she looked at him, touched with keen joy that he felt so strongly whatever she felt. But without pausing in her walk, she said,—

"And now, Tito, I wish you to leave me, for the *cugina* and I shall be less noticed if we enter the piazza alone."

"Yes, it were better you should leave us," said Monna Brigida; "for to say the truth, Messer Tito, all eyes follow you, and let Romola muffle herself as she will, every one wants to see what there is under her veil, for she has that way of walking like a procession. Not that I find fault with her for it, only it doesn't suit my steps. And, indeed, I would rather not have us seen going to San Marco, and that's why I am dressed as if I were one of the Piagnoni themselves, and as old as Sant' Anna; for if it had been anybody but poor Dino, who ought to be forgiven if he's dying, for what's the use of having a grudge against dead people?—make them feel while they live, say I——"

No one made a scruple of interrupting Monna Brigida, and Tito, having just raised Romola's hand to his lips, and said, "I understand, I obey you," now turned away, lifting his cap —a sign of reverence rarely made at that time by native Florentines, and which excited Bernardo del Nero's contempt for Tito as a fawning Greek, while to Romola, who loved homage, it gave him an exceptional grace.

He was half glad of the dismissal, half disposed to cling to Romola to the last moment in which she would love him without suspicion. For it seemed to him certain that this brother would before all things want to know, and that Romola would before all things confide to him, what was her father's position and her own after the years which must have brought so much change. She would tell him that she was soon to be publicly betrothed to a young scholar, who was to fill up the place left vacant long ago by a wandering son. He foresaw the impulse that would prompt Romola to dwell on that prospect, and what would follow on the mention of the future husband's name. Fra Luca would tell all he knew and conjectured, and Tito saw no possible falsity by which he could now ward off the worst consequences of his former dissimulation. It was all over with his prospects in Florence. There was Messer Bernardo del Nero, who would be delighted at seeing confirmed the wisdom of his advice about deferring the betrothal until Tito's character and position had been established by a longer residence; and the history of the young Greek professor, whose benefactor was in slavery, would be the talk under every loggia. For the first time in his life he felt too fevered and agitated to trust his power of self-command; he gave up his intended visit to Bardo, and walked up and down under the walls until the yellow light in the west had quite faded, when, without any distinct purpose, he took the first turning, which happened to be the Via San Sebastiano, leading him directly toward the Piazza dell' Annunziata.

He was at one of those lawless moments which come to us all if we have no guide but desire, and if the pathway where desire leads us seems suddenly closed; he was ready to follow any beckoning that offered him an immediate purpose.

CHAPTER XIV.

THE PEASANTS' FAIR.

THE moving crowd and the strange mixture of noises that burst on him at the entrance of the piazza reminded Tito of what Nello had said to him about the Fierucoloni, and he pushed his way into the crowd with a sort of pleasure in the hooting and elbowing, which filled the empty moments, and dulled that calculation of the future which had so new a dreariness for him, as he foresaw himself wandering away solitary in pursuit of some unknown fortune, that his thought had even glanced toward going in search of Baldassarre after all.

At each of the opposite inlets he saw people struggling into the piazza, while above them paper lanterns, held aloft on sticks, were waving uncertainly to and fro. A rude monotonous chant made a distinctly traceable strand of noise, across which screams, whistles, gibing chants in piping boyish voices, the beating of drums, and the ringing of little bells, met each other in confused din. Every now and then one of the dim floating lights disappeared with a smash from a stone launched more or less vaguely in pursuit of mischief, followed by a scream and renewed shouts. But on the outskirts of the whirling tumult there were groups who were keeping this vigil of the Nativity of the Virgin in a more methodical manner than by fitful stone-throwing and gibing. Certain ragged men, darting a hard sharp glance around them while their tongues rattled merrily, were inviting country people to game with them on fair and open-handed terms; two masquerading figures on stilts, who had snatched lanterns from the crowd, were swaying the lights to and fro in meteoric fashion, as they strode hither and thither; a sage trader was doing a profitable business at a small covered stall, in hot *berlingozzi*, a favorite farinaceous delicacy; one man standing on a barrel, with his back firmly planted against a pillar of the loggia in front of the Foundling Hospital (Spedale degl' Innocenti), was selling efficacious pills, invented by a doctor of Salerno, warranted to prevent toothache and death by drowning; and not far off, against another pillar, a tumbler was showing off his tricks on a small platform; while a handful of 'prentices, despising the slack entertainment of guerilla stone-throwing, were having a private concentrated match of that favorite Florentine sport at the narrow entrance of the Via de' Febbrai.

Tito, obliged to make his way through chance openings in the crowd, found himself at one moment close to the trotting procession of barefooted, hard-heeled contadine, and could see their sun-dried, bronzed faces, and their strange, fragmentary garb, dim with hereditary dirt, and of obsolete stuffs and fashions, that made them look, in the eyes of the city people, like a way-worn ancestry returning from a pilgrimage on which they had set out a century ago. Just then it was the hardy, scant-feeding peasant-women from the mountains of Pistoia, who were entering with a year's labor in a moderate bundle of yarn on their backs, and in their hearts that meagre hope of good and that wide dim fear of harm, which were somehow to be cared for by the Blessed Virgin, whose miraculous image, painted by the angels, was to have the curtain drawn away from it on this Eve of her Nativity, that its potency might stream forth without obstruction.

At another moment he was forced away toward the boundary of the piazza, where the more stationary candidates for attention and small coin had judiciously placed themselves, in order to be safe in their rear. Among these Tito recognized his acquaintance Bratti, who stood with his back against a pillar, and his mouth pursed up in disdainful silence, eying every one who approached him with a cold glance of superiority, and keeping his hand fast on a serge covering which concealed the contents of the basket slung before him. Rather surprised at a deportment so unusual in an anxious trader, Tito went nearer and saw two women go up to Bratti's basket with a look of curiosity, whereupon the pedler drew the covering tighter, and looked another way. It was quite too provoking, and one of the women was fain to ask what there was in his basket.

"Before I answer that, Monna, I must know whether you mean to buy. I can't show such wares as mine in this fair for every fly to settle on and pay nothing. My goods are a little too choice for that. Besides, I've only two left, and I've no mind to sell them; for with the chances of the pestilence that wise men talk of, there is likelihood of their being worth their weight in gold. No, no: *andate con Dio*."

The two women looked at each other.

"And what may be the price?" said the second.

"Not within what you are likely to have in your purse, buona donna," said Bratti, in a compassionately supercilious tone. "I recommend you to trust in Messer Domeneddio and the saints: poor people can do no better for themselves."

"Not so poor!" said the second woman, indignantly, drawing out her money-bag. "Come, now! what do you say to a grosso?"

"I say you may get twenty-one quattrini for it," said Bratti, coolly; "but not of me, for I haven't got that small change."

"Come; two, then?" said the woman, getting exasperated, while her companion looked at her with some envy. "It will hardly be above two, I think."

After further bidding, and further mercantile coquetry, Bratti put on an air of concession.

"Since you've set your mind on it," he said, slowly raising the cover, "I should be loath to do you a mischief; for Maestro Gabbadeo used to say, when a woman sets her mind on a thing and doesn't get it, she's in worse danger of the pestilence than before. Ecco! I have but two left; and let me tell you, the fellow to them is on the finger of Maestro Gabbadeo, who is gone to Bologna—as wise a doctor as sits at any door."

The precious objects were two clumsy iron rings, beaten into the fashion of old Roman rings, such as were sometimes disinterred. The rust on them, and the entirely hidden character of their potency, were so satisfactory, that the grossi were paid without grumbling, and the first woman, destitute of those handsome coins, succeeded after much show of reluctance on Bratti's part in driving a bargain with some of her yarn, and carried off the remaining ring in triumph. Bratti covered up his basket, which was now filled with miscellanies, probably obtained under the same sort of circumstances as the yarn, and, moving from his pillar, came suddenly upon Tito, who, if he had had time, would have chosen to avoid recognition.

"By the head of San Giovanni, now," said Bratti, drawing Tito back to the pillar, "this is a piece of luck. For I was talking of you this morning, Messer Greco; but, I said, he is mounted up among the signori now—and I'm glad of it, for I was at the bottom of his fortune—but I can rarely get speech of him, for he's not to be caught lying on the stones now—not he! But it's your luck, not mine, Messer Greco, save and except some small trifle to satisfy me for my trouble in the transaction."

"You speak in riddles, Bratti," said Tito. "Remember, I don't sharpen my wits, as you do, by driving hard bargains for iron rings: you must be plain."

"By the Holy 'Vangels! it was an easy bargain I gave them. If a Hebrew gets thirty-two per cent, I hope a Christian may get a little more. If I had not borne a conscience, I should have got twice the money and twice the yarn. But, talking of rings, it is your ring—that very ring you've got on your finger—that I could get you a purchaser for; ay, and a purchaser with a deep money-bag."

"Truly?" said Tito, looking at his ring and listening.

"A Genoese who is going straight away into Hungary, as I understand. He came and looked all over my shop to see if I had any old things I didn't know the price of; I warrant you, he thought I had a pumpkin on my shoulders. He had been rummaging all the shops in Florence. And he had a ring on—not like yours, but something of the same fashion;

and as he was talking of rings, I said I knew a fine young man, a particular acquaintance of mine, who had a ring of that sort. And he said, 'Who is he, pray? Tell him I'll give him his price for it.' And I thought of going after you to Nello's to-morrow; for it's my opinion of you, Messer Greco, that you're not one who'd see the Arno run broth, and stand by without dipping your finger."

Tito had lost no word of what Bratti had said, yet his mind had been very busy all the while. Why should he keep the ring? It had been a mere sentiment, a mere fancy, that had prevented him from selling it with the other gems; if he had been wiser and had sold it, he might perhaps have escaped that identification by Fra Luca. It was true that it had been taken from Baldassarre's finger and put on his own as soon as his young hand had grown to the needful size: but there was really no valid good to anybody in those superstitious scruples about inanimate objects. The ring had helped toward the recognition of him. Tito had begun to dislike recognition, which was a claim from the past. This foreigner's offer, if he would really give a good price, was an opportunity for getting rid of the ring without the trouble of seeking a purchaser.

"You speak with your usual wisdom, Bratti," said Tito. "I have no objection to hear what your Genoese will offer. But when and where shall I have speech of him?"

"To-morrow, at three hours after sunrise, he will be at my shop, and if your wits are of that sharpness I have always taken them to be, Messer Greco, you will ask him a heavy price; for he minds not money. It's my belief he's buying for somebody else, and not for himself—perhaps for some great signor."

"It is well," said Tito. "I will be at your shop, if nothing hinders."

"And you will doubtless deal nobly by me for old acquaintance' sake, Messer Greco, so I will not stay to fix the small sum you will give me in token of my service in the matter. It seems to me a thousand years now till I get out of the piazza, for a fair is a dull, not to say a wicked thing, when one has no more goods to sell."

Tito made a hasty sign of assent and adieu, and moving away from the pillar, again found himself pushed toward the middle of the piazza and back again, without the power of determining his own course. In this zigzag way he was carried along to the end of the piazza opposite the church, where, in a deep recess formed by an irregularity in the line of houses, an entertainment was going forward which seemed to be especially attractive to the crowd. Loud bursts of laughter interrupted a monologue which was sometimes slow and oratorical, at others rattling and buffoonish. Here a girl was being pushed forward into the inner circle with apparent reluctance, and there a loud-laughing minx was finding a way with her own elbows. It was a strange light that was spread over the piazza. There were the pale stars breaking out above, and the dim waving lanterns below, leaving all objects indistinct except when they were seen close under the fitfully moving lights; but in this recess there was a stronger light, against which the heads of the encircling spectators stood in dark relief as Tito was gradually pushed toward them, while above them rose the head of a man wearing a white mitre with yellow cabalistic figures upon it.

"Behold, my children!" Tito heard him saying, "behold your opportunity! neglect not the holy sacrament of matrimony when it can be had for the small sum of a white quattrino—the cheapest matrimony ever offered, and dissolved by a special bull beforehand at every man's own will and pleasure. Behold the Bull!" Here the speaker held up a piece of parchment with huge seals attached to it. "Behold the indulgence granted by his Holiness Alexander the Sixth, who, being newly elected Pope for his peculiar piety, intends to reform and purify the Church, and wisely begins by abolishing that priestly abuse which keeps too large a share of this privileged matrimony to the clergy and stints the laity. Spit once, my sons, and pay a white quattrino! This is the whole and sole price of the indulgence. The quattrino is the only difference the Holy Father allows to be put any longer between us and the clergy—who spit and pay nothing."

Tito thought he knew the voice, which had a peculiarly sharp ring, but the face was too much in shadow from the lights behind for him to be sure of the features. Stepping as near as he could, he saw within the circle behind the speaker an altar-like table raised on a small platform, and covered with a red drapery stitched all over with yellow cabalistical figures. Half a dozen thin tapers burned at the back of this table, which had a conjuring apparatus scattered over it, a large open book in the centre, and at one of the front angles a monkey fastened by a cord to a small ring and holding a small taper, which in his incessant fidgety movements fell more or less aslant, whilst an impish boy in a white surplice occupied himself chiefly in cuffing the monkey, and adjusting the taper. The man in the mitre also wore a surplice, and over it a chasuble on which the signs of the zodiac were rudely marked in black upon a yellow ground. Tito was sure now that he recognized the sharp upward-tending angles of the face under the mitre: it was that of Maestro Vaiano, the mountebank, from whom he had rescued Tessa. Pretty little Tessa! Perhaps she too had come in among the troops of contadine.

"Come, my maidens! This is the time for the pretty who can have many chances, and for the ill-favored who have few. Matrimony to be had—hot, eaten, and done with as easily as *berlingozzi!* And see!" here the conjurer held up a cluster of tiny bags. "To every bride I give a *Breve* with a secret in it —the secret alone worth the money you pay for the matrimony. The secret how to—no, no, I will not tell you what the secret is about, and that makes it a double secret. Hang it round your neck if you like, and never look at it; I don't say *that* will not be the best, for then you will see many things you don't expect: though if you open it you may break your leg, *è vero*, but you will know a secret! Something nobody knows but me! And mark—I give you the *Breve*, I don't sell it, as many another holy man would: the quattrino is for the matrimony, and the *Breve* you get for nothing. *Orsù, giovanetti*, come like dutiful sons of the Church and buy the Indulgence of his Holiness Alexander the Sixth."

This buffoonery just fitted the taste of the audience; the *fierucola* was but a small occasion, so the townsmen might be contented with jokes that were rather less indecent than those they were accustomed to hear at every carnival, put into easy rhyme by the Magnifico and his poetic satellites; while the women, over and above any relish of the fun, really began to have an itch for the *Brevi*. Several couples had already gone through the ceremony, in which the conjurer's solemn gibberish and grimaces over the open book, the antics of the monkey, and even the preliminary spitting, had called forth peals of laughter; and now a well-looking, merry-eyed youth of seventeen, in a loose tunic and red cap, pushed forward, holding by the hand a plump brunette, whose scanty ragged dress displayed her round arms and legs very picturesquely.

"Fetter us without delay, Maestro!" said the youth, "for I have got to take my bride home and paint her under the light of a lantern."

"Ha! Mariotto, my son, I commend your pious observance...." The conjurer was going on, when a loud chattering behind warned him that an unpleasant crisis had arisen with his monkey.

The temper of that imperfect acolyte was a little tried by the over-active discipline of his colleague in the surplice, and a sudden cuff administered as his taper fell to a horizontal position caused him to leap back with a violence that proved too much for the slackened knot by which his cord was fastened. His first leap was to the other end of the table, from which position his remonstrances were so threatening that the imp in the surplice took up a wand by way of an equivalent threat, whereupon the monkey leaped on to the head of a tall woman in the foreground, dropping his taper by the way, and chattering with increased emphasis from that eminence. Great was the screaming and confusion, not a few of the spectators having a vague dread of the Maestro's monkey, as capable of more hidden mischief than mere teeth and claws could inflict; and the conjurer himself was in some alarm lest any harm should happen to his familiar. In the scuffle to seize the monkey's string, Tito got out of the circle, and, not caring to contend for his place again, he allowed himself to be gradually pushed toward the church of the Nunziata, and to enter amongst the worshippers.

The brilliant illumination within seemed to press upon his eyes with palpable force after the pale scattered lights and broad shadows of the piazza, and for the first minute or two he could see nothing distinctly. That yellow splendor was in itself something supernatural and heavenly to many of the peasant women, for whom half the sky was hidden by mountains, and who went to bed in the twilight; and the uninterrupted chant from the choir was repose to the ear after the hellish hubbub of the crowd outside. Gradually the scene became clearer, though still there was a thin yellow haze from incense mingling with the breath of the multitude. In a chapel on the left hand of the nave, wreathed with silver lamps, was seen unveiled the miraculous fresco of the Annunciation, which, in Tito's oblique view of it from the right-hand side of the nave, seemed dark with the excess of light around it. The whole area of the great church was filled with peasant women, some kneeling, some standing; the coarse bronzed skins, and the dingy clothing of the rougher dwellers on the mountains, contrasting with the softer-lined faces and white or red head-drapery of the well-to-do dwellers in the valley, who were scattered in irregular groups. And spreading high and far over the walls and ceiling there was another multitude, also pressing close against each other, that they might be nearer the potent Virgin. It was the crowd of votive waxen images, the effigies of great personages, clothed in their habit as they lived: Florentines of high name, in their black silk lucco, as when they sat in council; popes, emperors, kings, cardinals, and famous condottieri with plumed morion seated on their chargers; all notable strangers who passed through Florence or had aught to do with its affairs—Mohammedans, even, in well-tolerated companionship with Christian cavaliers; some of them with faces blackened and robes tattered by the corroding breath of centuries, others fresh and bright in new red mantle or steel corselet, the exact doubles of the living. And wedged in with all these were detached arms, legs, and other members, with only here and there a gap where some image had been removed for public disgrace, or had fallen ominously, as Lorenzo's had done six months before. It was a perfect resurrection-swarm of remote mortals and fragments of mortals, reflecting, in their varying degrees of freshness, the sombre dinginess and sprinkled brightness of the crowd below.

Tito's glance wandered over the wild multitude in search of

something. He had already thought of Tessa, and the white hoods suggested the possibility that he might detect her face under one of them. It was at least a thought to be courted, rather than the vision of Romola looking at him with changed eyes. But he searched in vain; and he was leaving the church, weary of a scene which had no variety, when, just against the doorway, he caught sight of Tessa, only two yards off him. She was kneeling with her back against the wall, behind a group of peasant women, who were standing and looking for a spot nearer to the sacred image. Her head hung a little aside with a look of weariness, and her blue eyes were directed rather absently toward an altar-piece where the Archangel Michael stood in his armor, with young face and floating hair, amongst bearded and tonsured saints. Her right hand, holding a bunch of cocoons, fell by her side listlessly, and her round cheek was paled, either by the light or by the weariness that was expressed in her attitude: her lips were pressed poutingly together, and every now and then her eyelids half fell: she was a large image of a sweet sleepy child. Tito felt an irresistible desire to go up to her and get her pretty trusting looks and prattle: this creature who was without moral judgment that could condemn him, whose little loving ignorant soul made a world apart, where he might feel in freedom from suspicions and exacting demands, had a new attraction for him now. She seemed a refuge from the threatened isolation that would come with disgrace. He glanced cautiously round, to assure himself that Monna Ghita was not near, and then, slipping quietly to her side, kneeled on one knee, and said, in the softest voice, "Tessa!"

She hardly started, any more than she would have started at a soft breeze that fanned her gently when she was needing it. She turned her head and saw Tito's face close to her: it was very much more beautiful than the Archangel Michael's, who was so mighty and so good that he lived with the Madonna and all the saints and was prayed to along with them. She smiled in happy silence, for that nearness of Tito quite filled her mind.

"My little Tessa! you look very tired. How long have you been kneeling here?"

She seemed to be collecting her thoughts for a minute or two, and at last she said,—

"I'm very hungry."

"Come, then; come with me."

He lifted her from her knees, and led her out under the cloisters surrounding the atrium, which were then open, and not yet adorned with the frescoes of Andrea del Sarto.

"How is it you are all by yourself, and so hungry, Tessa?"

"The Madre is ill; she has very bad pains in her legs, and sent me to bring these cocoons to the Santissima Nunziata, because they're so wonderful; see!"—she held up the bunch of cocoons, which were arranged with fortuitous regularity on a stem,—"and she had kept them to bring them herself, but she couldn't, and so she sent me because she thinks the Holy Madonna may take away her pains; and somebody took my bag with the bread and chestnuts in it, and the people pushed me back, and I was so frightened coming in the crowd, and I couldn't get anywhere near the Holy Madonna, to give the cocoons to the Padre, but I must—oh, I must."

"Yes, my little Tessa, you shall take them; but first come and let me give you some berlingozzi. There are some to be had not far off."

"Where did you come from?" said Tessa, a little bewildered. "I thought you would never come to me again, because you never came to the Mercato for milk any more. I set myself Aves to say, to see if they would bring you back, but I left off, because they didn't."

"You see I come when you want some one to take care of you, Tessa. Perhaps the Aves fetched me, only it took them a long while. But what shall you do if you are here all alone? Where shall you go?"

"Oh, I shall stay and sleep in the church—a great many of them do—in the church and all about here—I did once when I came with my mother; and the *patrigno* is coming with the mules in the morning."

They were out in the piazza now, where the crowd was rather less riotous than before, and the lights were fewer, the stream of pilgrims having ceased. Tessa clung fast to Tito's arm in satisfied silence, while he led her toward the stall where he remembered seeing the eatables. Their way was the easier because there was just now a great rush toward the middle of the piazza, where the masked figures on stilts had found space to execute a dance. It was very pretty to see the guileless thing giving her cocoons into Tito's hand, and then eating her berlingozzi with the relish of a hungry child. Tito had really come to take care of her, as he did before, and that wonderful happiness of being with him had begun again for her. Her hunger was soon appeased, all the sooner for the new stimulus of happiness that had roused her from her languor, and, as they turned away from the stall, she said nothing about going into the church again, but looked round as if the sights in the piazza were not without attraction to her now she was safe under Tito's arm.

"How can they do that?" she exclaimed, looking up at the dancers on stilts. Then, after a minute's silence, "Do you think Saint Christopher helps them?"

"Perhaps. What do you think about it, Tessa?" said Tito, slipping his right arm round her, and looking down at her fondly.

"Because Saint Christopher is so very tall; and he is very good: if anybody looks at him he takes care of them all day. He is on the wall of the church—too tall to stand up there—but I saw him walking through the streets one San Giovanni, carrying the little Gesù."

"You pretty pigeon! Do you think anybody could help taking care of *you*, if you looked at them?"

"Shall you always come and take care of me?" said Tessa, turning her face up to him, as he crushed her cheek with his left hand. "And shall you always be a long while first?"

Tito was conscious that some bystanders were laughing at them, and though the license of street fun, among artists and young men of the wealthier sort as well as among the populace, made few adventures exceptional, still less disreputable, he chose to move away toward the end of the piazza.

"Perhaps I shall come again to you very soon, Tessa," he answered, rather dreamily, when they had moved away. He was thinking that when all the rest had turned their backs upon him, it would be pleasant to have this little creature adoring him and nestling against him. The absence of presumptuous self-conceit in Tito made him feel all the more defenceless under prospective obloquy: he needed soft looks and caresses too much ever to be impudent.

"In the Mercato?" said Tessa. "Not to-morrow morning, because the *patrigno* will be there, and he is so cross. Oh! but you have money, and he will not be cross if you buy some salad. And there are some chestnuts. Do you like chestnuts?"

He said nothing, but continued to look down at her with a dreamy gentleness, and Tessa felt herself in a state of delicious wonder; everything seemed as new as if she were being carried on a chariot of clouds.

"Holy Virgin!" she exclaimed again presently. "There is a holy father like the Bishop I saw at Prato."

Tito looked up too, and saw that he had unconsciously advanced to within a few yards of the conjurer, Maestro Vaiano, who for the moment was forsaken by the crowd. His face was turned away from them, and he was occupied with the apparatus on his altar or table, preparing a new diversion by the time the interest in the dancing should be exhausted. The monkey was imprisoned under the red cloth, out of reach of mischief, and the youngster in the white surplice was holding a sort of dish or salver, from which his master was taking some ingredient. The altar-like table, with its gorgeous cloth, the row of tapers, the sham episcopal costume, the surpliced attendant, and even the movements of the mitred figure, as he alternately bent his head and then raised something before the lights, were a sufficiently near parody of sacred things to rouse poor little Tessa's veneration; and there was some additional awe produced by the mystery of their apparition in this spot, for when she had seen an altar in the street before, it had been on Corpus Christi Day, and there had been a procession to account for it. She crossed herself and looked up at Tito, but then, as if she had had time for reflection, said, "It is because of the Natività."

Meanwhile Vaiano had turned round, raising his hands to his mitre with the intention of changing his dress, when his quick eye recognized Tito and Tessa, who were both looking at him, their faces being shone upon by the light of his tapers, while his own was in shadow.

"Ha! my children!" he said, instantly, stretching out his hands in a benedictory attitude, "you are come to be married. I commend your penitence—the blessing of Holy Church can never come too late."

But whilst he was speaking, he had taken in the whole meaning of Tessa's attitude and expression, and he discerned an opportunity for a new kind of joke which required him to be cautious and solemn.

"Should you like to be married to me, Tessa?" said Tito, softly, half enjoying the comedy, as he saw the pretty childish seriousness on her face, half prompted by hazy previsions which belonged to the intoxication of despair.

He felt her vibrating before she looked up at him and said, timidly, "Will you let me?"

He answered only by a smile, and by leading her forward in front of the *cerretano*, who, seeing an excellent jest in Tessa's evident delusion, assumed a surpassing sacerdotal solemnity, and went through the mimic ceremony with a liberal expenditure of *lingua furbesca* or thieves' Latin. But some symptoms of a new movement in the crowd urged him to bring it to a speedy conclusion and dismiss them with hands outstretched in a benedictory attitude over their kneeling figures. Tito, disposed always to cultivate good-will, though it might be the least select, put a piece of four grossi into his hand as he moved away, and was thanked by a look which, the conjurer felt sure, conveyed a perfect understanding of the whole affair.

But Tito himself was very far from that understanding, and did not, in fact, know whether, the next moment, he should tell Tessa of the joke and laugh at her for a little goose, or whether he should let her delusion last, and see what would come of it—see what she would say and do next.

"Then you will not go away from me again," said Tessa, after they had walked a few steps, "and you will take me to where you live." She spoke meditatively, and not in a questioning tone. But presently she added, "I must go back once to the Madre, though, to tell her I brought the cocoons, and that I am married, and shall not go back again."

Tito felt the necessity of speaking now; and in the rapid thought prompted by that necessity, he saw that by undeceiving Tessa he should be robbing himself of some at least of that pretty trustfulness which might, by and by, be his only haven from contempt. It would spoil Tessa to make her the least particle wiser or more suspicious.

"Yes, my little Tessa," he said, caressingly, "you must go back to the Madre; but you must not tell her you are married —you must keep that a secret from everybody; else some very great harm would happen to me, and you would never see me again."

She looked up at him with fear in her face.

"You must go back and feed your goats and mules, and do just as you have always done before, and say no word to any one about me."

The corners of her mouth fell a little.

"And then, perhaps, I shall come and take care of you again when you want me, as I did before. But you must do just what I tell you, else you will not see me again."

"Yes, I will, I will," she said, in a loud whisper, frightened at that blank prospect.

They were silent a little while; and then Tessa, looking at her hand, said,—

"The Madre wears a betrothal ring. She went to church and had it put on, and then after that, another day, she was married. And so did the cousin Nannina. But then *she* married Gollo," added the poor little thing, entangled in the difficult comparison between her own case and others within her experience.

"But you must not wear a betrothal ring, my Tessa, because no one must know you are married," said Tito, feeling some insistence necessary. "And the *buona fortuna* that I gave you did just as well for betrothal. Some people are betrothed with rings, and some are not."

"Yes, it is true, they would see the ring," said Tessa, trying to convince herself that a thing she would like very much was really not good for her.

They were now near the entrance of the church again, and she remembered her cocoons which were still in Tito's hand.

"Ah, you must give me the *boto*," she said; "and we must go on, and I must take it to the Padre, and I must tell the rest of my beads, because I was too tired before."

"Yes, you must go in, Tessa; but I will not go in. I must leave you now," said Tito, too feverish and weary to re-enter that stifling heat, and feeling that this was the least difficult way of parting with her.

"And not come back? Oh, where do you go?" Tessa's mind had never formed an image of his whereabouts or his doings when she did not see him: he had vanished, and her thought, instead of following him, had stayed in the same spot where he was with her.

"I shall come back some time, Tessa," said Tito, taking her under the cloisters to the door of the church. "You must not cry—you must go to sleep, when you have said your beads. And here is money to buy your breakfast. Now kiss me, and look happy, else I shall not come again."

She made a great effort over herself as she put up her lips to kiss him, and submitted to be gently turned round, with her face toward the door of the church. Tito saw her enter; and then, with a shrug at his own resolution, leaned against a pillar, took off his cap, rubbed his hair backward, and wondered where Romola was now, and what she was thinking of him. Poor little Tessa had disappeared behind the curtain among the crowd of peasants; but the love which formed one web with all his worldly hopes, with the ambitions and pleasures that must make the solid part of his days—the love that was identified with his larger self—was not to be banished from his consciousness. Even to the man who presents the most elastic resistance to whatever is unpleasant there will come moments when the pressure from without is too strong for him, and he must feel the smart and the bruise in spite of himself. Such a moment had come to Tito. There was no possible attitude of mind, no scheme of action, by which the uprooting of all his newly planted hopes could be made otherwise than painful.

CHAPTER XV.

THE DYING MESSAGE.

WHEN Romola arrived at the entrance of San Marco she found one of the Frati waiting there in expectation of her arrival. Monna Brigida retired into the adjoining church, and Romola was conducted to the door of the chapter-house in the outer cloister, whither the invalid had been conveyed; no woman being allowed admission beyond this precinct.

When the door opened, the subdued external light blending with that of two tapers placed behind a truckle-bed showed the emaciated face of Fra Luca, with the tonsured crown of golden hair above it, and with deep-sunken hazel eyes fixed on a small crucifix which he held before him. He was propped up into nearly a sitting posture; and Romola was just conscious, as she threw aside her veil, that there was another monk standing by the bed, with the black cowl drawn over his head, and that he moved toward the door as she entered; just conscious that in the background there was a crucified form rising high and pale on the frescoed wall, and pale faces of sorrow looking out from it below.

The next moment her eyes met Fra Luca's as they looked up at her from the crucifix, and she was absorbed in that pang of recognition which identified this monkish emaciated form with the image of her fair young brother.

"Dino!" she said, in a voice like a low cry of pain. But she did not bend toward him; she held herself erect, and paused at two yards' distance from him. There was an unconquerable repulsion for her in that monkish aspect; it seemed to her the brand of the dastardly undutifulness which had left her father desolate—of the grovelling superstition which could give such undutifulness the name of piety. Her father, whose proud sincerity and simplicity of life had made him one of the few frank pagans of his time, had brought her up with a silent ignoring of any claims the Church could have to regulate the belief and action of beings with a cultivated

THE DYING MESSAGE. 163

reason. The Church, in her mind, belonged to that actual life of the mixed multitude from which they had always lived apart, and she had no ideas that could render her brother's course an object of any other feeling than incurious, indignant contempt. Yet the lovingness of Romola's soul had clung to that image in the past, and while she stood rigidly aloof, there was a yearning search in her eyes for something too faintly discernible.

But there was no corresponding emotion in the face of the monk. He looked at the little sister returned to him in her full womanly beauty with the far-off gaze of a revisiting spirit.

"My sister!" he said, with a feeble and interrupted but yet distinct utterance, "it is well thou hast not longer delayed to come, for I have a message to deliver to thee, and my time is short."

Romola took a step nearer: the message, she thought, would be one of affectionate penitence to her father, and her heart began to open. Nothing could wipe out the long years of desertion; but the culprit, looking back on those years with the sense of irremediable wrong committed, would call forth pity. Now, at the last, there would be understanding and forgiveness. Dino would pour out some natural filial feeling; he would ask questions about his father's blindness—how rapidly it had come on? how the long dark days had been filled? what the life was now in the home where he himself had been nourished?—and the last message from the dying lips would be one of tenderness and regret.

"Romola," Fra Luca began, "I have had a vision concerning thee. Thrice I have had it in the last two months: each time it has been clearer. Therefore I came from Fiesole deeming it a message from Heaven that I was bound to deliver. And I gather a promise of mercy to thee in this, that my breath is preserved in order to——"

The difficult breathing which continually interrupted him would not let him finish the sentence.

Romola had felt her heart chilling again. It was a vision, then, this message—one of those visions she had so often heard her father allude to with bitterness. Her indignation rushed to her lips.

"Dino, ‑ thought you had some words to send to my father. You forsook him when his sight was failing; you made his life very desolate. Have you never cared about that? never repented? What is this religion of yours, that places visions before natural duties?"

The deep-sunken hazel eyes turned slowly toward her and rested upon her in silence for some moments, as if he were meditating whether he should answer her.

"No," he said at last: speaking as before, in a low passionless tone, as of some spirit not human, speaking through dying human organs. "No; I have never repented fleeing from the stifling poison-breath of sin that was hot and thick around me and threatened to steal over my senses like besotting wine. My father could not hear the voice that called me night and day; he knew nothing of the demon tempters that tried to drag me back from following it. My father has lived amidst human sin and misery without believing in them: he has been like one busy picking shining stones in a mine, while there was a world dying of plague above him. I spoke, but he listened with scorn. I told him the studies he wished me to live for were either childish trifling—dead toys—or else they must be made warm and living by pulses that beat to worldly ambitions and fleshly lusts, for worldly ambitions and fleshly lusts made all the substance of the poetry and history he wanted me to bend my eyes on continually."

"Has not my father led a pure and noble life, then?" Romola burst forth, unable to hear in silence this implied accusation against her father. "He has sought no worldly honors; he has been truthful; he has denied himself all luxuries; he has lived like one of the ancient sages. He never wished you to live for worldly ambitions and fleshly lusts; he wished you to live as he himself has done, according to the purest maxims of philosophy, in which he brought you up."

Romola spoke partly by rote, as all ardent and sympathetic young creatures do; but she spoke with intense belief. The pink flush was in her face, and she quivered from head to foot. Her brother was again slow to answer; looking at her passionate face with strange passionless eyes.

"What were the maxims of philosophy to me? They told

me to be strong, when I felt myself weak; when I was ready, like the blessed Saint Benedict, to roll myself among thorns, and court smarting wounds as a deliverance from temptation. For the Divine love had sought me, and penetrated me, and created a great need in me; like a seed that wants room to grow. I had been brought up in carelessness of the true faith; I had not studied the doctrines of our religion; but it seemed to take possession of me like a rising flood. I felt that there was a life of perfect love and purity for the soul; in which there would be no uneasy hunger after pleasure, no tormenting questions, no fear of suffering. Before I knew the history of the saints, I had a foreshadowing of their ecstasy. For the same truth had penetrated even into pagan philosophy: that it is a bliss within the reach of man to die to mortal needs, and live in the life of God as the Unseen Perfectness. But to attain that I must forsake the world; I must have no affection, no hope, wedding me to that which passeth away; I must live with my fellow-beings only as human souls related to the eternal unseen life. That need was urging me continually: it came over me in visions when my mind fell away weary from the vain words which record the passions of dead men: it came over me after I had been tempted into sin and had turned away with loathing from the scent of the emptied cup. And in visions I saw the meaning of the Crucifix."

He paused, breathing hard for a minute or two: but Romola was not prompted to speak again. It was useless for her mind to attempt any contact with the mind of this unearthly brother: as useless as for her hand to try and grasp a shadow. When he spoke again, his heaving chest was quieter.

"I felt whom I must follow: but I saw that even among the servants of the Cross who professed to have renounced the world, my soul would be stifled with the fumes of hypocrisy, and lust, and pride. God had not chosen me, as he chose Saint Dominic and Saint Francis, to wrestle with evil in the Church and in the world. He called upon me to flee: I took the sacred vows, and I fled—fled to lands where danger and scorn and want bore me continually, like angels, to repose on the bosom of God. I have lived the life of a hermit, I have ministered to pilgrims; but my task has been short: the veil has worn very thin that divides me from my everlasting rest. I came back to Florence that——"

"Dino, you *did* want to know if my father was alive," interrupted Romola, the picture of that suffering life touching her again with the desire for union and forgiveness.

"——That before I died I might urge others of our brethren to study the Eastern tongues, as I had not done, and go out to greater ends than I did; and I find them already bent on the work. And since I came, Romola, I have felt that I was sent partly to thee—not to renew the bonds of earthly affection, but to deliver the heavenly warning conveyed in a vision. For I have had that vision thrice. And through all the years since first the Divine voice called me, while I was yet in the world, I have been taught and guided by visions. For in the painful linking together of our waking thoughts we can never be sure that we have not mingled our own error with the light we have prayed for; but in visions and dreams we are passive, and our souls are as an instrument in the Divine hand. Therefore listen, and speak not again—for the time is short."

Romola's mind recoiled strongly from listening to this vision. Her indignation had subsided, but it was only because she had felt the distance between her brother and herself widening. But while Fra Luca was speaking, the figure of another monk had entered, and again stood on the other side of the bed, with the cowl drawn over his head.

"Kneel, my daughter, for the Angel of Death is present, and waits while the message of Heaven is delivered: bend thy pride before it is bent for thee by a yoke of iron," said a strong, rich voice, startlingly in contrast with Fra Luca's.

The tone was not that of imperious command, but of quiet self-possession and assurance of the right, blended with benignity. Romola, vibrating to the sound, looked round at the figure on the opposite side of the bed. His face was hardly discernible under the shadow of the cowl, and her eyes fell at once on his hands, which were folded across his breast and lay in relief on the edge of his black mantle. They had a marked physiognomy which enforced the influence of the voice; they were very beautiful and almost of transparent delicacy. Romola's disposition to rebel against command, doubly active in the presence of monks, whom she had been taught to despise, would have fixed itself on any repulsive detail as a point of support. But the face was hidden, and the hands seemed to have an appeal in them against all hardness. The next moment the right hand took the crucifix to relieve the fatigued grasp of Fra Luca, and the left touched his lips with a wet sponge which lay near. In the act of bending, the cowl was pushed back, and the features of the monk had the full light of the tapers on them. They were very marked features, such as lend themselves to popular description. There was the high arched nose, the prominent under lip, the coronet of thick dark hair above the brow, all seeming to tell of energy and passion; there were the blue-gray eyes, shining mildly under auburn eyelashes, seeming, like the hands, to tell of acute sensitiveness. Romola felt certain they were the features of Fra Girolamo Savonarola, the prior of San Marco, whom she had chiefly thought of as more offensive than other monks, because he was more noisy. Her rebellion was rising against the first impression, which had almost forced her to bend her knees.

"Kneel, my daughter," the penetrating voice said again; "the pride of the body is a barrier against the gifts that purify the soul."

He was looking at her with mild fixedness while he spoke, and again she felt that subtle mysterious influence of a personality by which it has been given to some rare men to move their fellows.

Slowly Romola fell on her knees, and in the very act a tremor came over her; in the renunciation of her proud erectness, her mental attitude seemed changed, and she found herself in a new state of passiveness. Her brother began to speak again:—

"Romola, in the deep night, as I lay awake, I saw my father's room—the library—with all the books, and the marbles, and the leggio, where I used to stand and read; and I saw you—you were revealed to me as I see you now, with fair long hair, sitting before my father's chair. And at the leggio stood a man whose face I could not see. I looked and looked, and it was a blank to me, even as a painting effaced; and I saw him move and take thee, Romola, by the hand; and then I saw thee take my father by the hand; and you all three went down the stone steps into the streets, the man whose face was a blank to me leading the way. And you stood at the altar in Santa Croce, and the priest who married you had the face of death; and the graves opened, and the dead in their shrouds rose and followed you like a bridal train. And you passed on through the streets and the gates into the valley, and it seemed to me that he who led you hurried you more than you could bear, and the dead were weary of following you, and turned back to their graves. And at last you came to a stony place where there was no water, and no trees or herbage; but instead of water, I saw written parchment unrolling itself everywhere, and instead of trees and herbage I saw men of bronze and marble springing up and crowding round you. And my father was faint for want of water, and fell to the ground; and the man whose face was a blank loosed thy hand and departed: and as he went I could see his face; and it was the face of the Great Tempter. And thou, Romola, didst wring thy hands and seek for water, and there was none. And the bronze and marble figures seemed to mock thee and hold out cups of water, and when thou didst grasp them and put them to my father's lips, they turned to parchment. And the bronze and marble figures seemed to turn into demons and snatch my father's body from thee, and the parchments shrivelled up, and blood ran everywhere instead of them, and fire upon the blood, till they all vanished, and the plain was bare and stony again, and thou wast alone in the midst of it. And then it seemed that the night fell, and I saw no more. . . . Thrice I have had that vision, Romola. I believe it is a revelation meant for thee: to warn thee against marriage as a temptation of the enemy; it calls upon thee to dedicate thyself——"

His pauses had gradually become longer and more frequent, and he was now compelled to cease by a severe fit of gasping, in which his eyes were turned on the crucifix as on a light that was vanishing. Presently he found strength to speak again, but in a feebler, scarcely audible tone:

"To renounce the vain philosophy and corrupt thoughts of the heathens: for in the hour of sorrow and death their pride will turn to mockery, and the unclean gods will——"

The words died away.

In spite of the thought that was at work in Romola, telling her that this vision was no more than a dream, fed by youthful memories and ideal convictions, a strange awe had come over her. Her mind was not apt to be assailed by sickly fancies; she had the vivid intellect and the healthy human passion which are too keenly alive to the constant relations of things to have any morbid craving after the exceptional. Still the image of the vision she despised jarred and distressed her like painful and cruel cries. And it was the first time she had witnessed the struggle with approaching death: her young life had been sombre, but she had known nothing of the utmost human needs; no acute suffering—no heart-cutting sorrow; and this brother, come back to her in his hour of supreme agony, was like a sudden awful apparition from an invisible world. The pale faces of sorrow in the fresco on the opposite wall seemed to have come nearer, and to make one company with the pale face on the bed.

"Frate," said the dying voice.

Fra Girolamo leaned down. But no other word came for some moments.

"Romola," it said next.

She leaned forward too: but again there was silence. The words were struggling in vain.

"Fra Girolamo, give her——"

"The crucifix," said the voice of Fra Girolamo.

No other sound came from the dying lips.

"Dino!" said Romola, with a low but piercing cry, as the certainty came upon her that the silence of misunderstanding could never be broken.

"Take the crucifix, my daughter," said Fra Girolamo, after a few minutes. "His eyes behold it no more."

Romola stretched out her hand to the crucifix, and this act appeared to relieve the tension of her mind. A great sob burst from her. She bowed her head by the side of her dead brother and wept aloud.

It seemed to her as if this first vision of death must alter the daylight for her for evermore.

Fra Girolamo moved toward the door, and called in a lay brother who was waiting outside. Then he went up to Romola and said in a tone of gentle command: "Rise, my daughter, and be comforted. Our brother is with the blessed. He has left you the crucifix, in remembrance of the heavenly warning—that it may be a beacon to you in the darkness."

She rose from her knees, trembling, folded her veil over her head, and hid the crucifix under her mantle. Fra Girolamo then led the way out into the cloistered court, lit now only by the stars and by a lantern which was held by some one near the entrance. Several other figures in the dress of the dignified laity were grouped about the same spot. They were some of the numerous frequenters of San Marco, who had come to visit the Prior, and having heard that he was in attendance on the dying brother in the chapter-house, had awaited him here.

Romola was dimly conscious of footsteps and rustling forms moving aside: she heard the voice of Fra Girolamo saying, in a low tone, "Our brother is departed"; she felt a hand laid on her arm. The next moment the door was opened, and she was out in the wide piazza of San Marco, with no one but Monna Brigida, and the servant carrying the lantern.

The fresh sense of space revived her, and helped her to recover her self-mastery. The scene which had just closed upon her was terribly distinct and vivid, but it began to narrow under the returning impressions of the life that lay outside it. She hastened her steps, with nervous anxiety to be again with her father—and with Tito—for were they not together in her absence? The images of that vision, while they clung about her like a hideous dream not yet to be shaken off, made her yearn all the more for the beloved faces and voices that would assure her of her waking life.

Tito, we know, was not with Bardo; his destiny was being shaped by a guilty consciousness, urging on him the despairing belief that by this time Romola possessed the knowledge which would lead to their final separation.

And the lips that could have conveyed that knowledge were

forever closed. The prevision that Fra Luca's words had imparted to Romola had been such as comes from the shadowy region where human souls seek wisdom apart from the human sympathies which are the very life and substance of our wisdom; the revelation that might have come from the simple questions of filial and brotherly affection had been carried into irrevocable silence.

CHAPTER XVI.

A FLORENTINE JOKE.

EARLY the next morning Tito was returning from Bratti's shop in the narrow thoroughfare of the Ferravecchi. The Genoese stranger had carried away the onyx ring, and Tito was carrying away fifty florins. It did just cross his mind that if, after all, Fortune, by one of her able devices, saved him from the necessity of quitting Florence, it would be better for him not to have parted with his ring, since he had been understood to wear it for the sake of peculiar memories and predilections; still, it was a slight matter, not worth dwelling on with any emphasis, and in those moments he had lost his confidence in fortune. The feverish excitement of the first alarm which had impelled his mind to travel into the future had given place to a dull, regretful lassitude. He cared so much for the pleasures that could only come to him through the good opinion of his fellow-men that he wished now he had never risked ignominy by shrinking from what his fellow-men called obligations.

But our deeds are like children that are born to us; they live and act apart from our own will. Nay, children may be strangled, but deeds never: they have an indestructible life both in and out of our consciousness; and that dreadful vitality of deeds was pressing hard on Tito for the first time.

He was going back to his lodgings in the Piazza di San Giovanni, but he avoided passing through the Mercato Vecchio, which was his nearest way, lest he should see Tessa. He was not in the humor to seek anything; he could only await the first sign of his altering lot.

The piazza with its sights of beauty was lit up by that warm morning sunlight under which the autumn dew still lingers, and which invites to an idlesse undulled by fatigue. It was a festival morning, too, when the soft warmth seems to steal over one with a special invitation to lounge and gaze. Here, too, the signs of the fair were present; in the spaces round the octagonal baptistery, stalls were being spread with fruit and flowers, and here and there laden mules were standing quietly absorbed in their nose-bags, while their drivers were perhaps gone through the hospitable sacred doors to kneel before the blessed Virgin on this morning of her Nativity. On the broad marble steps of the Duomo there were scattered groups of beggars and gossiping talkers: here an old crone with white hair and hard sunburnt face encouraging a round-capped baby to try its tiny bare feet on the warmed marble, while a dog sitting near snuffed at the performance suspiciously; there a couple of shaggy-headed boys leaning to watch a small pale cripple who was cutting a face on a cherrystone; and above them on the wide platform men were making changing knots in laughing desultory chat, or else were standing in close couples gesticulating eagerly.

But the largest and most important company of loungers was that toward which Tito had to direct his steps. It was the busiest time of the day with Nello, and in this warm season and at an hour when clients were numerous, most men preferred being shaved under the pretty red-and-white awning in front of the shop rather than within narrow walls. It is not a sublime attitude for a man, to sit with lathered chin thrown backward, and have his nose made a handle of; but to be shaved was a fashion of Florentine respectability, and it is astonishing how gravely men look at each other when they are all in the fashion. It was the hour of the day, too, when yesterday's crop of gossip was freshest, and the barber's tongue was always in its glory when his razor was busy; the deft activity of those two instruments seemed to be set going by a common spring. Tito foresaw that it would be impossible for him to escape being drawn into the circle, he must smile and retort, and look perfectly at his ease. Well! it was but the ordeal of swallowing bread and cheese pills after all. The man who let the mere anticipation of discovery choke him was simply a man of weak nerves.

But just at that time Tito felt a hand laid on his shoulder, and no amount of previous resolution could prevent the very unpleasant sensation with which that sudden touch jarred him. His face, as he turned it round, betrayed the inward shock; but the owner of the hand that seemed to have such evil magic in it broke into a light laugh. He was a young man about Tito's own age, with keen features, small close-clipped head, and close-shaven lip and chin, giving the idea of a mind as little encumbered as possible with material that was not nervous. The keen eyes were bright with hope and friendliness, as so many other young eyes have been that have afterward closed on the world in bitterness and disappointment; for at that time there were none but pleasant predictions about Niccolò Macchiavelli, as a young man of promise, who was expected to mend the broken fortunes of his ancient family.

"Why, Melema, what evil dream did you have last night, that you took my light grasp for that of a *sbirro* or something worse?"

"Ah, Messer Niccolò!" said Tito, recovering himself immediately; "it must have been an extra amount of dulness in my veins this morning that shuddered at the approach of your wit. But the fact is, I have had a bad night."

"That is unlucky, because you will be expected to shine without any obstructing fog to-day in the Rucellai Gardens. I take it for granted you are to be there."

"Messer Bernardo did me the honor to invite me," said Tito; "but I shall be engaged elsewhere."

"Ah! I remember, you are in love," said Macchiavelli, with a shrug, "else you would never have such inconvenient engagements. Why, we are to eat a peacock and ortolans under the loggia among Bernardo Rucellai's rare trees; there are to be the choicest spirits in Florence and the choicest wines. Only, as Piero de' Medici is to be there, the choice spirits may happen to be swamped in the capping of impromptu verses. I hate that game; it is a device for the triumph of small wits, who are always inspired the most by the smallest occasions."

"What is that you are saying about Piero de' Medici and small wits, Messer Niccolò?" said Nello, whose light figure was at that moment predominating over the Herculean frame of Niccolò Caparra.

That famous worker in iron, whom we saw last with bared muscular arms and leathern apron in the Mercato Vecchio, was this morning dressed in holiday suit, and as he sat submissively while Nello skipped round him, lathered him, seized him by the nose, and scraped him with magical quickness, he looked much as a lion might if it had donned linen and tunic and was preparing to go into society.

"A private secretary will never rise in the world if he couples great and small in that way," continued Nello. "When great men are not allowed to marry their sons and daughters as they like, small men must not expect to marry their words as they like. Have you heard the news Domenico Cennini, here, has been telling us?—that Pagolantonio Soderini has given Ser Piero da Bibbiena a box on the ear for setting on Piero de' Medici to interfere with the marriage between young Tommaso Soderini and Fiammetta Strozzi, and is to be sent ambassador to Venice as a punishment?"

"I don't know which I envy him most," said Macchiavelli, "the offence or the punishment. The offence will make him the most popular man in all Florence, and the punishment will take him among the only people in Italy who have known how to manage their own affairs."

"Yes, if Soderini stays long enough at Venice," said Cennini, "he may chance to learn the Venetian fashion, and bring it home with him. The Soderini have been fast friends of the Medici, but what has happened is likely to open Pagolantonio's eyes to the good of our old Florentine trick of choosing a new harness when the old one galls us; if we have not quite lost the trick in these last fifty years."

"Not we," said Niccolò Caparra, who was rejoicing in the free use of his lips again. "Eat eggs in Lent and the snow will melt. That's what I say to our people when they get noisy over their cups at San Gallo, and talk of raising a *romor* (insurrection): I say, never do you plan a *romor;* you may as well try to fill Arno with buckets. When there's water enough Arno will be full, and that will not be till the torrent is ready."

"Caparra, that oracular speech of yours is due to my excellent shaving," said Nello. "You could never have made it with that dark rust on your chin. Ecco, Messer Domenico, I am ready for you now. By the way, my bel erudito," continued Nello, as he saw Tito moving toward the door, "here has been old Maso seeking for you, but your nest was empty. He will come again presently. The old man looked mournful, and seemed in haste. I hope there is nothing wrong in the Via de' Bardi."

"Doubtless Messer Tito knows that Bardo's son is dead," said Cronaca, who had just come up.

Tito's heart gave a leap—had the death happened before Romola saw him?

"No, I had not heard it," he said, with no more discomposure than the occasion seemed to warrant, turning and leaning against the doorpost, as if he had given up his intention of going away. "I knew that his sister had gone to see him. Did he die before she arrived?"

"No," said Cronaca; "I was in San Marco at the time, and saw her come out from the chapter-house with Fra Girolamo, who told us that the dying man's breath had been preserved as by a miracle, that he might make a disclosure to his sister."

Tito felt that his fate was decided. Again his mind rushed over all the circumstances of his departure from Florence, and he conceived a plan of getting back his money from Cennini before the disclosure had become public. If he once had his money he need not stay long in endurance of scorching looks and biting words. He would wait now, and go away with Cennini and get the money from him at once. With that project in his mind he stood motionless—his hands in his belt, his eyes fixed absently on the ground. Nello, glancing at him, felt sure that he was absorbed in anxiety about Romola, and thought him such a pretty image of self-forgetful sadness that he just perceptibly pointed his razor at him, and gave a challenging look at Piero di Cosimo, whom he had never forgiven for his refusal to see any prognostics of character in his favorite's handsome face. Piero, who was leaning against the other doorpost, close to Tito, shrugged his shoulders: the frequent recurrence of such challenges from Nello had changed the painter's first declaration of neutrality into a positive inclination to believe ill of the much-praised Greek.

"So you have got your Fra Girolamo back again, Cronaca? I suppose we shall have him preaching again this next Advent," said Nello.

"And not before there is need," said Cronaca, gravely. "We have had the best testimony to his words since the last Quaresima; for even to the wicked wickedness has become a plague; and the ripeness of vice is turning to rottenness in the nostrils even of the vicious. There has not been a change since the Quaresima, either in Rome or at Florence, but has put a new seal on the Frate's words—that the harvest of sin is ripe, and that God will reap it with a sword."

"I hope he has had a new vision, however," said Francesco Cei, sneeringly. "The old ones are somewhat stale. Can't your Frate get a poet to help out his imagination for him?"

"He has no lack of poets about him," said Cronaca, with quiet contempt, "but they are great poets and not little ones; so they are contented to be taught by him, and no more think the truth stale which God has given him to utter than they think the light of the moon is stale. But perhaps certain high prelates and princes who dislike the Frate's denunciations might be pleased to hear that, though Giovanni Pico, and Poliziano, and Marsilio Ficino, and most other men of mark in Florence, reverence Fra Girolamo, Messer Francesco Cei despises him."

"Poliziano?" said Cei, with a scornful laugh. "Yes, doubtless he believes in your new Jonah; witness the fine orations he wrote for the envoys of Sienna, to tell Alexander the Sixth that the world and the Church were never so well off as since he became Pope."

"Nay, Francesco," said Macchiavelli, smiling, "a various scholar must have various opinions. And as for the Frate, whatever we may think of his saintliness, you judge his preaching too narrowly. The secret of oratory lies, not in saying new things, but in saying things with a certain power that moves the hearers—without which, as old Filelfo has said, your speaker deserves to be called, 'non oratorem, sed aratorem.' And, according to that test, Fra Girolamo is a great orator."

"That is true, Niccolò," said Cennini, speaking from the shaving-chair, "but part of the secret lies in the prophetic visions. Our people—no offence to you, Cronaca—will run after anything in the shape of a prophet, especially if he prophesies terrors and tribulations"

"Rather say, Cennini," answered Cronaca, "that the chief secret lies in the Frate's pure life and strong faith, which stamp him as a messenger of God."

"I admit it—I admit it," said Cennini, opening his palms, as he rose from the chair. "His life is spotless: no man has impeached it."

"He is satisfied with the pleasant lust of arrogance," Cei burst out bitterly. "I can see it in that proud lip and satisfied eye of his. He hears the air filled with his own name—Fra Girolamo Savonarola, of Ferrara; the prophet, the saint, the mighty preacher, who frightens the very babies of Florence into laying down their wicked bawbles."

"Come, come, Francesco, you are out of humor with waiting," said the conciliatory Nello. "Let me stop your mouth with a little lather. I must not have my friend Cronaca made angry: I have a regard for his chin; and his chin is in no respect altered since he became a Piagnone. And for my own part, I confess, when the Frate was preaching in the Duomo last Advent, I got into such a trick of slipping in to listen to him that I might have turned Piagnone too, if I had not been hindered by the liberal nature of my art; and also by the length of the sermons, which are sometimes a good while before they get to the moving point. But, as Messer Niccolò here says, the Frate lays hold of the people by some power over and above his prophetic visions. Monks and nuns who prophesy are not of that rareness. For what says Luigi Pulci? 'Dombruno's sharp-cutting cimiter had the fame of being enchanted; but,' says Luigi, 'I am rather of opinion that it cut sharp because it was of strongly tempered steel.'

Yes, yes; Paternosters may shave clean, but they must be said over a good razor."

"See, Nello!" said Macchiavelli, "what doctor is this advancing on his Bucephalus? I thought your piazza was free from those furred and scarlet-robed lackeys of death. This man looks as if he had had some such night adventure as Boccaccio's Maestro Simone, and had his bonnet and mantle pickled a little in the gutter; though he himself is as sleek as a miller's rat."

"A-ah!" said Nello, with a low long-drawn intonation, as he looked up toward the advancing figure—a round-headed, round-bodied personage, seated on a raw young horse, which held its nose out with an air of threatening obstinacy, and by a constant effort to back and go off in an oblique line showed free views about authority very much in advance of the age.

"And I have a few more adventures in pickle for him," continued Nello, in an undertone, "which I hope will drive his inquiring nostrils to another quarter of the city. He's a doctor from Padua; they say he has been at Prato for three months, and now he's come to Florence to see what he can net. But his great trick is making rounds among the contadini. And do you note those great saddle-bags he carries? They are to hold the fat capons and eggs and meal he levies on silly clowns with whom coin is scarce. He vends his own secret medicines, so he keeps away from the doors of the druggists; and for this last week he has taken to sitting in my piazza for two or three hours every day, and making it a resort for asthmas and squalling bambini. It stirs my gall to see the toad-faced quack fingering the greasy quattrini, or bagging a pigeon in exchange for his pills and powders. But I'll put a few thorns in his saddle, else I'm no Florentine. Laudamus! he is coming to be shaved; that's what I've waited for. Messer Domenico, go not away: wait; you shall see a rare bit of fooling, which I devised two days ago. Here, Sandro!"

Nello whispered in the ear of Sandro, who rolled his solemn eyes, nodded, and, following up these signs of understanding with a slow smile, took to his heels with surprising rapidity.

"How is it with you, Maestro Tacco?" said Nello, as the doctor, with difficulty, brought his horse's head round toward the barber's shop. "That is a fine young horse of yours, but something raw in the mouth, eh?"

"He is an accursed beast, the *vermocane* seize him!" said Maestro Tacco, with a burst of irritation, descending from his saddle and fastening the old bridle, mended with string, to an iron staple in the wall. "Nevertheless," he added, recollecting himself, "a sound beast and a valuable, for one who wanted to purchase, and get a profit by training him. I had him cheap."

"Rather too hard riding for a man who carries your weight of learning: eh, Maestro?" said Nello. "You seem hot."

"Truly, I am likely to be hot," said the doctor, taking off his bonnet, and giving to full view a bald low head and flat broad face, with high ears, wide lipless mouth, round eyes, and deep arched lines above the projecting eyebrows, which altogether made Nello's epithet "toad-faced" dubiously complimentary to the blameless batrachian. "Riding from Peretola, when the sun is high, is not the same thing as kicking your heels on a bench in the shade, like your Florence doctors. Moreover, I have had not a little pulling to get through the carts and mules into the Mercato, to find out the husband of a certain Monna Ghita, who had had a fatal seizure before I was called in; and if it had not been that I had to demand my fees——"

"Monna Ghita!" said Nello, as the perspiring doctor interrupted himself to rub his head and face. "Peace be with her angry soul! The Mercato will want a whip the more if her tongue is laid to rest."

Tito, who had roused himself from his abstraction, and was listening to the dialogue, felt a new rush of the vague half-formed ideas about Tessa which had passed through his mind the evening before: if Monna Ghita were really taken out of the way, it would be easier for him to see Tessa again—whenever he wanted to see her.

"*Gnaffè*, Maestro," Nello went on, in a sympathizing tone, "you are the slave of rude mortals, who, but for you, would die like brutes, without help of pill or powder. It is pitiful to see your learned lymph oozing from your pores as if it were mere vulgar moisture. You think my shaving will cool and disencumber you? One moment and I have done with Messer Francesco here. It seems to me a thousand years till I wait upon a man who carries all the science of Arabia in his head and saddle-bags. Ecco!"

Nello held up the shaving-cloth with an air of invitation, and Maestro Tacco advanced and seated himself under a preoccupation with his heat and his self-importance which made him quite deaf to the irony conveyed in Nello's officiously polite speech.

"It is but fitting that a great medicus like you," said Nello, adjusting the cloth, "should be shaved by the same razor that has shaved the illustrious Antonio Benevieni, the greatest master of the chirurgic art."

"The chirurgic art!" interrupted the doctor, with an air of contemptuous disgust. "Is it your Florentine fashion to put the masters of the science of medicine on a level with men who do carpentry on broken limbs, and sew up wounds like tailors, and carve away excrescences as a butcher trims meat? *Via!* A manual art, such as any artificer might learn, and which has been practised by simple barbers like yourself—on a level with the noble science of Hippocrates, Galen, and Avicenna, which penetrates into the occult influences of the stars and plants and gems!—a science locked up from the vulgar!"

"No, in truth, Maestro," said Nello, using his lather very deliberately, as if he wanted to prolong the operation to the utmost, "I never thought of placing them on a level: I know your science comes next to the miracles of Holy Church for mystery. But there, you see, is the pity of it"—here Nello fell into a tone of regretful sympathy—"your high science is sealed from the profane and the vulgar, and so you become an object of envy and slander. I grieve to say it, but there are low fellows in this city—mere *sgherri*, who go about in night-caps and long beards, and make it their business to sprinkle gall in every man's broth who is prospering. Let me tell you —for you are a stranger—this is a city where every man had need carry a large nail ready to fasten on the wheel of Fortune when his side happens to be uppermost. Already there are stories—mere fables doubtless—beginning to be buzzed about concerning you, that make me wish I could hear of your being well on your way to Arezzo. I would not have a man of your metal stoned, for though San Stefano was stoned, he was not great in medicine like San Cosmo and San Damiano. . . ."

"What stories? what fables?" stammered Maestro Tacco. "What do you mean?"

"*Lasso!* I fear me you are come into the trap for your cheese, Maestro. The fact is, there is a company of evil youths who go prowling about the houses of our citizens carrying sharp tools in their pocket;—no sort of door, or window, or shutter but they will pierce it. They are possessed with a diabolical patience to watch the doings of people who fancy themselves private. It must be they who have done it—it must be they who have spread the stories about you and your medicines. Have you by chance detected any small aperture in your door or window-shutter? No? Well, I advise you to look; for it is now commonly talked of that you have been seen in your dwelling at the Canto di Paglia, making your secret specifics by night: pounding dried toads in a mortar, compounding a salve out of mashed worms, and making your pills from the dried livers of rats which you mix with saliva emitted during the utterance of a blasphemous incantation—which indeed these witnesses profess to repeat."

"It is a pack of lies!" exclaimed the doctor, struggling to get utterance, and then desisting in alarm at the approaching razor.

"It is not to me, or any of this respectable company, that you need to say that, doctor. *We* are not the heads to plant such carrots as those in. But what of that? What are a handful of reasonable men against a crowd with stones in their hands? There are those among us who think Cecco d'Ascoli was an innocent sage—and we all know how he was burnt alive for being wiser than his fellows. Ah, doctor, it is not by living at Padua that you can learn to know Florentines. My belief is, they would stone the Holy Father himself, if they could find a good excuse for it; and they are persuaded that you are a necromancer, who is trying to raise the pestilence by selling secret medicines—and I am told your specifics have in truth an evil smell."

"It is false!" burst out the doctor, as Nello moved away

his razor; "it is false! I will show the pills and the powders to these honorable signori—and the salve—it has an excellent odor—an odor of—of salve." He started up with the lather on his chin, and the cloth round his neck, to search in his saddle-bag for the belied medicines, and Nello in an instant adroitly shifted the shaving-chair till it was in the close vicinity of the horse's head, while Sandro, who had now returned, at a sign from his master placed himself near the bridle.

"Behold, Messeri!" said the doctor, bringing a small box of medicines and opening it before them. "Let any signor apply this box to his nostrils, and he will find an honest odor of medicaments—not indeed of pounded gems, or rare vegetables from the East, or stones found in the bodies of birds; for I practise on the diseases of the vulgar, for whom Heaven has provided cheaper and less powerful remedies according to their degree. and there are even remedies known to our science which are entirely free of cost—as the new *tussis* may be counteracted in the poor, who can pay for no specifics, by a resolute holding of the breath. And here is a paste which is even of savory odor, and is infallible against melancholia, being concocted under the conjunction of Jupiter and Venus; and I have seen it allay spasms."

"Stay, Maestro," said Nello, while the doctor had his lathered face turned toward the group near the door, eagerly holding out his box, and lifting out one specific after another; "here comes a crying contadina with her baby. Doubtless she is in search of you; it is perhaps an opportunity for you to show this honorable company a proof of your skill. Here, buona donna! here is the famous doctor. Why, what is the matter with the sweet *bimbo?*"

This question was addressed to a sturdy-looking, broad-shouldered contadina with her head-drapery folded about her face so that little was to be seen but a bronzed nose and a pair of dark eyes and eyebrows. She carried her child packed up in the stiff mummy-shaped case in which Italian babies have been from time immemorial introduced into society, turning its face a little toward her bosom, and making those sorrowful grimaces which women are in the habit of using as a sort of pulleys to draw down reluctant tears.

"Oh, for the love of the Holy Madonna!" said the woman, in a wailing voice; "will you look at my poor *bimbo?* I know I can't pay you for it, but I took it into the Nunziata last night, and it's turned a worse color than before; it's the convulsions. But when I was holding it before the Santissima Nunziata, I remembered they said there was a new doctor come who cured everything; and so I thought it might be the will of the Holy Madonna that I should bring it to you."

"Sit down, Maestro, sit down," said Nello. "Here is an opportunity for you; here are honorable witnesses who will declare before the Magnificent Eight that they have seen you practising honestly and relieving a poor woman's child. And then if your life is in danger, the Magnificent Eight will put you in prison a little while just to insure your safety, and after that, their sbirri will conduct you out of Florence by night, as they did the zealous Frate Minore who preached against the Jews. What! our people are given to stone-throwing; but we have magistrates."

The doctor, unable to refuse, seated himself in the shaving-chair, trembling, half with fear and half with rage, and by this time quite unconscious of the lather which Nello had laid on with such profuseness. He deposited his medicine-case on his knees, took out his precious spectacles (wondrous Florentine device!) from his wallet, lodged them carefully above his flat nose and high ears, and lifting up his brows, turned toward the applicant.

"O Santiddio! look at him," said the woman with a more piteous wail than ever, as she held out the small mummy, which had its head completely concealed by dingy drapery wound round the head of the portable cradle, but seemed to be struggling and crying in a demoniacal fashion under this imprisonment. "The fit is on him! *Ohimè!* I know what color he is; it's the evil eye—oh!"

The doctor, anxiously holding his knees together to support his box, bent his spectacles toward the baby, and said cautiously, "It may be a new disease; unwind these rags, Monna!"

The contadina, with sudden energy, snatched off the encircling linen, when out struggled—scratching, grinning, and screaming—what the doctor in his fright fully believed to be a demon, but what Tito recognized as Vaiano's monkey, made more formidable by an artificial blackness, such as might have come from a hasty rubbing up the chimney.

Up started the unfortunate doctor, letting his medicine-box fall, and away jumped the no less terrified and indignant monkey, finding the first resting-place for his claws on the horse's mane, which he used as a sort of rope-ladder till he had fairly found his equilibrium, when he continued to clutch it as a bridle. The horse wanted no spur under such a rider, and, the already loosened bridle offering no resistance, darted off across the piazza, with the monkey, clutching, grinning, and blinking, on his neck.

"*Il cavallo! Il Diavolo!*" was now shouted on all sides by the idle rascals who gathered from all quarters of the piazza, and was echoed in tones of alarm by the stall-keepers, whose vested interests seemed in some danger; while the doctor, out of his wits with confused terror at the Devil, the possible stoning, and the escape of his horse, took to his heels with spectacles on nose, lathered face, and the shaving-cloth about his neck, crying—"Stop him! stop him! for a powder—a florin—stop him for a florin!" while the lads, outstripping him, clapped their hands and shouted encouragement to the runaway.

The *cerretano*, who had not bargained for the flight of his monkey along with the horse, had caught up his petticoats with much celerity, and showed a pair of party-colored hose above his contadina's shoes, far in advance of the doctor. And away went the grotesque race up the Corso degli Adimari —the horse with the singular jockey, the contadina with the remarkable hose, and the doctor in lather and spectacles, with furred mantle outflying.

It was a scene such as Florentines loved, from the potent and reverend signor going to council in his lucco, down to the grinning youngster who felt himself master of all situations when his bag was filled with smooth stones from the convenient dry bed of the torrent. The gray-headed Domenico Cennini laughed no less heartily than the younger men, and Nello was triumphantly secure of the general admiration.

"Aha!" he exclaimed, snapping his fingers when the first burst of laughter was subsiding. "I have cleared my piazza of that unsavory fly-trap, *mi pare*. Maestro Tacco will no more come here again to sit for patients than he will take to licking marble for his dinner."

"You are going toward the Piazza della Signoria, Messer Domenico," said Macchiavelli. "I will go with you, and we shall perhaps see who has deserved the *palio* among these racers. Come, Melema, will you go too?"

It had been precisely Tito's intention to accompany Cennini, but before he had gone many steps, he was called back by Nello, who saw Maso approaching.

Maso's message was from Romola. She wished Tito to go to the Via de' Bardi as soon as possible. She would see him under the loggia, at the top of the house, as she wished to speak to him alone.

CHAPTER XVII.

UNDER THE LOGGIA.

THE loggia at the top of Bardo's house rose above the buildings on each side of it, and formed a gallery round quadrangular walls. On the side toward the street the roof was supported by columns; but on the remaining sides, by a wall pierced with arched openings, so that at the back, looking over a crowd of irregular, poorly built dwellings toward the hill of Bogoli, Romola could at all times have a walk sheltered from observation. Near one of those arched openings, close to the door by which he had entered the loggia, Tito awaited her, with a sickening sense of the sunlight that slanted before him and mingled itself with the ruin of his hopes. He had never for a moment relied on Romola's passion for him as likely to be too strong for the repulsion created by the discovery of his secret; he had not the presumptuous vanity which might have hindered him from feeling that her love had the same root with her belief in him. But as he imagined her coming toward him in her radiant beauty, made so lovably mortal by her soft hazel eyes, he fell into wishing that she had been something lower, if it were only that she might let him clasp her and kiss her before they parted. He had had no real caress from her—nothing but now and then a long glance, a kiss, a pressure of the hand; and he had so often longed that they should be alone together. They were going to be alone now; but he saw her standing inexorably aloof from him. His heart gave a great throb as he saw the door move: Romola was there. It was all like a flash of lightning: he felt, rather than saw, the glory about her head, the tearful appealing eyes; he felt, rather than heard, the cry of love with which she said, "Tito!"

And in the same moment she was in his arms, and sobbing with her face against his.

How poor Romola had yearned through the watches of the night to see that bright face! The new image of death; the strange bewildering doubt infused into her by the story of a life removed from her understanding and sympathy; the haunting vision, which she seemed not only to hear uttered by the low gasping voice, but to live through, as if it had been her own dream, had made her more conscious than ever that it was Tito who had first brought the warm stream of hope and gladness into her life, and who had first turned away the keen edge of pain in the remembrance of her brother. She would tell Tito everything; there was no one else to whom she could tell it. She had been restraining herself in the presence of her father all the morning; but now that long-pent-up sob might come forth. Proud and self-controlled to all the world beside, Romola was as simple and unreserved as a child in her love for Tito. She had been quite contented with the days when they had only looked at each other; but now, when she felt the need of clinging to him, there was no thought that hindered her.

"My Romola! my goddess!" Tito murmured with passionate fondness, as he clasped her gently, and kissed the thick golden ripples on her neck. He was in paradise: disgrace, shame, parting—there was no fear of them any longer. This happiness was too strong to be marred by the sense that Romola was deceived in him; nay, he could only rejoice in her delusion; for, after all, concealment had been wisdom. The only thing he could regret was his needless dread; if, indeed, the dread had not been worth suffering for the sake of this sudden rapture.

The sob had satisfied itself, and Romola raised her head. Neither of them spoke; they stood looking at each other's faces with that sweet wonder which belongs to young love— she with her long white hands on the dark brown curls, and he with his dark fingers bathed in the streaming gold. Each was so beautiful to the other; each was experiencing that undisturbed mutual consciousness for the first time. The cold pressure of a new sadness on Romola's heart made her linger the more in that silent soothing sense of nearness and love; and Tito could not even seek to press his lips to hers, because that would be change.

"Tito," she said at last, "it has been altogether painful, but I must tell you everything. Your strength will help me to resist the impressions that will not be shaken off by reason."

"I know, Romola—I know he is dead," said Tito; and the long lustrous eyes told nothing of the many wishes that would have brought about that death long ago if there had been such potency in mere wishes. Romola only read her own pure thoughts in their dark depths, as we read letters in happy dreams.

"So changed, Tito! It pierced me to think that it was Dino. And so strangely hard: not a word to my father; nothing but a vision that he wanted to tell me. And yet it was so piteous —the struggling breath, and the eyes that seemed to look toward the crucifix, and yet not to see it. I shall never forget it; it seems as if it would come between me and everything I shall look at."

Romola's heart swelled again, so that she was forced to break off. But the need she felt to disburden her mind to Tito urged her to repress the rising anguish. When she began to speak again, her thoughts had travelled a little.

"It was strange, Tito. The vision was about our marriage, and yet he knew nothing of you."

"What was it, my Romola? Sit down and tell me," said Tito, leading her to the bench that stood near. A fear had come across him lest the vision should somehow or other relate to Baldassarre; and this sudden change of feeling prompted him to seek a change of position.

Romola told him all that had passed, from her entrance into San Marco, hardly leaving out one of her brother's words, which had burnt themselves into her memory as they were spoken. But when she was at the end of the vision, she paused; the rest came too vividly before her to be uttered, and she sat looking at the distance, almost unconscious for the moment that Tito was near her. *His* mind was at ease now; that vague vision had passed over him like white mist, and left no mark. But he was silent, expecting her to speak again.

"I took it," she went on, as if Tito had been reading her thoughts, "I took the crucifix; it is down below in my bedroom."

"And now, my Romola," said Tito, entreatingly, "you will banish these ghastly thoughts. The vision was an ordinary monkish vision, bred of fasting and fanatical ideas. It surely has no weight with you."

"No, Tito; no. But poor Dino, *he* believed it was a divine message. It is strange," she went on meditatively, "this life of men possessed with fervid beliefs that seem like madness to their fellow-beings. Dino was not a vulgar fanatic; and Fra Girolamo—his very voice seems to have penetrated me with a sense that there is some truth in what moves them: some truth of which I know nothing."

"It was only because your feelings were highly wrought, my Romola. Your brother's state of mind was no more than a form of that theosophy which has been the common disease of excitable dreamy minds in all ages; the same ideas that your father's old antagonist, Marsilio Ficino, pores over in the New Platonists; only your brother's passionate nature drove him to act out what other men write and talk about. And for Fra Girolamo, he is simply a narrow-minded monk, with a gift of preaching and infusing terror into the multitude. Any words or any voice would have shaken you at that moment. When your mind has had a little repose, you will judge of such things as you have always done before."

"Not about poor Dino," said Romola. "I was angry with

him; my heart seemed to close against him while he was speaking; but since then I have thought less of what was in my own mind and more of what was in his. Oh, Tito! it was very piteous to see his young life coming to an end in that way. That yearning look at the crucifix when he was gasping for breath—I can never forget it. Last night I looked at the crucifix a long while, and tried to see that it would help him, until at last it seemed to me by the lamplight as if the suffering face shed pity."

"My Romola, promise me to resist such thoughts; they are fit for sickly nuns, not for my golden-tressed Aurora, who looks made to scatter all such twilight fantasies. Try not to think of them now; we shall not long be alone together."

The last words were uttered in a tone of tender beseeching, and he turned her face toward him with a gentle touch of his right hand.

Romola had had her eyes fixed absently on the arched opening, but she had not seen the distant hill; she had all the while been in the chapter-house, looking at the pale images of sorrow and death.

Tito's touch and beseeching voice recalled her; and now in the warm sunlight she saw that rich dark beauty which seemed to gather round it all images of joy—purple vines festooned between the elms, the strong corn perfecting itself under the vibrating heat, bright winged creatures hurrying and resting among the flowers, round limbs beating the earth in gladness with cymbals held aloft, light melodies chanted to the thrilling rhythm of strings—all objects and all sounds that tell of Nature revelling in her force. Strange, bewildering transition from those pale images of sorrow and death to this bright youthfulness, as of a sun-god who knew nothing of night! What thought could reconcile that worn anguish in her brother's face—that straining after something invisible—with this satisfied strength and beauty, and make it intelligible that they belonged to the same world? Or was there never any reconciling of them, but only a blind worship of clashing deities, first in mad joy and then in wailing? Romola for the first time felt this questioning need like a sudden uneasy dizziness and want of something to grasp; it was an experience hardly longer than a sigh, for the eager theorizing of ages is compressed, as in a seed, in the momentary want of a single mind. But there was no answer to meet the need, and it vanished before the returning rush of young sympathy with the glad loving beauty that beamed upon her in new radiance, like the dawn after we have looked away from it to the gray west.

"Your mind lingers apart from our love, my Romola," Tito said, with a soft reproachful murmur. "It seems a forgotten thing to you."

She looked at the beseeching eyes in silence, till the sadness all melted out of her own.

"My joy!" she said, in her full clear voice.

"Do you really care for me enough, then, to banish those chill fancies, or shall you always be suspecting me as the Great Tempter?" said Tito, with his bright smile.

"How should I not care for you more than for everything else? Everything I had felt before in all my life—about my father, and about my loneliness—was a preparation to love you. You would laugh at me, Tito, if you knew what sort of man I used to think I should marry—some scholar with deep lines in his face, like Alamanno Rinuccini, and with rather gray hair, who would agree with my father in taking the side of the Aristotelians, and be willing to live with him. I used to think about the love I read of in the poets, but I never dreamed that anything like that could happen to me here in Florence in our old library. And then *you* came, Tito, and were so much to my father, and I began to believe that life could be happy for me too."

"My goddess! is there any woman like you?" said Tito, with a mixture of fondness and wondering admiration at the blended majesty and simplicity in her.

"But, dearest," he went on, rather timidly, "if you minded more about our marriage, you would persuade your father and Messer Bernardo not to think of any more delays. But you seem not to mind about it."

"Yes, Tito, I will, I do mind. But I am sure my godfather will urge more delay now, because of Dino's death. He has never agreed with my father about disowning Dino, and you know he has always said that we ought to wait until you have been at least a year in Florence. Do not think hardly of my godfather. I know he is prejudiced and narrow, but yet he is very noble. He has often said that it is folly in my father to want to keep his library apart, that it may bear his name; yet he would try to get my father's wish carried out. That seems to me very great and noble—that power of respecting a feeling which he does not share or understand."

"I have no rancor against Messer Bernardo for thinking you too precious for me, my Romola," said Tito: and that was true. "But your father, then, knows of his son's death?"

"Yes, I told him—I could not help it. I told him where I had been, and that I had seen Dino die; but nothing else; and he has commanded me not to speak of it again. But he has been very silent this morning, and has had those restless movements which always go to my heart; they look as if he were trying to get outside the prison of his blindness. Let us go to him now. I had persuaded him to try to sleep, because he slept little in the night. Your voice will soothe him, Tito: it always does."

"And not one kiss? I have not had one," said Tito, in his gentle reproachful tone, which gave him an air of dependence very charming in a creature with those rare gifts that seem to excuse presumption.

The sweet pink blush spread itself with the quickness of light over Romola's face and neck as she bent toward him. It seemed impossible that their kisses could ever become common things.

"Let us walk once round the loggia," said Romola, "before we go down."

"There is something grim and grave to me always about Florence," said Tito, as they paused in the front of the house, where they could see over the opposite roofs to the other side of the river, "and even in its merriment there is something shrill and hard—biting rather than gay. I wish we lived in Southern Italy, where thought is broken, not by weariness, but by delicious languors such as never seem to come over the 'ingenia acerrima Florentina.' I should like to see you under that southern sun, lying among the flowers, subdued into mere enjoyment, while I bent over you and touched the lute and sang to you some little unconscious strain that seemed all one with the light and the warmth. You have never known that happiness of the nymphs, my Romola."

"No; but I have dreamed of it often since you came. I am very thirsty for a deep draught of joy—for a life all bright like you. But we will not think of it now, Tito; it seems to me as if there would always be pale sad faces among the flowers, and eyes that look in vain. Let us go."

CHAPTER XVIII.

THE PORTRAIT.

When Tito left the Via de' Bardi that day in exultant satisfaction at finding himself thoroughly free from the threatened peril, his thoughts, no longer claimed by the immediate presence of Romola and her father, recurred to those futile hours of dread in which he was conscious of having not only felt but acted as he would not have done if he had had a truer foresight. He would not have parted with his ring; for Romola, and others to whom it was a familiar object, would be a little struck with the apparent sordidness of parting with a gem he had professedly cherished, unless he feigned as a reason the desire to make some special gift with the purchase-money; and Tito had at that moment a nauseating weariness of simulation. He was well out of the possible consequences that might have fallen on him from that initial deception, and it was no longer a load on his mind; kind fortune had brought him immunity, and he thought it was only fair that she should. Who was hurt by it? The results to Baldassarre were too problematical to be taken into account. But he wanted now to be free from any hidden shackles that would gall him, though ever so little, under his ties to Romola. He was not aware that that very delight in immunity which prompted resolutions not to entangle himself again, was deadening the sensibilities which alone could save him from entanglement.

But, after all, the sale of the ring was a slight matter.

Was it also a slight matter that little Tessa was under a delusion which would doubtless fill her small head with expectations doomed to disappointment? Should he try to see the little thing alone again and undeceive her at once, or should he leave the disclosure to time and chance? Happy dreams are pleasant, and they easily come to an end with daylight and the stir of life. The sweet, pouting, innocent, round thing! It was impossible not to think of her. Tito thought he should like some time to take her a present that would please her, and just learn if her stepfather treated her more cruelly now her mother was dead. Or, should he at once undeceive Tessa, and then tell Romola about her, so that they might find some happier lot for the poor thing? No: that unfortunate little incident of the *cerretano* and the marriage, and his allowing Tessa to part from him in delusion, must never be known to Romola, and since no enlightenment could expel it from Tessa's mind, there would always be a risk of betrayal; besides even little Tessa might have some gall in her when she found herself disappointed in her love—yes, she *must* be a little in love with him, and that might make it well that he should not see her again. Yet it was a trifling adventure such as a country girl would perhaps ponder on till some ruddy contadino made acceptable love to her, when she would break her resolution of secrecy and get at the truth that she was free. *Dunque*—good-by, Tessa! kindest wishes! Tito had made up his mind that the silly little affair of the *cerretano* should have no further consequences for himself; and people are apt to think that resolutions taken on their own behalf will be firm. As for the fifty-five florins, the purchase-money of the ring, Tito had made up his mind what to do with some of them; he would carry out a pretty ingenious thought which would set him more at ease in accounting for the absence of his ring to Romola, and would also serve him as a means of guarding her mind from the recurrence of those monkish fancies which were especially repugnant to him; and with this thought in his mind, he went to the Via Gualfonda to find Piero di Cosimo, the artist who at that time was pre-eminent in the fantastic mythological design which Tito's purpose required.

Entering the court on which Piero's dwelling opened, Tito

found the heavy iron knocker on the door thickly bound round with wool and ingeniously fastened with cords. Remembering the painter's practice of stuffing his ears against obtrusive noises, Tito was not much surprised at this mode of defence against visitors' thunder, and betook himself first to tapping modestly with his knuckles, and then to a more importunate attempt to shake the door. In vain! Tito was moving away, blaming himself for wasting his time on this visit, instead of waiting till he saw the painter again at Nello's, when a little girl entered the court with a basket of eggs on her arm, went up to the door, and standing on tiptoe, pushed up a small iron plate that ran in grooves, and putting her mouth to the aperture thus disclosed, called out in a piping voice, "Messer Piero!"

In a few moments Tito heard the sound of bolts, the door opened, and Piero presented himself in a red night-cap and a loose brown serge tunic, with sleeves rolled up to the shoulder. He darted a look of surprise at Tito, but without further notice of him stretched out his hand to take the basket from the child, re-entered the house, and presently returning with the empty basket, said, "How much to pay?"

"Two grossoni, Messer Piero; they are all ready boiled, my mother says."

Piero took the coin out of the leathern scarsella at his belt, and the little maiden trotted away, not without a few upward glances of awed admiration at the surprising young signor.

Piero's glance was much less complimentary as he said,—

"What do you want at my door, Messer Greco? I saw you this morning at Nello's; if you had asked me then, I could have told you that I see no man in this house without knowing his business and agreeing with him beforehand."

"Pardon, Messer Piero," said Tito, with his imperturbable good humor; "I acted without sufficient reflection. I remembered nothing but your admirable skill in inventing pretty caprices, when a sudden desire for something of that sort prompted me to come to you."

The painter's manners were too notoriously odd to all the world for this reception to be held a special affront; but even if Tito had suspected any offensive intention, the impulse to resentment would have been less strong in him than the desire to conquer good will.

Piero made a grimace which was habitual with him when he was spoken to with flattering suavity. He grinned, stretched out the corners of his mouth, and pressed down his brows so as to defy any divination of his feelings under that kind of stroking.

"And what may that need be?" he said, after a moment's pause. In his heart he was tempted by the hinted opportunity of applying his invention.

"I want a very delicate miniature device taken from certain fables of the poets, which you will know how to combine for me. It must be painted on a wooden case—I will show you the size—in the form of a triptych. The inside may be simple gilding: it is on the outside I want the device. It is a favorite subject with you Florentines—the triumph of Bacchus and Ariadne; but I want it treated in a new way. A story in Ovid will give you the necessary hints. The young Bacchus must be seated in a ship, his head bound with clusters of grapes, and a spear intwined with vine-leaves in his hand: dark-berried ivy must wind about the masts and sails, the oars must be thyrsi, and flowers must wreathe themselves about the poop; leopards and tigers must be crouching before him, and dolphins must be sporting round. But I want to have the fair-haired Ariadne with him, made immortal with her golden crown—that is not in Ovid's story, but no matter, you will conceive it all—and above there must be young Loves, such as you know how to paint shooting with roses at the points of their arrows——"

"Say no more!" said Piero. "I have Ovid in the vulgar tongue. Find me the passage. I love not to be choked with other men's thoughts. You may come in."

Piero led the way through the first room, where a basket of eggs was deposited on the open hearth, near a heap of broken egg-shells and a bank of ashes. In strange keeping with that sordid litter, there was a low bedstead of carved ebony, covered carelessly with a piece of rich Oriental carpet, that looked as if it had served to cover the steps to a Madonna's throne; and a carved *cassone*, or large chest, with painted devices on its sides and lid. There was hardly any other furniture in the large room, except casts, wooden steps, easels and rough boxes, all festooned with cobwebs.

The next room was still larger, but it was also much more crowded. Apparently Piero was keeping the Festa, for the double door underneath the window which admitted the painter's light from above, was thrown open, and showed a garden, or rather thicket, in which fig-trees and vines grew in tangled trailing wildness among nettles and hemlocks, and a tall cypress lifted its dark head from a stifling mass of yellowish mulberry leaves. It seemed as if that dank luxuriance had begun to penetrate even within the walls of the wide and lofty room; for in one corner, amidst a confused heap of carved marble fragments and rusty armor, tufts of long grass and dark feathery fennel had made their way, and a large stone vase, tilted on one side, seemed to be pouring out the ivy that streamed around. All about the walls hung pen and oil sketches of fantastic sea-monsters; dances of satyrs and mænads; Saint Margaret's resurrection out of the devouring dragon; Madonnas with the supernal light upon them; studies of plants and grotesque heads; and on irregular rough shelves a few books were scattered among great drooping bunches of corn, bullocks' horns, pieces of dried honeycomb, stones with patches of rare-colored lichen, skulls and bones, peacocks' feathers, and large birds' wings. Rising from amongst the dirty litter of the floor were lay figures. one in the frock of a Vallombrosan monk, strangely surmounted by a helmet with barred visor, another smothered with brocade and skins hastily tossed over it. Amongst this heterogeneous still life, several speckled and white pigeons were perched or strutting, too tame to fly at the entrance of men; three corpulent toads were crawling in an intimate friendly way near the door-stone; and a white rabbit, apparently the model for that which was frightening Cupid in the picture of Mars and Venus placed on the central easel, was twitching its nose with much content on a box full of bran.

"And now, Messer Greco," said Piero, making a sign to Tito that he might sit down on a low stool near the door, and then standing over him with folded arms, "don't be trying to see everything at once, like Messer Domeneddio, but let me know how large you would have this same triptych."

Tito indicated the required dimensions, and Piero marked them on a piece of paper.

"And now for the book," said Piero, reaching down a manuscript volume.

"There's nothing about the Ariadne there," said Tito, giving him the passage; "but you will remember I want the crowned Ariadne by the side of the young Bacchus: she must have golden hair."

"Ha!" said Piero, abruptly, pursing up his lips again. "And you want them to be likenesses, eh?" he added, looking down into Tito's face.

Tito laughed and blushed. "I know you are great at portraits, Messer Piero; but I could not ask Ariadne to sit for you, because the painting is a secret."

"There it is! I want her to sit to me. Giovanni Vespucci wants me to paint him a picture of Œdipus and Antigone at Colonos, as he has expounded it to me; I have a fancy for the subject, and I want Bardo and his daughter to sit for it. Now, you ask them; and then I'll put the likeness into Ariadne."

"Agreed, if I can prevail with them. And your price for the Bacchus and Ariadne?"

"*Baie!* If you get them to let me paint them, that will pay me. I'd rather not have your money: you may pay for the case."

"And when shall I sit for you?" said Tito; "for if we have one likeness, we must have two."

"I don't want *your* likeness; I've got it already," said Piero, "only I've made you look frightened. I must take the fright out of it for Bacchus."

As he was speaking, Piero laid down the book and went to look among some paintings, propped with their faces against the wall. He returned with an oil-sketch in his hand.

"I call this as good a bit of portrait as I ever did," he said, looking at it as he advanced. "Yours is a face that expresses fear well, because it's naturally a bright one. I noticed it the first time I saw you. The rest of the picture is hardly sketched; but I've painted *you* in thoroughly."

Piero turned the sketch, and held it toward Tito's eyes. He saw himself with his right hand uplifted, holding a wine-cup, in the attitude of triumphant joy, but with his face turned away from the cup with an expression of such intense fear in the dilated eyes and pallid lips, that he felt a cold stream through his veins, as if he were being thrown into sympathy with his imaged self.

"You are beginning to look like it already," said Piero, with a short laugh, moving the picture away again. "He's seeing a ghost—that fine young man. I shall finish it some day, when I've settled what sort of ghost is the most terrible—whether it should look solid, like a dead man come to life, or half transparent, like a mist."

Tito, rather ashamed of himself for a sudden sensitiveness strangely opposed to his usual easy self-command, said carelessly,—

"That is a subject after your own heart, Messer Piero—a revel interrupted by a ghost. You seem to love the blending of the terrible with the gay. I suppose that is the reason your shelves are so well furnished with death's-heads, while you are painting those roguish Loves who are running away with the armor of Mars. I begin to think you are a Cynic philosopher in the pleasant disguise of a cunning painter."

"Not I, Messer Greco: a philosopher is the last sort of animal I should choose to resemble. I find it enough to live, without spinning lies to account for life. Fowls cackle, asses bray, women chatter, and philosophers spin false reasons—that's the effect the sight of the world brings out of them. Well, I am an animal that paints instead of cackling, or braying, or spinning lies. And now, I think, our business is done; you'll keep to your side of the bargain about the Œdipus and Antigone?"

"I will do my best," said Tito—on this strong hint immediately moving toward the door.

"And you'll let me know at Nello's. No need to come here again."

"I understand," said Tito, laughingly, lifting his hand in sign of friendly parting.

CHAPTER XIX.

THE OLD MAN'S HOPE.

MESSER BERNARDO DEL NERO was as inexorable as Romola had expected in his advice that the marriage should be deferred till Easter, and in this matter Bardo was entirely under the ascendency of his sagacious and practical friend. Nevertheless, Bernardo himself, though he was as far as ever from any susceptibility to the personal fascination in Tito which was felt by others, could not altogether resist that argument of success which is always powerful with men of the world. Tito was making his way rapidly in high quarters. He was especially growing in favor with the young Cardinal Giovanni de' Medici, who had even spoken of Tito's forming part of his learned retinue on an approaching journey to Rome; and the bright young Greek, who had a tongue that was always ready without ever being quarrelsome, was more and more wished for at gay suppers in the Via Larga, and at Florentine games in which he had no pretension to excel, and could admire the incomparable skill of Piero de' Medici in the most graceful manner in the world. By an unfailing sequence, Tito's reputation as an agreeable companion in "magnificent" society made his learning and talent appear more lustrous: and he was really accomplished enough to prevent an exaggerated estimate from being hazardous to him. Messer Bernardo had old prejudices and attachments which now began to argue down the newer and feebler prejudice against the young Greek stranger who was rather too supple. To the old Florentine it was impossible to despise the recommendation of standing well with the best Florentine families, and since Tito began to be thoroughly received into that circle whose views were the unquestioned standard of social value, it seemed irrational not to admit that there was no longer any check to satisfaction in the prospect of such a son-in-law for Bardo, and such a husband for Romola. It was undeniable that Tito's coming had been the dawn of a new life for both father and daughter, and the first promise had even been surpassed. The blind old scholar—whose proud truthfulness would never enter into that commerce of feigned and preposterous admiration which, varied by a corresponding measurelessness in vituperation, made the woof of all learned intercourse—had fallen into neglect even among his fellow-citizens, and when he was alluded to at all, it had long been usual to say that, though his blindness and the loss of his son were pitiable misfortunes, he was tiresome in contending for the value of his own labors; and that his discontent was a little inconsistent in a man who had been openly regardless of religious rites, and who in days past had refused offers made to him from various quarters, on the slight condition that he would take orders, without which it was not easy for patrons to provide for every scholar. But since Tito's coming, there was no longer the same monotony in the thought that Bardo's name suggested; the old man, it was understood, had left off his plaints, and the fair daughter was no longer to be shut up in dowerless pride, waiting for a *parentado*. The winning manners and growing favor of the handsome Greek who was expected to enter into the double relation of son and husband helped to make the new interest a thoroughly friendly one, and it was no longer a rare occurrence when a visitor enlivened the quiet library. Elderly men came from that indefinite prompting to renew former intercourse which arises when an old acquaintance begins to be newly talked about; and young men whom Tito had asked leave to bring once, found it easy to go again when they overtook him on his way to the Via de' Bardi, and, resting their hands on his shoulder, fell into easy chat with him. For it was pleasant to look at Romola's beauty; to see her, like old Firenzuola's type of womanly majesty, "sitting with a certain grandeur, speaking with gravity, smiling with modesty, and casting around, as it were, an odor of queenliness";[1] and she seemed to unfold like a

[1] "Quando una donna è grande, ben formata, porta ben sua persona, siede con una certa grandezza, parla con gravità, ride con modestia, e finalmente getta quasi un odor di Regina; allora noi diciamo quella donna pare una maestà, ella ha una maestà."—FIRENZUOLA: *Della Bellezza delle D...*

strong white lily under this genial breath of admiration and
homage; it was all one to her with her new bright life in
Tito's love.

Tito had even been the means of strengthening the hope in
Bardo's mind that he might before his death receive the
longed-for security concerning his library: that it should not
be merged in another collection; that it should not be trans-
ferred to a body of monks, and be called by the name of a
monastery; but that it should remain forever the Bardi Library, for the use of Florentines. For the old habit of trusting in the Medici could not die out while their influence was
still the strongest lever in the State; and Tito, once possessing the ear of the Cardinal Giovanni de' Medici, might do
more even than Messer Bernardo toward winning the desired
interest, for he could demonstrate to a learned audience the
peculiar value of Bardi's collection. Tito himself talked san-
guinely of such a result, willing to cheer the old man, and
conscious that Romola repaid those gentle words to her father
with a sort of adoration that no direct tribute to herself could
have won from her.

This question of the library was the subject of more than
one discussion with Bernardo del Nero when Christmas was
turned and the prospect of the marriage was becoming near—
but always out of Bardo's hearing. For Bardo nursed a vague
belief, which they dared not disturb, that his property, apart
from the library, was adequate to meet all demands. He
would not even, except under a momentary pressure of angry
despondency, admit to himself that the will by which he had
disinherited Dino would leave Romola the heir of nothing but
debts; or that he needed anything from patronage beyond the
security that a separate locality should be assigned to his
library, in return for a deed of gift by which he made it over
to the Florentine Republic.

"My opinion is," said Bernardo to Romola, in a consulta-
tion they had under the loggia, "that since you are to be
married, and Messer Tito will have a competent income, we
should begin to wind up the affairs, and ascertain exactly the
sum that would be necessary to save the library from being
touched, instead of letting the debts accumulate any longer.

Your father needs nothing but his shred of mutton and his macaroni every day, and I think Messer Tito may engage to supply that for the years that remain; he can let it be in place of the *morgen-cap*."

"Tito has always known that my life is bound up with my father's," said Romola, "and he is better to my father than I am: he delights in making him happy."

"Ah, he's not made of the same clay as other men, is he?" said Bernardo, smiling. "Thy father has thought of shutting woman's folly out of thee by cramming thee with Greek and Latin; but thou hast been as ready to believe in the first pair of bright eyes and the first soft words that have come within reach of thee, as if thou couldst say nothing by heart but Paternosters, like other Christian men's daughters."

"Now, godfather," said Romola, shaking her head playfully, "as if it were only bright eyes and soft words that made me love Tito! You know better. You know I love my father and you because you are both good, and I love Tito too because he is so good. I see it, I feel it, in everything he says and does. And if he is handsome, too, why should I not love him the better for that? It seems to me beauty is part of the finished language by which goodness speaks. You know *you* must have been a very handsome youth, godfather,"—she looked up with one of her happy, loving smiles at the stately old man—"you were about as tall as Tito, and you had very fine eyes; only you looked a little sterner and prouder, and——"

"And Romola likes to have all the pride to herself?" said Bernardo, not inaccessible to this pretty coaxing. "However, it is well that in one way Tito's demands are more modest than those of any Florentine husband of fitting rank that we should have been likely to find for you; he wants no dowry."

So it was settled in that way between Messer Bernardo del Nero, Romola, and Tito. Bardo assented with a wave of the hand when Bernardo told him that he thought it would be well now to begin to sell property and clear off debts; being accustomed to think of debts and property as a sort of thick wood that his imagination never even penetrated, still less got beyond. And Tito set about winning Messer Bernardo's respect by inquiring, with his ready faculty, into Florentine money matters, the secrets of the *Monti* or public funds, the values of real property, and the profits of banking.

"You will soon forget that Tito is not a Florentine, godfather," said Romola. "See how he is learning everything about Florence."

"It seems to me he is one of the *demoni*, who are of no particular country, child," said Bernardo, smiling. "His mind is a little too nimble to be weighted with all the stuff we men carry about in our hearts."

Romola smiled too, in happy confidence.

CHAPTER XX.

THE DAY OF THE BETROTHAL.

It was the last week of the Carnival, and the streets of Florence were at their fullest and noisiest: there were the masked processions, chanting songs, indispensable now they had once been introduced by Lorenzo the Magnificent; there was the favorite rigoletto, or round dance, footed "in piazza" under the blue frosty sky; there were practical jokes of all sorts, from throwing comfits to throwing stones—especially stones. For the boys and striplings, always a strong element in Florentine crowds, became at the height of Carnival-time as loud and unmanageable as tree-crickets, and it was their immemorial privilege to bar the way with poles to all passengers, until a tribute had been paid toward furnishing those lovers of strong sensations with suppers and bonfires; to conclude with the standing entertainment of stone-throwing, which was not entirely monotonous, since the consequent maiming was various, and it was not always a single person who was killed. So that the pleasures of the Carnival were of a checkered kind, and if a painter were called upon to represent them truly, he would have to make a picture in which there would be so much grossness and barbarity that it must be turned with its face to the wall, except when it was taken down for the grave historical purpose of justifying a reforming zeal which, in ignorance of the facts, might be unfairly condemned for its narrowness. Still there was much of that more innocent picturesque merriment which is never wanting among a people with quick animal spirits and sensitive organs: there was not the heavy sottishness which belongs to the thicker northern blood, nor the stealthy fierceness which in the more southern regions of the peninsula makes the brawl lead to the dagger-thrust.

It was the high morning, but the merry spirits of the Carnival were still inclined to lounge and recapitulate the last night's jests, when Tito Melema was walking at a brisk pace on the way to the Via de' Bardi. Young Bernardo Dovizi, who now looks at us out of Raphael's portrait as the keen-eyed Cardinal da Bibbiena, was with him; and as they went, they held animated talk about some subject that had evidently no relation to the sights and sounds through which they were pushing their way along the Por' Santa Maria. Nevertheless, as they discussed, smiled, and gesticulated, they both, from time to time, cast quick glances around them, and at the turning toward the Lung' Arno, leading to the Ponte Rubaconte, Tito had become aware, in one of these rapid surveys, that there was some one not far off him by whom he very much desired not to be recognized at that moment. His time and thoughts were thoroughly pre-occupied, for he was looking forward to a unique occasion in his life: he was preparing for his betrothal, which was to take place on the evening of this very day. The ceremony had been resolved upon rather suddenly; for although preparations toward the marriage had been going forward for some time—chiefly in the application of Tito's florins to the fitting up of rooms in Bardo's dwelling, which, the library excepted, had always been scantily furnished—it had been intended to defer both the betrothal and the marriage until after Easter, when Tito's year of probation, insisted on by Bernardo del Nero, would have been complete. But when an express proposition had come, that Tito should follow the Cardinal Giovanni to Rome to help Bernardo Dovizi with his superior knowledge of Greek in arranging a library, and there was no possibility of declining what lay so plainly on the road to advancement, he had become urgent in his entreaties that the betrothal might take place before his departure: there would be the less delay before the marriage on his return, and it would be less painful to part if he and Romola were outwardly as well as inwardly pledged to each other—if he had a claim which defied Messer Bernardo or any one else to nullify it. For the betrothal, at which rings were exchanged and mutual contracts were signed, made more than half the legality of marriage, to be completed on a separate occasion by the nuptial benediction. Romola's feeling had met Tito's in this wish, and the consent of the elders had been won.

And now Tito was hastening amidst arrangements for his departure the next day, to snatch a morning visit to Romola, to say and hear any last words that were needful to be said before their meeting for the betrothal in the evening. It was not a time when any recognition could be pleasant that was at all likely to detain him; still less a recognition by Tessa. And it was unmistakably Tessa whom he had caught sight of moving along, with a timid and forlorn look, toward that very turn of the Lung' Arno which he was just rounding. As he continued his talk with the young Dovizi, he had an uncomfortable undercurrent of consciousness which told him that Tessa had seen him and would certainly follow him: there was no escaping her along this direct road by the Arno, and over the Ponte Rubaconte. But she would not dare to speak to him or approach him while he was not alone, and he would continue to keep Dovizi with him till they reached Bardo's door. He quickened his pace, and took up new threads of talk; but all the while the sense that Tessa was behind him, though he had no physical evidence of the fact, grew stronger and stronger; it was very irritating—perhaps all the more so because a certain tenderness and pity for the poor little thing made the determination to escape without any visible notice of her, a not altogether agreeable resource. Yet Tito persevered and carried his companion to the door, cleverly managing his "addio" without turning his face in a direction where it was possible for him to see an importunate pair of blue eyes; and as he went up the stone steps, he tried to get rid of unpleasant thoughts by saying to himself that after all Tessa might not have seen him, or, if she had, might not have followed him.

But—perhaps because that possibility could not be relied on strongly—when the visit was over, he came out of the doorway with a quick step and an air of unconsciousness as to anything that might be on his right hand or his left. Our eyes are so constructed, however, that they take in a wide angle without asking any leave of our will; and Tito knew that there was a little figure in a white hood standing near the doorway—knew it quite well, before he felt a hand laid on his arm. It was a real grasp, and not a light, timid touch; for poor Tessa, seeing his rapid step, had started forward with a desperate effort. But when he stopped and turned toward her, her face wore a frightened look, as if she dreaded the effect of her boldness.

"Tessa!" said Tito, with more sharpness in his voice than she had ever heard in it before. "Why are you here? You must not follow me—you must not stand about doorplaces waiting for me."

Her blue eyes widened with tears, and she said nothing. Tito was afraid of something worse than ridicule, if he were seen in the Via de' Bardi with a girlish contadina looking pathetically at him. It was a street of high silent-looking dwellings, not of traffic; but Bernardo del Nero, or some one almost as dangerous, might come up at any moment. Even if it had not been the day of his betrothal, the incident would have been awkward and annoying. Yet it would be brutal—it was impossible—to drive Tessa away with harsh words. That accursed folly of his with the *cerretano*—that it should have lain buried in a quiet way for months, and now start up before him as this unseasonable crop of vexation! He could not speak harshly, but he spoke hurriedly.

"Tessa, I cannot—must not talk to you here. I will go on to the bridge and wait for you there. Follow me slowly."

He turned and walked fast to the Ponte Rubaconte, and there leaned against the wall of one of the quaint little houses that rise at even distances on the bridge, looking toward the way by which Tessa would come. It would have softened a much harder heart than Tito's to see the little thing advancing with her round face much paled and saddened since he had parted from it at the door of the "Nunziata." Happily it was the least frequented of the bridges, and there were scarcely any passengers on it at this moment. He lost no time in speaking as soon as she came near him.

"Now, Tessa, I have very little time. You must not cry. Why did you follow me this morning? You must not do so again."

"I thought," said Tessa, speaking in a whisper, and struggling against a sob that *would* rise immediately at this new voice of Tito's—"I thought you wouldn't be so long before you came to take care of me again. And the *patrigno* beats me, and I can't bear it any longer. And always when I come for a holiday I walk about to find you, and I can't. Oh, please don't send me away from you again! It has been so long, and I cry so now, because you never come to me. I can't help it, for the days are so long, and I don't mind about the goats and kids, or anything—and I can't——"

The sobs came fast now, and the great tears. Tito felt that he could not do otherwise than comfort her. Send her away—yes; that he *must* do, at once. But it was all the more impossible to tell her anything that would leave her in a state of hopeless grief. He saw new trouble in the background, but the difficulty of the moment was too pressing for him to weigh distant consequences.

"Tessa, my little one," he said, in his old caressing tones, "you must not cry. Bear with the cross *patrigno* a little longer. I will come back to you. But I'm going now to Rome—a long, long way off. I shall come back in a few weeks, and then I promise to come and see you. Promise me to be good and wait for me."

It was the well-remembered voice again, and the mere sound was half enough to soothe Tessa. She looked up at him with trusting eyes, that still glittered with tears, sobbing all the while, in spite of her utmost efforts to obey him. Again he said, in a gentle voice,—

"Promise me, my Tessa."

"Yes," she whispered. "But you won't be long?"

"No, not long. But I must go now. And remember what I told you, Tessa. Nobody must know that you ever see me, else you will lose me forever. And now, when I have left you, go straight home, and never follow me again. Wait till I come to you. Good-by, my little Tessa: I *will* come."

There was no help for it; he must turn and leave her without looking behind him to see how she bore it, for he had no time to spare. When he did look round he was in the Via de' Benci, where there was no seeing what was happening on the bridge; but Tessa was too trusting and obedient not to do just what he had told her.

Yes, the difficulty was at an end for that day, yet this return of Tessa to him, at a moment when it was impossible for him to put an end to all difficulty with her by undeceiving her, was an unpleasant incident to carry in his memory. But Tito's mind was just now thoroughly penetrated with a hopeful first love, associated with all happy prospects flattering to his ambition; and that future necessity of grieving Tessa could be scarcely more to him than the far-off cry of some little suffering animal buried in the thicket, to a merry cavalcade in the sunny plain. When, for the second time that day, Tito was hastening across the Ponte Rubaconte, the thought of Tessa caused no perceptible diminution of his happiness. He was well muffled in his mantle, less, perhaps, to protect him from the cold than from the additional notice that would have been drawn upon him by his dainty apparel. He leaped up the stone steps by two at a time, and said hurriedly to Maso, who met him,—

"Where is the damigella?"

"In the library; she is quite ready, and Monna Brigida and Besser Bernardo are already there with Ser Braccio, but none of the rest of the company."

"Ask her to give me a few minutes alone; I will await her in the *salotto*."

Tito entered a room which had been fitted up in the utmost contrast with the half-pallid, half-sombre tints of the library. The walls were brightly frescoed with "caprices" of nymphs and loves sporting under the blue among flowers and birds. The only furniture besides the red leather seats and the central table were two tall white vases, and a young faun playing the flute, modelled by a promising youth named Michelangelo Buonarotti. It was a room that gave a sense of being in the sunny open air.

Tito kept his mantle round him, and looked toward the door. It was not long before Romola entered, all white and gold, more than ever like a tall lily. Her white silk garment was bound by a golden girdle, which fell with large tassels; and above that was the rippling gold of her hair, surmounted by the white mist of her long veil, which was fastened on her brow by a band of pearls, the gift of Bernardo del Nero, and was now parted off her face so that it all floated backward.

"Regina mia!" said Tito, as he took her hand and kissed it, still keeping his mantle round him. He could not help going backward to look at her again, while she stood in calm delight, with that exquisite self-consciousness which rises under the gaze of admiring love.

"Romola, will you show me the next room now?" said Tito, checking himself with the remembrance that the time might be short. "You said I should see it when you had arranged everything."

Without speaking, she led the way into a long, narrow room, painted brightly like the other, but only with birds and flowers. The furniture in it was all old; there were old faded objects for feminine use or ornament, arranged in an open cabinet between the two narrow windows; above the cabinet was the portrait of Romola's mother; and below this, on the top of the cabinet, stood the crucifix which Romola had brought from San Marco.

"I have brought something under my mantle," said Tito, smiling; and throwing off the large loose garment, he showed the little tabernacle which had been painted by Piero di Cosimo. The painter had carried out Tito's intention charmingly, and so far had atoned for his long delay. "Do you know what this is for, my Romola?" added Tito, taking her by the hand, and leading her toward the cabinet. "It is a little shrine, which is to hide away from you forever that remembrancer of sadness. You have done with sadness now;

and we will bury all images of it—bury them in a tomb of joy. See!"

A slight quiver passed across Romola's face as Tito took hold of the crucifix. But she had no wish to prevent his purpose; on the contrary, she herself wished to subdue certain importunate memories and questionings which still flitted like unexplained shadows across her happier thought.

He opened the triptych and placed the crucifix within the central space; then closing it again, taking out the key, and setting the little tabernacle in the spot where the crucifix had stood, said,—

"Now, Romola, look and see if you are satisfied with the portraits old Piero has made of us. Is it not a dainty device? and the credit of choosing it is mine."

"Ah! it is you—it is perfect!" said Romola, looking with moist joyful eyes at the miniature Bacchus, with his purple clusters. "And I am Ariadne, and you are crowning me! Yes, it is true, Tito; you have crowned my poor life."

They held each other's hands while she spoke, and both looked at their imaged selves. But the reality was far more beautiful; she all lily-white and golden, and he with his dark glowing beauty above the purple red-bordered tunic.

"And it was our good strange Piero who painted it?" said Romola. "Did you put it into his head to paint me as Antigone, that he might have my likeness for this?"

"No, it was he who made my getting leave for him to paint you and your father, a condition of his doing this for me."

"Ah! I see now what it was you gave up your precious ring for. I perceived you had some cunning plan to give me pleasure."

Tito did not blench. Romola's little illusions about himself had long ceased to cause him anything but satisfaction. He only smiled and said,—

"I might have spared my ring; Piero will accept no money from me; he thinks himself paid by painting you. And now, while I am away, you will look every day at those pretty symbols of our life together—the ship on the calm sea, and the ivy that never withers, and those Loves that have left off wounding us and shower soft petals that are like our kisses;

and the leopards and tigers, they are the troubles of your life that are all quelled now; and the strange sea-monsters, with their merry eyes—let us see—they are the dull passages in the heavy books, which have begun to be amusing since we have sat by each other."

"Tito mio!" said Romola, in a half-laughing voice of love; "but you will give me the key?" she added, holding out her hand for it.

"Not at all!" said Tito, with playful decision, opening his scarsella, and dropping in the little key. "I shall drown it in the Arno."

"But if I ever wanted to look at the crucifix again?"

"Ah! for that very reason it is hidden—hidden by these images of youth and joy."

He pressed a light kiss on her brow, and she said no more, ready to submit, like all strong souls, when she felt no valid reason for resistance.

And then they joined the waiting company, which made a dignified little procession as it passed along the Ponte Rubaconte toward Santa Croce. Slowly it passed, for Bardo, unaccustomed for years to leave his own house, walked with a more timid step than usual; and that slow pace suited well with the gouty dignity of Messer Bartolommeo Scala, who graced the occasion by his presence, along with his daughter Alessandra. It was customary to have very long troops of kindred and friends at the *sposalizio*, or betrothal, and it had even been found necessary in time past to limit the number by law to no more than *four hundred*—two hundred on each side; for since the guests were all feasted after this initial ceremony, as well as after the *nozze*, or marriage, the very first stage of matrimony had become a ruinous expense, as that scholarly Benedict, Leonardo Bruno, complained in his own case. But Bardo, who in his poverty had kept himself proudly free from any appearance of claiming the advantages attached to a powerful family name, would have no invitations given on the strength of mere friendship; and the modest procession of twenty that followed the *sposi* were, with three or four exceptions, friends of Bardo's and Tito's selected on personal grounds.

Bernardo del Nero walked as a vanguard before Bardo, who was led on the right by Tito, while Romola held her father's other hand. Bardo had himself been married at Santa Croce, and had insisted on Romola's being betrothed and married there, rather than in the little church at Santa Lucia close by their house, because he had a complete mental vision of the grand church, where he hoped that a burial might be granted him among the Florentines who had deserved well. Happily the way was short and direct, and lay aloof from the loudest riot of the Carnival, if only they could return before any dances or shows began in the great piazza of Santa Croce. The west was red as they passed the bridge, and shed a mellow light on the pretty procession, which had a touch of solemnity in the presence of the blind father. But when the ceremony was over, and Tito and Romola came out on to the broad steps of the church, with the golden links of destiny on their fingers, the evening had deepened into struggling starlight, and the servants had their torches lit.

While they came out, a strange, dreary chant, as of a *Miserere*, met their ears, and they saw that at the extreme end of the piazza there seemed to be a stream of people impelled by something approaching from the Borgo de' Greci.

"It is one of their masked processions, I suppose," said Tito, who was now alone with Romola, while Bernardo took charge of Bardo.

And as he spoke there came slowly into view, at a height far above the heads of the onlookers, a huge and ghastly image of Winged Time with his scythe and hour-glass, surrounded by his winged children, the Hours. He was mounted on a high car completely covered with black, and the bullocks that drew the car were also covered with black, their horns alone standing out white above the gloom; so that in the sombre shadow of the houses it seemed to those at a distance as if Time and his children were apparitions floating through the air. And behind them came what looked like a troop of the sheeted dead gliding above blackness. And as they glided slowly, they chanted in a wailing strain.

A cold horror seized on Romola, for at the first moment it seemed as if her brother's vision, which could never be effaced from her mind, was being half fulfilled. She clung to Tito, who, divining what was in her thoughts, said,—

"What dismal fooling sometimes pleases your Florentines! Doubtless this is an invention of Piero di Cosimo, who loves such grim merriment."

"Tito, I wish it had not happened. It will deepen the images of that vision which I would fain be rid of."

"Nay, Romola, you will look only at the images of our happiness now. I have locked all sadness away from you."

"But it is still there—it is only hidden," said Romola, in a low tone, hardly conscious that she spoke.

"See, they are all gone now!" said Tito. "You will forget this ghastly mummery when we are in the light, and can see each other's eyes. My Ariadne must never look backward now—only forward to Easter, when she will triumph with her Care-dispeller."

CPSIA information can be obtained
at www.ICGtesting.com
Printed in the USA
BVOW09*1231261117
501182BV00006B/125/P

9 781297 812156